D1236874

# Jean Monnet

*Jean Monnet in Luxembourg, summer 1955*

# Jean Monnet

## Unconventional Statesman

### Sherrill Brown Wells

LYNNE
RIENNER
PUBLISHERS

BOULDER
LONDON

Frontispiece photo by Théo Mey. Courtesy of Fondation Jean Monnet
pour l'Europe. © Photothèque de la Ville de Luxembourg.


Published in the United States of America in 2011 by
Lynne Rienner Publishers, Inc.
1800 30th Street, Boulder, Colorado 80301
www.rienner.com

and in the United Kingdom by
Lynne Rienner Publishers, Inc.
3 Henrietta Street, Covent Garden, London WC2E 8LU

**Library of Congress Cataloging-in-Publication Data**
Wells, Sherrill Brown.
    Jean Monnet : unconventional statesman / Sherrill Brown Wells.
      p. cm.
    Includes bibliographical references and index.
    ISBN 978-1-58826-787-0 (hardcover : alk. paper)
    1. Monnet, Jean, 1888–1979.   2. European federation—History.
3. Statesmen—Europe—Biography.   4. Economists—Europe—
Biography.   I. Title.
    D413.M56W45   2011
    341.24'2092—dc23
    [B]
                                                    2011020127

**British Cataloguing in Publication Data**
A Cataloguing in Publication record for this book
is available from the British Library.


Printed and bound in the United States of America

   The paper used in this publication meets the requirements
         of the American National Standard for Permanence of
         Paper for Printed Library Materials Z39.48-1992.

    5   4   3   2   1

*To Lauren Wells Liers,*
*Christopher Wells, and*
*Samuel Wells*

# Contents

*List of Photographs*                                                            ix
*Preface*                                                                         xi

Introduction                                                                       1

**1**  Cognac Roots and Formative Experiences, 1888–1938                           5

**2**  Early Wartime Contributions, 1938–1943                                     45

**3**  Washington Assignments, 1943–1945                                          69

**4**  The Monnet Plan, 1945–1950                                                 95

**5**  Creation of the Coal and Steel Community, 1950–1952                       127

**6**  Losing the Battle for a European Defense Community,
       1952–1954                                                                 163

**7**  Regaining Momentum, 1954–1958                                             185

**8**  Promoting Closer Integration, 1958–1979                                   211

**9**  Jean Monnet: A Critical Assessment                                        243

*Bibliography*                                                                   255
*Index*                                                                          267
*About the Book*                                                                 279

# Photographs

Jean Monnet in Luxembourg, summer 1955     ii
Jean Monnet in Algiers, 1943     76
Jean Monnet and his team of collaborators at the
    Monnet Plan office, 1946 or 1947     106
Robert Schuman announces the Schuman Plan     131
Jean Monnet and Konrad Adenauer in Strasbourg, September 1952     166
Jean and Silvia Monnet at their home in Bricherhof,
    Luxembourg, 1953     171
Jean Monnet meeting at the White House with President
    Eisenhower and Secretary of State Dulles, June 3, 1953     174
Jean Monnet and Robert Schuman in Luxembourg, May 9, 1953     181
Jean Monnet and Paul-Henri Spaak, September 10, 1952     189
First session of the Action Committee for the United States of
    Europe, Paris, January 1956     195
Jean Monnet and Franz Etzel, mid-1950s     203
Jean Monnet and Max Kohnstamm in Luxembourg, May 9, 1953     214
President Kennedy and Jean Monnet at the White House,
    March 26, 1962     226
Jean Monnet at age eighty-four, outside his home in Houjarray,
    Luxembourg, November 1972     235

# Preface

My interest in Jean Monnet began in 1984 when the Office of the Historian of the Department of State sent me to Paris to do a study of French industrial policy. Minister-Counselor for Economic Affairs Michael E. C. Ely, at the US Embassy in Paris, helped me to gain access to the prominent statesmen who shaped French economic policy in the postwar period. Among those I was fortunate to interview were Robert Marjolin, Etienne Hirsch, and Pierre Uri, three of Monnet's most important colleagues, as well as many other French civil servants who worked with or knew Monnet. Later, in Washington, I became involved with the Jean Monnet Council created in 1988 to support studies of Monnet. Most of the members of the council were retired US diplomats who had worked closely with Monnet in Europe or in the United States. Spending time with these officials gave me a unique opportunity to conduct interviews and collect their personal papers containing correspondence with Monnet. Research in the Monnet archives in Lausanne and in other European archives helped me to understand the significance of this Frenchman who influenced the course of European events in the twentieth century.

Two comprehensive biographies of Monnet have been published. *Jean Monnet: The First Statesman of Interdependence* was written in 1994 by François Duchêne, British journalist and highly valued colleague of Monnet. The other, *Jean Monnet,* completed by the prominent French journalist and author Eric Roussel, was published in French in 1996. Roussel never knew Monnet but had privileged access to his family and other close friends. Valuable scholarship on Monnet's international roles written by scholars and officials who knew Monnet has been published in French as chapters in *Jean Monnet, l'Europe et les chemins de la Paix* edited by Gérard Bossuat and Andreas Wilkens (1999). Two other important collections of articles about

Monnet, including some written by his colleagues, are *Jean Monnet: The Path to European Unity* edited by Douglas Brinkley and Clifford P. Hackett (1991) and *Monnet and the Americans* edited by Hackett (1995), who was executive director of the Jean Monnet Council. In 2008, Clifford Hackett published a meticulously researched chronology of Monnet's life up to 1950 titled *A Jean Monnet Chronology*. Since the publication of these books, extensive work has been done on the institutions of the European Union (EU) and how they evolved from the seeds sown by Jean Monnet.

I chose to write a short political biography for the English-speaking world to show how this unconventional French statesman was instrumental in bringing peace to Europe and transforming the transatlantic relationship. Utilizing recent as well as previous scholarship, archives, and extensive interviews, I chronicle how this entrepreneurial genius combined influence and action in tackling complex international problems. Although Monnet's achievements are often overshadowed by those of Charles de Gaulle in their native France, I show how the visionary Monnet helped to shape French foreign policy in the postwar period, and I give special attention to the crucial role his US contacts and friendships played in the success of both his European and French initiatives.

The late Ernest R. May first suggested that I write about Monnet and showed a special interest in my work. Clifford Hackett nourished that idea by inviting me to write a chapter about four of Monnet's colleagues in his *Monnet and the Americans*. Three other scholars played an influential role in the evolution of this study, not only through their outstanding scholarship but also by their constant encouragement and advice. Richard F. Kuisel's monumental work on French economic history convinced me that Monnet's role in twentieth-century France needed further exploration. Desmond Dinan's extensive publications on the history of the European Union placed Monnet in perspective and ensured that I did not exaggerate his role in the integration process. And Thomas A. Schwartz's major study of John J. McCloy and the relationship between the United States and Germany after World War II demonstrated how the close relationship between McCloy and Monnet developed into a transnational partnership that played a critical role in transatlantic relations.

This volume benefited from the thoughtful comments of Desmond Dinan and George Sheridan, who reviewed the whole manuscript; Richard Kuisel, who read selected chapters; and Clifford Hackett, who read Chapter 1. I owe an intellectual debt to many scholars whose own work influenced my approach to this study, especially to Gérard Bossuat for his extensive scholarship on Monnet, as well as Pierre Hassner, Jean-Claude Casanova, Pierre Mélandri, Maurice Vaisse, André Kaspi, Georges-Henri Soutou, Élisabeth Du Réau, Hans-Peter Schwarz, Helga Haftendorn, Klaus Schwabe, Ludgar

Kuehnhardt, Herman Van der Wee, Piero Graglia, Pascaline Winand, Douglas Brinkley, Irwin Wall, David DiLeo, Charles Cogan, and John Gillingham.

I am indebted to Françoise Nicod, the head archivist at the Fondation Jean Monnet pour l'Europe in Lausanne, who generously and efficiently provided me with documents and photos over the years. The late Henri Rieben, president of the Fondation Jean Monnet when I began my work, always provided invaluable assistance. I wish to thank Idelle Nissila-Stone, who ably guided my work at the Ford Foundation Archives, and Martine Theisen, archivist at Photothèque de la Ville de Luxembourg, who assisted me with some of the photos. I am grateful to David Ettinger, international affairs and political science librarian at George Washington University's Gelman Library, and to Ann Sweeney, communications adviser at the European Union Delegation Library, for their help. I wish to thank Paul Hurwit, whose excellent translations of official Monnet documents facilitated my work. And I owe special thanks to Annie D. Grasso, whose limitless knowledge of the French language and its idiosyncrasies was invaluable. I thank those who have helped produce this volume, especially Lynne Rienner, publisher, whose sustained interest in the project kept me hopeful, and her able colleague, Shena Redmond, project editor. Kathy Kaiser, copyeditor, greatly improved the manuscript.

To those who have offered advice, assistance, and support at critical stages along the way, I owe more than I can express here: Michael Ely, Donald Lamm, Melinda Scrivner, Toni Dorfman, John Gaddis, Christian Ostermann, Bonnie Smith, David Schalk, Jenonne Walker, Robert Lehrman, Samuel Williamson, Anton DePorte, Stanley Crossick, Sue Wheeler, Clarissa Whitney, Deborah Kahn, Harris Miller, Renelle Gannon, Lauren Liers, and Christopher Wells. But I owe my deepest thanks to my husband, Samuel Wells, whose love, support, and constant encouragement enabled me to complete this study.

*—Sherill Brown Wells*

# Introduction

How did a brandy salesman from a small French provincial town, who left school at age sixteen, become one of the most influential European statesmen of the twentieth century? Jean Monnet never held an elective office, never joined a political party, and never developed any significant popular following in his native France. Yet, this unlikely Frenchman not only had a major impact on European politics and transatlantic relations, especially between 1945 and 1954, but was the single most important architect of European integration.

This political biography of the entrepreneurial internationalist demonstrates Monnet's significance in four realms: (1) reconstructing France, (2) effecting Franco-German reconciliation, (3) creating the European Union, and (4) constructing the transatlantic community. Monnet's role was central to each of these developments.

Monnet's accomplishments were numerous, diverse, and pathbreaking even before 1945. As a young man in his twenties, he demonstrated an ability to design innovative solutions to international problems. During World War I, he helped to create a program that enabled the British and French governments to coordinate their purchase of Allied supplies. After the war he became deputy head of the League of Nations, where his method of identifying obstacles and confronting problems enabled him to devise solutions to international disputes. He worked with European banks as an investment banker in the 1920s and helped Austria, Romania, and Poland to acquire international loans. In the 1930s his reputation as an international financier motivated Chinese Nationalist leader Chiang Kai-shek to invite him to China to help with reconstruction. During his six months in China, Monnet created a development bank designed to inject long-term Chinese and foreign public and private capital into the country's commercial and industrial ventures.

1

In the years just before and during the World War II, three heads of state sent Monnet on special diplomatic missions. French Prime Minister Edouard Daladier asked him in 1938 to go to Washington to negotiate the purchase of US planes to bolster French airpower. After France fell to the Germans in 1940, Monnet went to London, where British Prime Minister Winston Churchill sent him to the United States with a British passport to work with the British Purchasing Commission. Churchill believed that Monnet's experience in World War I could be valuable in hastening the acquisition of weapons and supplies needed to fight the new war. In 1943, President Franklin Roosevelt asked Monnet to go to Algiers to offer US support to France's General Henri Giraud. The president hoped that General Giraud could provide much-needed leadership for the French armed forces in North Africa. And with the help of his French colleagues exiled in Algiers, Monnet masterminded the negotiations between Giraud and the rival leader of the Free French, General Charles de Gaulle. These assignments from the French, British, and American heads of state helped to propel Monnet, by 1945, into the governing circles of Paris, London, and Washington and earned him the respect and reputation as a man of action and a skilled negotiator.

Monnet's international experience and the contacts he made prior to 1945 among French, British, and US statesmen, politicians, and civil servants enabled him to make his most important contributions to European peace after the end of World War II. He was the chief engineer of France's postwar recovery and the key architect of the European economic integration. He designed the two plans upon which the eventual European Union (EU) was built—the Monnet Plan to rebuild the French economy and the Schuman Plan to establish the European Coal and Steel Community (ECSC)—and then persuaded the leaders in power, de Gaulle in 1945 and Robert Schuman in 1950, to adopt his bold concepts. Once he was given the responsibility for implementing both these plans, he proved he could assemble teams of French and international civil servants to create effective organizations. As head of the Monnet Plan and later as president of the High Authority of the ECSC, Monnet continually pushed often reluctant French politicians to take the lead in economic integration. Even the failures of the two subsequent communities he designed and promoted—the European Defense Community (EDC) and the European Atomic Energy Community (Euratom)—helped spur European leaders to move forward with integration. By the end of 1954, his efforts had helped France reconstruct its economy and regain its influence on the continent, shape the use of Marshall Plan aid in Europe, recast Franco-German relations through the Schuman Plan, and moderate German recovery. All this positioned France to take a leading role in the Western Alliance and European integration. In 1955, Monnet and the Belgian Prime Minister Paul-Henri Spaak initiated the plans that brought the foreign ministers of the six ECSC countries together at Messina, Italy. This meeting in turn helped motivate the leaders of these nations to continue discussing forms of economic integration, which led to the Rome Treaties creating the common market, the forerunner of the EU.

This study captures a period in Franco-American relations between 1945 and 1954, when Monnet was a key interlocutor between France and the United States and an influence within each government. It demonstrates that French ministers often relied on Monnet to learn what US policymakers were thinking. American leaders in turn depended to a great extent on Monnet to sustain the progress toward European integration that they believed was essential to postwar peace and stability in Europe. Monnet's work contributed to the construction of the transatlantic community, which came to life in the 1945–1954 period with the general cross-Atlantic drive that included the Marshall Plan and the North Atlantic Treaty Organization (NATO). His use of the Marshall Plan funds to rebuild the French economy illustrates this transatlantic cooperation.

Beginning in 1954 and culminating with de Gaulle's ascent to power in 1958, Monnet's influence in Paris rapidly declined. However, while his leverage and influence on Western European leaders had significantly diminished by 1958, his influence on US policymakers continued through the Eisenhower and Kennedy administrations until the assassination of President Kennedy in 1963. His close friendships with many prominent Americans lasted until his death in 1979.

The pages that follow demonstrate why, in order to understand European integration—one of the most significant achievements of the twentieth century—it is essential to understand Jean Monnet's contribution to the process and to the events that influenced it.

# 1

# Cognac Roots and Formative Experiences, 1888–1938

**The man who** became known as "Mr. Europe" was neither eloquent nor flamboyant. Short and stocky with a bushy, brown mustache and piercing chestnut eyes, Jean Monnet was a problem solver and a highly unconventional statesman. His magnetism, acute intelligence, and subtle mind drew men of rare ability to him, and some loyally served as his brain trust throughout the most productive years of his life. Monnet was an avid reader of the press, though he had little knowledge of the literary currents of the time.[1] He was not a member of the intelligentsia or a gifted orator, found writing difficult, and preferred the telephone whenever possible. But he loved pondering political and international issues while walking briskly in the early morning hours in his long dark coat and battered gray felt hat. And without ever holding elective office, he labored to unite Europe as the path to peace and was instrumental in creating a new international organization that brought France and Germany together.

The warmth of close family ties and relatives nourished the young Monnet. Born on November 9, 1888, Jean was the first of four children of brandy salesman Jean-Gabriel Monnet. His father rose to be a minor member of the merchant aristocracy in the small town of Cognac in western France where a cooperative of small vine growers in the region had formed a society in 1838 to escape the purchasing monopoly of large brandy firms like the Martells and Hennessys. The largest shareholders in this cooperative called the United Vineyard Proprietors' Company of Cognac had asked Jean's father in 1897, when Jean was nine years old, to take over running their business. It then became known as J. G. Monnet and Company. They mandated important changes, including bottling, a significant departure from the traditional method of selling brandy in large wooden barrels.[2]

Jean Monnet extolled the virtues of his mother, who was a key influence on her son throughout his life. A tolerant, devout Catholic, Maria Demelle Monnet was thirteen years younger than her husband and only nineteen years old when Jean was born. Always close to her son, she treasured the detailed accounts of his travels that he regularly sent to her. "She distrusted ideas as such," recalled Monnet. "She wanted to know what was done with them." Monnet believed that his mother had inherited the moral qualities of her parents and exemplified the finest virtues, simple nobility, and "a sense of duty and a sense of proportion." Her father, a successful wine merchant and cellarman at Hennessy, lived with his much respected wife in a small house in the old part of Cognac. The warmth of his maternal grandparents engulfed Monnet as long as they lived, and their home was the first he visited whenever he returned to Cognac from his travels abroad. Viewed as somewhat strict during his childhood, his mother provided a balance to his imaginative, impatient, and irascible but never vindictive father who thrived on activity and travel. The elder Monnet was described in a magazine profile of his son as "a witty temperamental Prince charming whose one great aim in life was to see Monnet brandy cover the earth."[3] Jean learned from him to work for the public good and the importance of ideas. An optimist by nature who concentrated on developing the family business, Jean-Gabriel benefited from an education at Cognac's local college where he was sent to learn German, a skill that helped him expand his trade beyond the Rhine in later years.[4]

Tales of foreign lands heard at the Monnet family dinner table influenced young Jean. Never fond of school because he hated memorization, he found it hard to sit still. He liked to escape to the riverbank on his way home, dip his toes in the cool water, and watch the sunlight bouncing and flickering off the eddies. Counting the ripples made by the flat stones he skipped over the waves became a favorite pastime. He looked forward to Saturdays when the distillers from the countryside, who supplied his father with the eau de vie (or raw spirit), joined his family for meals. Business, friendship, and mutual trust brought these men to the Monnets' large dining room in the stately mansion owned by the company to which Jean's parents had moved when his father assumed direction of the business. Monnet and his three younger siblings—Gaston, Henriette, and Marie-Louise—enjoyed playing in the cooperative's large warehouse.

Because Cognac's salesmen traveled worldwide to sell their product, its population welcomed foreigners as family friends, unlike many other French communities, which were isolated and untouched by foreign influence. Visitors from all over the world, most frequently from Britain, Canada, Russia, Germany, Scandinavia, and the United States, spent the night in the vintners' homes as there were no hotels in Cognac.

Jean-Gabriel trained his two sons to run the family business. Since Jean was unhappy at school and lacked a desire to gain any specialized education such as studying the law, the elder Monnet acceded to his son's request to leave school and work in the family firm as an apprentice after his first baccalaureate at age sixteen.[5]

Life in Cognac shaped Monnet's pattern of thinking and judgment of people. As the guests enjoyed hot meat soup, freshly baked bread, and fine wine around the Monnets' dining table, Jean and his father listened attentively to the travelers' stories. Since their business was dependent upon the prosperity and tastes of people all over the world, Jean's father quizzed his guests about conditions in other countries. The young Monnet admired his father's endless questioning and curiosity about different customs and languages and learned how the senior Monnet assessed information gleaned from a traveler or salesman. "For Monnet, informal talk at mealtimes was one of the keys to work and work itself the passport to friendship," writes biographer François Duchêne, a British journalist and poet who worked with Monnet in the 1950s and 1960s. "Although in some respects his intelligence was very abstract, his approach to action latched almost physically on to the psychology of people and situations he faced. . . . It was an outlook very foreign to the university-educated mind." Duchêne portrays Monnet as a man with a peasant heritage but more squire than peasant. Valuing character and the individual, he "tied neither to rank. . . . His yardstick was the upright individual, of any class, deserving the respect of a local community which knew him from childhood."[6]

## Young Man in London

After working with the young apprentice for a few months, the senior Monnet sent his sixteen-year-old son to London in 1904 to expose him to British business practices. He wanted Jean to learn English, the language of the principal buyers of cognac, and continue his education through practical experience in their business circles and travel. After arranging a two-year apprenticeship with W. H. Chaplin and Co., wine merchants and spirit dealers who were the Monnet firm's agents in London, Jean sailed to London where he lived with the Chaplin family. The young Frenchman went daily with his host to the City of London, the financial center of Britain and the Western world on the banks of the Thames River. He observed business negotiations and how clients were handled. When accompanying Chaplin to restaurants and clubs, he learned that the City's businessmen were part of a socially exclusive circle bonded together by frequent contact at exclusive clubs, golf courses, and pubs. Business rivalry, he observed, was enmeshed in a web of personal relationships in this closely knit community.

This apprenticeship with the London merchants made an indelible impression on Monnet. From these London days the young man from Cognac gained a respect for Britain's industrial and financial power and a lifelong link to the English-speaking world. He returned home with some understanding of the British, fluency in the language of his family firm's most important clients, and a lifelong passion for tailored English suits. As the result of his experience as a worldwide salesman in the years that followed his return to France in 1906, he learned more about the financial district's exclusivity and organized strength and, above all, its effective use of what he termed "collective action." This contrasted sharply with French business attitudes, which favored individual action. In England, the young Frenchman had observed that companies could succeed only if they were collectively supported by the firms of the City.[7] Monnet also learned firsthand that the trading link between Cognac and London was based on personal, open family ties. Regardless of politics, it was important that the seller and the purchaser establish good relations with mutual respect for each other and the product. He believed the Cognac salesmen were on equal terms with the British, whereas in Paris, the pervasive feeling was that the French businessmen were somewhat under the influence of their counterparts in that universally respected economic power.[8]

## Travels as a Cognac Salesman

The senior Monnet decided that after London his eldest son should learn first-hand the demanding requirements of the family business. Sending him abroad to find new clients became the next step as the brand name of Monnet was still unfamiliar on the international market. In 1906, the eighteen-year-old Monnet boarded the ocean liner headed for Canada wearing a brand new bowler hat and lugging a large trunk full of samples of the family brandy. He traveled by train across Canada, visited old clients in several Canadian cities such as Winnipeg, and explored boomtowns, such as Moose Jaw, Saskatchewan, and Medicine Hat, Alberta, that had sprung up in the wake of the Klondike gold rush. One day in Calgary when looking for a horse and buggy to hire, he asked a stranger, who was hitching his horse to a post outside a saloon, where he could find a livery stable. The man asked, "Can you ride?" "Yes, I can," replied Monnet. "Then take my horse. When you're through, just hitch it back here again."[9] Monnet claimed later, with a smile, that this was his first lesson in the international pooling of resources. The young man trekked northward to Fort Selkirk in the Yukon Territory wearing a long raccoon coat that protected him from strong winds and the bitter cold of their winter. Inspired by the breathtaking vistas while climbing in the Rockies, he acquired a taste for long walks as an aid to serious thought. He remarked that they enabled "the concentration of mind that precedes action."[10] On his trip back across the continent from California to New York, he recalled that the spontaneity, unlimited confidence, and dynamism of the Canadians and Americans had impressed him.

On successive trips to North America between 1906 and 1914, Monnet enhanced the reputation of the family brandy, developed a retail network for the company, and expanded sales to trading posts and saloons. In September 1911, he negotiated an important agreement with the Hudson Bay Company (HBC), which had a flourishing business trading in furs and skins. Even though there was a legal ban on selling spirits to the Indians, the company found that selling brandy to the tribes increased their business with them.[11] HBC had been clients of his father's since the 1890s, but in 1911, J. G. Monnet and Co. became the sole suppliers of brandy to HBC's vast Canadian market. As a result of these negotiations, the twenty-three-year-old Frenchman developed close personal relationships with HBC's top officials. The most important of these was with the company's governor, Robert Kindersley, who would later become the chairman of the board of the investment bank Lazard Brothers of London and a member of the governing board of the Bank of England.[12] Monnet's trips to Scandinavia, Russia, Egypt, Greece, China, and other countries between 1906 and 1914 also broadened his perspective and experience. When rumors of war reached him in Canada in 1914, he sailed home.

## Contributions to World War I

Monnet made his first important contribution to European affairs during World War I, which raged from July 28, 1914, to November 11, 1918. This war was fought by two major power blocks—the Entente Powers, or "Allies," of the United Kingdom, France, and Russia against the Central Powers of Germany, Austro-Hungary, and Turkey. Monnet later claimed that, by the late summer of 1914, he realized that the lack of economic coordination among the Allies would become a major problem if the war dragged on. He saw that France was bearing the brunt of the battle on the ground, losing territory and important economic resources to Germany, and suffering disproportionate casualties. As he later wrote, his country was utterly dependent on foreign shipping for overseas supplies because it had lost vital agricultural land, two-thirds of its iron and steel, and half of its coal. The British situation was very different. Free from invading Germans, in command of the seas, and with the bulk of its merchant fleet intact, Britain carried on normal foreign trade. But British officials often found the French bidding against them for scarce overseas supplies, which inflated shipping rates and import prices. From his experience in London, where he heard the British merchants complain about French trading practices, Monnet knew that the protectionist views of France were incompatible with free-trading Britain, whose ships controlled access to resources. Yet he was confident that Britain would eventually organize a formidable army while retaining control of the seas. It troubled Monnet that, with severe French losses, his government believed the British should hand over resources to them, instead of jointly coordinating resource allocation. Since he was found medically unfit for military service because of respiratory problems, Monnet decided he could be useful to his nation in another way: he would focus on persuading the French and the British to cooperate in the purchase of war supplies to maximize the benefit of the combined effort.[13]

Since the young Monnet used his father as a sounding board for many of his ideas, they discussed his plan. Jean-Gabriel reflected the thinking of his generation by expressing that France and Britain, as two sovereign powers with separate armies, should each run its own war effort. He chided his son by declaring that even if he were right, the young man would have no way to influence "the big chiefs" in Paris.[14] The headstrong young man ignored his father's comments and acted on a principle that he would follow throughout his life: "First have an idea, then look for the man who can put it to work."[15] Precocious and self-confident, Monnet visited Fernand Benon, a lawyer and family friend in Cognac who was close to the French Prime Minister René Viviani. Open to new ideas, Benon offered to introduce the young man to the French leader.

In mid-September 1914, after devastating French losses at the Battle of the Marne where the swift German invasion of France was halted, Benon took Jean to meet the fifty-year-old prime minister in Bordeaux, where the central government had relocated soon after the war began. The visit was timely because the importance of a reliable source of supplies was becoming clearer as retreats and losses obliterated any hope of a short war. A man of strong character, austere manner, and high intelligence, Viviani listened carefully as Monnet argued the case for using Britain's economic power to its fullest capacity, a contribution that he believed would be decisive. Monnet floated the idea of setting up a joint Anglo-French body that could estimate the combined resources of the Allies and make real choices and decisions. He argued Allied solidarity "must be total" and neither side "must be free to use its men, its supplies, or its shipping in ways that haven't been agreed by both."[16]

Viviani asserted Monnet must understand how difficult it would be for the governments of Britain and France, each with divisive parliamentary interests, to make decisions simultaneously. Monnet brashly replied that he knew the British well enough to believe this was possible if the French appealed to their loyalty and "played fair." Because the British understood the terrible burden the French armies were bearing, Monnet argued they would agree to make the biggest contributions in the fields where they were supreme—production and shipping. Viviani acknowledged that approaching the British government at a time when the French were asking them to send more troops to aid their defensive front in the Lowlands was awkward. But he told the young man to try because "You seem to have an idea of how to go about it." The French leader told Monnet to call on Alexandre Millerand, the minister of war, and explain it was at his request.[17]

The prime minister may have been willing to see this young Frenchman because Monnet had proposed as early as August 14 that the HBC, headquartered in London, should become the French government's purchasing agent for vital civilian supplies. The firm's negotiator arrived in Bordeaux on September 25, about a week after Monnet's meeting with Viviani, and concluded a contract, signed October 19 with the French Ministry of Commerce and Supplies. The company credited the agreement to the initiative of Monnet, who took no commission for linking it to the French government.[18]

As a result of discussions with Millerand, Monnet was sent to London at the end of November 1914 to join the liaison mission of the French Civil Supplies Service headed by Quartermaster-General Eugène Mauclère. The boundless energy of the young Frenchman impressed Mauclère. Even Monnet's bilingual British secretary, whom he hired, spoke of Monnet as a "well-dressed workaholic." Monnet served as adviser and interpreter for Mauclère, traveled frequently back to its headquarters in Paris, and worked closely with Arthur Salter, a young civil servant in the British Transport Department in London.

Catapulted to a key position, Monnet described the existing chaotic, wasteful system of purchasing Allied supplies, especially food and grains, to his superiors.[19] As the chief source of troop supplies, Britain had provided, controlled, and often paid for the Allies' purchases from the earliest days of the war. Britain's importance as the wholesaler for the Allies resulted from the fact that it had the largest merchant shipping fleet in the world and had not been invaded or occupied. A small consultative committee, the International Supply Commission (Commission Internationale de Revitaillement, or CIR), had been set up in London in August 1914 with representatives of the British Admiralty, War Office, and Board of Trade and two representatives of the French government. The CIR heard offers made by manufacturers and suppliers, considered Allied needs, consulted the British government about the availability of transport and finance, and either placed the orders or identified the firms to which the orders should be given. Since the CIR's responsibilities were limited to troop supplies and did not include wheat, flour, meat, or sugar, each government was free to make whatever additional purchases it needed. Monnet soon discovered that the French and British supply services were competing against each other for wheat on the Australian and Argentine wheat markets to the detriment of their combined war efforts.[20]

The need for an Allied organization to purchase wheat became apparent in 1915, but little Anglo-French coordination was achieved until 1916. By midsummer of that year, the British government saw the need to change its wheat-purchasing policy and assume responsibility for importing wheat for the Italian and French troops and for rationing bread at home. Due to the poor autumn harvest of 1916, wheat prices had continued to rise, and the likelihood of crop failure in North and South America threatened a worldwide wheat deficit. German submarine warfare had continued to deplete the available shipping tonnage, and Britain's growing financial straits made it more difficult to purchase foreign wheat at reasonable prices. As a result, the British government, acting through a Royal Commission on Wheat Supplies, assumed complete control of the purchase, importation, and distribution of its wheat and other cereals in October 1916.[21]

Etienne Clémentel, who became the minister of commerce and posts in October 1915 and the real organizer of the French war effort, was the first cabinet minister to realize France's need for economic cooperation with the Allies. Idealistic as well as pragmatic, he understood in early 1916 that supply crises were developing. Shipping losses mounted, tonnage ran short, and private trading, especially competing French and British bids, caused prices to soar on the Australian and Argentine markets. Because their navy was small, the French were dependent on leasing ships from private traders or the British. So when the British began requisitioning the private ships the French had already leased, he became alarmed. Because Clémentel valued Monnet's advice, he appointed him head of his delegation in London. The minister often gave official backing to the young man's suggestions, including allowing the installation of a direct telephone line between their two offices. This helped establish a dialogue between London and Paris. Describing Clémentel as cultivated, clear-headed, and extremely articulate, Monnet found they shared the same goals and were willing to debate the means. "His greatest virtue in my eyes, obviously, was to be able to listen to advice and make up his mind when he judged that he had learned enough."[22]

Immediately after the British government assumed control over wheat, Clémentel, Monnet, and Salter seized the opportunity to solve the supply crisis by creating the Wheat Executive, which would coordinate and meet Allied requirements by purchasing, allocating, and transporting wheat. Monnet organized a series of meetings in late 1916 between Clémentel and Walter Runciman, president of the British Board of Trade, which enabled them to formalize this new body in an agreement signed November 29, 1916. While Salter claimed it was Monnet's original idea and Clémentel asserted Monnet prepared the negotiations, Monnet recorded that a great debt was owed to Salter, who gained British cooperation.[23] Runciman and Clémentel also signed the Navigation Act on December 3, 1916, which guaranteed France the right to the five hundred ships it had leased previously on the free market.[24]

The Wheat Executive became an important mechanism in Allied economic cooperation. Composed of three officials, one each from Britain, Italy, and France, this new body assessed each country's needs and available supplies, agreed on the allotment of each nation's shares, issued joint orders for the purchase of wheat, and arranged for its transport. The competence and authority of the Wheat Executive's members, each one of whom was in practice able to speak responsibly for his government and determine its action, made it function effectively. The governments usually accepted its decisions because it ensured wheat supplies, kept prices to a minimum, and enabled them to share the savings in shipping space. Combined purchases prevented competition between the largest buyers in the market, put a brake on rising prices, and ended the expensive, competitive scramble.[25] It proved to be such a success that it was soon extended to cover all cereals. The novelty of the agreement, wrote Monnet, was not only its provisions but the spirit in which it was conceived and applied by those responsible. He argued that the notion of national interests took second place to that of "the common interest."[26]

At Monnet's recommendation, the Allies in 1917 extended the wheat system to all shipping. Germany's resumption of unrestricted submarine warfare in January 1917 dramatized the need to coordinate all Allied supply needs, including food and munitions. Clémentel, who chaired the Allied conference in Paris in late 1917, strongly supported the plan of Monnet, his young adviser and liaison in the intense negotiations where powerful nationalistic egos surfaced and Britain's predominant economic role was challenged. But agreement was finally reached, and a comprehensive supply control organization modeled on the Wheat Executive, called the Allied Maritime Transport Council (AMTC), was created. Monnet's memorandum outlining the plan served as the basis of discussion for the final agreement on tonnage and imports.[27] According to Salter, the new advance was prepared by Monnet, who "had the flair to discern when the moment of possible action had come."[28]

Salter and Monnet subsequently set up a small directorate, the Allied Maritime Transport Executive, to run the AMTC, which enabled it to function effectively as an inter-Allied organization. Having denounced the lack of centralization that caused confusion, Monnet sought a remedy in this small, governing body. With Salter as chairman, along with the American George Rublee, the Italian Bernardo Attolico, and Monnet, representing France, these four young men were the core of a group that formed a kind of international civil service with the authority to act in AMTC's name. Each was committed to the same goals, trusted and respected one another, shared secret information, and had considerable influence as well as direct access to his own government's decisionmakers. Wishing to maintain the delicate balance between Allied and national interests, they worked closely together to implement Allied decisions.[29]

The AMTC's role proved critical because it pooled both supplies and ships and eased the transportation bottleneck of 1918. Calling it a successful experiment, Salter wrote that "a new instrument of allied administration was created, tested and proved effective in operation." He asserted that the Allied Maritime Transport Executive's four members continued to exercise authority in their national offices. The new Allied organization, he wrote, showed that national governments could be "integrated into the new inter-allied institution for a special purpose." British diplomat Harold Nicolson called it "the most advanced experiment yet made in international cooperation." Its creation also demonstrated Monnet's ability to think strategically about a wartime problem, help create a solution, and then persuade national leaders to adopt it. But the implementation of the Wheat Executive and the AMTC also underscored the limits of the power of an international authority. Because it was not devised to displace the authority of national governments, the organization was not given the full administrative powers Monnet believed were needed. And since the war had demonstrated France's vulnerability to international pressure, because of its reliance on shipping and trade, it helped Europeans like Clémentel and Monnet understand the limits of their nation's economic sovereignty. It also underscored the realization that total war required more resources than any nation could alone provide.[30]

Because he had become a member of the French inner circle of decision-makers, Monnet aroused some opposition in Paris. While continuing in 1918 as France's representative on the Allied Maritime Transport Executive, Monnet also served since the end of 1916 as head of the French Mission in London for food and shipping, an organization of one hundred officials. Louis Loucheur, the minister of armaments who detested Clémentel, tried to have Monnet removed from his London posts. But Prime Minister Georges Clemenceau listened to Clémentel, personally summoned Monnet to Paris to question him on his work, was satisfied by the young man's report, and then ignored Loucheur's pleas. Moreover, the French government, under attack in the fall of 1918 in the National Assembly, utilized Monnet's British ties and asked him to secure extra shipping for relief and reconstruction in the northern part of France. After Monnet promptly arranged for the transfer of half a million tons of British shipping, he was officially thanked.[31]

## Participation in the Paris Peace Conference

Monnet's participation in the 1919 Paris Peace Conference, due to his close relationship with Clémentel and Clemenceau, gained him valuable experience as well as lifelong friends. While some other delegations viewed him as being outside the French establishment, these two top French leaders considered him a reliable source of information and their private spokesman. When the Allied leaders created the Supreme Economic Council, which had replaced the AMTC, Clémentel designated Monnet as France's representative in the Council's Supply Section headed by American Herbert Hoover. At the Peace Conference, the young Frenchman met some important individuals who later became influential and remained lifelong friends. New York lawyer John Foster Dulles, who was acting legal counsel to Bernard Baruch, the US representative on the Reparations Commission, remained especially close to Monnet and corresponded with him until the American's death in 1959. Others included Allen Dulles, Foster Dulles's brother and the director of the CIA in the Eisenhower administration, and prominent British economist John Maynard Keynes. Monnet also developed a close relationship with the US banker of J. P. Morgan, Dwight Morrow, with whom he had worked in London when the financier was an adviser attached to the US section of the AMTC. The Morrows and the Monnets developed close family ties and often visited each other's homes. The Morrows' daughter, writer Anne Morrow, and her husband Charles Lindbergh, were often Monnet's guests in Paris.[32]

Monnet strongly supported Clémentel's proposals to extend Allied wartime cooperation to the postwar reconstruction period and his plan for worldwide control of raw material supplies. Clémentel's real aim was to contain German economic power after the war and protect France against the superior strength of Germany in any Franco-German relationship. While it is unclear whether Monnet had any role in shaping these ideas, he argued for Allied economic planning as well as the continuation of wartime economic controls in the reconstruction period. But British and US opposition killed these proposals because the two countries wanted to return to free trade. Not wanting to perpetuate the wartime system of rationing supplies, those nations wished to maintain a free hand in the distribution of postwar relief, which the Americans knew would be funded largely by them.[33]

## Contributions to the League of Nations

Established on June 28, 1919, when the Treaty of Versailles was signed, the League of Nations was to prevent war through collective security and disarmament, and to settle international disputes through negotiation and arbitration. Its Council, composed of representatives of nine sovereign states, governed this intergovernmental organization by unanimous decisions. The Permanent Secretariat, located in Geneva, was composed of representatives from member nations who were experts in various spheres. Called the "motor" of the League of Nations, that body assisted the Council in its work while the forty-seven-nation Assembly could issue only opinions, resolutions, and recommendations.[34]

Monnet's wartime activities in London led to his appointment as a top administrator of the League of Nations. Because of his important role in creating and administering the inter-Allied institutions during the war, his name surfaced on both British and French leaders' lists as a possible candidate for a key job. Although he was suggested by the wartime British Minister of Blockade Lord Robert Cecil, it was Sir Eric Drummond, British diplomat and the League's designated secretary general, who personally chose Monnet among other nominations to be the highest ranking of four undersecretaries of the Secretariat and in the number two position allocated to a Frenchman.[35]

Drummond, Monnet, and Raymond Fosdick, the designated US League representative, were members of the committee that met to set up the Secretariat during the summer of 1919. Meeting at their headquarters in the London mansion called Sutherland House, these men believed that the League's authority was based on reason and cooperative goodwill. They idealistically clung to the hope its will would prevail by sheer moral strength and force of habit and significantly appeal to public opinion. In a letter to his wife that summer, Fosdick wrote that since his generation was in a "race with international anarchy," he and Monnet had stressed that the world had "very little time in which to set up the framework of international government and establish the habit of teamwork."[36] Fosdick, who served as undersecretary general of the League, left this post shortly after the US Senate voted on March 19, 1920, not to ratify the Versailles Treaty.

Monnet understood the shortcomings of the League: it had no powers of enforcement and had to rely on persuasion. Nevertheless, he clung to the belief then and throughout his life that change was possible. Writing in a May 27, 1919, memorandum, he asserted that cooperation among nations would grow from their getting to know each other better and "from the interpenetration between their constituent elements and those of their neighbors."[37] Both Monnet and Arthur Salter, who later joined the Secretariat as head of the Economic and Finance Division, saw the League "as a means to organize peace." Monnet believed a quality Secretariat with good contacts in governments would invite the states to "appreciate the problem as a whole in the light of the general interest."[38] Dwight Morrow also shared Monnet's faith in the Secretariat and his belief that it was a much more important body than either the League Council or Assembly. "Keep the organization a fact-finding body, and let its power grow, and keep in mind that it takes a very long time to accomplish anything that is to be permanent," he wrote Monnet. "Your League of Nations may not get started, or it may get started and it may fail, but men will come back to the work that you did in London during the war and will turn over the precedents that you made, and some of them will be used in the real concert that will last."[39]

Having lived in England for almost five years and traveling back and forth to Paris often during the war, Monnet had a growing interest in international problems, and he welcomed the new challenge. He moved to Geneva at the end of 1920 and soon became Drummond's principal aide, presided in his absence, and was later promoted to deputy secretary general. During the League's first three years Monnet, who brought an able international staff with him including French colleagues, made a substantial contribution to its birth and work.[40] As a League official, the thirty-one-year-old Frenchman designed innovative ways to solve complex international problems arising from war.

Monnet created a strategy to solve the heated dispute between Poland and Germany over coal-rich Upper Silesia, which had become one of the most important industrial areas of Europe by the end of the nineteenth century. Both nations laid claim to the land as well as to its coal and steel facilities. One-third of the over two million people living there were German, mainly the landed proprietors and owners of the industries, while two-thirds were Polish, largely workers or peasants. The Poles claimed the region was theirs, but the Germans insisted on holding on to their assets, approximately a quarter of Germany's total output. Both sides refused partition because each wanted control over the whole area. The British, backing Germany, and the French, backing Poland, handed this dispute to the League in August of 1921 and agreed to accept arbitration. The decision was then entrusted to a commission of the League composed of a Japanese chairman and representatives from four countries that had no part in the dispute—Brazil, China, Spain, and Belgium. This group turned to Monnet for the solution.[41]

In less than a month, he and his French colleague Pierre Denis produced a report outlining a pragmatic plan. They recommended that a transitional regime composed of two joint Polish-German institutions be established to govern the territory. One was a managing commission composed of two Germans and two Poles plus a League representative. The other, an arbitration tribunal composed of one expert from each government and a president appointed by the League, was to settle disputes. The two bodies would jointly run the disputed area for fifteen years on both sides of a proposed borderline dividing the area between the countries. Their mandate was to manage transport, distribution of water and electricity, currency, social security, trade unions, and other essential services. With regard to the tribunal, Monnet stipulated that the League chairman would possess the deciding vote in case of an impasse. Despite stormy opposition in the Reichstag, the German-Polish Convention on Silesia, which endorsed the plan containing 606 items, was signed on May 15, 1922. The managing commission backed by the arbitration tribunal worked well for fifteen years. In Monnet's view, the solution was not to start a process of change but to stabilize situations inherited from the war.[42]

Monnet also tackled the League's problem of rebuilding war-torn Austria. For three years, the Allies had done nothing to help that conquered country of 6.5 million German-speaking people recover from the war. But in 1921, the League was commissioned to restore the country's finances in order to combat inflation and unemployment. The Secretariat's financial committee determined that the monetary situation had to be stabilized first by the Austrian government before foreign loans could be secured. This involved budget cuts, a domestic loan, and an independent institute to control the flow of money. Even though the Austrian officials accepted these austere measures, the fear of political upheaval and the partition of Austria by Italy and Czechoslovakia had discouraged institutions from giving loans to revitalize its economy. Monnet thought that if the threat of external intervention were removed and if nations agreed to respect that country's independence and territorial integrity, loans would flow into the country. Monnet's idea was adopted, and Basil Blackwell, a respected British treasury official, was enlisted to design a recovery plan. He persuaded Great Britain, France, Italy, and Czechoslovakia to sign a "protocol of abstention" agreeing to respect Austria's territorial integrity and independence, and helped raise funds while the League supervised the operation. After Monnet persuaded the director of the prestigious and powerful Bank of England, Montagu Norman, to back the US$130 million Austrian loan, other banks in Geneva, Paris, and New York willingly subscribed.[43] Monnet wrote that he learned the value of "collective action" from this endeavor and "the need to associate in a common enterprise as equals, both victors and vanquished, both givers and receivers of aid."[44] He observed that by accepting outside help, Austria lost none of its independence but was strengthened by international guarantees and domestic reforms. The success of the Austrian settlement, the first time an international organization sponsored a program of reconstruction, triggered efforts to stabilize the Hungarian economy, which also had been badly damaged during the war. It also stimulated hopes that the League would help initiate changes in the international system.[45]

Monnet earned praise from European diplomats and French leaders for his League work. To many who worked in this international organization, he was the "kingpin" of the organization because he demonstrated that the League had real power to arbitrate disputes or to find solutions to problems. He was active in the delineation of the Geneva Protocol, a 1925 treaty prohibiting the first use of chemical and biological weapons; helped organize a conference on international financial questions; and chaired the League's Economic Committee. He opposed the location of League headquarters in Geneva, Switzerland, because he believed it was too far from the power centers of Europe and tried, to no avail, to help restructure German reparations. Even though his name was attached to the ill-fated Saar policy (allowing France to gain economic control of that region until a referendum fifteen years hence), which he had opposed, he received other commendations. Through close collaboration, he earned the respect of many of his League colleagues such as French diplomats Henri Bonnet and René Massigli, French academic Paul Mantoux, young French civil servants Pierre Comert and Pierre Denis, as well as members of the international elite with whom he worked. Among these were Englishman Albert Thomas, Norwegian diplomat Eric Colban, and Polish doctor Ludwik Rajchman. Louis Joxe, who was later secretary general of the French Foreign Ministry and worked in both the Secretariat and French delegation to the League, wrote that the French, from Foreign Minister Aristide Briand downward, "swore by Jean Monnet who was their guide and conscience." Joxe remarked that when Monnet left, "the great names of the day . . . could hardly conceive of life in Geneva without referring to his example."[46] Georges Bonnet, the French foreign minister of Munich in September 1938, noted that Monnet "enjoyed an extraordinary reputation as a clever diplomat."[47] While his colleagues noted this young man had great charm, determination, energy, and a fiery temper when opposed, Monnet's friend Louise Weiss wrote that his "flashes of genius" assured that the League had "remarkable power." The Spanish essayist Salvador de Madariaga argued that, besides Drummond, Monnet was the "creator" of the League of Nations and remarked that he seemed to have moral and physical "equilibrium" and "poise." He described Monnet as a bourgeois who remained in French history as "the model of all that the French bourgeoisie have given France and the world: positive intelligence, disinterested action, integrity, a sense of public service and responsibility."[48]

Monnet's contributions to the League of Nations demonstrated his capacity to think strategically and design innovative ways to diffuse complex international disputes. More importantly, the experience of working there inspired his thinking about ways to solve international controversies and earned him an international reputation. He confessed later in his life that the League supplied "little solutions to big problems" and that he disliked the administrative work. He was especially frustrated by the League's fatal flaw: its inability to enforce a decision over a national veto. Heads of governments searched for solutions that suited their national interests, not solutions to problems, and this veto power was both the cause and the symbol of a nation's inability "to go beyond national interest." He wrote he was concerned about "the power of a nation to say no to an international body that had no supranational power."[49]

## Rescuing J. G. Monnet and Co.

At the end of 1922, thirty-four-year-old Monnet resigned from the Secretariat of the League to rescue his family's business from bankruptcy. His sister Marie-Louise had traveled to Geneva to beg her brother to return to take charge of J. G. Monnet and Co. Drummond and other League officials pleaded with him to stay and claimed that his departure would compromise the development of that institution. But he did not change his mind. His family was extremely important to him, and he could not ignore this obligation. Drummond especially regretted his departure as they had collaborated closely, viewed many issues from a similar perspective, and had become great friends. Monnet had enjoyed working with him in the new international organization and felt more could usefully be done. But he wrote to Drummond that he knew the team he left behind would continue the work of the Secretariat, which like "all institutions, would outlive its founders." He claimed he left because his father was old and needed him, not out of disenchantment with the League's weakness, which he said he comprehended more fully later in his life. While he thrived at the epicenter of tough negotiations and enjoyed puzzling through solutions to international disputes, he had learned that he was not born to be an administrator and was content to leave that aspect of his League work behind.[50]

Because the British market for cognac had declined due to increased duties on spirits after the war and a shift in British tastes to whiskey, J. G. Monnet and Co. was in financial trouble. In addition, the US market fell in the early 1920s as a result of prohibition. In his effort to save the firm, Monnet made several important decisions. The first, which was painful to him but especially to the elder Monnet, was to abandon his father's conservative business practice of tying up much of the firm's capital in the barrels of brandy stored in their cellars and selling only small amounts of older brandy to connoisseurs. He had to free up more capital through increased sales of the company's vast stocks while expanding the sale of younger spirits. In addition, he created a brandy syndicate that allowed him to sell shares in brandy "futures" to his British and US friends, which helped the firm recover and keep it from bankruptcy.[51] He also reorganized the firm to increase its efficiency. But two other remedial efforts did not work. His attempt to buy the assets of the Mumm champagne company came to nothing. And his brother Gaston's request to Ivar Kreuger, a Swede who controlled 75 percent of the world's match industry, for a guarantee of a loan to cover obligations from the franc's fall was turned down. This came as a surprise because Gaston's Swedish wife, Helmi, and her family were close to the Kreugers. And the Monnet brothers thought that because their family firm had the sole right of importing wine and spirits into Sweden, this might have brought a different result.[52]

Another request for a loan did succeed. Before leaving the League in March 1922, Monnet had requested a loan from the HBC headed by Robert Kindersley. Although the long-standing relationship between the firm and HBC was cordial, it improved after the younger Monnet negotiated HBC's 1911 agreement with the family firm and spearheaded its 1914 agreement with the French government for supplies. As a result, the firm's London headquarters responded rapidly to his request, and J. G. Monnet and Co. was granted a loan of 2 million francs (about $160,000). Monnet agreed to repay the loan, but the HBC board told him it would be treated as a gift if not repaid because Monnet had consistently refused any commission on that firm's war profits, which had exceeded 1 million pounds (about $5 million). Recovery came gradually. Production in the Cognac region had fallen, brandy prices rose, and the British market revived slowly. By the end of 1925 and early 1926, the Monnet firm became financially sound again. The business was turned over to his cousins, Robert and Georges Monnet, after his brother Gaston's death in 1927. Jean sold his house on the river to Robert but continued to maintain shares and involvement in the company's policies and received annual income of about $25,000 for the rest of his life. In September 1930, the HBC loan was repaid with interest, twelve years before it was due. But since the agreement mandated repayment in francs, which had lost about 60 percent of their value, J. G. Monnet and Co.'s reimbursement was really less than 40 percent of principal and interest. This substantial, timely loan probably saved the Monnet company.[53]

## Investment Banking Experience

Having stabilized his family company and rescued it from bankruptcy, Monnet seriously considered a new financial opportunity. A New York investment bank and one of the leading finance houses investing in Europe, Blair and Company, asked him to set up a joint European affiliate with Chase National, the Blair and Company foreign corporation. While on a trip to the United States and Canada with his cousin George for the family firm's business in January 1926, he discussed the offer with some of his American friends. As he was unable to consult Dwight Morrow, he later wrote him that he had accepted the offer of vice president and managing partner of European Blair in Paris in August 1926.[54]

Between 1924 and 1930, the US financial community greatly expanded its investments in Europe. Because the financial structure of the continent was threatened by the near-collapse of the Weimar Republic, its rampant inflation, and its default on its reparations installment in 1923, US policymakers were willing, by the end of that year, to play a significant role in the financial rehabilitation of Germany and the stabilization of European currencies. Banker and politician Charles G. Dawes, a member of the Allied Reparations Commission in 1923, chaired the international committee of experts that was mandated by this commission to find a solution to the crisis. This committee devised the Dawes Plan in 1924, which provided US finance largely through loans to revive the German economy, reduce somewhat the burden of its reparations, and stabilize the European currencies. The policymakers assumed that as Germany's economic growth resumed and European economies began to recuperate, they were laying the basis for US prosperity as well as the framework for a stable and peaceful world order.[55]

In the mid-1920s, powerful New York investment bankers extended their interests in Europe. They floated loans for industrial firms or governments that by themselves were unable to raise the credit needed for capital investment. Blair was one of the leading financial houses providing US investment in Europe, which fueled this period of rapid growth. While most of the money came from open capital markets, the consortia formed for each of their loans had the prior backing of the four major central banks—those of the United Kingdom, France, United States, and Germany, headed by strong, powerful governors.[56]

Monnet became the chief negotiator for a loan to the Polish government in which a consortium of US banks—Blair, Banker's Trust, Chase National, and Kuhn Loeb—decided to organize an international issue of bonds. The Polish plan was to use the money for an internal economic reform program designed to counter inflation and stimulate a period of stable economic growth. While the Bank of England had been weakened by World War I, its strong governor, Montagu Norman, behaved as though his nation's pre-1914 preeminence had not been lost. Wishing to exert British influence, Norman believed his bank and no other should act as the financial guardian and settle the Polish question. While on good terms with Norman, Monnet regarded him as an imperialist with a superiority complex. Emile Moreau, governor of the Bank of France, a staunch rival of Norman's and competitor for influence and power in Europe, fostered hopes to bolster his country's relations with Eastern European countries as bulwarks against Germany. In July 1926, Monnet had helped Moreau with the stabilization of the franc by serving as intermediary among Moreau, French Prime Minister Raymond Poincaré, and Benjamin Strong, the US Federal Reserve Bank chairman. After bluntly sharing with Moreau the view that the Americans favored him, Monnet facilitated a meeting among the US treasury secretary, other US officials, and Strong, who agreed to help the French. The excellent relationship Strong thereby established with Moreau pleased them both.[57]

Ludwik Rajchman, a cultivated Polish doctor who was the health director of the League of Nations, alerted his former French colleague to the Poles' fears that Norman intended to make political demands on Poland. Rajchman hoped Monnet and Blair and Co. would help Poland resist British insistence that its existing borders with Germany be revised. During most of 1927, when negotiating with the Polish government in Warsaw, Monnet wrote, "I found myself at the crossroads of rival influences emanating from London, Paris, Berlin, and Washington, since the big central banks all felt it their duty to supervise the parity at which the Polish currency was fixed."[58] John Foster Dulles of Sullivan and Cromwell of New York, one of the largest law firms in the country, served as the principal US lawyer and legal adviser in these negotiations. With the help of his American friend, Monnet navigated through the web of rivalries and negotiated a solution satisfactory to all parties. He was able to establish himself at the center of the negotiations because he was trusted by Strong and succeeded in persuading Moreau and the French bank to become a counterweight to British influence. In the battles over the loan to Poland, Strong settled the British-French dispute by taking the lead and forcing the two governors to follow. As Moreau noted in his diary, Monnet told him that US bankers had decided that the Bank of England would no longer be their sole channel for loans to European governments. But Monnet also warned Moreau against revealing France's political aim in Eastern Europe to the Americans, whose interests were economic and financial. In establishing a Franco-American alliance in these financial negotiations, "It is not clear how much Monnet acted as an American banker or extracurricular Frenchman," Duchêne concludes.

"The two were compatible. Either way, aligning with Americans to overcome European opposition was prophetic of his later career."[59]

The Polish loan for $72 million, based on $20 million contributed by the four central banks, was signed in Warsaw at the end of 1927 with no strings attached but a demand for severe domestic reform measures. Monnet recalled with amusement the final negotiation, which took place in the office of President Marshal Józef Pilsudski of Poland. The president, recorded Monnet, decked in "his tight, gray military tunic ribbed with red, expostulated against our demands. He refused an interest rate of 7 1/2 %. We got up, ready to break off negotiations. 'Wait a moment,' he said. We sat down again. 'Look,' he said smiling, 'Surely you'll let me have half a point for Wanda?'" After revealing she was his daughter, the bankers willingly complied and agreed to a loan at 7 percent.[60]

In January 1928, Monnet became the key negotiator for Blair and Co. on a loan made to Romania to stabilize its currency and revive its economy. While the strategy resembled that of the Polish loan, it proved more difficult. The sum was $100 million, and US willingness to invest in foreign securities diminished after the stock market decline of 1928, precursor to the crash of October 1929. Businessman Ivar Kreuger, the Swedish "match king" and an important client of J. G. Monnet and Co., saved the day by promising the final $30 million needed to conclude the loan in February 1929. As the whole Kreuger empire was founded on secret speculation and fraud, it began to crumble after the 1929 stock market crash and then totally collapsed. Because of this, Kreuger shot himself in Paris in March 1932.[61]

Monnet's investment banking experience from 1926 to 1932 initiated him into the culture of the financial world and underscored the intense nationalism of the period, the political nature of the loans, and rivalries among the central banks. It also provided important European contacts and expanded his network of influential Americans. René Pleven, later the French prime minister in the early 1950s, served as Monnet's main assistant in Blair and Co.'s financial dealings from 1925 to 1929 and worked periodically for him until 1940. Pleven later expressed how much he learned from his early experience of working with his friend from Cognac. "Monnet was my guide during the early years of my life," wrote Pleven. "He was one of the great men who marked our time" not only because of his "extraordinary clairvoyance and the sureness of his judgment" but because "his indomitable spirit was never dampened by events. . . . He was above all a man of action."[62]

In the 1920s, Monnet's fascination with the United States never abated. His friendship with prominent Americans in New York like Dulles and Morrow, who also worked on the European loans, deepened during the lengthy negotiations. The Frenchman met the young lawyer John McCloy, who joined the New York law firm Cravath in 1924, through Donald Swatland, McCloy's Harvard Law School classmate and lawyer for Blair and Co. When he headed the Paris office for Cravath in 1930, McCloy had frequent contact with Monnet. During these years, Walter Lippmann, a prominent US journalist of worldwide prominence who had befriended Monnet at the Versailles Conference, became in the 1920s one of few individuals Monnet considered his equal. These two men corresponded regularly until Lippmann's death in 1963 and met often in Paris, New York, or Washington. Frequently dining in each other's homes, their wives also became good friends. Lippmann often sent the Frenchman his articles from the *New York Herald,* and Monnet occasionally sent to this American the policy statements he had written in hopes of getting coverage in the US press.[63]

## Loss of Risky Investment

Not all of Monnet's US contacts proved advantageous to him in the long run. After signing the Romanian loan in February 1929, Monnet returned to New York. He found his US colleague, the head of Blair in New York, Elisha Walker, wanting to take advantage of the optimistic and expansionist mood of US financial circles. The banker was searching for new financial opportunities and found a like-minded partner in Amadeo Giannini. This well-known sixty-year-old Italian financier, an imposing figure with "a lion's mane of grizzled hair," had built the Bank of America in San Francisco into the largest banking network outside of New York, with many holding companies in Europe and America. In hopes of creating a bank with worldwide reach, these two men fused the assets of the two financial houses and established a vast holding company called Transamerica. Walker signed an agreement in March 1929 with Transamerica Corp., the parent company of Bank of America, to merge with Blair and Co. In the consolidation, Blair and Co. received $86 million in the form of 363,637 shares of Bank of America, making the total shares of Transamerica 1,363,637. In May, the agreement came into effect under the name of Bancamerica-Blair Corp., with Walker as president and chairman of Transamerica's executive committee and Monnet as vice chairman. While Walker argued it was neither a sale nor an absorption but a consolidation, the *New York Times* reported that it was the first merger of a private bank and a national bank and that the new corporation would have capitalization of $125 million, with half coming from Blair and Co. Soon after he made his deal with Walker, Giannini retired to Austria on what he claimed to be a badly needed two-year vacation.[64]

The month of August 1929 turned out to be pivotal in Monnet's life. News of the Transamerica merger caused its share prices to soar throughout the summer. On August 23, Transamerica Corp. declared a 150 percent dividend, and the stock continued to rise in September. On top of that good news, Monnet met "the light of his life"—Silvia de Bondini Giannini—that same month. He had invited his Italian colleague, Francesco Giannini (no relation to Amadeo Giannini), a senior official of Blair and Co. in Rome, for dinner at his Paris home. "That night, I saw his young wife for the first time," wrote Monnet. "She was very beautiful. We forgot the other guests. . . . I think I can trace back to that first meeting the beginning of a love that was mutual and indestructible. I was forty years old; she was little more than twenty. We soon decided that we must be together for life."[65] While Monnet's *Memoirs* were written by his friend François Fontaine in the 1970s and then reviewed and approved by Monnet, the description of this meeting and Monnet and Giannini's love was composed by the couple themselves. As he was always private about their marriage, he did not want anything more written about it in his memoirs.[66]

We do not know if Silvia returned the Frenchman's infatuation immediately because little is written about her. The daughter of an Italian publisher of a French-language weekly who grew up speaking French and Greek as well as Italian, she had married Giannini in Italy only four months earlier. But the eligible French bachelor focused his charm on her. This intelligent, passionate, strikingly beautiful woman with long dark hair, a magnetic smile, and sparkling eyes became the center of his life and dreams.

When the stock market crashed on October 24, 1929, Monnet and Walker precipitously lost the fortune they had made in only five months as a result of the merger. In January 1930, the two men discovered that the declared assets of Transamerica were fraudulent and seriously overvalued. Having failed to investigate Giannini's assets or to talk to the accountants before the merger, Walker and Monnet found balance sheets replete with double booking. Transamerica shares tumbled from $165 in September 1929 to $2 a share by the end of 1931. Moreover, the company's worth plummeted in the same period, and the whole venture collapsed. With the help of Swatland, Monnet and Walker reorganized Transamerica, isolated it from Giannini's other commercial holdings, and settled the financial disputes and problems.

But Monnet and Walker had also underestimated the guile and energy of this wily Italian. He accused Walker and Monnet of trying to take the corporation from him in a "diabolical conspiracy," which he claimed had caused the share price to sink. In February 1932 Giannini regained control of the company through a carefully staged campaign to woo the stockholders and won a cleverly planned proxy fight. Monnet and Walker left Transamerica with heavy hearts and empty pockets and returned to New York with the other Blair managers, leaving their company behind. Having been a millionaire for a brief period, Monnet lost the entire sum he had acquired in that venture. He later remarked, "I may have been good at making [money] perhaps, but certainly not at keeping it."[67]

## Challenges in China

Between 1932 and 1936, influential friends like Dulles and the Lazard Bank partners Kindersley and Baron Robert Brand helped Monnet survive financially after the collapse of the Transamerica venture. At Dulles's recommendation, Monnet was invited to represent the creditors as one of five members of a board chosen to liquidate Kreuger's match empire from September 1932 to July 1933. The Lazard partners also steered some jobs his way. Because their bank had benefited from collaboration with Monnet on the purchase of supplies during World War I, they gave him direct financial assistance for several years after his Transamerica debacle in the form of a substantial loan.[68]

Rajchman, Monnet's League of Nations colleague, generated an unusual financial opportunity for the Frenchman in China in 1933. Rajchman had become a close friend of T. V. Soong, the Harvard-educated finance minister of the Chinese Nationalist government. In the 1930s, the Nationalist Chinese government, headed by the wily General Chiang Kai-shek, took steps to Westernize its economy. Soong, brother of the general's wife, who belonged to one of the most powerful families in China, had traveled widely in Europe and the United States and acquired an interest in Western ways and culture. A strong advocate of modernizing China, he wished to free his nation from the financial tutelage of the so-called China Consortium, a cartel of US, British, French, and Japanese banks backed by their governments. Rajchman, who had visited China in 1925 and again as the League health official in 1929, had been charmed and wooed by Soong, and returned to Geneva a champion of China and its modernization. Rajchman became convinced that there was a great need to attack China's serious public health and sanitary issues along with its financial and economic problems.

In the early 1930s, Soong turned to Rajchman and requested advice about reconstruction from the League of Nations' economic experts. The Pole arranged to have Arthur Salter, who had become director of the League's Economic and Financial Department, sent to China to advise Soong on developing a reconstruction plan of Chinese design. Soong also sought his advice on the establishment of a central body to coordinate the efforts of the various ministries. With Salter's help in 1931, Soong set up the National Economic Council to handle some investments in projects for roads, agriculture, education, and public health. But Salter was skeptical that the council would succeed. "To one who came like myself as a technical adviser on [an] official policy visit to China," he wrote in his memoirs, "[the reaction] was bound to be first of fascinating interest and then of disillusionment." The technical problems "were soluble," he noted, but "the indispensable basis was peace, external and internal, and reasonably good government. Without this, all financial and economic schemes were useless."[69]

Two years later, Soong followed Rajchman's recommendation and invited Monnet to come to China as an economic consultant. The offer was relayed by the Polish doctor sometime in late 1932 or early 1933. Monnet seriously considered the offer and met several times with Soong after his arrival in the United States in May 1933 in Washington before and after the minister's scheduled exploratory meetings with Wall Street officials and bankers and the State Department. Monnet continued his discussions with the Chinese minister in early June when they sailed on the same ship to Britain. Together they met on June 14 at Lazard Bank in London with Brand, Kindersley, and British financier Charles Addis.[70] During those discussions, Soong revealed he had made Lazard Bank the sole purchasing agent in England for Nationalist China, a deal probably made as a result of Monnet's close contacts with these men. This meant the Frenchman and the Chinese minister shared an important financial connection. Monnet also understood that the underlying assumption of these London-based bankers was that, in exchange for financially supporting Monnet with substantial loans over the years, the bank expected him to generate business in China and channel some of it to them.[71]

Monnet continued discussions with Soong in July 1933. The Chinese official wanted Monnet to come to China to propose an economic development strategy and a comprehensive reconstruction plan. Moreover, he wanted Monnet to bring US and European groups together to provide China with loans, technical assistance, and funds to finance economic development. The minister's declared goal was to create a "Consultative Committee," an international corporation for investment, which would attract both Chinese and international capital, represent foreigners and Chinese in equal numbers, and exclude the Japanese. This idea of creating an international corporation was probably Monnet's. Soong's offer included substantial remuneration. In a May 19, 1933, agreement, Soong stated he would pay Monnet $150,000 a year and cover the cost of his offices in China, Paris, London, and New York related to the construction plan as well as the expenses of cable and travel.

In a second agreement of July 18, Monnet agreed to develop the international corporation and expressed his willingness to assist the Chinese government in reorganizing its foreign purchases through a central department.[72] Soong asked Monnet to chair this committee or corporation, which he envisioned would be composed of US, Belgian, British, Chinese, French, German, and Italian members. Monnet was a logical choice because of his close association with Rajchman and Lazard Bank and his own reputation in international finance.[73]

Monnet pondered the unknown factors surrounding this mission and carefully weighed the advice of his British and US friends. As the League had rejected the Chinese minister's request that Monnet be sent to China on an official mission, the risks were totally his. The fact that Soong, whom he barely knew, had made a financial arrangement with his close friends at Lazard must have been reassuring to him and played some role in his acceptance of the unusual offer. And his dream of marrying his beloved Silvia Giannini as soon as possible meant he badly needed money to finance a new family. Monnet finally accepted the challenge because his financial needs were great and there were no other immediate job offers.[74]

He sailed from New York via San Francisco for Shanghai in November 1933 with two British colleagues. Arthur Salter, who had returned to Geneva in 1931 from his first mission to China for Soong, accompanied Monnet on this trip because he had been asked to write a report on the Chinese economy for the League. David Drummond, son of Eric Drummond, was also on board as he had been invited to assist Monnet during his seven-month stay. They arrived in China's financial capital three weeks later, where Soong warmly welcomed them. The Chinese minister had arranged with his local French agent and representative of the Bank of Indochina, Henri Mazot, to house the trio in a comfortable villa in the city's French enclave. With its French restaurants and lotteries, the area, wrote Monnet, had "the atmosphere of a French provincial town."[75]

Teeming with Chinese on bicycles and foreigners, the large international port city of Shanghai pulsated with mystery and intrigue. Western resources, enterprise, and manufactures streamed into this economic center of the Chinese economy. As the trio explored the city, they saw Chinese workers scurrying around the docks and unloading cargo as ships came and went. On its dark streets, they found nightclubs flourishing. Beautiful Chinese women with sleek, shining black hair moved gracefully in sheath dresses, serving drinks, while the international patrons puffed on long, thin opium pipes and listened to Chinese jazz bands playing popular American tunes.

Soong introduced Monnet to many Chinese customs and to prominent Chinese bankers and officials in Shanghai. Traveling to other key cities in China, the Frenchman wished to garner information firsthand. He found the Chinese very different from Westerners and impossible to understand. But he gradually learned how to win their confidence, and that, he believed, was more important than understanding them. He found their pride had been deeply wounded by the intrusion of powerful European firms that had treated China like a colonial territory. This had made them wary of foreigners and many were xenophobic. But his secret was "to act as you speak, so that there is never any contradiction between what you say and what you do." He found that once he had won their confidence and established good personal relations, "everything becomes simple and there are no misunderstandings."[76]

Monnet's own experience in international finance, combined with advice from his Chinese contacts, made it clear to him early on that it would be impossible to invest foreign capital in the reconstruction of China without Chinese capital. He also knew that the repayment of loans could be guaranteed only if the Chinese were part of the financial operation. What was needed, he decided, was a wholly Chinese financial corporation to be organized by the principal banks themselves, a body that would be able to participate in bond issues on Western markets and with which European financial interests could deal on a large-scale operation in China.[77] He believed it essential that this corporation create an alliance between foreign and Chinese capital. Such an insti-

tution would also give the Chinese an equal stake in the success of the operations that were needed to modernize their country, another essential requirement. Investment in China's infrastructure, especially the expansion of communications and transport such as railways in that vast country, should be the
bank's first priority before financing other industry, he argued.[78]

Many obstacles confronted Monnet as he tried to implement his pragmatic
plan. Much opposition came from Chinese bankers themselves because his
recommendations violated long-established traditional practices and plunged
him into the midst of personal and political alliances and rivalries. The Chinese elites and bankers were suspicious of his motives and were especially
wary of foreigners like himself serving as intermediaries between Chinese and
foreign banks. And there were other problems. Even though Shanghai was the
financial and business capital of China, Monnet was shocked to discover it had
no bank capable of floating loans but only deposit banks where many south-
ern Chinese kept their savings and where many of the wealthiest banks were
Chinese, not foreign. Officials challenged his argument that it was necessary
to bring the Bank of China, which was controlled by the central government
with the ability to pressure private banks, together with not only public and
private banks but also foreign ones. A number of officials did not believe rival
banks could cooperate and work together in this venture. In addition, there was
much resistance to his assertion that it was necessary for Chinese banks to pay
their outstanding debts first before trying to obtain new credits. Because the
Chinese had defaulted often on the principal as well as the interest of their foreign debts, Chinese credit was nonexistent, and, between 1928 and 1933,
China had failed to raise a single loan.[79]

Monnet faced other difficult challenges. He had arrived in China in the
midst of its own civil war and Japanese aggression. The Nationalist Chinese
government in 1933, led by Chiang Kai-shek, had won the battle against its
Chinese opponents, but it was still fighting continuous Japanese advances in
the north, Communists in the central part of the country, and political opposition in the south. The political instability affected the financial sector, and, as
Monnet wrote, "Revolutionary ferment was universal."[80]

In the late nineteenth century, the Japanese had methodically extended
their influence in Asia by occupying parts of Mongolia and establishing control over Taiwan in 1895 and later over the Korean peninsula in 1905. Japan
began its long, drawn-out intermittent war with China in the 1930s and was
moving rapidly to consolidate its empire by invading Manchuria in 1931 and
annexing it in 1932. In the 1920s, a series of treaties, known as the Washington Conference System, were signed by eight nations to uphold China's independence and integrity and maintain the principle of equal opportunity for its
economic development. Even though Japan was a member of this treaty
regime, under which the European signatories steadily made concessions
demanded by China, Japanese elites feared being at the mercy of outside

forces as well as alienation from the international community. Japan wished to limit the demands of the Chinese Nationalists and to make China's rich natural resources available for its own use.[81]

Japan remained a serious obstacle to Monnet's plan because its officials were hostile to any foreign penetration of China that rivaled their own. Moreover, the Japanese had no interest in China's growth and were suspicious of Monnet's motives. Although he arrived in Shanghai as a private individual, Monnet's association with Rajchman, who was known to be hostile to Japan, made it hard for the Japanese to believe Monnet operated independently of the Polish doctor. They mistrusted Monnet's repeated assurances to their consul in Nanking, Yakichiro Suma, that he was not working as a League representative nor was he anti-Japanese. Suspicions of Monnet and his efforts to stimulate Chinese development came also from his close association with Soong, whom the Japanese intensely disliked because he wanted to exclude the Japanese from certain investments in China.[82]

Fully aware of the problem, Monnet was open about his work and careful to keep Suma informed at every stage. But Suma and the Japanese government remained intractable and insisted on having a say on matters such as how the Chinese should manage their debt. They continually demanded that their imperialistic claim in China be recognized by the other powers, that the Nationalist government of Chiang Kai-shek sign a preferential trade agreement with them, and that in any loan agreement they have the lion's share of the business. On April 17, 1934, the head of Japan's Foreign Ministry's Information Section issued a declaration that "we oppose . . . any attempt on the part of China to avail herself of the influence of any other country in order to resist Japan."[83] The Japanese not only worried about Monnet's and Soong's activities but also feared that the United States wished for a prominent role in China and believed that behind Monnet lay US financial power.[84]

Rumors of intrigue, false accusations, and deception surrounded Monnet as he worked to establish a Chinese development corporation. His plan was viewed with suspicion not only by many Chinese and the Japanese but by officials representing the French and British governments in Nanking and Shanghai. French diplomat and Asia expert Henri Hoppenot, who distrusted Rajchman, feared China could not make the reforms necessary for Monnet's scheme to work. With the approval of the secretary general of the French Foreign Ministry in Paris, Philippe Berthelot, Hoppenot ordered Philip Baudet, French consul in Nanking, to talk to Monnet in Shanghai and report on his activities. Baudet informed his government that the Frenchman's plans were adventurous, illusory, fragile, and had little chance of being implemented. Baudet warned that, while Monnet's project was underwritten by private Chinese banks with a lot of disposable capital, the sums were insufficient and would therefore prevent foreign investors from obtaining the necessary guarantees on their investment. The consul also expressed his own doubts about the willingness of the Chinese to pay their outstanding debts and whether Japanese resistance could be overcome. If the Japanese allowed Monnet's proposed bank to be created, Baudet argued, there was the possibility that there would be pressure by the Chinese financiers not to repay and thus cause their guarantees to foreigners to evaporate.[85]

Both Suma and Baudet played a double game, conveying false information about Monnet's endeavors not only to their own governments but also to the British. Suma reported to a British diplomat that Monnet's bank would run into problems of debt repayment, that it was a company "on paper only," and that it was incapable of fulfilling Soong's goal of constructing a capitalist regime in China. Even Drummond's own dispatches defending and explaining his colleague's scheme to the British Foreign Office fell on deaf ears. His reports failed to disprove Suma's and Baudet's exaggerated, damaging claims, partly because the British viewed the French as rivals in China, where the British were the largest investors and remained determined to safeguard their interests. Moreover, the British Foreign Office viewed Monnet's plan to build the transportation infrastructure by financing Chinese railways as direct competition. Foreign Office official Alexander Cadogan wrote that he believed the reports that Monnet's plan existed only on paper and that its author, while being a capable financier, had no sense of political realities. Other British officials held the view that the Frenchman was elusive, bothersome, and adventurous. They also complained about the unwillingness of Monnet's financial sponsor, Soong, to disclose his own dependence on British financial institutions.[86]

Defying his competitors, skeptics, and perpetrators of false information, Monnet confounded his detractors in June 1934 and secured agreement from the principal Chinese banks to participate in and to underwrite a new development bank he created called the China Development Finance Corporation (CDFC). Just seven months after arriving in this bustling Chinese city, his new institution was designed to combine long-term Chinese public and private capital with foreign capital and inject the latter into public and private commercial and industrial ventures. The French entrepreneur had steadfastly adhered to the operating principles he had originally outlined to Soong: (1) the need for Chinese participation in the institution's creation and to share in its profits, and (2) the need for the bank to grant equal opportunity to all foreign banks to participate in and to profit equally from the enterprise without discrimination. With the help of Soong's strong pressure on the banks, Monnet had secured the agreement of the main Chinese private banks and the four government-controlled ones, including the powerful Bank of Shanghai and Hong Kong, to be participants in the new Shanghai-based institution. The real powers behind the CDFC, among the ninety-eight persons attending the first shareholder meeting on June 2, 1934, at the Shanghai Bankers Club, were the members of the Soong family: the three brothers T. V., T. L., and T. A. Soong and their brother-in-law, H. H. Kung, who was married to Chiang Kai-shek's older sister.[87]

Monnet knew he could not finalize the agreement without the concurrence of General Chiang Kai-shek, so in May he visited him several times at his home on the Yangtze River. It was located "well away from the intrigues of the capital," wrote Monnet. As the general spoke only Chinese, his wife translated his words and asked her own questions. During one visit, she told Monnet, "The General thinks you would make an excellent general. But he has one criticism: you are too soft with your friends." On another occasion, she reported, "The General likes you. He says there is something Chinese in you."[88] While the general had been skeptical at first, he became more sympathetic to the CDFC idea. On May 23, he supported it but insisted that Soong's younger brother, T. L. Soong, become its general manager. Monnet later reported to his US friend William Bullitt, whom he had met in Paris during the Versailles Conference, that T. V. Soong was dismissed as finance minister because the general wanted to establish his own dominance over the Soong dynasty.[89]

Monnet had earlier won the approval of Kung, head of the National Bank. Drummond and Monnet suspected that Kung had persuaded the general not to oppose the creation of this corporation. When the final agreement was reached and the documents drawn up, Monnet decided to complete the deal and set the date for signing by going to see Mr. Cheng, head of the Bank of China, whom he had met several times before to discuss the new bank. But Cheng refused to set a date. Under the impression that the powerful banker was no longer prepared to help create this institution, Monnet consulted a Chinese friend. He was told that Chinese custom required him to ask Cheng three times. Monnet followed this advice and the corporation was set up, with the Soong family and their associates among its main shareholders.[90]

Incorporated on July 4, 1934, the CDFC had some early success in raising money in Europe and China for projects to open up the country, including railroads where large investments were urgently needed. Since the most important locally based British banks had grown increasingly alarmed at the influence of Japan in China and had hoped to use the Chinese to fight their economic battles, they reversed their earlier opposition to Monnet's plans and made investments in Monnet's bank. CDFC's first railway bond issue in 1934 with the Bank of Shanghai and Hong Kong was heavily oversubscribed. The railroad line from Shanghai to Ningpo, with its bridge over the Fuchun River, became the first step in creating the southeast Chinese rail network. A second line—the Shanghai-Hangchow-Minhow Railway—was also financed and constructed with money raised by the CDFC. Moreover, the British Foreign Office preferred Monnet's proposals for redeeming China's railway debt to those proposed by the British Shanghai banks. And the support of the Foreign Office helped Monnet obtain in October 1934 agreement in principle for unusual credit agreements from Washington's Export-Import Bank, which enabled China to import equipment for modernization.[91]

Using his influential connections, his experience in international finance, and his innate pragmatism, Monnet demonstrated in Shanghai his ability to bring disparate economic interests and officials together to create a workable institution that was new and useful to China. He had found it extremely difficult to penetrate the Chinese banking community and could not have succeeded without Soong's powerful influence or the support of Lazard Bank, which he leveraged wisely. As his colleague Drummond noted, Monnet displayed great patience in these difficult negotiations and demonstrated he was a "rare combination of a visionary and a pragmatic man of action." Duchêne argues that, "without being spectacular, Monnet's solution shifted the assumptions of the day." Because no one had thought of making Shanghai, China's most important financial center, the base for a reconstruction program or dared attempt a mixed corporation of the principal Chinese banks, public and private, the CDFC was novel at the time. Moreover, the idea of an investment partnership with the Chinese was alien to many Westerners. But Monnet changed the context by designing a new framework—a new institution in which rival banks were brought together and allowed to work toward a common and profitable goal. The CDFC committed Chinese and Western financiers to joint ventures, and these projects made an initial contribution to the modernization of China by improving the transportation sector.[92]

## His Marriage, the Important Transaction

Monnet never stopped dreaming about his future life with Silvia Giannini. After meeting the charismatic entrepreneur from Cognac in the summer of 1929, she remained with her Italian husband for two more years. But once she gave birth in April 1931 to Anna, her husband's child, she and Monnet began to make serious plans to be together. In the 1930s, divorce was nearly impossible in Italy as well as in France. As efforts to obtain an annulment of her marriage from the Catholic Church failed, Monnet became impatient and increasingly upset. Tired of their separation and courtship by "cable and transatlantic phone," in 1934 he began searching for a country that would permit divorce and allow Silvia to retain custody of Anna, who under Italian law and other countries of Roman law, belonged to the father. Monnet wanted to have "the legitimacy of a big country" supporting their union. But he rejected the United States as he believed that a Reno, Nevada–style divorce lacked dignity. Rajchman once again proved useful to him. The Polish doctor wrote him that the Soviet Union had minimal residency requirements, and that once sworn in, new citizens were permitted to divorce and remarry immediately thereafter. This seemed the best possible option, so Monnet decided to investigate it.

In July 1934, after the CDFC had been established, Monnet left Shanghai for Moscow by traveling across the vast Soviet continent on the Trans-Siberian

Railway. The prospective groom planned his own marriage, noted Duchêne, like he was negotiating among great powers. In typical Monnet fashion, he contacted the French and US ambassadors in Moscow, Charles Alphand and William Bullitt, respectively, and asked their help in paving the way for his marriage. He did not know Alphand personally, but he knew Bullitt quite well. Rajchman and the Soviet ambassador in China had also contacted the Soviet government on his behalf. The forty-six-year-old worldly bachelor arrived in Moscow ill from the long train ride and stayed with Bullitt a week longer than planned in order to recover. Thanks to the advance preparations made by his friends and contacts, he found the Soviets cooperative and completed the necessary forms and plans without difficulty. In later years, Monnet mused that the Soviets had probably calculated that because he was well-known in international circles, assisting him might prove to be good public relations.[93]

After leaving Moscow, Monnet arrived in Paris at the end of July 1934 in order to spend August there with Silvia and Anna. They had arrived from Switzerland where they had been staying with Silvia's mother. Silvia's husband strongly opposed her plans for divorce and her decision to keep Anna with her. To hide from her husband while awaiting Monnet's arrival in Paris, the two were living clandestinely with Monnet's sister Marie-Louise, a Catholic nun, in a cloister outside the city. Shortly after Monnet returned from Moscow, Silvia took Anna to the Soviet embassy in Paris where mother and daughter both were sworn in and became citizens.

At the end of August, Monnet sailed to New York and visited Washington. At the State Department, he met with the top China specialist and head of its Division of Far Eastern Affairs, Stanley Hornbeck, to inform him and his colleagues about the situation in Shanghai. He had kept these officials informed of his CDFC activities while in Shanghai and tried, while in the United States, to obtain additional loans for China. In October 1934, he and Drummond went to London to assist in the CDFC negotiations with the Bank of Shanghai and Hong Kong for an additional large loan to that country.[94]

After the marriage documents and visas arrived early in November 1934, Jean and Silvia headed for Moscow. Monnet took the train from Paris while Silvia traveled from Switzerland, where she had been staying with her mother and child. Monnet waited at the station to meet Silvia's train, which arrived a few hours late. Excited to be together at last, they walked hand in hand around Red Square leaving large footprints in the fresh snow that blanketed the city. They marveled at the distinctive architecture of the Orthodox churches and wandered into Saint Basil's Cathedral whose snowcapped onion domes sparkled in the sunlight.

Since Silvia was already a Soviet citizen, she was granted a divorce from her Italian husband on November 13, and she and Monnet were married in a civil ceremony immediately after in the same building. They were surrounded by colorful bouquets of flowers held by French and US embassy officials who enthusiastically toasted the newlyweds with champagne. Bullitt had written Monnet that he regretted not being able to attend the wedding because of a trip to Japan and China but had instructed his embassy colleagues to assist his friend. Immediately after the ceremony, the couple left for Paris. After collecting three-year-old Anna from Silvia's mother, who had brought the child from Switzerland to France, they traveled together in Europe for three weeks and sailed for New York in early December.[95]

Silvia's initiation into Monnet's peripatetic life of constant traveling among countries and continents came swiftly. After four months in the United States, they sailed for Shanghai in March 1935. They stayed just nine months before moving back to New York in January 1936. Silvia's ex-husband made several attempts to regain custody of his child, but he never succeeded. By hiding for a week in the Soviet consulate in Shanghai with her daughter, Silvia successfully foiled one of his plots to abduct Anna. She finally won a lawsuit for Anna's custody in New York in 1937. But as the ruling was not recognized in Europe, she could not return to the continent with the child until June 1939 when she became a naturalized French citizen. After the death of Silvia's first husband in 1974, the Monnets celebrated the religious wedding they had always wanted in the cathedral at Lourdes.[96]

Silvia, an intelligent, forceful woman, remained an influential partner to her husband throughout their forty-five-year marriage. Since her opinion mattered more to Monnet than that of anyone else, he consulted her almost daily on most business matters, lauded her keen mind, and always valued her judgment. Because Monnet was a private person and wanted to keep his life with Silvia and family out of the public eye, little is known about their personal lives except that she was the most important person in his life. As he loved living in the countryside and most of his friends were colleagues in his public life, her relatively sequestered life could not have been easy for her, and his long periods away from her and Anna must have been extremely trying for both of them. To combat her loneliness when he was away, she immersed herself in painting, which she loved. Her life was enlivened in the early years in New York by close relationships with some of the wives of Monnet's American friends, to whom she remained close for the rest of her life.[97]

## Monnet's New Venture in Private Financial Consulting

In February 1935, before Monnet and his Italian bride left New York and sailed back to Shanghai, he embarked on a new stage in his career. He became a partner in a private financial consulting firm in New York with George Murnane, a partner in Boston's investment bank of Lee, Higginson and Co. and an old friend and business associate of John Foster Dulles. Murnane had met Monnet during World War I when he had been deputy commissioner of the US

Red Cross in France, and each held the other in high regard. Murnane been a casualty of the Kreuger empire's collapse because his bank had invested heavily in the Swede's ventures. Having joined the Transamerica board, he, like Monnet, had lost his investment and was removed from the board. In addition to the two partners, the new consulting firm consisted of David Drummond in London, Pierre Denis in Paris, and Henri Mazot in Shanghai. Monnet proposed salaries for each of the partners of $36,000, a hefty sum in 1935.[98]

The firm of Monnet, Murnane, and Co. could not have been created without the financial help of Dulles, who occasionally invested in enterprises or individuals. The highly respected New York lawyer was always concerned about the well-being of his French friend, whom he considered one of the most brilliant men he knew. Dulles had persuaded his senior partner, William N. Cromwell, in his law firm Sullivan and Cromwell, to join him in investing in this small corporation. Dulles argued it "should produce a large amount of legal business for us" and personally invested $25,000, while asking his firm to invest $50,000. Dulles, who had confidence in the business talents of Murnane and Monnet, wrote Cromwell that he had taken the initiative to bring the two men together because he felt they would make an ideal combination and that they would be exceedingly successful. Although Cromwell had doubts about the venture, he wrote Dulles that he would join him. But, he added, "My motive is solely to help the firm and yourself." He added that his consent rested upon Dulles's reassurance that this corporation "will not constitute a partnership with us." Cromwell explained that he was concerned that "both Monnet and Murnane had reached middle age and neither has been able to accumulate but meager personal assets." Moreover, he argued that "their death, retirement or incapacity would inevitably result in loss of all our investment unless you somehow protect us by life insurance." Dulles and Cromwell finally agreed to invest $100,000—each donating $50,000—in Monnet, Murnane, and Co., which was incorporated in Prince Edward Island, Canada.[99]

Monnet returned to China with his family in the spring of 1935 wishing to continue to invest, under Murnane's auspices, in Chinese ventures through CDFC. Fairly optimistic about the new Chinese development bank he had created, Monnet wanted to contribute to its success, to make deals that would cover some of Murnane's initial operating expenses, and to make substantial personal profits. He believed the Murnane partnership was advantageously positioned because of his own knowledge and experience, his many contacts, and CDFC's ability to tap numerous financial centers.[100] In some ways, he saw his partnership as a means to continue his work in China, which both frustrated and fascinated him.

In 1934, Monnet had believed that development opportunities were great, and the bank did well that year. But upon returning to Shanghai in 1935, Monnet found his bank's financial circumstances had changed in the six months he had been away. As the civil war continued to create political instability, foreign investment in CDFC had fluctuated but declined overall, and Monnet found Kung and Soong pessimistic. They claimed China had become too dependent on Great Britain, which controlled 56 percent of the foreign capital invested in China outside Manchuria. But in spite of that negative view of the British, these Chinese officials had asked both London and Washington for financial assistance without Monnet's knowledge and then complained profusely about Britain's slow response. Although their secretive ploy annoyed Monnet, he finally agreed to write the British, supporting the request for a loan. But British Foreign Office officials did not completely trust Monnet because he considered Japan a threat to China, while they wished to appease Japan and were not interested in any type of bilateral aid to China. Kung and Soong continually carped to Monnet about the Japanese, who they feared would undercut CDFC in order to gain a stronger and more permanent foothold in their country.[101]

By the end of 1935 and early 1936, Monnet's personal interest in the CDFC declined. Its ventures had not proved to be very profitable, and Soong had reneged on some payments to him. In addition, the Frenchman continued to find himself in the middle of leadership struggles among the Soongs. Consequently, Monnet decided to leave China for good in January of 1936 and brought his family back to New York. Hoping to provide a more stable family life where Silvia and Anna were legally secure, he rented a comfortable apartment overlooking Central Park, which they all enjoyed. But their worries about Anna's future arose immediately after their return as Silvia's first husband, Francesco Giannini, filed a lawsuit in New York courts to regain custody of his child. Monnet hired a top lawyer in Dulles's firm to fight the claim, and the lawsuit failed. This continuous custody battle made the Monnets' first years of marriage difficult and unsettling.[102]

From 1936 to 1938, Monnet worked in both the New York and Paris offices of his new company. While Murnane basically ran the US side of the business and Monnet the European, the Frenchman spent much of his time in New York with his family. At Dulles's initiative, Murnane and Drummond negotiated the sale of most of the industrial fortune from the coal mines of the Petschek family to prominent German interests. The sale was completed in 1938 in order to rescue part of this Czechoslovakian Jewish family's assets so as to prevent its confiscation by the Nazis after the family fled to the United States. The Petschek family obtained $6.25 million, only a fourth of their worth, but it was a large amount considering the circumstances in Germany in 1938. The firm earned $250,000 for the sale, the largest commission they apparently ever received. The Murnane firm also undertook, in the event of war, to protect the assets of American Bosch, a subsidiary of the German electrical engineering firm run by Robert Bosch. Monnet was not a principal in these arrangements, as Murnane sensed that "indirect contact" with Bosch headquarters "might have been distasteful" to his French partner.[103] In August

1939, Murnane negotiated on his firm's behalf to prevent the sale of American Bosch to hostile interests, a negotiation that would later pose problems for Monnet in his wartime dealings with Washington.[104]

Once back in New York in early 1936, Monnet did not abandon his Chinese interests entirely, and the Murnane firm's work with the CDFC in China continued for several more years through a local agent. But due to the civil war, which made the political and economic situation precarious in China in the late 1930s, the transactions did not generate the income that the two partners and their investors anticipated. Neither the Chinese nor European endeavors proved very successful. Moreover, relations between Monnet and T. L. Soong, the manager of CDFC who had earlier replaced his brother T. V. Soong as finance minister, had reached a crisis. The new manager claimed he had no obligation to Monnet. Moreover, the two Soong brothers quarreled over Monnet's repeated requests in 1939 for compensation for Murnane's work with CDFC and ignored his pleas.[105] Discouraged by the lack of continued financial success in China and bored with international financial affairs, which had interested him earlier, Monnet spent more time in Paris than New York during his four years with the firm. As a result, he turned his focus to Europe and ended his active role in the partnership with Murnane late in 1939.[106] This partnership was dissolved in 1949 when it became Murnane & Co.[107]

Monnet's years as an entrepreneur and partner in private enterprise with Murnane are hard to evaluate because he recounts little about them in his memoirs. Sadly, many of his papers relating to his activities before World War II were burned by his family to prevent retaliation against him and his family during the German occupation. Their action is understandable because the Nazi commandant in charge of the Cognac area, along with several other soldiers, actually lived in the Monnets' home. Monnet, Murnane, and Co., a financial consultancy where governments and corporations as well as individuals could seek financial advice, was quite rare before World War II. The firm gave Monnet valuable firsthand professional experience in the private sector, increased his appreciation of the complexities of the financial world, and boosted his self-confidence, which strengthened his future performance in the public sector. However, his original goal of helping the Chinese develop their railroad through the CDFC had made little headway, and he was relieved to be able to put the venture behind him and turn his attention to Europe.[108]

By 1938, at the age of fifty, Monnet had gained a reputation in international circles as a man of considerable talents with influential friends and contacts on both sides of the Atlantic. In his work during World War I and with the League of Nations, he exhibited brilliance and proved himself a strategic thinker who could design innovative solutions to international problems as well as be a good negotiator. His sound business sense and good judgment, honed by working for his father's company, underlay the pragmatism of many of his diplomatic and financial schemes. Monnet never much concerned himself with his own income, which came fairly regularly from his family firm, or profit for its own sake. But, as he liked to live comfortably and had expensive tastes, he was grateful for the generosity of his American friends, especially Dulles, whose help enabled him to survive financially after the failure of his Transamerica venture.

Monnet's political thinking was shaped by his early work within international groups and organizations. World War I dramatically demonstrated the negative aspects of unchecked nationalism that had led to armed conflict among states. But the tasks assigned him and the organizations in which he played a role had also shown the "power of collective action" and the benefits of nations pursuing their "common interest" as opposed to their purely national interests. Also apparent to him were the benefits of collective decisionmaking, international authority, close Allied cooperation, and nations forced to work together and share national sovereignty to achieve a common goal. Since the Allies had rejected such powers for the AMTC and were totally absent in the League, he saw the need for a new organization, an international authority with the powers of enforcement to bridle nationalism and override a national veto. The myriad experiences during the first half of his life in both the public and private sectors helped to prepare this entrepreneur "in the public interest"[109] for the challenges he would face during World War II.

## Notes

1. Monnet's close collaborator François Fontaine stated the only political theorists Monnet was familiar with were John Jay, Alexander Hamilton, and James Madison and that he kept copies of the *Federalist Papers* in his office, read newspapers and *Kon-Tiki*, Iban Saud, and two anthologies prepared by Fontaine on Europeans and French regionalism. Frederic Fransen, *The Supranational Politics of Jean Monnet* (Westport, CT: Greenwood Press, 2001), p. 5. Max Kohnstamm stated Monnet gave people poems and took notes on the writings of French philosopher and mathematician Blaise Pascal. Max Kohnstamm, interview by the author, November 19, 2005.

2. Jean Monnet, *Memoirs* (New York: Doubleday, 1978), pp. 36–39; François Duchêne, *Jean Monnet: The First Statesman of Interdependence* (New York: W. W. Norton, 1994), p. 28.

3. Duchêne, *Jean Monnet*, p. 28.

4. Monnet, *Memoirs*, pp. 36–41.

5. Ibid., pp. 38, 43.

6. Ibid., pp. 39–41; Duchêne, *Jean Monnet*, pp. 28–30.

7. Monnet, *Memoirs*, p. 43.

8. Ibid., pp. 43–44.

9. Richard Mayne, "Father of Europe: The Life and Times of Jean Monnet," unpublished manuscript, p. 14.

10. Monnet, *Memoirs*, pp. 45–47.

11. Mayne, "Father of Europe," p. 15.

12. Duchêne, *Jean Monnet*, pp. 31–32.

13. Ibid., pp. 48–49; W. W. Rostow, "Jean Monnet: The Innovator as Diplomat," in *The Diplomats, 1939–1979,* ed. Gordon A. Craig and Francis Lowenheim (Princeton, NJ: Princeton University Press, 1994), pp. 262–263. Some authorities claim that Monnet suffered from nephritis, or inflammation of the kidneys.

14. Monnet, *Memoirs,* pp. 49–50.

15. Ibid., p. 50.

16. Duchêne, *Jean Monnet,* p. 33; Monnet, *Memoirs,* pp. 50–52.

17. Monnet, *Memoirs,* p. 52.

18. Duchêne, *Jean Monnet,* pp. 33–34. Monnet reveals nothing about this in his memoirs. Duchêne speculates he maintained silence about his role because he did not want his war record associated in any way with profits.

19. Monnet, *Memoirs,* pp. 53–54; Duchêne, *Jean Monnet,* pp. 35–36; Eric Roussel, *Jean Monnet* (Paris: Librairie Artheme Fayard, 1996), p. 83.

20. Kathleen Burk, *Britain, America, and the Sinews of War, 1914–1918* (Boston: George Allen and Unwin, 1985), pp. 44–45; Duchêne, *Jean Monnet,* p. 36; Monnet, *Memoirs,* pp. 53–55.

21. Burk, *Britain, America,* p. 50; James Arthur Salter, *Allied Shipping Control, an Experiment in International Administration* (Oxford, UK: Clarendon Press, 1921), p. 109.

22. Monnet, *Memoirs,* p. 55; Duchêne, *Jean Monnet,* pp. 35–39; Roussel, *Jean Monnet,* pp. 56–60. By the end of the war, Clémentel was responsible for industry, transport, and supply as well as trade.

23. Jean-Baptiste Duroselle, "Deux types de grands hommes: Le Général de Gaulle et Jean Monnet," *Collection "Conférences,"* no. 15 (Genève: Institut Universitaire de Hautes Etudes Internationales, 1977), p. 7. Duroselle argues that Monnet invented the Wheat Executive.

24. Etienne Clémentel, *La France et la politique économique interalliée* (Paris: Presses Universitaires, 1931), p. 109; Duchêne, *Jean Monnet,* pp. 36–37; Monnet, *Memoirs,* pp. 58–59.

25. Salter, *Allied Shipping Control,* pp. 109–110.

26. Monnet, *Memoirs,* p. 59.

27. Nicole Piétri, "Jean Monnet et les organismes interalliés durant la première guerre mondiale," in *Jean Monnet, l'Europe et les chemins de la paix,* ed. Gérard Bossuat and Andreas Wilkens (Paris: Publications de la Sorbonne, 1999), pp. 27–28; see also Georges-Henri Soutou, *L'Or et le sang: Les Buts de guerre économique de la première guerre mondiale* (Paris: Fayard, 1989).

28. Salter, *Allied Shipping Control,* pp. 113–114, 151–156.

29. Piétri, "Jean Monnet et les organismes interalliés," p. 28; Salter, *Allied Shipping Control,* pp. 113–115; Monnet, *Memoirs,* pp. 68–69.

30. Piétri, "Jean Monnet et les organismes interalliés," p. 28; Salter, *Allied Shipping Control,* p. 122; Monnet, *Memoirs,* pp. 68–69; Harold Nicolson, *Dwight Morrow* (New York: Harcourt, Brace, 1935), p. 204; Fransen, *The Supranational Politics of Jean Monnet,* pp. 23–27.

31. Monnet, *Memoirs,* pp. 70–71; Duchêne, *Jean Monnet,* pp. 37–38.

32. Monnet-Morrow correspondence, Series I, 1900–1931, Dwight Morrow Papers, Amherst College Library; John Foster Dulles to Monnet, telegram, September 23, 1931, and report from Dulles to Monnet, November 14, 1940, John Foster Dulles Papers, Princeton University Library; Duchêne, *Jean Monnet,* p. 40; Nicolson, *Dwight Morrow,* pp. 240–241; Fransen, *The Supranational Politics of Jean Monnet,* pp. 27–28.

33. Duchêne, *Jean Monnet,* pp. 39–40; see also Soutou, *L'Or et le sang* (Paris: Fayard, 1989).

34. Antoine Fleury, "Jean Monnet au Secrétariat de la Société des Nations" in *Jean Monnet, l'Europe et les chemins de la paix*, ed. Bossuat and Wilkens, p. 35.

35. Ibid, pp. 34–35.

36. Raymond B. Fosdick, *Letters on the League of Nations* (Princeton, NJ: Princeton University Press, 1966), pp. 17–18; Monnet, *Memoirs,* pp. 80–82.

37. Fleury, "Jean Monnet au Secrétariat," pp. 34–41; for a copy of the May 27, 1919, memorandum, see "Memorandum par Jean Monnet sur le Secrétariat de la Société des Nations," in Bossuat and Wilkens, pp. 441–445; Monnet, *Memoirs,* p. 83.

38. Monnet, *Memoirs,* pp. 82–83; Duchêne, *Jean Monnet,* p. 41.

39. Dwight Morrow to Jean Monnet, letter, November 10, 1919, Dwight Morrow Papers, Amherst College Library. See also Morrow's letter to Monnet of August 2, 1920, Dwight Morrow Papers.

40. Fleury, "Jean Monnet au Secrétariat," pp. 34–41; Roussel, *Jean Monnet,* pp. 80–85.

41. Lubor Jílek, "Rôle de Jean Monnet dans les règlements d'Autriche et de Haute-Silésie," in *Jean Monnet, l'Europe et les chemins de la paix*, ed. Bossuat and Wilkens, pp. 43–56; Roussel, *Jean Monnet,* pp. 92–98; Duchêne, *Jean Monnet,* p. 41.

42. Jílek, "Rôle de Jean Monnet," pp. 43–56; Duchêne, *Jean Monnet,* p. 41; Monnet, *Memoirs,* pp. 85–91.

43. Monetary equivalents are in US dollars unless otherwise noted.

44. Monnet, *Memoirs,* p. 92.

45. Jílek, "Rôle de Jean Monnet," pp. 56–61; Duchêne, *Jean Monnet,* pp. 41–43; Monnet, *Memoirs,* pp. 87–95.

46. Louis Joxe, *Victoires sur la nuit: Mémoires 1940–1966* (Paris: Fayard, 1981), p. 97.

47. Duchêne, *Jean Monnet,* p. 43.

48. Roussel, *Jean Monnet,* pp. 88–89, 102–103.

49. Monnet, *Memoirs,* pp. 95–99.

50. Roussel, *Jean Monnet,* pp. 104–105; Monnet, *Memoirs,* pp. 99–101.

51. Morrow and Kindersley each planned to invest 5,000 pounds, Monnet 3,000, and Robert Brand 2,000 in the brandy syndicate. See Clifford Hackett, *A Jean Monnet Chronology* (Washington, DC: Jean Monnet Council, 2008), p. 55.

52. Roussel, *Jean Monnet,* pp. 102–105; Duchêne, *Jean Monnet,* pp. 31–32.

53. Duchêne, *Jean Monnet,* pp. 31–32, 43–44; Monnet, *Memoirs,* pp. 95–99; Roussel, *Jean Monnet,* pp. 102–105.

54. Eric Bussière, "Jean Monnet et la stabilisation monétaire roumaine de 1929: Un 'outsider' entre l'Europe et l'Amerique," in *Jean Monnet, l'Europe et les chemins de la paix,* ed. Bossuat and Wilkens, pp. 63–76; Duchêne, *Jean Monnet,* pp. 44–47; Monnet, *Memoirs,* pp. 102–104; Roussel, *Jean Monnet,* pp. 115–123; Hackett, *Jean Monnet Chronology,* p. 56.

55. Melvin P. Lefler, *The Elusive Quest: America's Pursuit of European Stability and French Security, 1919–1933* (Chapel Hill: University of North Carolina Press, 1979), pp. 82–157; William E. Leuchtenburg, *The Perils of Prosperity, 1914–1932,* 2nd ed. (Chicago: University of Chicago Press, 1993), pp. 111–112; Melvin P. Lefler, "1921–1932: Expansionist Impulses and Domestic Constraints," in *Economics and World Power: An Assessment of American Diplomacy Since 1789,* ed. William H. Becker and Samuel F. Wells, Jr. (New York: Columbia University Press, 1984), pp. 225–275. For a comprehensive analysis of the significance of the Dawes Plan, see Patrick O. Cohrs, *The Unfinished Peace After World War I: America, Britain, and the Stabilisation of Europe, 1919–1932* (Cambridge, UK: Cambridge University Press, 2006), pp. 137–142.

56. Bussière, "Jean Monnet et la stabilisation monétaire roumaine de 1929," pp. 63–76; Duchêne, *Jean Monnet*, pp. 44–47; Monnet, *Memoirs*, pp. 102–104; Roussel, *Jean Monnet*, pp. 115–123; Hackett, *Jean Monnet Chronology*, p. 56.

57. Roussel, *Jean Monnet*, pp. 114–116; Lefler, *Elusive Quest*, pp. 142–157.

58. Monnet, *Memoirs*, p. 104.

59. Duchêne, *Jean Monnet*, pp. 44–47; Roussel, *Jean Monnet*, pp. 115–123.

60. Monnet, *Memoirs*, pp. 102–104.

61. Bussière, "Jean Monnet et la stabilisation monétaire roumaine de 1929," pp. 63–76; Duchêne, *Jean Monnet*, pp. 44–47; Monnet, *Memoirs*, pp. 102–104; Roussel, *Jean Monnet*, pp. 115–123; Hackett, *Jean Monnet Chronology*, pp. 63–65.

62. René Pleven, "Témoignage de René Pleven," in *Témoignages à la mémoire de Jean Monnet* (Lausanne, Switzerland: Fondation Jean Monnet pour l'Europe Centre de recherches européennes, 1989), pp. 391–392.

63. See, for example, the telegram from Monnet to Walter Lippmann, April 16, 1943, and letters from Lippmann to Monnet, September 30, 1948, December 30, 1948, January 10, 1949, and June 1, 1950, Walter Lippmann Papers, Yale University Library.

64. Hackett, *Jean Monnet Chronology*, p. 68.

65. Monnet, *Memoirs*, pp. 109–110.

66. Clifford Hackett, interview by the author, November 3, 2010. Hackett was told by Fontaine that Monnet allowed only the two short paragraphs they composed together about their meeting and marriage to be included in his *Memoirs*. He did not want anything else written about their marriage.

67. Roussel, *Jean Monnet*, pp. 125–132; Duchêne, *Jean Monnet*, p. 49.

68. Duchêne, *Jean Monnet*, p. 51.

69. Salter, *Memoirs*, pp. 219–220.

70. Hackett, *Jean Monnet Chronology*, pp. 80–85; Duchêne, *Jean Monnet*, pp. 51–53.

71. Duchêne, *Jean Monnet*, p. 51.

72. Hackett, *Jean Monnet Chronology*, pp. 84–85.

73. Hackett, *Jean Monnet Chronology*, pp. 82–86; Roussel, *Jean Monnet*, pp. 139–140; Duchêne, *Jean Monnet*, pp. 51–52.

74. Roussel, *Jean Monnet*, pp. 139–143; Hackett, *Jean Monnet Chronology*, pp. 82–86.

75. Monnet, *Memoirs*, pp. 110–114; Roussel, *Jean Monnet*, p. 143.

76. Monnet, *Memoirs*, pp. 110–115.

77. Hungdah Su, "The Father of Europe in China: Jean Monnet and the Creation of the C.D.F.C. (1933–1936)," *Journal of European Integration History* 13 (2007), p. 18.

78. Monnet, *Memoirs*, pp. 111–112; Roussel, *Jean Monnet*, pp. 143–147.

79. Duchêne, *Jean Monnet*, p. 53.

80. Monnet, *Memoirs*, p. 112.

81. Akira Iriye, *The Origins of the Second World War in Asia and the Pacific* (London: Longman, 1987), pp. 1–40.

82. Hackett, *Jean Monnet Chronology*, pp. 96–97; *FRUS*, 1934, vol. 3, pp. 403–405.

83. Hackett, *Jean Monnet Chronology*, p. 92.

84. Roussel, *Jean Monnet*, pp. 138–146, 148–164; Duchêne, *Jean Monnet*, pp. 50–54; Monnet, *Memoirs*, pp. 102–115.

85. Roussel, *Jean Monnet*, pp. 144–150.

86. Ibid., pp. 149–150.

87. Ibid., pp. 150–151; Hackett, *Jean Monnet Chronology*, p. 94.

88. Monnet, *Memoirs,* pp. 110–114.

89. Ibid.; Hackett, *Jean Monnet Chronology*, pp. 94–96.

90. Monnet, *Memoirs,* pp. 110–114; Roussel, *Jean Monnet,* pp. 151–156.

91. Roussel, *Jean Monnet*, pp. 138–164; Duchêne, *Jean Monnet*, pp. 50–54; Monnet, *Memoirs,* pp. 109–115.

92. Roussel, *Jean Monnet*, pp. 162–164; Duchêne, *Jean Monnet*, pp. 53–54.

93. Duchêne, *Jean Monnet*, pp. 54–56; Hackett, *Jean Monnet Chronology*, pp. 95–97, 112; Monnet, *Memoirs*, pp. 109–110.

94. Hackett, *Jean Monnet Chronology*, pp. 98–100.

95. Duchêne, *Jean Monnet*, pp. 54–56; Monnet, *Memoirs*, pp. 109–110; Hackett, *Jean Monnet Chronology*, pp. 99–100.

96. Duchêne, *Jean Monnet*, pp. 54–56; Monnet, *Memoirs*, pp. 109–110.

97. Robert Nathan, Walt Rostow, and Edna Rostow, interviews by the author in 1994. Monnet's closest colleagues rarely spoke or wrote about the Monnets' marriage, and the comments were always positive about Silvia.

98. Hackett, *Jean Monnet Chronology*, pp. 102–103.

99. William Cromwell in Paris to Dulles, cable, January 30, 1935, Murnane File, and letter from Dulles to Monnet and George Murnane, February 2, 1935, Monnet File, Papers of John Foster Dulles, Princeton University Library; Duchêne, *Jean Monnet*, pp. 56–57.

100. Monnet to Pierre Denis and David Drummond, letter, March 13, 1935, Papers of Lord Perth, European Institute Archives.

101. Duchêne, *Jean Monnet*, pp. 57–58; Roussel, *Jean Monnet*, pp. 161–164.

102. Duchêne, *Jean Monnet*, pp. 57–58; Roussel, *Jean Monnet*, pp. 161–162; Hackett, *Jean Monnet Chronology*, p. 14.

103. Duchêne, *Jean Monnet*, p. 60.

104. Ibid, pp. 60–61; Hackett, *Jean Monnet Chronology*, pp. 125, 163–167.

105. Duchêne, *Jean Monnet*, p. 59; Hackett, *Jean Monnet Chronology*, pp. 106–125, 136, 144, 163.

106. Duchêne, *Jean Monnet*, pp. 59–60.

107. Hackett, *Jean Monnet Chronology*, pp. 132, 134, 195.

108. Duchêne, *Jean Monnet*, pp. 57–61.

109. Ibid., p. 63.

# 2

# Early Wartime Contributions, 1938–1943

Efforts by France to strengthen its air defense for possible war with Germany propelled Jean Monnet into service for his country in 1938. From the mid-1930s on, Monnet believed Adolf Hitler's menacing proclamations about expanding German power and his antidemocratic, authoritarian one-party state system threatened European peace. At a dinner with John Foster Dulles at George Murnane's Long Island home in New York in September 1935, Monnet expressed his horror at the Nazi dictator's decrees against Jews. Monnet spent a lot of time in Paris between 1936 and 1939 on business for Monnet, Murnane, and Co. There he added his voice to the chorus of outspoken French officials who were alarmed by Hitler's remilitarization of the Rhineland in 1936 and France's shortage of aircraft in comparison to Germany, which had been expanding its army and building an air force.[1] All of them advocated greater military preparedness to counter France's vulnerability. From January 1938 onward, René Pleven, Monnet's capable assistant at Blair and Co. in the late 1920s and future prime minister, observed Monnet's "desperate efforts to close our gap in air power" with Germany. Monnet tried "with might and main to awaken the British and French leaders to the need to take immediate action to correct the weakness of their air forces," Pleven wrote. "I never admired Monnet as a man of action more than in the years preceding 1939. . . . He was unyieldingly clear-sighted" and "profoundly anti-Hitler."[2]

Monnet lunched with his good friend William Bullitt nearly every time he was in Paris between 1936 and 1938. This American, who had campaigned for President Franklin Roosevelt's reelection, had been appointed US ambassador to France in August 1936 after serving as ambassador in Moscow. Monnet and Bullitt constantly shared their fears about Hitler's aggressive behavior. It was Bullitt who persuaded Monnet to get involved with a group working on the airpower gap, which was linked to Guy La Chambre, the young, energetic air minister. Monnet likely shared with the group a paper he had written while in Paris in the spring of 1938 titled "Note on the possible establishment of an aeronautical industry abroad out of reach of enemy attack," meaning in North America.[3]

French Prime Minister Edouard Daladier, the tough, willful politician from Provence who had held various ministerial posts in the 1920s and 1930s, rose rapidly to become chairman of the Radical Socialist Party and prime minister for the second time in April 1938. This burly, dark-complected French leader also enjoyed the company of Bullitt, who was fluent in French. He often discussed with the US diplomat the growing German threat and his preoccupation with building up France's air and ground defenses. Proud of the armament program he had sponsored as both war minister and defense minister in earlier governments, the prime minister was convinced that it would have a deterrent effect on Hitler.[4]

Monnet first met Daladier in early 1938 at a friend's dinner party. The man from Cognac came with a League of Nations colleague, Pierre Comert, who along with the young diplomat Henri Bonnet had worked in the League's cultural and information section. It is entirely possible and in character for Monnet to have worked his way into Daladier's entourage because of his concerns about German rearmament and French military weakness. Whatever the circumstances, Monnet wrote that he and the French leader "became friendly." After Daladier and British Prime Minister Neville Chamberlain signed the act of appeasement with Hitler at the Munich conference on September 28–29, 1938, the French prime minister returned home filled with a sense of humiliation. He said he had not been fooled by the German leader's insincere assurances and claimed that the meeting with Hitler would never have happened if he had had 3,000 to 4,000 planes at his disposal.[5]

Monnet and his wife, Silvia, were visiting Paris at the time of the Munich conference. Their close friends, Anne Morrow Lindbergh and her famous aviator husband Charles Lindbergh, arrived in Paris September 30, the day after the Munich meeting. Morrow recorded in her diary that they went straight to the US embassy and were met by "two close friends" who were very distraught about Munich: Bullitt appeared "white and tired" and Monnet "rather gray." She wrote that Bullitt "wants C [Lindbergh] to help in organizing some kind of air rearmament for France . . . in the USA" and Monnet to "organize it." They discussed with La Chambre, who joined them for lunch, Bullitt's idea of France building aircraft factories in Canada with both US technology and skilled labor. "The French . . . are very depressed," she wrote. "They do not trust Germany," and Monnet and Lindbergh "never seem to agree."[6]

On October 1, Monnet and Lindbergh met with La Chambre at his ministry office, along with Roger Hoppenot, a French government economist, to discuss opening aircraft factories in Canada. Two days later, Bullitt hosted a luncheon meeting at the US embassy for Daladier with Monnet, Lindbergh, and La Chambre. At the end of the meal, Daladier asked Monnet to go to Washington for urgent secret talks with Roosevelt about the French government's plan to purchase US warplanes. This initiative was sparked by the prime minister's hope that the US president would support his rearmament campaign.[7] Daladier's government was pursuing two lines of policy—while still hoping that Hitler was ready for some kind of détente, the government redoubled its efforts to arm France for a war that might come within months— and Monnet's mission was a critical part of this strategy.[8]

The Lindberghs dined at the Monnets' Paris apartment several times in the week before Jean's departure for the United States on October 11. That same day Lindbergh left for his third trip to Germany, this time to discuss the possibility of France buying German aircraft engines. Monnet thought his idea was pure folly. Lindbergh had toured Germany's air bases and factories on a previous visit at the invitation of the German General Hermann Goering and told the French air staff they were underestimating German capabilities.[9] Anne Morrow recorded in her diary some of their conversations. She described Silvia as charming and wrote, "Nice talk with Silvia . . . about women's struggle between husband and children." She noted, Monnet "is such a rare person . . . a true balanced wisdom into life itself. And he has that wonderful French quickness and lightness that makes communication with him such a joy. He thinks it is very much overrated that children need their mothers all the time. Yes, I say, it is true, neglected children always turn out well. While, says Jean, neglected husbands do not!" In December, Monnet invited the Lindberghs to Cognac where Anne found Monnet's father "a wonderful old man—gay, quick, full of love, and humor. Much joking between him and Jean."[10]

Daladier chose Monnet to meet with Roosevelt largely because of Bullitt's strong recommendation. The ambassador had kept his president apprised of France's serious shortage of airpower, and, in his September 28 cable, he wrote that France had 600 warplanes, Germany 65,000, and Italy 2,000. Bullitt told Roosevelt that La Chambre had asked him for advice on who could help France immediately find the badly needed additional military aircraft. He reported he had suggested Monnet because he believed that his friend was the man best qualified to organize this effort on behalf of France. He explained that the Frenchman was "an intimate friend of mine, whom I trust as a brother." Daladier was persuaded to follow Bullitt's advice because Monnet brought additional advantages to the task: anonymity, negotiating skills, and extensive knowledge of America.[11] Monnet was pleased to have been asked to undertake this purchasing mission he deemed extremely important to French national interests. Always enjoying being close to the corridors of French power, he also relished the opportunity to meet the US president whom he admired for his handling of the depressed US economy.

Having traveled in secret by ship to the United States, Monnet, accompanied by Bullitt, met with Roosevelt at his family home in Hyde Park on October

19, 1938. Seated in his wheelchair, the president extended his hand and warmly welcomed Monnet. Isolationism was strong in the country, he explained, and his hands were tied legally by the Johnson Act of 1933, which prohibited loans for arms to any country that had failed to pay its World War I dollar debts, which included France. The president added that the Neutrality Act of 1935 forbade sales of complete weapons to belligerents. However, Hitler had to be stopped. Roosevelt told Monnet he had already asked the Air Corps for expanded aircraft production and directed the State Department to study the removal of the arms embargo from the Neutrality Act. He said he believed that the Germans could produce 40,000 planes a year, Britain together with Canada 20,000, and France 15,000. He declared that 20,000 to 30,000 extra planes "will be needed to achieve decisive superiority over Germany and Italy: and they'll have to be found here in the United States." He argued that the Neutrality Act could be circumvented if the French set up assembly plants near Montreal with the Americans shipping parts across the frontier, and even pointed to possible locations on a map. The president's charm and intelligence seduced Monnet. Roosevelt's sincere tone, his "exceptionally wide-ranging mind," and belief that the dangers amassing in Europe also threatened the New World deeply impressed the Frenchman. "So much attention to detail showed the importance he attached to the problem," concluded the emissary from France.[12]

Before Monnet's meeting with Roosevelt, the French had made direct contact with Roosevelt in January 1938 through French Senator François-Amaury de La Grange. From an aristocratic family with economic interests in the United States, the senator had met Roosevelt before World War I through his marriage to an American. He had kept in touch with Roosevelt and visited him several times at Hyde Park after he became president. In early 1938, La Grange drew Roosevelt's attention to France's aeronautical weakness and its consequences, and reported to his government that Roosevelt understood France's dilemma.[13]

The president sent Monnet to Henry Morgenthau, Jr., his treasury secretary and the only senior person in his administration the president could trust to fight the isolationists. When Monnet and Bullitt met Morgenthau on October 22, Morgenthau was skeptical that the French could produce sufficient dollars to cover the cost of the planes. But he remained open to the use of private French investments available in the United States, a sum later identified by the Treasury as $500 million. Bullitt wrote Daladier that the negotiations with both Morgenthau and Roosevelt had gone well.

Monnet returned to France at the end of the month. In a report on November 14, he stated that if orders were placed for existing types of aircraft by the end of 1938, 1,000 US planes could be delivered by July 1939 and another 1,500 by February 1940. Canadian assembly plants could be built outside Montreal, staffed with US skilled labor, and the United States could help France build more engines. Daladier faced strong opposition to this idea.

French Air Ministry experts were skeptical that the US planes would meet French standards, and Paul Reynaud, the new finance minster, refused to allow the use of private French funds deposited in the United States to be used as payment. But Daladier was encouraged by Roosevelt's goodwill. He remained convinced that this purchase of US planes was necessary and sent Monnet back to Washington on December 9 to purchase the planes.[14]

Monnet arrived in the US capital with authorization to buy 1,000 planes for up to $65 million and set up a Canadian corporation. When the details of the plan hit the press there was opposition from the US military and isolationists, but Roosevelt ignored the protests and proclaimed the French orders good for the aircraft industry, US defense, and its workers because they provided jobs. The president overcame the opposition of the Army Air Corps to the release of its new models of planes to the French and the opposition of Congress. The French mission received support from US editorial writers across the country because many believed the Europeans needed help to preserve democracy against Hitler.

In February 1939, the French purchasing team, which included Monnet and two future French prime ministers, René Pleven and René Mayer, then representing the armaments industry, placed firm orders for 555 combat planes and trainers and another 1,000 in 1940. The French invested heavily in the expansion of US plants because they remained secure from German bombardment.[15] By May 10, 1940, when the Germans attacked France, the plants in Canada had produced only several hundred planes. Yet the French orders benefited the Allies, argues Duchêne, by quadrupling "American monthly production capacity in less than a year." Most significantly, they "laid the foundations for the gigantic later expansion of the US aircraft industry."[16] As Daladier's biographer Élisabeth Du Réau argues, Monnet's mission was fruitful because "a dynamic was born, a real dialogue had been established, and relations had been forged." This initial joint action, she writes, led to greater Anglo-French cooperation and the future Atlantic triangle of Paris-London-Washington.[17]

## Advocating for Anglo-French Cooperation

As he had done during World War I, Monnet spearheaded Anglo-French economic planning early in World War II. On September 3, 1939, the day Britain and France declared war on Germany in response to its invasion of Poland two days earlier, Monnet declined a request from Daladier to embark on a fourth mission to the United States to buy more planes. Instead, he wrote two memoranda for the prime minister pointing out the need to increase US productive capacity and implement Anglo-French economic planning to strengthen the Allied war effort. Monnet believed that the only way to win the war, "like the first war, was to pool the two countries' material resources and productive potential." US production, he argued, needed to be doubled or quadrupled as soon as Roosevelt persuaded Congress to repeal the Neutrality Act. Because the increase had to be achieved by an Anglo-French effort, Allied economic cooperation was therefore essential. Urging the lessons of the first war be learned, he proposed the creation of institutional structures similar to those of 1917 and 1918: "strong inter-Allied executive committees, one for each sector," with policy councils of relevant ministers over them and an economic council, composed of one British and one French minister, such as the prime minister, to oversee the effort.[18]

On September 12, 1939, at the first meeting of the Anglo-French Supreme War Council, established to oversee joint military strategy, Daladier proposed that a "Frenchman who is a friend of Roosevelt" take charge of joint Allied purchases abroad. On September 20, Daladier sent the British prime minister, Neville Chamberlain, proposals almost identical to Monnet's of September 3, asking that Monnet meet in London those working on essential imports in order to avoid the mistakes of the first war. The British prime minister agreed and said all London doors to appropriate authorities would be open to him. Monnet attended the second Supreme War Council on September 22 and traveled the next day to London with French official René Mayer. Sir Edward Bridges, the secretary of the British War Cabinet, who made all the arrangements for Monnet's talks with British officials, accompanied them. Monnet immediately began lobbying intensely for far-reaching coordination of economic strategy. On October 1, he outlined for Bridges the structure of the Anglo-French committee he proposed to set up based upon his first war experience. He underlined the problems they would face, such as a shipping shortage and financing foreign imports.[19] From late September to early December, Monnet was the main author of the letters, memoranda, minutes of official meetings, and notes of informal discussions that, according to British official historians, created the "logical and genuinely combined structure of economic planning."[20]

Top Whitehall officials initially resisted many of Monnet's ideas and insisted on retaining the power to decide what Britain could supply. But they finally accepted the need for a coordinating committee of civil servants to have a permanent, independently appointed chairman. While many opposed his appointment because they disliked his autocratic style and single-mindedness and argued he lacked ministerial stature, Monnet secured the chair of what was called the Anglo-French Coordinating Committee (AFCOC) by having himself appointed jointly by the French and British prime ministers. This high-level backing was necessary, he believed, in order to preserve his independence, to protect himself from bureaucratic infighting and opposition, and to dramatize that his function derived from no single government. At the first meeting on December 6, 1939, he declared himself an Allied, not a French, official.[21]

Talented men worked with Monnet to coordinate Allied economic policies and to pool resources and purchases from neutral nations in the early critical months of the war. As chairman, Monnet exploited his position by managing the comprehensive committee structure he designed and used his power to ensure that the nine separate executive committees under him (food, shipping, oil, production and purchasing, etc.) functioned efficiently. The British members of these executives were the civil servants who headed ministries. Its French members, Monnet noted, were "outstanding colleagues" and included Pleven, his deputy on the French economic mission who chaired the Aviation Executive; Mayer, who was in charge of the Armaments and Raw Materials Executives; and Robert Marjolin, the dark-haired young economist and socialist planner in the 1930s whose intelligence impressed Monnet. Marjolin served as statistician for the committee and assembled figures on the requirements of the Allied armies and civilian populations. Monnet issued rational, clear instructions asking each executive to inventory resources, establish how best to use those resources for the Allies' benefit, and formulate joint import programs. Even though the executives focused on imports, the key issue in supplies, the Allied countries continued to compete on foreign markets for items such as tallow, silk, and flax, which provoked crises and inefficiencies. But the degree of Anglo-French economic and financial cooperation reached in the first three months of the war reflected an important achievement in the inter-Allied economic effort. It even exceeded what was achieved during World War I after four years of effort.[22]

One of Monnet's major achievements was to persuade the British to join the French in large joint orders for US aircraft in March 1940. He helped overcome resistance to these purchases on both sides of the Channel by using the classic "balance sheet" or business planning tool of analysis he had learned from his father. This analytical method assessed estimated needs over a period of time, in this case four years, and balanced them against available resources. It usually employed statistical tables for clarity and helped leaders face problems realistically, see needs clearly, and establish broad priorities. This kind of analysis made it harder to resist the needed remedial measures.

In order to overcome resistance to purchasing policies in the United States, Monnet had requested, in an October 6, 1939, memorandum to Daladier, that statistics comparing German and Allied airpower and rates of production, both actual and prospective, be produced. While it took four months, the figures showed the Germans outnumbered the British and French together 1.5 to 1 in fighters and 2 to 1 in bombers. As historian Ernest May has argued, Monnet and almost everyone else had fallen victim to a German deception campaign and overestimated German strength. The Luftwaffe was not nearly as strong as the French, British, and Americans believed.[23] But the statistics compiled by the French government, though erroneous, silenced British treasury and military opposition. And, on March 29, 1940, the Supreme War Council approved a joint program to purchase 4,700 airframes and 8,000 engines by 1941 from the United States at a cost of $614 million. Added to earlier French orders, these again "increased U.S. manufacturing capacity."[24]

In the late spring of 1940, British officials began to see the benefits of Anglo-French cooperation through Monnet's committee, which connected London and Paris. Monnet commented thirty years later that AFCOC's limitations meant "coordination enabled discussion but did not enable decisions."[25] Yet he acknowledged that despite the problems, it achieved some positive results. After Daladier fell from power that March and Monnet informed new Prime Minister Paul Reynaud about the AFCOC's work, London requested that Monnet continue to lead it. A British diplomat in Paris admitted that while he did not care for Monnet, "in England they think him the cat's pajamas."[26] Like many in his country who looked down on the French, the British author Anthony Sampson commented with a smile that Monnet reminded him of Hercule Poirot, British mystery writer Agatha Christie's caricature of a pre–World War I Frenchman, who spoke English with a strong French accent.[27]

## Concocting the Anglo-French Union Proposal

The June 16, 1940, proposal from Winston Churchill, the new British prime minister, to Reynaud for an indissoluble Anglo-French union emerged as a desperate effort to keep France in the war after it fell to Germany on June 9. Monnet, who with the British Foreign Minister Lord Halifax concocted the proposed instant union of Britain and France, believed surrendering to the Germans would be suicidal. He argued that the continuity of the French government after the war had to be preserved, that the French navy had to be saved, as much material as possible protected from capture by the Germans, and that Britain was the logical place to turn for support. Monnet together with Salter, his prime British collaborator during World War I who was serving as vice chairman of the AFCOC, drafted this proposal for a union of their two countries on June 13 and 14, 1940. It was used by Sir Robert Vansittart, the chief diplomatic adviser to the British government, in his June 14 draft of the Declaration of Union for the prime minister. While Churchill remained skeptical of the idea, thinking it was merely a propaganda appeal intended to stiffen morale, he went along with the British War Cabinet, which approved the text.[28]

Monnet and the French ambassador in London, Charles Corbin, persuaded General Charles de Gaulle, recently appointed undersecretary of national defense and a liaison with the British government by Prime Minister Reynaud, to support the idea of the union.[29] The general had come to London on June 16 to make arrangements to transport the French government and

troops to North Africa and telephoned Monnet upon his arrival. He acce
an invitation to dinner at Monnet's apartment where these men had their ....
encounter. When Silvia asked him how long his mission would last, de Gaulle
replied, "I am not here on a mission, Madame. I am here to save the honor of
France."[30]

In a brief morning meeting of June 16, de Gaulle, accompanied by Monnet and Pleven, asked Churchill to relay this proposal to unite the two nations
to Prime Minister Reynaud immediately. Initially impressed by this tall, lanky
French general whom he had just recently met, Churchill agreed and asked de
Gaulle to telephone Reynaud in Bordeaux where the French government had
relocated. Both Churchill and de Gaulle had approved the text of the Declaration of Union as each wished to encourage France to continue fighting in
North Africa, to bolster Reynaud, and to avoid a rupture between the Allies.
Churchill also agreed that it was necessary to keep the French fleet and
colonies in the war against Germany. From 10 Downing Street, where the
British cabinet was also meeting, de Gaulle telephoned Reynaud the final text
as Pleven translated it for him line by line into French. When de Gaulle fin-
ished, Churchill picked up the phone and reassured Reynaud he had approved
the declaration.[31]

After this call, Monnet and de Gaulle conversed with Churchill. While the
prime minister declined Monnet's request to send Britain's air forces to defend
France, Monnet informed the British leader of his plan to transfer all French
munitions contracts in the United States to Britain if France made a separate
peace. "He evidently expected this," noted Churchill, "and wished to save as
much as possible from what seemed to him to be the wreck of the world. His
whole attitude in this respect was most helpful."[32] The "Constable of France,"
as Churchill nicknamed de Gaulle, flew to Bordeaux the night of June 16 to
convince the French cabinet to accept the offer of the Declaration of Union and
personally deliver the text. But he was too late. The proposal had failed in the
French cabinet moments before. Reynaud had resigned and Marshal Philippe
Pétain replaced him as head of the Vichy government that capitulated to the
Germans. Monnet had persuaded Churchill to send him in a British plane to
Bordeaux that same day, accompanied by Pleven and Marjolin, with an offer to
transport members of the Reynaud cabinet to North Africa if they wished to
continue the fighting. But upon arrival, they found the French leadership in dis-
array and unwilling to move, so Monnet's group returned to London.[33]

Monnet understood that his effort to preserve the sovereignty of France
through the instant union of France and Britain had no chance of success. It
was a desperate attempt to maintain the French fighting spirit and the will to
resist conquest, which failed. But the ideas it encompassed were underscored
to British and US leaders and to de Gaulle. The recognition that the economic
resources of the United States would be needed in the battle against the enemy,
that French sovereignty and government based on "the principles of liberty

and democracy" must be preserved, and that the union must not collapse at the end of hostilities demonstrated Monnet's concern for the future of France. He also believed that economic integration should be a positive postwar goal and had propagated the idea of turning the Anglo-French economic collaboration already achieved into a permanent political union.[34]

Monnet's several discussions in London with de Gaulle in June and July 1940 demonstrated how concerned they each were for their nation's future. They both were determined to restore France's independence as a sovereign nation and to prevent it from abandoning the struggle against the Germans. But they disagreed on how to achieve this. Monnet believed resistance must be organized in North Africa, on French soil, under the authority of French leaders who were not under German control. He opposed de Gaulle's efforts to set up a French organization in London, which might appear in France "as an authority established under British protection." Monnet understood de Gaulle's "own conception of the historic role he felt called upon to play." This imposing military figure passionately proclaimed over BBC radio on June 18 that France would remain in the war and that French people should rally around him. The Vichy government declared de Gaulle outside the law and sentenced him to prison for refusing to obey an order from Pétain to return to France. Monnet wrote de Gaulle on June 23 about his disagreement with the general's idea to set up a French authority in Britain. In replying to Monnet the next day, de Gaulle wrote, "My dear friend, At such a time as this, it would be absurd for us to cross one another, because our fundamental aim is the same, and together perhaps we can do great things. Come and see me, wherever you choose. We shall agree."[35]

Monnet noted that de Gaulle "criticized my decision" to go to the United States to secure the armaments and essential material resources the Allies "at present lacked," but "he respected my choice as I admired his determination." The man from Cognac understood it had taken "great strength of character for him, a traditional soldier, to cross the great dividing-line of disobedience to orders from above." Monnet added, "He was the only man of his rank with the courage to do so; and in the painful isolation felt by those Frenchmen who had decided to continue the Allied struggle, de Gaulle's rare example was a source of great moral strength." But Monnet also realized de Gaulle was a strong-headed, complex, ambitious personality who believed France's role and his own were indissolubly linked.[36]

## Working with the British Purchasing Commission in Washington

The British North American Supply Committee (NAS) chaired by Arthur Salter replaced Monnet's AFCOC in July 1940. In his last act as chair of that committee on June 17, Monnet telegrammed Arthur Purvis, a Canadian businessman who had just opened the Anglo-French Purchasing Board in New York, to divert all further US orders intended for France to the United Kingdom. Purvis and Jean-Frédéric Bloch-Lainé, the head of the French Purchasing Commission in the United States, rushed the transfer of the contracts from the French to British hands with the help of a lawyer whom Dulles had recommended. While this action prevented the cancellation of the French aircraft contracts that Monnet had so carefully nurtured, it also required the British to pay the $612 million for them.[37]

After submitting his resignation as head of the AFCOC to Pétain in July, Monnet asked Churchill if he could "serve the true interests of his country" by continuing his work on supply coordination as a member of the British Purchasing Commission (BPC) in North America. While initially viewing Monnet simply as a high official, Churchill learned that the Frenchman had experience with both supply issues and the United States, which could potentially be advantageous to the Allied cause. The British prime minister therefore agreed to Monnet's request, and provided him with a passport signed by Churchill himself and a salary of $10,000 a year drawn on the Ministry of Supply.[38]

Between mid-August 1940 when he left London and February 1943, Monnet helped initiate and expand the US mobilization program as delegate-at-large on the BPC in Washington. Since he had been supervising the BPC from London as director of the AFCOC and was familiar with US decision-making processes, he became an indispensable coordinator of British and US efforts to match munitions and supplies needed by the British with US capabilities. With knowledge of French and British requirements and a strategic vision of future Allied needs, he helped plan US production capacity for the demands of the war in Europe.

When Monnet returned to the US capital in September 1940 with his wife and daughter, he faced opposition on several fronts. Canadian and British BPC officials complained because they were not consulted about his appointment. Some of the British were suspicious of this Frenchman at the center of Allied war planning while others feared he was a disciple of de Gaulle. Among the US opponents, the isolationists loudly proclaimed their nation could avoid European involvement and advocated staying clear of Britain's cause. The country was also preoccupied by a divisive political campaign over a third term for Roosevelt, who ran on the theme that his experienced hand would keep the United States out of war.

Once the president won reelection in November 1940, Monnet knew his efforts to secure supplies for the Allies had strong support from the White House. He believed he had forged a working relationship with Roosevelt when he personally delivered Daladier's request for airplanes two years earlier. While he never abused the privilege, he felt free to call on the president. Monnet also thought he understood to a large degree the difficult task facing the president in the years 1939–1941. Roosevelt had to balance his nation's desire to stay out of war with the contradictory need to defeat the Nazis. "Roosevelt's solution was not to intensify the conflict by choosing one goal over the other but rather to weave the two goals together," writes historian Robert Dallek. The president repeatedly urged the nation to believe that "the surest road to peace . . . was material aid to the Allies." And, Dallek argues, even when he concluded in the spring of 1941 that his country would have to join the battle, Roosevelt showed "caution and restraint" in edging the country toward war. But his appointment of John G. Winant, a former Republican governor of New Hampshire, in 1941 as the US ambassador in London signaled, contends Dallek, his definite commitment to Britain and the Allies in the continental battle waging in Europe.[39]

Monnet was very much persona grata in the inner circle of the British military staff in Washington, the circle around Sir John Dill, chief military representative to Washington from 1941 to 1944. In the crucial early period of the war, Dill helped coordinate the military policies of the United Kingdom and the United States, and his friendship with US Army Chief of Staff George Marshall did much to cement Anglo-American solidarity. Brigadier Vivian Dykes, the British secretary of the Combined Chiefs of Staff in Washington during the war, had a positive relationship with Monnet. He wrote in his diary in early January 1942, "Went out with [Brig] Ian [Jacob] to dine with Monnet. . . . Monnet is a very shrewd fellow. He stresses the importance of the Dill-Marshall liaison. I think he is right that the Yanks won't work to organizations—they deal only in personalities." Monnet and Dykes regularly consulted about tactics in their efforts to obtain supplies for Britain and the Allies, and Dykes kept Dill informed.[40]

Unruffled by any opposition, Monnet moved easily into the center of the Washington policymaking and social circles soon after his arrival because of his many American contacts. His close relationship based on "total trust" continued with journalist Walter Lippmann, who had a formidable influence on public opinion in the US capital. He also renewed his contact with Felix Frankfurter, the Supreme Court justice. Monnet had met this revered lawyer and scholar in 1927 at a dinner party given in Washington by George T. Rublee, the US member of the Allied Maritime Transport Council, which Monnet and Salter had created in London in 1918. Frankfurter, the leading educator of a generation of US jurists with a reputation as an aloof intellectual, became a trusted and useful friend. He operated in Washington through his network of former students and was in frequent contact with the White House. Frankfurter's real preoccupation "was with power . . . and he gloried in a power which was personal and exercised over the elite at close quarters," writes historian Eliot Janeway.[41]

At Rublee's party, Monnet also met Dean Acheson, the thirty-four-year-old international lawyer known for his powerful intellect and sharp wit. Acheson had brought his Harvard Law School mentor, Frankfurter, along to meet one of the senior partners in Covington, Burling, and Rublee, the prominent international firm with many European clients where Acheson worked.[42] Acheson's appointment by Roosevelt as assistant secretary of state for economic affairs in February 1941 meant he participated in all Lend-Lease arrangements with countries receiving US military and civilian aid. The work and social life of both Acheson and Monnet during these war years brought them into frequent contact and resulted in a mutual, lifelong respect for one another's ideas and dedication. "Both shared a profound and single-minded devotion to international cooperation," writes historian Douglas Brinkley. "Monnet must have been an inspiration to Acheson as to what could be accomplished by sheer dint of personality, persuasion, and connections." Acheson called Monnet "one of the brilliant men of his generation," and admired his "action-oriented, no nonsense, get-the-job-done approach to every assignment or project he undertook." Brinkley also notes that Acheson compared Monnet to General George Marshall because "each had a global reputation as a prestigious statesman of great consequence while usually managing to remain above the fray of partisan politics."[43]

Frankfurter introduced Monnet to many prominent personalities, such as Katharine and Phil Graham, who later became the owners and publishers of the *Washington Post*. Many mornings Graham strolled with this Frenchman through Rock Creek Park, a vast wooded area close to the Monnets' large rented Foxhall Road home. They had moved from a hotel suite to this comfortable but not elegant house in this prized suburban neighborhood with their daughter and cook-and-butler couple and were very happy there. Monnet loved Rock Creek Park and treated it like his own garden. The influential newspaper magnate compared Monnet to Benjamin Franklin because of the power of his intelligence and his competence.

The entrepreneur from Cognac wined and dined with the social elite that included old friends with whom he corresponded for many years as well as future influential foreign policy players and advisers who lived in or traveled frequently to Washington. Among them were the respected journalists brothers Joseph and Stewart Alsop, and James Reston, reporter for the *New York Times*, and his wife, Sally; Foster Dulles and his wife, Janet; the Dean Achesons; poet and writer Archibald Macleish and his wife; Averell Harriman, the railroad magnate; as well as the Walter Lippmanns.[44] Katharine Graham later captured in her memoirs the views of many of the Frenchman's American friends:

> Monnet was proof positive that if someone is brilliant, political, and concentrated, he can make a power base where none exists. . . . His mode of operation was to know the right people—those who had the knowledge, the power, and the will to move things—then to learn what made things move and to be constantly pushing the levers of power. He was very selective about whom

he saw and how he used his time. He never made small talk, and he always kept to the point in his discussions, at meetings, or even at dinners.[45]

Almost daily Monnet visited Frankfurter's office at the Supreme Court where they swapped ideas on how to strengthen US support of Great Britain. "We were soon united by deep friendship as well as common ideals," wrote Monnet, "and I was able to count on his full support."[46] Frankfurter admired the "resolution" and "will" Monnet displayed in accomplishing his tasks. He remarked that Monnet had "blinders on" and focused on his goal. "For the things that he's interested in, he doesn't dissipate his energies, or doesn't take time off, or doesn't listen to anything else." The Justice recounted that Monnet had a powerful will. "In government affairs the realization of objects depends on the resolution of men—that's the difference between statesmen who matter and statesmen who don't—resolution, pertinacity, patience, and persistence." Resolution, he added, was "manifested" in Monnet "to an extreme intensity."[47] Their families dined together often at the Monnets' house, and their wives became good friends. On occasion the Monnets even lent the Frankfurters their French cook-and-butler couple.

Monnet met Milton Katz, an assistant general counsel to the War Production Board, who described how Monnet adjusted to life in wartime Washington in 1941 just after the board was created by Roosevelt. "I enjoyed him," recalled Katz, "and found him interesting on so many questions. . . . He plainly had great influence." When Katz apologized for assigning Monnet to an office that was less comfortable than others in the building that housed the board, the Frenchman replied, "My young friend . . . I've learned that there is no international problem whatever that can compare in difficulty with the allocation of office space. . . . Don't be concerned. I'm very happy here." This lawyer wrote about lunching with the Monnets in their "lovely house on Foxhall Road with a lovely garden and serious paintings on the walls." To Monnet, Katz exclaimed, "I marvel at this camp of yours. Here you are, in an exceedingly transient situation, your country has fallen, you don't know what you'll do next, and you're here for a job, the duration of which none of us can forecast. And yet you live this way." Monnet replied that he had decided years ago that wherever you happen to be, for however brief a tenure, you should always organize your life as if you were going "to live there permanently. Because if you don't, you'll spend your entire life camping. . . . I'm now living the way I choose to live, whatever the circumstances." Katz quipped, "This was vintage Monnet."[48]

This lawyer recalled that Silvia had been concerned about their daughter Anna, then eleven years old, who performed well in her US school except for failing French. When confronted, the headmistress exclaimed that the child just could not master the grammar. Knowing Anna spoke excellent French, Silvia invited the teacher to come to the house when the child came home for lunch and asked her to hide behind a screen. The child, as always, spoke perfect French with her parents at lunch, proving her mother's point. As Katz observed, "It was perfectly clear. The child had become an ardent American and was determined not to be anything but an American."[49]

Frankfurter assisted Monnet's work in Washington immeasurably, including introducing him to Harry Hopkins, Roosevelt's closest adviser. When sent by the president to London to make contact with Churchill, Hopkins followed Monnet's advice and was successful in establishing himself as a link between the prime minister and the president. Hopkins harbored a dislike for British aristocrats and the Churchill legend, but Monnet told him to set his prejudices aside and deal with the prime minister, who made the key decisions. A grateful Hopkins later inveigled an invitation to Monnet's home, claiming he wanted to get to know his host "a little better," and they soon became good friends. When the Lend-Lease Act was passed in March 1941 eliminating legal restrictions on sales to belligerents, Hopkins was put in charge of arms aid to the Allies. From then on, when the British had a problem with the Americans, they briefed Monnet and sent him to see Hopkins. This method always produced a solution. Because of his facilitating role, Monnet deserves much of the credit for making the Lend-Lease program work.[50]

Monnet faced lingering distrust from Morgenthau, whom he had met in 1938. Roosevelt's treasury secretary believed the Frenchman had questionable German connections because the firm of Monnet, Murnane, and Co. had worked to preserve the assets of German subsidiaries in America in 1939. But his suspicions did not diminish Monnet's influence with Roosevelt or other high policy officials. When Morgenthau approached the British ambassador, Lord Halifax, about his suspicions, Halifax asked Frankfurter for an evaluation of Monnet and his services. The Justice reported to Halifax that he had heard

no higher praise of any official entrusted with British interests than what has been accorded Monnet by men charged with ultimate responsibility. I have heard Harry Hopkins, Secretary Stimson, the two assistant secretaries of war, McCloy and Lovett, and leading men in the army, Lend Lease Administration . . . speak of Monnet in terms of the highest esteem and admiration. He has been a creative and energizing force in our defense program. As one important official put it, "Monnet has really been a teacher to our defense administration." Another top official wrote me that "he has been responsible more than anyone connected with the British mission for the orientation of the men with whom he comes in contact in the War Department to the primary task which the United States must perform if it is to act effectively in the war. . . . [He] is the only one from their shop who talks and presses to the point almost of irritation the broad picture of the U.S. obligation. He spares himself no indignity or rebuff but before long has the Army officers repeating his arguments. He thinks on the basis of wide experience and wide contacts with the men of influence in three different governments, all of whom struggled with the problems of supply in war, not only in this war but in the last, and the quality and plane of his thinking shows it. . . . There is no mystery about the source of his achievement. He possesses an extraordinary clarity of mind, a power of concentration that is almost consecration, pertinacity, experience with technical defense problems, as well as large experience in the delicate task of carrying on successful collaboration between our two governments. . . . he brings the advantage of enjoying the friendship and confidence of Americans . . . in key places. . . . [E]veryone to whom I have spoken who has worked with Monnet has absolute confidence in him and in his trustworthiness, discretion, and single-minded devotion to the cause he is serving.[51]

Just as he had done in London as head of the Anglo-French Coordinating-Committee, Monnet lobbied for coordination of economic strategy. Working with Purvis and Salter, who joined the committee, and using access to the president's inner circles, this trio worked hard to persuade the British government to acknowledge its dependency upon the United States for additional raw materials, manpower, and resources. This closely knit group had to counter British reluctance to increase its war production significantly and persuade Britain to combine resources with the United States, as Monnet had tried to do in June 1940. They asked the British to estimate their requirements by using Monnet's planning device or balance sheet, officially known as the Anglo-American Combined Statement. They deemed these figures essential in order to underscore British needs for Roosevelt and his advisers and thereby motivate them to act. They advocated two of Monnet's principles: that there were practically no limits to the amount of munitions that could be produced by the vast US economy and that a war-winning armaments strategy, defined as what was necessary to overwhelm the enemy, without regard to cost, had to be adopted.

But the British Ministry of Supply refused to state Britain's arms needs because attempts to garner that information would have caused upheavals within the British industrial leadership, forced changes in manufacturing methods, and created an acknowledged dependence on the United States. And as historian John Gillingham asserts, Churchill assumed that the North Americans would "do those things economically necessary to win the war" and did not appear to focus on the consequences of failing to modernize British production, or to "override entrenched interests" in the British armaments economy.[52]

The supply group dramatized Allied as well as British needs to Roosevelt's decisionmakers in order to stimulate US production. Lacking British help, Purvis and Monnet made their own estimates of British requirements and gave the figure of $15 billion to Roosevelt on December 30, 1940, which was revised upward by the British Purchasing Commission to $18.85 billion in February 1941. Roosevelt showed great interest in a Purvis statement about Britain's arms deficiency and ordered that same month that US requirements be drawn up to meet the projected supply and arms needs of the British in combined Anglo-American programs. Having facilitated the French purchase of US airplanes, the president had continued to prepare his nation's industry for war by sending an appropriations bill to Congress in July 1940. By calling for a buildup of the armed forces, it launched a wave of government spending. But the president faced strong opposition from many quarters, especially from the War Department and private industry where there was an unwillingness to take the risks of wartime investment.[53]

In April 1941, Monnet developed another influential link to Roosevelt's cabinet following the appointment of Henry Stimson as secretary of war. Monnet had known Stimson in the early 1930s when he was secretary of state under President Herbert Hoover. This connection was strengthened when Stimson appointed Monnet's friend, John J. McCloy, as his assistant secretary of war. McCloy and Monnet had worked together in Paris in the late 1920s when McCloy opened a Paris law office, and their relationship deepened in 1941. Conversing either by phone or in McCloy's office nearly every day, they were consumed by the problems of mobilizing US industrial power.[54]

Soon after his appointment, Stimson insisted that all military orders from foreign countries be handled by the War Department. While McCloy strongly supported a greater US production effort and facilitated Monnet's requests, some Washington officials, such as Secretary of State Cordell Hull, never trusted Monnet. A former Tennessee congressman with little knowledge of foreign affairs, Hull saw Monnet as de Gaulle's agent. But Stimson reassured the secretary that Monnet was being treated by the War Department "purely as an agent here to purchase supplies (and) his authority and our authority was limited to that subject in all our talks." Stimson never admitted to Hull that Monnet personally kept him informed about the French political situation in North Africa, that he found Monnet's clear analyses very useful, or that he passed on these memoranda to others in the US government.[55]

## Making New Contacts

Monnet had a talent for finding persons in positions of influence who could be useful to him. Having learned about Robert Nathan, the tall, dark-haired, New Deal economist, Monnet arranged to meet him. Nathan had become associate director of the Bureau of Research and Statistics of the National Defense Advisory Commission. His job was to collect information on military requirements, analyze the productive capacity of the economy, and determine what critical components would be needed if all-out defense mobilization became necessary.

Nathan grew to admire this Frenchman who stressed the urgency of America's mobilization. He recalled,

Monnet was truly a great strategist and always full of ideas. He loved to debate, argue, and disagree, and he stimulated you to take different approaches. He was always initiating and discussing ideas, but he also was anxious to know what you thought. Monnet was a patient listener who tried to find practical solutions to problems. He was not an economist but a doer, and he believed in an orderly process.[56]

Whether on an early morning walk in Rock Creek Park or sipping cognac at his home, Monnet repeatedly stressed the consequences for the Allies as well as for Western democracy if the United States did not expand material output massively and quickly. "Monnet had one goal in Washington: to impress upon American decisionmakers that American production was needed to stop Hitler," recalled Nathan. "He never suggested the United States send troops or advocated our nation become involved. He just wanted Europe to be able to help defend itself with massive American production."[57]

Throughout 1941, Nathan and Monnet met often to discuss ways to obtain large and speedy increases in US production. Nathan explained it was hard to get specific requirements from the military services and that, without this information, the US government could not get support to build and convert large industrial facilities. But after the British sank the German battleship *Bismarck* on May 27, 1941, Roosevelt declared "an unlimited national emergency" and demanded data from the military. By the spring of 1941, Roosevelt knew he had to bring his nation into the war to fight beside his Allies but could not yet declare war because of the pervasive isolationist sentiment in the United States. McCloy, Monnet, and economist-statistician Stacy May, a Monnet disciple, began to prepare war orders for a comprehensive Anglo-American balance sheet, the method of planning for war supplies introduced by the Frenchman. It enabled them to compare US and British resources with estimates of German strength and potential. Working closely with Nathan, Monnet persistently urged him to elevate the figures because he saw his role as matching the Allies' needs with the pace of wartime production. But Nathan refused. He stressed their analyses would be useless if their US figures did not accurately reflect production capacity and underscored that feasibility was essential for a successful mobilization.

"Monnet was an impatient man because he knew better than most the grave jeopardy of Great Britain," wrote Nathan, who sometimes tired of Monnet's prodding, brusque style, and single-mindedness.[58]

In early September 1941, the balance sheet was completed. As historian William K. Hancock wrote, the Anglo-American Combined Statement, as it came to be known, "was never intended as an end in itself, but was on the contrary always intended to give leverage in shifting the obstructions which impeded an expansion and acceleration of war production."[59] It clearly demonstrated the limits of US rearmament by showing that US production lagged behind Britain and Canada and that there were serious deficiencies in the number of heavy bombers and tanks. Monnet argued that this statement underscored the need to develop plans at once "for the production some time by the end of 1942 of sufficient weapons, tanks, planes, etc. to exceed German material strength without any doubt whatever."[60]

These conclusions helped motivate Roosevelt to approve the mobilization plan for US war production to meet Allied needs for the army and navy on September 25, 1941. By mid-October, Nathan had designed a production schedule for the successive years 1942, 1943, and 1944 to dramatically increase US military output. Roosevelt adopted the Victory Program of increased war production ten days after the December 7 Japanese attack on Pearl Harbor. Historian John Gillingham argues, "The Victory Program thus conceived by Monnet, brought into the world by Donald Nelson [head of the War Production Board], and baptized by Roosevelt, would enable the United States to win the war with comfortable margins to spare."[61] As Monnet noted, this meant an "immense increase in US strength and, by implication, a decisive US impact on the future course of the war."[62] In one of his "fireside chats" at the end of December, Roosevelt described his country as an "arsenal of democracy," a phrase purported to be coined by Monnet.[63]

In another initiative, Monnet, May, and Nathan demonstrated in December 1941 and later to Roosevelt through Hopkins that the US production schedule in most types of weapons could be increased by an additional 50 percent in 1942. Monnet also showed that even this expanded Victory Program fell well behind the mobilization already achieved by the United Kingdom. At the first war planning meeting of Churchill and Roosevelt from December 28 through January 5, 1942, the well-briefed leaders agreed to elevate their production, despite protests from the industrialists who were reluctant to risk the required investments. In his speech to Congress January 6, 1942, just one month after Pearl Harbor, Roosevelt called for the mammoth production of airplanes and tanks, which significantly increased US industrial expansion. "On that day, more than any other time in my life," wrote Monnet, "I felt the satisfaction of having contributed to a decision that would change the course of events."[64]

Once the United States entered the war, the challenge for US officials was to calculate specific British, Soviet, and US military requirements as well as the pace at which items could be produced under maximum effort. After Pearl Harbor, Nathan was made chairman of the Planning Committee of the War Production Board where he designed and submitted a feasibility study of the US mobilization and production effort with the help of McCloy and Monnet. By spring of 1942, the success of the production program and the creation of the Combined Production and Resources Board helped increase Anglo-American cooperation.[65]

Monnet described his main contribution to the war effort at this time as tackling the enormous mobilization problems, stating them in simple terms, and bringing them "into wide-ranging discussion." He wrote, "This time I had no difficulty in finding men who were ready to listen and to turn into practical decisions the plans we worked out together." Nathan and Hopkins credit Monnet with being one of "the most important single contributors to the Allied victory in World War II. If it hadn't been for Monnet and his Victory Program effort, we would have lost months . . . of vital production." Nathan argues that "Monnet should be given credit for getting the Victory Program through." After the war, Halifax wrote Frankfurter that Monnet "was, with such as Harry Hopkins, one of the real architects of our victory." John Maynard Keynes, the wartime British treasury official, reported Monnet's efforts "may well have shortened the war by a year."[66]

Monnet was just one of many individuals in Washington seeking US help for Britain during the early years of the war. While Monnet preached the doctrine of "all out production," other British citizens labored to persuade Roosevelt to enter the war. Churchill had sent William Stephenson, code-named "Intrepid," to head a secret intelligence organization, the British Security Coordination (BSC), as part of his covert plan to prod the country into action. According to the organization's official history, Stephenson was empowered to "do all that was not being done and could not be done by overt means" to ensure aid for Britain and counter the enemy's plans in the Western Hemisphere.[67] Among those recruited during the war to be part of this spy ring were British playwright Noel Coward, author Ian Fleming, advertising businessman David Ogilvy, and Roald Dahl, the young, intelligent, handsome RAF pilot who later became a novelist and famed children's author. These men gained access to Washington society and government by becoming friends with influential wartime leaders such as Henry Morgenthau and members of Congress. They helped the BSC conduct covert action campaigns to weaken the isolationist forces in the United States and influence US policy in favor of Britain. They planted propaganda in US newspapers, radio stations, and wire services and influenced leading columnists such as Drew Pearson, Walter Lippmann, and Walter Winchell. Dahl, who was officially attached to the British Air Mission, even befriended Eleanor Roosevelt and thereby became a regular guest at the White House and Hyde Park. His reports on his conversations with the president were sent back to Churchill, who was desperately trying to engage this US leader. However controversial this spy ring later became, Churchill believed that as Britain's only hope of survival depended on US assistance, he had to do everything possible to ensure that aid.[68]

While Monnet and British spies labored in Washington, three prominent Americans worked tirelessly from London to convince Roosevelt and a reluctant US public to support the British in their greatest hour of need. Writer Lynne Olson, in her recent book *Citizens of London*, contends that Roosevelt sent John Winant to England as the US ambassador to keep an eye on Churchill. Arriving in London in the spring of 1941, Winant played a key role in shaping and maintaining the alliance between the United States and Britain during World War II. Averell Harriman, the ambitious chairman of the Union Pacific Railroad, arrived soon after Winant to be the administrator of the US Lend-Lease aid to Britain. Edward R. Murrow, head of CBS News in London, continually broadcast to Americans the extent of the destruction caused by the repeated bombing of London and Londoners' courage and resourcefulness. While the prime minister courted Winant, Harriman, and Murrow because he knew how important these men were to his nation's survival, all three had close personal links to Churchill and his family. Once Roosevelt declared war, all three men urged the US president to provide as much aid as possible to Britain. Their tireless advocacy of the need to help Britain survive the war helped lay the groundwork for the Anglo-American partnership that developed in 1941 and maintain it once the United States entered the war.[69]

Assignments from the prime ministers of France and Great Britain between 1938 and 1942 catapulted Monnet into the governing circles of Paris, London, and Washington and earned him a reputation as a man of both strategic vision and action. He demonstrated that he could, with foresight, identify a problem in the rapidly changing international situation, design a solution, and then implement it. Monnet utilized his World War I experience and the French and British wartime predicaments in 1939–1940 to coordinate the Allied supply effort. He had understood earlier than many the extent of Allied dependency on the United States as a source of supplies and war materials and that the fate of Europe would be determined by the industrial and agricultural power of the United States. Because of his knowledge, persistence, and persuasive abilities, first Churchill and then US officials listened to him. He incessantly propagated his belief in the ability of the US economy to expand almost without limit. And because Roosevelt found many of the Frenchman's views compatible with his own, he was encouraged by Monnet to take bold and dramatic steps to increase US wartime production and thereby helped spur mobilization of the US economy. By becoming the wartime supplier for the Allies, the United States helped the Allies hold the line against Germany until it could join the effort.

During these diplomatic missions, Monnet forged relationships and gained knowledge and contacts in London and Washington that would assist him in his later postwar efforts to reconstruct the French economy and restore France to a position of influence in Europe. Having established close relations with Hopkins, Stimson, and McCloy, and having won the respect of many influential US and British officials, he helped to lay the foundation for a lasting transatlantic relationship that was needed to beat the Germans.[70] He also appears to have demonstrated to de Gaulle and other Allied leaders that the preservation of French sovereignty during the combat, even if it involved union with Britain, was very much on his mind.

Moreover, his success at winning the respect and trust of the US president as well as Hopkins enabled him to utilize this access to influence Roosevelt in

1943 and gain an assignment from him that proved beneficial to his own divided country, which was suffering from a humiliating defeat.

## Notes

1. Jean Monnet, *Memoirs* (New York: Doubleday, 1978), pp. 116–118; Ernest R. May, *Strange Victory* (New York: Hill and Wang, 2000), pp. 27–37.
2. René Pleven, "Témoignage de René Pleven," in *Témoignages à la mémoire de Jean Monnet* (Lausanne, Switzerland: Fondation Jean Monnet pour l'Europe Centre de recherches européennes, 1989), pp. 391–392.
3. François Duchêne, *Jean Monnet: The First Statesman of Interdependence* (New York: W. W. Norton, 1994), pp. 64–67.
4. May, *Strange Victory*, pp. 113–126.
5. Monnet, *Memoirs*, pp. 116–118; Duchêne, *Jean Monnet*, pp. 64–67; Elisabeth du Réau, "Jean Monnet, le Comité de coordination franco-britannique et le projet d'Union franco-britannique: Les Moyens de vaincre le nazisme (septembre 1939–juin 1940)," in *Jean Monnet, l'Europe et les chemins de la paix,* ed. Gérard Bossuat and Andreas Wilkens (Paris: Publications de la Sorbonne, 1999), p. 78.
6. Diaries of Anne Morrow Lindbergh, cited in Clifford Hackett, *A Jean Monnet Chronology* (Washington, DC: Jean Monnet Council, 2008), pp. 112–114.
7. Monnet, *Memoirs*, pp. 117–118; du Réau, "Jean Monnet, le Comité de coordination franco-britannique," p. 78.
8. Monnet, *Memoirs*, pp. 116–117; May, *Strange Victory*, pp. 146, 179; Élisabeth Du Réau, *Edouard Daladier* (Paris: Fayard, 1993), pp. 345–346; Eric Roussel, *Jean Monnet* (Paris: Librairie Artheme Fayard, 1996), pp. 167, 172–173; Duchêne, *Jean Monnet*, p. 65; Hackett, *Jean Monnet Chronology,* pp. 113–114.
9. May, *Strange Victory*, p. 164.
10. Diaries of Anne Morrow Lindbergh, cited in Hackett, *Jean Monnet Chronology*, pp. 112–116.
11. May, *Strange Victory*, pp. 146, 179; Du Réau, *Daladier*, pp. 345–346; Roussel, *Jean Monnet*, pp. 167, 172–173; Duchêne, *Jean Monnet*, p. 65; Hackett, *Jean Monnet Chronology*, p. 112.
12. Monnet, *Memoirs*, pp. 118–119; Duchêne, *Jean Monnet*, p. 67; Roussel, *Jean Monnet*, p. 170; Jean-Louis Mandereau, "Témoignage de Jean-Louis Mandereau," in *Témoignages à la mémoire de Jean Monnet* (Lausanne, Switzerland: Fondation Jean Monnet pour l'Europe Centre de recherches européennes, 1989), pp. 335–346.
13. Roussel, *Jean Monnet*, pp. 173–175.
14. Duchêne, *Jean Monnet*, pp. 67–68; Du Réau, "Jean Monnet, le Comité de coordination franco-britannique," pp. 80–81; Roussel, *Jean Monnet*, pp. 175–176.
15. Irwin M. Wall, *The United States and the Making of Postwar France, 1945–1954* (Cambridge, UK: Cambridge University Press, 1991), pp. 16–17; see also John M. Haight, Jr., *American Aid to France, 1938–1940* (New York: Atheneum, 1970).
16. Duchêne, *Jean Monnet*, pp. 68–70.
17. Du Réau, "Jean Monnet, le Comité de coordination franco-britannique," pp. 80–82.
18. Monnet, *Memoirs*, pp. 18, 124–126; Duchêne, *Jean Monnet*, pp. 70–71.
19. Du Réau, *Daladier*, p. 383; Jean Monnet to Sir Edward Bridges, letter, October 1, 1939, Roosevelt Papers, Roosevelt Library; Duchêne, *Jean Monnet*, p. 71; Monnet, *Memoirs*, p. 126.

20. W. K. Hancock and M. M. Gowing, *The British War Economy: UK History of the Second World War* (London: H.M.S.O., 1975), pp. 187–189.

21. Duchêne, *Jean Monnet*, pp. 72–73.

22. Monnet, *Memoirs*, pp. 209–210; Hancock and Gowing, *British War Economy*, pp. 187–190; Duchêne, *Jean Monnet*, pp. 73–77; du Réau, "Jean Monnet, le Comité de coordination franco-britannique," p. 84; du Réau, *Daladier*, pp. 384–385.

23. May, *Strange Victory*, pp. 109–110, 174–175, 245, 352–354.

24. Duchêne, *Jean Monnet*, pp. 74–75.

25. Ibid., p. 75.

26. Clifford Hackett, "Jean Monnet and the Roosevelt Administration," in *Monnet and the Americans*, ed. Clifford Hackett (Washington, DC: Jean Monnet Council, 1995), p. 34.

27. Duchêne, *Jean Monnet*, p. 30.

28. François Duchêne, interview by the author, October 16, 1994; Frederic Fransen, *The Supranational Politics of Jean Monnet* (Westport, CT: Greenwood Press, 2001), pp. 34–36; Avi Shlaim, "Prelude to Downfall: The British Offer of Union to France, June 1940," *Journal of Contemporary History* 9 (1974), p. 44; Winston S. Churchill, *Their Finest Hour* (Boston: Houghton Mifflin, 1949), pp. 204–208.

29. Charles Cogan, *Charles de Gaulle: A Brief Biography with Documents* (Boston: Bedford Books of St. Martin's Press, 1996), pp. 28–29.

30. Monnet, *Memoirs*, pp. 23–24.

31. Shlaim, "Prelude to Downfall," pp. 45–60.

32. Churchill, *Finest Hour*, pp. 214–215; Fransen, *Supranational Politics of Jean Monnet*, p. 39.

33. Monnet, *Memoirs*, pp. 30–35.

34. Fransen, *Supranational Politics of Jean Monnet*, pp. 40–46; John Davenport, "M. Jean Monnet of Cognac," *Fortune* 2, no. 30 (1944), pp. 125ff.

35. Monnet, *Memoirs*, pp. 143–146; Cogan, *De Gaulle*, pp. 41–42.

36. Monnet, *Memoirs*, pp. 146–147.

37. Hackett, "Jean Monnet," pp. 33–35; Duchêne, *Jean Monnet*, p. 83.

38. Monnet to Churchill, letter, July 2, 1940, and Churchill to Monnet, letter, July 16, 1940, Roosevelt Papers, Roosevelt Library. See also Monnet, *Memoirs*, pp. 147–149; Duchêne, *Jean Monnet*, pp. 83–84; Hackett, "Jean Monnet," pp. 35–36.

39. Robert Dallek, *Franklin D. Roosevelt and American Foreign Policy, 1932–1945* (New York: Oxford University Press, 1979), pp. 529–533.

40. Vivian Dykes, diary entry of January 11, 1942, in *Establishing the Anglo-American Alliance: The Second World War Diaries of Brigadier Vivian Dykes,* ed. Alex Danchev (London: 1990: Brassey's Defense Publishers, Ltd.), p. 89. See also Alex Danchev, *Very Special Relationship: Field-Marshal Sir John Dill and the Anglo-American Alliance, 1941–1944* (London: Brassey's Defense Publishers, 1986); Alex Danchev, interview by the author, July 1, 2009.

41. Eliot Janeway, *The Struggle for Survival: A Chronicle of Economic Mobilization in World War II* (New Haven, CT: Yale University Press, 1951), p. 140.

42. Douglas Brinkley, "Dean Acheson and Jean Monnet," in *Monnet and the Americans*, ed. Clifford Hackett (Washington, DC: Jean Monnet Council, 1995), pp. 74–76.

43. Ibid., p. 78.

44. Monnet, *Memoirs,* pp. 154–155; Monnet to Walter Lippmann, letter, April 29, 1926, Walter Lippmann Papers, Yale University; Joseph Alsop to Monnet, letter, February 26, 1965, and Monnet to Alsop, letter, March 4, 1965, Joseph Alsop Papers, Library of Congress; Roussel, *Jean Monnet*, pp. 155–156.

45. Katharine Graham, *Personal History* (New York: Vintage Books, 1998), p. 128.

46. Hackett, "Jean Monnet," p. 37; Duchêne, *Jean Monnet,* p. 88; Monnet, *Memoirs*, pp. 153–154.

47. Felix Frankfurter, *Felix Frankfurter Reminisces: Recorded in Talks with Dr. Harlan B. Phillips* (New York: Reynal, 1960), pp. 184–185.

48. Professor Milton Katz, interview by Leonard Tennyson, January 28, 1988, Fondation Jean Monnet.

49. Ibid.

50. John Gillingham, *Coal, Steel, and the Rebirth of Europe, 1945–1955* (Cambridge, UK: Cambridge University Press, 1991), pp. 50–51; Hackett, "Jean Monnet," pp. 41–47; Duchêne, *Jean Monnet*, p. 91.

51. Felix Frankfurter to Lord Halifax, letter, November 14, 1941, Felix Frankfurter Papers, Library of Congress. Frankfurter's letter contains a long quote from John McCloy's letter to the Chief Justice. See Thomas Schwartz, "The Transnational Partnership: Jean Monnet and Jack McCloy," in *Monnet and the Americans* (Washington, DC: Jean Monnet Council, 1995), pp. 171–177.

52. Gillingham, *Coal, Steel,* pp. 50–52, 81–82; Hancock, *British War Economy*, p. 185; Duchêne, *Jean Monnet*, pp. 87–91.

53. Ibid.

54. Schwartz, "Transnational Partnership," pp. 172–173.

55. Hackett, "Jean Monnet," pp. 39–41; Schwartz, "Transnational Partnership," p. 173.

56. Robert Nathan, interview by the author, April 17, 1989.

57. Ibid.

58. Sherrill B. Wells, "Monnet and 'The Insiders': Nathan, Tomlinson, Bowie, and Schaetzel," in *Monnet and the Americans*, ed. Clifford Hackett (Washington, DC: Jean Monnet Council, 1995), pp. 199–200; Duchêne, *Jean Monnet*, p. 90; Robert Nathan, "An Unsung Hero of World War II," in *Jean Monnet: The Path to European Unity*, ed. Douglas Brinkley and Clifford Hackett (New York: St. Martin's Press, 1991), pp. 75–76.

59. Hancock, *British War Economy*, pp. 187–189.

60. Quoted in Duchêne, *Jean Monnet*, p. 92.

61. Gillingham, *Coal, Steel*, p. 89.

62. Monnet, *Memoirs,* p. 172.

63. Hackett, "Jean Monnet," p. 47; Duchêne, *Jean Monnet*, pp. 91–92; Schwartz, "Transnational Partnership," pp. 172–173.

64. Monnet, *Memoirs,* p. 174; Duchêne, *Jean Monnet*, p. 93; Hancock, *British War Economy*, pp. 187–189.

65. Wells, "Insiders," p. 200.

66. Ibid.; Nathan, interview; Duchêne, *Jean Monnet,* p. 97; Monnet, *Memoirs*, p. 177; see also John Gillingham, "Jean Monnet et le 'Victory Program' américain," in *Jean Monnet, l'Europe et les chemins de la paix,* ed. Gérard Bossuat and Andreas Wilkens (Paris: Publications de la Sorbonne, 1999), pp. 98, 109.

67. Jennet Conant, *The Irregulars: Roald Dahl and the British Spy Ring in Wartime Washington* (New York: Simon and Schuster, 2008), pp. xii–xiv.

68. Ibid., pp. 1–369.

69. Lynne Olson, *Citizens of London: The Americans Who Stood with Britain in Its Darkest, Finest Hour* (New York: Random House, 2010).

70. Du Réau, *Daladier*, pp. 345–346.

# 3

# Washington Assignments,
# 1943–1945

By July of 1942 British Prime Minister Churchill and President Roosevelt decided the Allies would launch an attack on the Germans from French North Africa. The Vichy collaborationist government in Algiers, a port city on the Algerian coast and the temporary home of many French exiles, had become consumed by factional strife. To implement their strategy Roosevelt and Churchill realized it was necessary to resolve the divisions among both the French military and the civilians living in North Africa. These leaders sent Allied Commander General Dwight Eisenhower in November to establish headquarters in Algiers and prepare for a peripheral attack on the Axis forces. His challenge was to bring some political and military organization to French North Africa in order to make it a safe base for forthcoming operations. To help the Allies implement their military strategy and unite the French, Roosevelt sent Monnet to Algiers in February 1943.

Disputes within the US government over its policy toward France had arisen soon after the French surrender to Germany in June 1940. Washington had recognized Marshal Philippe Pétain's Vichy collaborationist government in hopes of encouraging French resistance to the Germans. The British, on the other hand, supported the Free French movement of General Charles de Gaulle whose efforts from London to rally his countrymen to resist the German occupation made him a traitor to Pétain. But the State Department distrusted de Gaulle, whom they believed was a potential dictator. This view of the general, fueled by exile Alexis Léger, former secretary general of the French Foreign Ministry who lived in Washington, reflected Roosevelt's own view and made US policy hostile toward the Free French.

By late 1942, it was clear to the Allies that the Vichy government was not thwarting Hitler. And when the Allied troops landed in North Africa on

November 8, 1942, they were stunned to find that the French troops fought against them. As several of the senior French military leaders who were neither collaborationist nor Gaullist were competing to lead a French faction in North Africa, the Roosevelt administration had begun focusing on General Henri Honoré Giraud. This handsome, mild-tempered French military man with a saber-toothed mustache had escaped from a German prison camp with the Allies' help. Secretly transported on a submarine to Gibraltar, he was then flown to northern Algeria to cooperate with the Allies. With Roosevelt's approval, General Eisenhower gave Giraud the title of commander-in-chief of the French forces. After Admiral Jean Louis Darlan, Petain's provisional administrator in Algiers, was assassinated on Christmas Day, Giraud assumed the title of civil and military commander-in-chief of French interests in North Africa. Since US Consul General Robert Murphy's negative reports from Algiers on Gaullism had reinforced Roosevelt's dislike of the volatile French general in London, Giraud became a possible alternative French leader in the eyes of the US government.[1]

After the Allied landings in North Africa, Monnet became increasingly preoccupied with the problems facing France under German occupation. He thought that de Gaulle might be more interested in his own political power than the fate of their nation. He was also concerned that the administration of the Vichy government in Algiers had become so divided that Allied plans to regain North Africa from the Germans appeared threatened. Moreover, that government's antidemocratic, anti-Semitic, and reactionary character deeply troubled him. As an Allied victory in the war looked more likely, Monnet understood the need to persuade the US government to safeguard French sovereignty and to reassure the French people about their political future and their rights to self-determination promptly after the war.[2]

The confused situation in North Africa put France on the agenda of the Casablanca conference in January 1943 when Roosevelt and Churchill met to coordinate Allied war efforts. Churchill persuaded de Gaulle to fly to Casablanca for a brief meeting with Giraud and the Allied leaders on January 22. This meeting exposed the wide divergence of views between the two generals. It underscored the urgency of the problem even though they publicly voiced agreement to work together to defeat the Axis powers and posed for a widely publicized photograph shaking hands. Talks with Giraud convinced Roosevelt that the general needed help if he was to play a useful role in the Allied North Africa operation. His lack of sound political judgment and his deeply entrenched military authoritarianism worried the British as well as the other Americans. Eisenhower had thought he had an exceptional ally in Giraud, one who could win him the cooperation of the French forces and the administration. But he was disappointed to discover that Giraud received a cold reception by the French in Africa. Moreover, Giraud had poisoned the whole atmosphere by refusing to condemn Pétain or his collaboration schemes. De Gaulle, who had chafed under Giraud's command in the late 1930s, regarded this military rival with a mixture of suspicion and condescension. He believed Giraud was not only unacceptable as a leader but had no political value since his command derived from US authorities. A few weeks later, de Gaulle wrote his personal representative in Algiers and close friend General Georges Catroux, stating that only "Free France is capable of generating the spirit of war," to make the effort of the nation "constant and resolute," and to be "the hope of the resistance."[3]

Monnet believed he could play a role in Algiers that was useful to the Allies, the US government, and France. Since his arrival in Washington from London in August 1940, his close friends Henry Stimson and John McCloy had shown him Murphy's dispatches to Roosevelt and had given him firsthand knowledge of the complex situation in Algiers. Both of these officials also regularly consulted him about the likelihood of some of the French there splitting from Vichy. Monnet shared with these two men his concern that once the Germans were beaten, French unity would be at stake during the rest of the war and at its end. Since Allied policy tended to accentuate the quarrels and divisions among the French, Monnet saw that his task "was to preserve the chances of bringing together all those who wanted to take part in their country's liberation." With foresight, Monnet argued it was critical to look ahead "to the moral and material reconstruction of Europe."[4] He was convinced that a stable, strong, and united France would be important to the European continent and felt compelled to go to Algiers to influence the evolving political situation there and to help reunite the French. Therefore, early in 1943, Monnet engineered an assignment to be Roosevelt's emissary in the Europeanized picturesque Mediterranean city of Algiers.[5]

On Christmas Eve, Monnet wrote Harry Hopkins and Felix Frankfurter a long memorandum, intended for Roosevelt, in an attempt to focus the president's attention on France before the January meeting with Churchill. Monnet stressed the need to make the large French army in North Africa part of the Allied forces and at the service of the French government that would be set up after the liberation of France. He argued that the French people had a right to determine for themselves what kind of government and leaders should replace the collaborationist Vichy regime, which had destroyed theirs. Great Britain and the United States, he stressed, must preserve the right of the French to self-determination after liberation. He drew a distinction between French support for de Gaulle as a symbol of the fight against Germany and support for de Gaulle as head of a postwar government. Any rivalry between de Gaulle's London Committee and Algiers must be discouraged, and the French fighting forces must be given resources produced by the "arsenal of democracy."[6] Acutely aware of Secretary of State Cordell Hull's and Roosevelt's distaste for de Gaulle's presumption that he spoke for all Frenchmen, Monnet stressed that French sovereignty must not be usurped by any pretender to political authority inside or outside France. He proposed the formation of a governing body composed of both Free French and former Vichy supporters that would be placed under Allied supervision but limited to local administration. The main Allied effort would be focused on the creation of a French national army.[7]

Monnet asked Hopkins, Roosevelt's adviser, whether he could be sent to Algiers on behalf of the Munitions Assignment Board to assist Giraud, and Hopkins passed the suggestion on to Roosevelt at Casablanca. "I judged that my most useful role," Monnet wrote, "would be at the heart of French affairs."[8] Roosevelt consulted Hull, writing, "Apparently Giraud lacks the administrative ability, and the French army officers will not recognize de Gaulle's authority. Since there are no French civilians readily available in this area, what would be your opinion of having Jean Monnet come here? [to N. Africa] It appears he has kept his skirts clear of political entanglements in recent years and my impression of him is very favorable." The president added, "I am particularly anxious that the mention of Monnet be kept completely secret as everything will be spoiled if there is any leak."[9]

Roosevelt talked with Giraud on January 17 in Casablanca about the plan to form a three-man Committee for the Liberation of France with Giraud as the civil and military head, de Gaulle as military deputy, and a third man a civil deputy for administration. The president added that Monnet best represented France and the French spirit in North America. Meanwhile Monnet, leaving no stone unturned, arranged for Giraud to cable Washington that he would welcome Monnet. While the general did not know him personally, Monnet had provided his political adviser direct access to Hopkins in December 1942, which helped Giraud obtain arms for a new French army. When informed of Monnet's help, Giraud asked his adviser to telegram Washington in early February that he wanted Monnet to come to Algiers.[10]

Roosevelt shared some of Monnet's concern about French unity and France's political future. In a February 12, 1943, speech to White House correspondents, Roosevelt commented on the need to safeguard French sovereignty and the right of the French to self-determination after the war. On February 20, following the advice of Hopkins, Stimson, and McCloy, and ignoring Hull, the president asked Monnet to go to Algiers as his emissary, nominally on behalf of the Munitions Assignment Board chaired by Hopkins, to manage the rearmament of the French forces by handling Lend-Lease supplies.[11] He indicated he had complete confidence in the Frenchman to carry out this mission. Roosevelt's line of reasoning is revealed in part in his February 22 message to Eisenhower in which he stated that Monnet would be good for Giraud for two reasons. First, he was in "close touch with the activities of all our combined boards. . . . I have discussed all arms matters" with him. Second, while Monnet "has never been identified with the Free French or any other faction, he has devoted himself exclusively to war" and "can be useful to Giraud," Murphy, and Harold Macmillan, a junior member of the British government.

Macmillan had been sent to Algiers by Churchill as minister-resident to keep an eye on Murphy. After Monnet's arrival, Eisenhower replied that he was delighted by Monnet's presence and had been impressed by his character and his account of the situation in Algiers since his arrival.[12]

The president sent Monnet to Algiers to bolster Giraud by serving as his political adviser and to help end the divisions among the French. This meant acquainting the general with US views, assisting in rearming the French forces there, and trying to reconcile Giraud and de Gaulle. Monnet, remarked a US colleague with a smile, was in fact "entrusted with the task of being Henri Giraud's thinker."[13] Always planning ahead, Monnet personally telegrammed Giraud that he had been assigned "a special mission in North Africa by the Mutual Assignments Board" to assist "the rearming of French forces." To maximize his leverage with the general and to facilitate his difficult task, he stressed, "This mission has been given me with the assent of the President and of the British government."[14]

Before leaving Washington on February 23, 1943, Monnet talked with French and US colleagues about his goal of uniting the French. To his friend Hervé Alphand, whom he described as "an outstandingly brilliant diplomat," he expressed his belief that the Free French factions needed to unite to preserve their country. Frankfurter urged him to maintain his independence "and not throw his weight completely behind Giraud." After his arrival in Algiers February 28, Monnet told Murphy that he had "come to Algiers not so much to serve Giraud as to seek a solution which would create unity among all French factions." But Murphy learned only later that Monnet's idea of French unity challenged Roosevelt's conception.[15]

## Meeting the Challenges of Algiers

In this delicate mission, Monnet benefited initially from the observations, actions, and advice of John McCloy. The US official had been sent to Algiers on behalf of the War Department two weeks earlier to ensure the creation of a strong French army to assist the Allies in liberating Europe. McCloy pressed on Giraud the need to purge his administration of Vichy collaborators and paved the way for Monnet by arranging for the two of them to meet together with Giraud. McCloy also informed Eisenhower he would get "real help in Monnet," and urged the US general to keep in touch with the French adviser. McCloy's wife, Ellen, had volunteered, while Monnet was in North Africa, to look after Silvia, Anna, and their new baby daughter Marianne, born in November 1941.[16]

Macmillan, Murphy, and Monnet all pressed reforms on Giraud. Describing his first meeting with the general, Macmillan wrote, "His blue eyes, his noble stature, his fluent and almost classical French, his obvious sincerity—

all these struck me forcibly. But they could not conceal . . . his unsuitability for the difficult and complex task which he had assumed."[17] He found Giraud "a horse very much in the second class."[18] René Pleven, in Algiers in 1943 with Monnet, noted that Giraud was purely a military man who was not politically astute. Maurice Couve de Murville, a French statesman and supporter of de Gaulle, observed that because Giraud lacked political judgment, he was not the caliber of person needed to lead the French. As a result, it was an unequal battle between the two generals.[19] Alphand noted, "No possible comparison with de Gaulle, that furious, violent, unrestrained force, that figure which breaks with the whole of the past, that explosion against mistakes, faults, and betrayals."[20]

Monnet liked and respected Giraud's character and ability and found him courageous and upright. But as he noted in his *Memoirs*, this general was stubborn, vain, conservative, and naive in politics—"a man with a fine bearing and clear and empty eyes, aware of his great standing as a heroic officer, unyielding on military problems, hesitant on others. I shall give no opinion upon his intelligence, which was that of a general long schooled in desert affairs and inclined to simplify things." Monnet discovered Giraud was "incapable of rejuvenating the army—it had 185 generals—or of eradicating the men of Vichy." He had "neither the inclination nor the ability to run the large-scale administration that we had to prepare for postwar France." Moreover, Monnet reported, Giraud had little knowledge of the world and of global relations. "I have tried to give him general principles and to dispel his suspicions of the United States and Britain," he wrote. "In egocentricity, Giraud had nothing to learn from de Gaulle. . . . Each believed that he had a sacred mission. Both were obsessed by the need for France to be independent; and I can testify that Giraud felt no more committed to the Americans than de Gaulle to the British. Each exploited the main Power which seemed likely to bring him and France to the top."[21] Giraud, in turn, saw Monnet as the one who could obtain the necessary military supplies. But as Monnet warned him, if there were no reforms, there would be no equipment for the troops.

By using this threat as well as British pressure, and mustering his powers of persuasion, Monnet convinced Giraud to enact the needed reforms, break with Vichy, and repudiate the 1940 armistice. Under Monnet's careful shepherding and the drafting of various speeches and decrees, Giraud gradually dismantled the Vichy regime in Algiers. He abrogated Vichy laws and reestablished democratic laws, sacked Vichy generals, declared the goal to be elections by universal suffrage, and abolished political censorship. Historian André Kaspi states that after negotiating every word with the general over a two-week period, Monnet basically wrote Giraud's important March 14 address and worked with Murphy and Macmillan on the final draft.[22] In this speech, Giraud called for French union and cleared the way for negotiations on unity with de Gaulle. Monnet had persuaded Giraud to take the three decisive steps favored by de Gaulle: denounce the armistice and the legitimacy of the Vichy regime, stress French sovereignty, and pay tribute to democracy.

Moreover, Giraud had publicly voiced the political principles upon which Monnet believed France's survival would depend: unity, restoration of its sovereignty, and the preservation of the democratic process. Giraud accomplished this by calling for the restoration of human liberties under the law, declaring that modifications to French political institutions be undertaken only by the French people, insisting that a consultative council of French resistance be created, and stressing the preservation of territorial integrity.[23] As Monnet later wrote, "Giraud's speech was both the prologue and the first act in reuniting the French."[24] It launched the negotiations that made unity possible.

Giraud hoped his speech would ingratiate him with the Fighting French and prove him a worthwhile partner. But it so stunned Giraud's supporters that they offered to resign. Their reaction, in turn, shocked Giraud who exclaimed, "But come, I don't believe a word of what I said in it: that was only politics!" Shortly after, Giraud wrote to General Catroux about his March 14 speech.[25] In the eyes of the French community in Algiers, the five-star general was a highly respected man of principle who had had political and military experience as a prewar governor general of Indochina. This friend of de Gaulle's understood that military and political problems were intertwined and could not be separated.

Louis Joxe, a former League of Nations colleague who worked with Monnet again in the spring of 1943 and later became a prominent French statesman, found Catroux a man of strong character. He not only knew de Gaulle well, wrote Joxe, but Catroux never "confused legend and abstraction with concrete reality."[26] Many of the exiles recognized that as an Algerian himself, Catroux's presence there was important in their search for a solution. On behalf of de Gaulle, Catroux wrote back to Giraud and inquired about his intentions. Giraud, in his reply drafted by Monnet, stated that he wanted to assure the general in London that he "particularly wished to set out the principles that direct my conduct. No misunderstanding therefore remains between us." Giraud claimed, "I am ready to welcome General de Gaulle in order to give the union a concrete form."[27]

## Carefully Orchestrating the Negotiations

Kaspi has described in illuminating detail the complicated negotiations masterminded by Monnet, Macmillan, and Catroux in Algiers among Giraud and de Gaulle and their advisers, which led to the establishment of the French Committee for National Liberation (CFLN) in June 1943.[28] While Monnet kept Murphy informed, he sometimes contacted the White House directly

*Jean Monnet in Algiers, 1943. Monnet is standing at far left. Seated from left to right: General Georges Catroux, General Charles de Gaulle, Winston Churchill, General Henri Giraud, Anthony Eden; back row: André Philip, Harold Macmillan, General Joseph Georges, Sir Allan Brooke, Admiral Sir Andrew Cunningham, Réné Massigli.*

through Hopkins, knowing that this account of the talks would reach Roosevelt. Macmillan was Monnet's interlocutor with the British government.[29]

Each of the two strong-willed contenders felt compelled to negotiate with the other. De Gaulle feared being marginalized by Giraud if the latter headed a large French army built up by Americans. Giraud knew he had to deal with the self-proclaimed leader of the Free French because de Gaulle was an important symbol with a substantial following among French citizens and the resistance. Backed by his large army, Giraud believed the Gaullists could join him, but he had no intention of joining them. It is not clear whether he understood the implications of his invitation to de Gaulle to join forces, stated in his March 14 speech, or the fact that he would have to make concessions. Nevertheless, the next day Giraud invited de Gaulle to talks in Algiers.

Monnet sought the opinion of the "eminent men" among the exiles then in Algiers on how best to set up a provisional French administration governed "by the laws of the Republic."[30] These included prominent Frenchmen such as Joxe and Charles Ettori, who was also a member of the Council of State. Joxe recounted how Monnet had persuaded Giraud to recall him from eastern Algeria where Giraud had earlier exiled Joxe for "Gaullist intrigues." He wrote that the man from Cognac, with whom he had worked twice, was an important influence on him.[31]

Monnet insisted on two central institutional safeguards in his negotiations with the two generals. First was that any council or authority set up should be collegial, make decisions by majority vote, observe collective responsibility, and act like an institution but not lead to a one-man or two-man rule. The second was that this authority should not have a free hand to organize elections after the liberation of France and thereby be prevented from seizing power. The council's tenure must be limited, and the elections should be organized by a grassroots, legitimate administration. Monnet put these two safeguards in a paper he had drafted for Giraud, who reluctantly accepted them. Catroux delivered this April 1 message to de Gaulle in London on April 9, and in his formal reply on April 15, de Gaulle agreed to these ideas. But he insisted that copresidents be created, with Giraud either as first president and de Gaulle as second in charge of the resistance or commander-in-chief, but not both. De Gaulle also proposed an executive committee of five or seven men, including two generals and Monnet.[32]

Monnet recalled that the mediators—Catroux, Macmillan, and himself—worked persistently to unite the warring French factions but had only one course to follow. That was to bring about a gradual change, if not in the minds of the two rival leaders, at least in the context or framework within which they were operating.[33] Monnet wrote Giraud's April 27 reply accepting de Gaulle's idea of equal copresidents and a new council or executive committee of seven chosen by the two generals. It would not be a provisional government but would operate by majority voting. De Gaulle proclaimed he was willing to collaborate with Giraud but also insisted that a provisional government be the central power and that the military be subordinate to civil power. After explosive outbursts from both generals over the timing and location of the talks, de Gaulle issued a more temperate note on May 3 in which he insisted on the subordination of the military to civilian power. By early May, the three mediators observed that Giraud's attitude toward compromise had hardened and become less compliant. They agreed that since the critical policy issues were nearly settled, the time had arrived for de Gaulle to come to Algiers to negotiate personally with Giraud.[34]

Monnet managed his operations in Algeria from three locations. One was his six-room apartment in Algiers, which, at McCloy's request, came with six domestic staff provided by the military and through which everyone who counted for anything passed through, Joxe recalled. The Giraud administration also gave him an official office in that city. But Monnet's preferred base of operation was far from town, a small hotel in Tipasa, about fifty miles west of Algiers. Between the multiple negotiation sessions with Giraud, Monnet retreated to his small bay town on the rugged, indented coastline west of Algiers to think and sleep. He loved to be close to nature and found the green hilly landscape along the coast both a stimulant and soothing respite as it was so close to the ocean. This was also a favorite spot of Albert Camus, the distinguished

French literary figure, who wrote about his love for this jagged coastline that was constantly lapped by the waves. In Alphand's words, it was a spot "beside the soft and shining sea, in a beautiful setting of Roman ruins, scented by wild thyme, under a clear Mediterranean light, with a profusion of flowers and birds." The future French ambassador to the United States added, "You will see Monnet there, in shorts, with American shoes and socks, talking, thinking aloud, dictating, playing a different part with each of his colleagues, trying his ideas out on all of them, taking care not to limit his options."[35]

Joxe also described some of Monnet's odd behavior in Algeria and wrote,

> His charm was enhanced by compulsive little habits he pretended to take lightly, attributing sovereign virtues to a certain mineral water imported by the crate-load from the United States, and claiming to be restored to health after the first sip. To feel at ease and calm in spirit he would, at the right moment, draw on thick red woolen socks. He drank no alcohol, ate little, slept anywhere, spent entire days questioning people or thinking alone by the sea, hours also writing his wife, whose opinion mattered to him more than anyone else's. Then, abruptly, he would lift the telephone and call Giraud or Bob [Murphy] in Algiers, John McCloy or Robert Sherwood in the States, talking to them as if they were neighbors on the landing.[36]

Joxe described how dependent Monnet was on his wife's advice and judgment. Not only did he love and admire Silvia profoundly because she was cultured, an artist who appreciated creativity in all forms, and a painter who captured multiple shades of light and shadows on her canvases, but she also provided an order and perspective within which he could formulate his ideas. Since he was living far from her, he wrote her constantly and always awaited the arrival of the postman in hopes of receiving a reply. At his modest apartment in Algiers, he had created a small family museum filled with photographs, books, and objects belonging to his infant daughter and had hung a pair of Marianne's shoes on the fireplace.[37]

Monnet's innate distrust of the political ambitions of military leaders was known to his close colleagues. "This rather small, stocky, thickset man," recalled Joxe, "whose vertical gap between his eyebrows showed he had powers of concentration and curiosity and who listened carefully and spoke little, was a wise man." A young democrat raised in England, being "steeped in the writings of Washington, Jefferson, and Lincoln gave him an advantage over European men of action." Monnet also distrusted soldiers who took political power, and in some ways his thoughts "reflected those of a republican with radical tendencies."[38]

Monnet and Macmillan retreated to the small hotel in the hills near Tipasa the second week of May to work out the final terms of the memorandum that laid the basis of the de facto French government. Together they swam, sunned, dined, and debated between intervals of drafting. After presenting it to Giraud on May 17, he reluctantly endorsed their terms. In return for coming to Algiers, de Gaulle was asked to approve the principle stating that the committee or council to be created must work under rules of cabinet responsibility, and when France was free, be limited by the *loi Tréveneuc*. This 1872 law appealed to Monnet because it provided the legal basis for the establishment of a future provisional government. It stated that, in the event of an absence of the organizations representing national sovereignty, the task of appointing new authorities should be entrusted to the representatives of elected councils in France's departments. As Monnet wrote to Hopkins on May 9, the collective responsibility of the executive committee or council was vital before France's liberation, and the loi Treveneuc after it. "This [last] question will really decide whether personal power or democratic institutions are going to govern France after the war. . . . There can be no compromise. . . . If de Gaulle agrees, there will I hope be unity. If he does not agree, then there will be a break."[39]

Catroux, a moderating influence on de Gaulle, helped to prepare the self-proclaimed leader of the Free French for this important meeting. De Gaulle valued the general's judgment and advice. In his May 11 letter to de Gaulle, Catroux wrote that it was important that this encounter "be dominated by a spirit of union and not suspicion." He asked that his friend remember he had "consented to collective responsibility in an organization of government that replaces the provisional government under the *loi Tréveneuc*." On May 17 Catroux informed de Gaulle that while Giraud insisted on the primary leadership spot in Algiers, he was trying to lead Giraud "towards an honorable compromise." But he reminded de Gaulle that the current atmosphere was conducive "less towards concessions than maintaining the status quo." He added that he did not think the United States would oppose the union if Giraud is given a position of "equal rank to you" and if the government formed "conforms to the democratic spirit and presents a personal power exercise."[40]

Before leaving London for Algiers, de Gaulle had called on British Foreign Secretary Anthony Eden to bid him farewell. "Nothing is more likeable than your nation," exclaimed de Gaulle. "I do not always think the same of your policy." Eden retorted, "Do you know you have given us more difficulty than all our European Allies?" The general replied, smiling, "I have no doubt of it. France is a great power."[41] The temperamental general had been bolstered by the news two weeks earlier that his chief agent and resistance leader, Jean Moulin, had united all the resistance groups in France, formed a National Council, and recognized de Gaulle as their political leader. As a result of this news, de Gaulle arrived in Algiers in high spirits on May 30 accompanied by a few of his faithful followers, including diplomat René Massigli and socialist André Philip.[42]

De Gaulle had responded to Giraud on May 27 and stated he had accepted the loi Treveneuc and collective responsibility in the new executive. At a luncheon given upon de Gaulle's arrival, Monnet sat next to him. De Gaulle later wrote that Monnet had "tackled me at once with economic questions." In recalling this conversation, Macmillan noted that de Gaulle had argued that "Anglo-Saxon domination of Europe was a mounting threat, and that if it continued, France after the war would have to lean towards Germany and Russia. Monnet still finds it difficult to make up his mind as to whether the general is a dangerous demagogue or mad or both."[43]

Unknown to de Gaulle, Churchill's antipathy to him had ballooned into such anger by the end of May that he recommended his government abandon its support for the overpowering general. The prime minister had become alarmed by intelligence reports that de Gaulle had become unfriendly to both Britain and the United States. He sent a telegram to Eden and urged his cabinet "to consider urgently whether we should not now eliminate de Gaulle as a political force."[44] In a memorandum to both his Deputy Prime Minister Clement Attlee and Eden, Churchill argued the French leader was an Anglophobe and agreed with Washington's fears that he was too dictatorial. But the British War Cabinet followed Eden's advice and refused to withdraw support for de Gaulle, warning that such a radical change in policy might cause the Free French forces to break away from the Allies, forcing Churchill to continue his support for him.[45]

Unaware of Churchill's hostility, de Gaulle confronted Giraud in Algiers on May 31 in a meeting run by Monnet. De Gaulle was accompanied by Catroux, Massigli, and Philip, and Giraud by Monnet and General Joseph Georges, a respected French general in Algiers. When Giraud refused to agree to dismiss three ex-Vichy governors, de Gaulle stormed out of the meeting. Macmillan later criticized Monnet for failing to make a motion formally constituting the new committee, and Monnet admitted he had mismanaged the meeting.[46]

Hot, dusty Algiers on May 31, noted Monnet, was riddled with intrigue and plots. When it was known the next day that de Gaulle had provoked the resignation of the governor general of Algeria without consulting Giraud, Catroux was furious. He criticized de Gaulle for encroaching upon Giraud's rights and offered to resign. Moreover, Giraud reacted to de Gaulle's action with such vehemence that Macmillan concluded the general had lost "his wits." Giraud believed de Gaulle was launching a putsch. But Monnet and Catroux persuaded Giraud to do nothing rash, countered rumors, and assuaged de Gaulle's fears for his personal security. Monnet had earlier squelched widely circulating rumored threats to his own life, especially that he was to be arrested in a "counter-revolutionary Army putsch," by calling a meeting of Giraud's assistants to warn them that such rumors would only delay the arming of French troops. Monnet later learned that McCloy, when he heard rumors of an uprising, had arranged military protection for him.[47]

Fears of assassination plots were real. Eisenhower's aide Harry Butcher wrote in his diary on June 1 that "there are a lot of hotheads in the de

Gaulle–Giraud camps and we wouldn't be surprised if there is at least an attempted assassination."[48] Monnet's chauffeur, Fernand Javel, reported that one of his friends in French counterintelligence came to warn him that his boss was in danger. Javel recounted that one morning coming back from Tipasa to Algiers, "at a place called La Trappe with a crossing at a half-turn in the road ... a lorry, ignoring the right of way, suddenly bore down on us out of the side-road. . . . I just got by, weaving sharply."[49]

De Gaulle's provocative actions on May 31 reminded Monnet that his character had not changed since their last meeting in London in 1940. He later wrote,

> It was the same mixture of practical intelligence that could only command respect, and a disquieting tendency to overstep the bounds of common sense. He was by turns intimate, using his undoubtable charm, and distant, impervious to argument when carried away by patriotic honor or personal pride. I agreed with his analysis of things, but only up to a point; beyond that point I could no longer follow him in his bursts of egocentricity. His conflict with Roosevelt, and in a lesser degree with Churchill, had become an obsession.[50]

## Creating the French Committee for National Liberation

As tempers cooled and the immediate crisis subsided in the next two days, the assembled members of the French resistance in Algiers met on June 2. They formed the new executive committee, the French Committee for National Liberation (CFLN), by adopting the framework outlined in the May 17 document carefully crafted by Monnet and Macmillan and accepted by de Gaulle and Giraud. The CFLN was formally constituted on June 3, and this new de facto centralized French government issued its official communiqué on June 4. The CFLN immediately voted to dismiss the remaining Vichy governors by a vote of five (which included Monnet) to two, with only one general on Giraud's side, demonstrating Giraud's isolation.[51]

On June 5 the CFLN met to increase its members to fourteen. Among its members were three Giraudists—French official René Mayer; Dr. Jules Abadie, a local dignitary chosen by Giraud; and Couve de Murville—and four Gaullists: Pleven; two other exiles, André Diethelm and Adrien Tixier, whom de Gaulle called back from Washington; and Henri Bonnet, a French diplomat who had served with Monnet at the League in the 1920s. De Gaulle's victory over Giraud now became clear as all fourteen members, including Mayer, voted with de Gaulle on future issues. De Gaulle's actions were moderated by the middle-of-the-road and mostly constructive activities of the three Gaullistically inclined Giraudists—Monnet, Couve de Murville, and Mayer—and the three moderate Gaullists—Catroux, Massigli, and Bonnet. [52] Joxe became the secretary general of the CFLN along with two deputies. "It was a good, well-balanced administrative team," wrote Monnet, "in which a consensus could be secured for decisions in the general interest."[53]

Other disagreements ensued, but Monnet; Philip, who was asked to be in charge of the internal policies; and Massigli, in charge of foreign affairs, worked out a compromise, which the two generals accepted on June 17. Giraud was to remain commander-in-chief, but a committee of the CFLN, including de Gaulle and Giraud, along with their respective chiefs of army, air, and naval staffs, were to handle defense policy. This enabled de Gaulle to have a say in military matters, which he lacked earlier.[54] The British prime minister had flown to Algiers before de Gaulle's arrival to stimulate anti-Gaullist sentiment among the officials there because he disliked that general so much. After inviting the two generals to a luncheon on June 6, Churchill told de Gaulle he had come to prevent "some too sudden shock as for example if you had eaten Giraud up in one go." De Gaulle replied, "That was not my intention at all. I meant to proceed by stages."[55]

Disputes over the division of power between the two generals continued, but by the end of June, de Gaulle was the real head of CFLN. He acknowledged in his memoirs that Monnet "was the prime mover in this development." Ten years later he paid Monnet a backhanded tribute when he wrote, "The 'inspirer' (Monnet) came up with a scheme to confound general Giraud and general de Gaulle in a single government. . . . The fact is what followed came as a surprise to no one—doubtless not even to the 'inspirer.'"[56]

In a July letter to Roosevelt, Murphy forcefully criticized Monnet's actions that had put de Gaulle in charge and declared France independent. "Monnet arrived with a definite objective—to sell French unity. He succeeded." But Murphy argued that while Monnet "respects the United States and Britain and . . . will avoid giving offense to us," he is "out to gain every advantage for the French he possibly can." Because Monnet "knows our methods so well," Murphy feared that he would benefit from "every opportunity we offer him to seize advantage. . . . Monnet is loyal neither to Giraud nor to de Gaulle but he is loyal to France and to Monnet."[57]

Murphy's remarks reflected the bitter disappointment of US officials, including Roosevelt, who placed their hopes in Monnet's mission and in Giraud. But Roosevelt and others understood seven months later that Giraud lacked the political and administrative skills necessary to lead the French. As Joxe argues, "Giraud himself was primarily responsible for his own loss" and "the members of the CFLN were nearly unanimous in their support of de Gaulle."[58] Monnet's success won him praise from McCloy and Frankfurter who attributed the formation of the CFLN to "Monnet's infinite patience and complete disinterestedness and extraordinary resourcefulness."[59] Frankfurter dismissed Hull's charges that Monnet sold out to de Gaulle and exclaimed, in a conversation with Stimson, that Hull's remarks were "all rubbish of the worst sort, that de Gaulle, as everyone knows, is the most powerful single symbol in the effort of French liberation, that Monnet is not selling out to him, because he is single-minded about France and therefore is trying to prevent a French civil war." Frankfurter records Stimson replied that it "was entirely his view and that it is very difficult to talk with Hull [as] he is so touchy and 'irrational on this subject.'"[60]

The other prominent French leaders assembled in Algiers in 1943 shared Monnet's goal of French unity under democratic conditions. The CFLN could not have been created without their agreement and willingness to work together for the same goal. As Pleven wrote, "It was a talented team . . . the equal or superior of most regularly constituted governments."[61] Monnet and Catroux, along with Macmillan, worked together and ran a peaceful meeting that resulted in a compromise between the two generals, without physical clashes or violence, and ended with the likelihood that de Gaulle would emerge in time as the leader. Monnet and the other leaders succeeded because they changed the context of the battle for power between the two generals and their contending factions by focusing on the design of the postwar governing institutions, not the generals' egotistical personalities or their personal power. Monnet along with Catroux and the other pragmatists supported de Gaulle's ascendancy in the CFLN because they knew he was more able and better positioned to unify the French and thereby best serve their nation's interest. But their emphasis on unity and postwar institutions to govern their nation meant they believed there was a need to constrain de Gaulle's authoritarian tendencies by forcing him to agree to certain provisions.[62]

Catroux and Monnet were the two main mediators who made French union possible. They were moderates, noted Joxe, "not candidates for power but volunteers for French unity," and had indeed helped to prevent discord and possible civil war.[63] Working with the talented group of Frenchmen, Monnet had judiciously fulfilled his mission: to unify his people and lay the groundwork for restoring French sovereignty under liberal, democratic principles. "I had come to Algiers to help reunite the French—to help them work together for victory and for the recovery of France. . . . I had the feeling that I would go back to the nerve-center of the war effort, to consolidate the machinery that would surely bring us to the end of the war, and to prepare now for the reconstruction of France after the Liberation."[64] He believed that

> in obtaining the restoration of Republican liberty and legality, my purpose had not been merely to satisfy Roosevelt, any more than it had been to make overtures to de Gaulle. I was neither fulfilling a particular mission nor answering a particular memorandum. I was simply acting on my convictions, in the certainty of thereby preparing the climate that was needed if we were to continue the war and build the subsequent peace. But there was more to it than that. My convictions also made me vigilant against any premature bid for power and any *fait accompli* that might be presented at the Liberation, from whichever quarter it might come.[65]

Monnet explained in his *Memoirs* his concern about de Gaulle's intention to assume leadership of a provisional government, "which would negotiate with the Allies and establish itself in France, when the time came, in order to prepare for elections." Monnet found it hard to accept "de Gaulle's attempt to freeze, in his own interests, a situation that was still fluid and to politicize an effort at wartime reorganization that had scarcely begun." De Gaulle's attitude had unfortunately "confirmed Churchill's and especially Roosevelt's misgivings," which "to me, quite frankly, seemed exaggerated." De Gaulle, he noted, "was not by nature a dictator. But he was openly a candidate for power; and his impatience and intolerance seemed to incline him towards certain forms of personal authority. Slight as the risk might be, it had to be averted in the interests of France."[66]

Monnet received wide praise from the French statesmen who were working with him in Algiers in the spring of 1943. Joxe observed not only that Monnet had close relationships with Churchill and Roosevelt and their representatives in Algeria but that the president believed Monnet represented the best in France, North Africa, and the French spirit. Joxe praised Monnet for being able to think ahead and in many directions at once. But, above all, he said Monnet believed it essential to preserve democratic principles in the future French government and always to maintain the distinction between military and civilian power.[67]

Couve de Murville credits Monnet's "powers of persuasion" as a factor in the success of the negotiations. He describes him as a simple man who expressed his ideas simply and repeatedly and as a result was an extraordinary force of nature who inspired confidence.[68] Pleven declared that Monnet's presence in Algiers was "certainly useful to everyone, to the CFLN, and to de Gaulle." And, as an adviser to Giraud, the man from Cognac was able to tone down and ameliorate the relationship between the two generals. Pleven argues that Monnet's ability to always think about the future—at least five years ahead—was useful to France. The differences of opinion among the CFLN members were not a problem because each realized "it was necessary to succeed. . . . We were all conscious of the fact that Giraud lacked the essential political qualities."[69]

## Pondering Postwar Policy

During the summer of 1943, signs that the war had at last turned in favor of the Allies spurred the future French leaders exiled in Algiers to debate ideas for the CFLN's postwar European policy. Monnet's small group—which included Alphand, Marjolin, Mayer, and Etienne Hirsch, a chemical engineer who had joined them—generated and debated numerous memoranda. Monnet's August 5, 1943, memorandum addressed to the CFLN outlined France's special responsibilities as well as its real opportunity to make a new and different peace from that of World War I. In it, he stressed the need to produce ideas for a new European order that could harness nationalism, the main cause of war, such as the formation of a European federation of states. He wrote:

> Only France can be the architect of the design for a new European order and the driving force that makes this possible . . . at the very least to launch the enterprise to carry off a partial success. . . . Accordingly, we must act before the enemy crumbles. We must act now. This is the duty of the French Committee of National Liberation. It must decide on a course of conduct, sound out the Allies, not necessarily to gain their consent but to reflect in the final formulation the position it will take . . . for allied cooperation—or at least the assistance of some of them—is essential to the success of our enterprise. . . . The goals are these: the restoration, or establishment, in Europe of democratic regimes and the economic and political structuring of a "European entity." These two events are essential to the creation of the conditions for making the European peace a normal state of affairs. There will be no peace in Europe if there remains the possibility of instituting regimes under which the right of opposition is not adhered to and free elections are not held. These two conditions are essential to the restoration and preservation of all the fundamental freedoms of speech, assembly, association, etc., which form the basis for the progress of Western Civilization. . . . The requisite prosperity and social progress will be impossible, unless the States of Europe join together in a federation or a "European entity" that molds them into a common economic unit.[70]

Hirsch discovered Monnet one morning pointing to the regions of the Ruhr and Lorraine on a map of Europe. Monnet exclaimed that all the trouble came from that part of the world where France and Germany had "forged the instruments of war" and he proposed extracting the two regions from these countries to prevent another war. "What I was thinking of," Monnet explained in his later years while contemplating writing his memoirs, "was a system whereby the former Reich would be stripped of part of its industrial potential, so that the coal and steel resources of the Ruhr could be placed under a European authority and used for the benefit of all nations involved, including a demilitarized Germany." He wanted to see "a true yielding of sovereignty by European nations to some kind of central union—a union that could cut down tariffs, create a great internal European market, and prevent that race of nationalism, the curse of the modern world."[71] These ruminations, discussed in Algeria during wartime with his colleagues, show that finding a way to bring peace to Europe constantly preoccupied him and that a "union" of European nations seemed the best path to take to achieve that goal.

Being an introspective as well as a contemplative person, Monnet also wrote during these summer months a memorandum titled "Psychology: Reflective Note," in which he analyzed some of his strengths and weaknesses quite immodestly. "Your real strength lies in your objective, disinterested, comprehensive assessment of a particular problem and of the solution you propose," he wrote in second person to himself. "This is the real contribution you make . . . but this requires preparation—concentration, and, finally, a conclusion. . . . The abilities you marshal to reach these conclusions equals your psychological capacity for negotiation and persuasion [which] is actually either a weakness, whenever you're looking for a solution based on common consent in order to resolve the immediate difficulty, or, alternatively, a very great strength, if you enlist it in the cause of achieving the goal you have proposed." Revealing his own negotiating style, he concluded, "To make it a strength, you need to confine yourself to always setting the objective, formulating the plan, and staying constantly focused, while at the same time you remain mistrustful of your natural abilities to negotiate and to persuade."[72] This confident man understood that he possessed analytical and negotiating skills and seemed to justify his perceived need to be single-mindedly focused when solving a problem or devising a solution to it.

## Back to Washington

The newly constituted de facto French government, CFLN, appointed Monnet to head two cabinet committees—Programs and Reconstruction—in order to supervise the delivery and deployment of Lend-Lease supplies for the Allied troops in North Africa. In September, it accepted his request to be sent back to Washington to influence decisions "on the massive aid programs which France so badly needed." He believed he had to prepare for the postwar reconstruction of France and lay the foundations for bilateral Franco-American agreements "to safeguard our economic and financial future."[73] At a luncheon given by de Gaulle on October 17, 1943, before his departure, Monnet discussed his idea of a federation of European states united "as a single free trade zone" based on equality among its members. He recommended that Germany be divided into several states that should be treated as equals in order to diminish the pressure to reconstitute a single state. He also argued that the coal and steel industries should be placed under international authority. In response, de Gaulle argued it would be hard to see the French and Germans belonging to the "same economic union." On the other hand, the general favored an economic union of "France with the Benelux, perhaps the Rhineland detached from Germany, perhaps Italy, Spain and Switzerland, in close understanding with the Soviet Union and Britain," with France taking the lead.[74]

As a full member of the CFLN accompanied by Marjolin and Alphand, his deputy, Monnet returned to Washington in November 1943. He was delighted to be reunited with his family and especially glad to see his baby daughter, Marianne, and be present for her second birthday celebration. Silvia had turned a spare room into a studio where she could paint and was pleased that Monnet enjoyed her many colorful paintings that now covered the living and dining room walls.

Monnet had been given a mandate to handle many of the military and civil issues raised by the expected landing of Allied troops in France. These included the administration of occupied France by a French authority to prepare for the Allied armies; provision of food, emergency relief, and supplies to the liberated people; establishment of currency arrangements in the transition from German occupation to sovereignty; and de facto recognition of the CFLN as the prospective government of France, which would lead to full recognition. Monnet believed gaining recognition for the CFLN was the next critical step in his effort to preserve French sovereignty and control over its affairs. Experience, influence, and connections made Monnet better able than any other Frenchman to serve his nation's interests in Washington that fall of 1943, for he knew where decisions were made and who made them. McCloy, at the War Department, chaired the Combined Civil Affairs Board and its subcommittee for France, and Hopkins and Stimson, noted Monnet, remained eager to help him.[75]

Dean Acheson, as assistant secretary of state for economic affairs, continued to be heavily involved in the Lend-Lease negotiations and chaired the planning committee of the United Nations Relief and Rehabilitation Agency, which was formally created to provide humanitarian relief such as food, clothing, shelter, and fuel to postwar nations. The delegates of this organization's forty-four nations met for the first time in Atlantic City from November 10 to December 1, 1943. As Monnet represented France, it was during these meetings, dinners, and walks together that Acheson first learned of Monnet's vision for postwar Europe and his wide-ranging ideas about reconstruction. Historian Douglas Brinkley asserts that it was Monnet, "perhaps more than any other catalyst, who influenced the way Acheson perceived the rebuilding and restructuring process for postwar Europe." He added that Acheson, like Monnet, "revered innovative and contributive action."[76] State Department adviser Henry Owen remarked that Monnet's "optimism, his dedication to action, were in a way more American than European."[77]

Despite his network of influential friends, Monnet faced a formidable political obstacle in Washington because Roosevelt refused to recognize the CFLN. The president's almost visceral anti-Gaullism and often expressed views of the general as a "fool," "fanatic," and "prima donna"[78] continually thwarted Monnet's efforts to gain any statement that would imply recognition. These difficulties and Monnet's failure to obtain US acquiescence to de Gaulle's terms on the currency question eroded his stature in the CFLN. The US Treasury issued banknotes to be used by the Allied expeditionary force landing in France. But de Gaulle claimed this currency was imposed "by force" and refused to recognize it because there was no mention of its being issued by the authority of the CFLN. The US officials replied that there was no French currency because there was no French government in the eyes of the Allies. This attitude of Roosevelt and Monnet's failure to change the president's mind especially disappointed de Gaulle, who was extremely sensitive about the question of recognition.[79] Alphand, who returned to Algiers in March 1944, discovered the depth of the CFLN's dismay at Monnet's lack of success in Washington and wrote that "the disappointment here, in the wake of the hopes raised by the press, by our friends and by our telegrams from Washington, is pretty deep." De Gaulle directed Monnet to return to Algiers at the end of June to report.[80]

De Gaulle experienced the depth of Roosevelt's personal hostility toward him when they met at the White House in July 1944. Roosevelt clearly conveyed his own view that Europe, and especially France, mattered little and said Great Britain, China, and the United States would settle the world's problems. Europe, he declared, was clearly subordinate to the other powers. De Gaulle countered with the argument that Roosevelt's plan did not acknowledge the centrality and greatness of Europe and that it endangered the whole Western world. The French general, who had been slighted by the president, returned home with the impression that the United States was already trying to rule the world.[81]

After his two-month stay in Algiers in the summer of 1944, Monnet and eight other ministers were dismissed on September 9 from the cabinet of the CFLN, which had become the Provisional Government of the French Republic (GPRF) on June 2, 1944. To be dropped by the government he had helped create was a bitter disappointment for Monnet, but he knew de Gaulle blamed him for not gaining Roosevelt's recognition of France's provisional government. But the GPRF officials sent Monnet back to Washington at the end of September 1944 as commissioner-at-large on special assignment to negotiate about civil imports into France and Lend-Lease agreements with the Americans on terms that made him more than an ordinary high official. At his own suggestion, he was given the title of chairman of the Committee for Imports because it enabled him to use the services of the French Supply Council, which had been created in 1943. Titles did not normally interest him, but having one for this assignment made his job of gaining continuing US economic support slightly easier.[82]

Monnet recalled that he was fortunate to have had colleagues of "outstanding technical ability" working with him on seeking aid and supplies—Marjolin in Washington, Hirsch in London, and Alphand who had been sent to Paris—"but my real hope was to set them to work on building the future, when everything would have to be refashioned and rethought."[83] On October 22, 1944, Roosevelt finally recognized GPRF. Commenting on Monnet's influence, Alphand noted, "Jean Monnet amazes me. It is he who drafts the memoranda . . . to the President . . . he who incites Eisenhower to send telegrams to shift the balance in our favor. . . . I will be the only Frenchman to know how much we owe him in this phase of the war."[84]

Tensions between Roosevelt and the French Provisional Government delayed the Lend-Lease negotiations, but on February 28, 1945, an agreement was signed. It provided $2.575 billion, a sum that exceeded the $1 billion for all US supplies previously made available to France. It allotted $1.675 billion in current supplies of food and raw materials, previously paid for in dollars, but now under Lend-Lease. The cost of a French import program, established by Monnet in November 1944 and designed to continue in effect through January 1, 1946, was calculated in the Lend-Lease accords. In memoranda to Monnet, Hirsch had sent estimates of the kinds of items needed once the liberating armies had arrived in France. In addition to foodstuffs, he listed sweaters, underwear, clothes for prisoners, fuel, industrial oils and fats, shoes, clothing, and medical supplies.[85] The remaining $900 million was for equipment and machinery for reconstruction, officially for prosecuting the war. The French had to pay 20 percent of the price on delivery, and the rest was to be reimbursed on favorable terms over thirty years, at 2.375 percent interest. Both sides in the negotiations understood quickly "what Monnet had made the central tenet of his postwar activity," notes historian Irwin Wall: "France would modernize, and the United States, one way or another, would provide much of the financing."[86]

In early September 1945, Monnet took over the chairmanship of the French Supply Council, which had grown to 500 officials. He transformed it from an organization dealing with the US administration to one dealing directly with US suppliers through commercial contracts and put his French friend, Leon Kaplan, in charge. He made George Ball, a US lawyer he had met in the Lend-Lease Administration, the legal counsel for the Supply Council, and obtained a retainer from the French government for him.[87] In December he negotiated a supplementary Lend-Lease takeout loan of $550 million from the Export-Import Bank on Lend-Lease terms. Monnet knew this was just a temporary solution and wrote,

> So beyond the immediate question of supplies for the French, I was concerned to give them the means with which they could recover their strength and independence for themselves. To achieve this, it was essential to rebuild the country's stocks of raw materials and to replace capital investments that had been run down or destroyed. But I realized that a mere return to prewar production levels would be inadequate if the French were to regain their position in the modern world.[88]

Monnet demonstrated both in Algiers and later in Washington that he was a visionary strategist who was able to plan for the future. Because he believed preserving French sovereignty was critical, he understood that concrete steps had to be taken in 1943 to ensure France's political future and to prepare for its postwar needs. Using his persuasive powers, he astutely engineered the Algiers assignment from Roosevelt to bolster Giraud. And leveraging the US government's backing to achieve his goals in Algiers to the benefit of France, he had worked pragmatically and methodically to unify the factions under liberal, democratic conditions. Even though he was there as Roosevelt's emissary, he was not hemmed in by any specified US policy because one had not yet been developed. As a result, he was left to deal with Giraud and de Gaulle more or less as his own instincts and circumstances dictated, and he handled them judiciously. In addition, Giraud and his followers did not constitute an organized movement or policy and never clearly sided with either Vichy or the Allies. As Giraud lacked the qualities of leadership that de Gaulle had in abundance—charisma, clear goals, powers of persuasion, political astuteness, commanding presence, and vision—Giraud was easily outmaneuvered by Monnet. Roosevelt's emissary persuaded the general to take steps whose ramifications he did not understand but which resulted in the establishment of clear terms for the negotiations. Without the leverage of US support and supplies for his troops, Giraud might not have bowed so readily to Monnet's recommendations. If Monnet had not had US equipment to bolster Giraud's role as proclaimed head of the French armed forces in North Africa, he might not have obtained de Gaulle's agreement to the written pledges establishing a democratic CFLN and postwar institutions.

Being realistic and flexible, Monnet utilized Catroux, whose moderating influence on de Gaulle in the negotiations was also critical to the success of the mission. By working closely with both Macmillan and Catroux, Monnet changed the context of the dispute by shifting the discussion from personalities to institutions. Monnet's efforts to overcome the divisions in Algiers were supported by his French colleagues exiled in Algiers—Joxe, Ettori, Pleven, Couve de Murville, Mayer, and the others, who collectively designed the institutional framework of the CFLN. By structuring the negotiations between the two generals and establishing a de facto French government, Monnet and his colleagues gave their support to the most qualified military man able to unite the factions. In so doing, his coalition of exiles also helped avert a possible future civil war and went a long way to ensuring that French sovereignty would be reestablished under liberal, democratic principles after the battles ceased. Monnet was able to succeed in Algiers because he wisely utilized and leveraged the power given him by the US president and by his American friends like McCloy and Hopkins who were in positions of influence. But he could not have succeeded without the pragmatism, intelligence, and support of his French colleagues.

By siding with de Gaulle in the CFLN, Monnet won some grudging respect from the domineering general because he had demonstrated he was the "kingmaker" and a match for the willful military man. As Alphand recorded in his diary, Monnet was enough of a power center on the committee that "I am to some extent a buffer (is he aware of it?), a peace-maker, between him (Monnet) and de Gaulle."[89] While the conversations between de Gaulle and Monnet in Algiers delineated areas of disagreement on the contours of a future Europe, the events there in 1943 served as a pivotal juncture in their long, complex relationship.

Monnet clearly gained prestige and respect from his French colleagues for his leadership and achievements in Algiers and Washington from 1943 to 1945. Despite Roosevelt's dislike of de Gaulle, Monnet had successfully used his own contacts and influence to obtain provisions for France through a Lend-Lease program and a loan. He lobbied hard for US recognition of the CFLN, which for him symbolized the embodiment of French sovereignty, by pragmatically beginning with an effort to gain de facto recognition. This reservoir of respect and admiration from his nation's future leaders and politicians in turn became an asset in his future efforts to reconstruct France after the war and implement his long-term goals of bringing peace to Europe. Always thinking about the future and foremost the interests of France, Monnet during these years shared with some colleagues his thinking about bringing peace to Europe through a federation of nation-states, a peace that would in turn permit France to thrive.

## Notes

1. François Duchêne, *Jean Monnet: The First Statesman of Interdependence* (New York: W. W. Norton, 1994), pp. 99–103; Jean Lacouture, *De Gaulle, the Rebel, 1890–1944*, trans. Patrick O'Brien (New York: W. W. Norton and Co., 1990), pp. 389–393; Thomas A. Schwartz, "The Transnational Partnership: Jean Monnet and Jack McCloy," in *Monnet and the Americans*, ed. Clifford Hackett (Washington, DC: Jean Monnet Council, 1995), pp. 175–176.

2. Duchêne, *Jean Monnet*, pp. 98–105; Richard Mayne, "Jean Monnet: A Biographical Essay," in *Monnet and the Americans*, ed. Clifford Hackett (Washington, DC: Jean Monnet Council, 1995), p. 15. American journalist Walter Lippmann condemned Vichy leader Marcel Peyrouton, governor general in Algeria, for his antidemocratic views in an April 27, 1943, message to Monnet, AME 27/4/18, R329, Fondation Jean Monnet pour l'Europe Centre de recherches européennes, Lausanne, Switzerland.

3. Memorandum summarizing the January 22, 1943, meeting of the generals and letter from de Gaulle to Catroux, February 23, 1943, papers of General George Catroux, Archives nationales, Paris; Lacouture, *De Gaulle*, pp. 415–433; Charles G. Cogan, *Charles de Gaulle: A Brief History with Documents* (Boston: Bedford Books of St. Martin's Press, 1996), pp. 48–53.

4. Jean Monnet, *Memoirs* (New York: Doubleday, 1978), p. 181.

5. Duchêne, *Jean Monnet*, pp. 98–108; Eric Roussel, *Jean Monnet* (Paris: Librairie Artheme Fayard, 1996), pp. 280–293; Schwartz, "Transnational Partnership," pp. 175–176.

6. Monnet, *Memoirs*, pp. 181–183; Robert Sherwood, *Roosevelt and Hopkins* (New York: Harper and Brothers, 1948), pp. 680–681.

7. Monnet, *Memoirs*, pp. 181–183; Schwartz, "Transnational Partnership," p. 176; Clifford Hackett, "Jean Monnet and the Roosevelt Administration," in *Monnet and the Americans*, ed. Clifford Hackett (Washington, DC: Jean Monnet Council, 1995), pp. 52–53; Sherwood, *Roosevelt*, pp. 680–681.

8. Monnet, *Memoirs*, p. 183; Hackett, "Jean Monnet," p. 55.

9. President Roosevelt to Cordell Hull, cable, January 16, 1943, in Sherwood, *Roosevelt*, pp. 678–679.

10. Duchêne, *Jean Monnet*, pp. 104–105; Lacouture, *De Gaulle*, p. 391.

11. Sherwood, *Roosevelt*, p. 679; Schwartz, "Transnational Partnership," p. 176.

12. President Roosevelt to Dwight Eisenhower, letter, February 22, 1943, and Eisenhower to Harry Hopkins, letter, March 3, 1943, Papers of Harry Hopkins, Roosevelt Library; Duchêne, *Jean Monnet*, p. 105; Roussel, *Jean Monnet*, pp. 291–294.

13. Lacouture, *De Gaulle*, p. 435.

14. Duchêne, *Jean Monnet*, p. 105.

15. Monnet, *Memoirs*, pp. 194–195; Schwartz, "Transnational Partnership," pp. 176–177. See also McCloy's March 8, 1943, memorandum of his interview with Giraud, McCloy Papers, Amherst College Library.

16. Schwartz, "Transnational Partnership," pp. 176–178.

17. Harold Macmillan, *The Blast of War, 1939–1945* (New York: Harper and Row, 1967), p. 175.

18. Ibid., 145.

19. René Pleven, interview by Roger Massip, May 28, 1980, and Maurice Couve de Murville, interview by Antoine Marès, January 16, 1984, Fondation Jean Monnet.

20. Lacouture, *De Gaulle*, p. 435.

21. Monnet, *Memoirs*, pp. 206–207.

22. André Kaspi, *La Mission de Jean Monnet à Alger* (Paris: Richelieu, 1972), pp. 81–108; André Kaspi, interview by the author, September 24, 2008. Kaspi stated there were seven versions of this speech written by Monnet.

23. Monnet, *Memoirs*, pp. 186–187; Lacouture, *De Gaulle*, pp. 441–442.

24. Monnet, *Memoirs*, p. 186.

25. Lacouture, *De Gaulle*, p. 442.

26. Louis Joxe, interview with Roger Massip, May (n.d.), 1982, Fondation Jean Monnet.

27. Lacouture, *De Gaulle*, p. 442; Kaspi, *La Mission*, pp. 81–108; Monnet, *Memoirs*, pp. 186–191; Pleven, interview.

28. Kaspi, *La Mission de Jean Monnet*, pp. 81–186.

29. Duchêne, *Jean Monnet*, pp. 115–121; Roussel, *De Gaulle*, pp. 295–299.

30. Monnet, *Memoirs*, p. 189.

31. Joxe, interview.

32. Monnet, *Memoirs*, pp. 188–189; Duchêne, *Jean Monnet*, pp. 117–118; Lacouture, *De Gaulle*, pp. 442–443.

33. Monnet, *Memoirs*, p. 193.

34. Ibid., pp. 190–193.

35. Duchêne, *Jean Monnet*, pp. 112–113; see also Louis Joxe, *Victoires sur la nuit: Mémoires, 1940–1966* (Paris: Flammarion, 1981).

36. Duchêne, *Jean Monnet*, p. 113; Joxe, interview, May 1982.

37. Joxe, interview.

38. Ibid.

39. Monnet to Hopkins, letter, May 9, 1943, quoted in Duchêne, *Jean Monnet*, pp. 117–119; Frederic Fransen, *The Supranational Politics of Jean Monnet* (Westport, CT: Greenwood, 2001), pp. 55–56; Monnet, *Memoirs*, pp. 190–191.

40. George Catroux to Charles de Gaulle, letters, May 11 and 17, 1943, Catroux Papers, Archives nationales, Paris.

41. Lacouture, *De Gaulle*, p. 445.

42. Ibid.; Monnet, *Memoirs*, p. 196.

43. Duchêne, *Jean Monnet*, p. 120.

44. Lacouture, *De Gaulle*, p. 432.

45. Anthony Eden, *The Memoirs of the Rt. Hon. Sir Anthony Eden*, Vol. 2 (London: Cassell, 1962), p. 386.

46. Lacouture, *De Gaulle*, p. 446; Monnet, *Memoirs,* pp. 197–199.

47. Lacouture, *De Gaulle*, pp. 446–447; Monnet, *Memoirs,* p. 199; Schwartz, "Transnational Partnership," p. 178.

48. Duchêne, *Jean Monnet*, p. 114.

49. Ibid., pp. 120–121.

50. Monnet, *Memoirs*, pp. 198–199.

51. Duchêne, *Jean Monnet*, pp. 120–121.

52. Lacouture, *De Gaulle*, p. 448; Monnet, *Memoirs*, p. 202.

53. Monnet, *Memoirs*, p. 203.

54. Duchêne, *Jean Monnet*, p. 121.

55. Lacouture, *De Gaulle*, pp. 438, 448.

56. Duchêne, *Jean Monnet*, p. 125.

57. Murphy to Roosevelt, letter, July 6, 1943, Roosevelt Papers, Roosevelt Library.

58. Joxe, interview.

59. Schwartz, "Transnational Partnership," p. 178.

60. Joseph P. Lash, *From the Diaries of Felix Frankfurter* (New York: W. W. Norton, 1975), p. 260.

61. Duchêne, *Jean Monnet*, p. 123.

62. Ibid., pp. 123–125.

63. Ibid., p. 124.

64. Monnet, *Memoirs*, p. 208.

65. Ibid., p. 191.

66. Ibid., pp. 191–192.

67. Joxe, interview.

68. Couve de Murville, interview.

69. Pleven, interview.

70. Monnet, "Memorandum from Algiers," August 5, 1943, AME 33/1/4 (Lausanne, Switzerland: Fondation Jean Monnet).

71. Etienne Hirsch, *Ainsi va la vie* (Lausanne, Switzerland: Fondation Jean Monnet pour l'Europe, 1988), pp. 78–79; see also Monnet, *Memoirs,* pp. 222–223.

72. Monnet, "Psychologie, note de réflection, Tipaza," July 23, 1943, Fondation Jean Monnet.

73. Monnet, *Memoirs*, p. 209.

74. Monnet–de Gaulle conversation, October 17, 1943, Fondation Jean Monnet; Duchêne, *Jean Monnet*, pp. 127–128.

75. Duchêne, *Jean Monnet*, p. 128; Monnet, *Memoirs*, pp. 211–216.

76. Douglas Brinkley, "Dean Acheson and Jean Monnet: On the Path to Atlantic Partnership," in *Monnet and the Americans*, ed. Clifford Hackett (Washington, DC: Jean Monnet Council, 1995), pp. 78–80.

77. Henry Owen, interview by Leonard Tennyson, June 30, 1981, Fondation Jean Monnet.

78. John L. Harper, *American Visions of Europe* (Cambridge: Cambridge University Press, 1994), p. 113.

79. Monnet, *Memoirs,* pp. 216–218.

80. Duchêne, *Jean Monnet*, pp. 136–137.

81. Harper, *American Visions*, pp. 114–115.

82. Ibid., p. 137; Clifford Hackett, *A Jean Monnet Chronology* (Washington, DC: Jean Monnet Council, 2008), pp. 203–204.

83. Monnet, *Memoirs,* pp. 224–225.

84. Duchêne, *Jean Monnet*, p. 132.

85. Etienne Hirsch to Monnet, memorandum, October 26, 1944, Etienne Hirsch papers, files 7-1, 7-2, European University Institute, Florence, Italy.

86. Irwin Wall, "Jean Monnet, the United States and the French Economic Plan," in *Jean Monnet: The Path to European Unity*, ed. Douglas Brinkley and Clifford Hackett (New York: St. Martin's Press, 1991), pp. 88–89.

87. Hackett, *Monnet Chronology*, p. 212; Duchêne, *Jean Monnet*, pp. 143–144.

88. Monnet, *Memoirs*, p. 227.

89. Duchêne, *Jean Monnet*, p. 123.

# 4

# The Monnet Plan,
# 1945–1950

**World War II changed** the economic thinking of the political leadership of France. The elites emerged from the chaos with a general consensus that drastic changes had to be made in the structure of their economy if France were to survive, eliminate its vulnerability to attack, and recover its status as a major power. Economic renewal and reconstruction, therefore, became the prime objectives of French leaders and the new generation of men who came to power in government and business after 1945.[1] "France had come out of the war plundered and completely exhausted," declared economist Robert Marjolin. "There was a change of spirit after the war," he continued. "This new generation was anxious not to repeat the mistakes of the interwar period and to progress as quickly as possible."[2]

While the French postwar leadership favored economic reconstruction, it lacked a plan and the money to finance it. Jean Monnet developed both a strategy for reconstruction and a method of financing it. The abrupt end to the US Lend-Lease program on September 2, 1945, which had sent monetary aid to France for the previous six months, forced provisional President Charles de Gaulle to focus on French postwar recovery in the near and long term. The Monnet Plan arose out of the need to draw up an economic program to justify to the US government access to more of the aid that Lend-Lease no longer provided.[3]

## Planning for Modernization

De Gaulle became head of the Provisional Government of the French Republic (GPRF) in August 1944. The embodiment of French patriotism during the

95

war, he unified the country. He was proclaimed provisional president with such unanimity that he was able to rule as a temporary dictator by general consent. He even succeeded in gaining support from the Communists by giving posts in his 1944 cabinet to two party members. In the referendum of October 1945, the voters confirmed him as combined president and prime minister and called for a new set of political institutions.[4]

In several meetings with de Gaulle in the last half of 1945, Monnet stressed the need for France to modernize. A conversation in Washington between these two men in August 1945 appears to have been the origin of the Monnet Plan. At the invitation of President Harry Truman, de Gaulle came to Washington for talks at the White House about the political and economic situation in France.[5] Monnet, who was in the US capital overseeing the final month of negotiations for US supplies under Lend-Lease, recalled his meeting with the French leader on August 23:

> I had not seen him for the past six months and I took the opportunity to expound to him my ideas about the future of France. "You speak of greatness. There will only be greatness when the French are of a stature to warrant it. That is how they are. . . . [T]hey must modernize themselves—because at the moment they are not modern. They need more production and greater productivity. Materially, the country needs to be transformed.[6]

Monnet believed that during the previous year, de Gaulle had realized the limits of French power and had become aware of how completely its economy had been destroyed by the war. The day before their meeting, de Gaulle had begun talks with the Export-Import Bank about the loan Monnet had been assigned to negotiate. The French president had confessed to Monnet that "America's dazzling prosperity" had astonished him since his arrival, that his knowledge of "this enormous country had previously been limited and imperfect." Monnet wrote that de Gaulle "listened to me very attentively, and replied, 'You are certainly right, but do you really want to try?' I answered, I don't know what I shall be able to achieve, but I'll certainly do my best."[7]

In August of 1945, US officials told the French government it would have to formulate a program to renovate its economy in order to continue to receive US aid. "Return to capitalism or head toward socialism," Undersecretary of State William Clayton told the head of one of the French purchasing commissions. "But in either case the government must . . . formulate a precise program proving its desire to give France an economy that will permit it to reach international production costs calculated in man hours." He declared, "If it . . . demonstrates to us the seriousness of its program, we shall help your country, for its prosperity is necessary to peace."[8]

Monnet drafted a memorandum for de Gaulle to send to Truman. It outlined France's plan to settle its Lend-Lease debt through a loan and stated his government's intention to request further loans for new equipment. Attempting to reassure the Americans, Monnet had written, for de Gaulle's signature, "We intend to submit to you in the near future our industrial equipment program aimed at modernizing our production." By tying aid to a modernization program and making the French accountable, the US government hastened the French planning process.[9]

Back in Paris in November of 1945, Monnet convinced de Gaulle of the need to reconstruct France in a systematic way and obtain US aid to accomplish it. Monnet argued there was "no mystery about our plight and no miracle could cure it." He told de Gaulle he was worried about the important psychological problem of disappointing those who believed France's liberation would bring prosperity. It would take time, he asserted, to rebuild cities and repair the railways. When the general stated he was anxious to ensure that "our efforts" not be relaxed, Monnet argued, "It will take very great willpower and an immense effort of explanation before people realize what is really wrong,— which is that our capital equipment and production methods are out of date." De Gaulle replied, "That is a task for the authorities. Make a proposal to them." Monnet replied, "I don't know exactly what has to be done, but I am sure of one thing. The French economy can't be transformed unless the French people take part in its transformation. And when I say 'the French people,' I don't mean an abstract entity: I mean trade unionists, industrialists, and civil servants. Everyone must be associated in an investment and modernization plan." De Gaulle told Monnet to send his proposals before the end of the year[10] and that same month announced his government's intention to frame "a grand plan" for reconstruction and renovation. The French and US governments exchanged letters setting the stage for the plan and for comprehensive negotiations on financial questions and commercial policy.[11]

Monnet brought Silvia and his two daughters back to France early in the fall of 1945. He had given up renting the expensive Foxhall Road house and moved his family to Wakefield, Rhode Island, in November of 1944 to reduce the family's costs of living in Washington.[12] But with a mandate from de Gaulle to work on reconstructing France in the fall of 1945, he was happy to move his family back home. After searching for a place in the countryside, he and Silvia bought a restored farmhouse with a thatched roof. It stood in the middle of a large garden in the village of Houjarray, near the Rambouillet forest, which is about twenty-seven miles southwest of Paris. John McCloy found all four members of the family happily ensconced there when he visited them in early October 1945.[13]

Monnet immediately began planning a strategy for reconstructing the French economy and enlisted some of his ablest colleagues to help. Working at this stage out of the Bristol Hotel on the rue du Faubourg St. Honoré in Paris with Marjolin, Etienne Hirsch, and Félix Gaillard, a young politician from Monnet's Clarente region and future prime minister, these men consulted many people and debated ideas and drafts long into many autumn nights. Marjolin outlined the challenge facing them:

> For the country to emerge from the abyss into which it had been plunged by a history of backwardness in the movement towards industrialization, by a profound decline during the thirties, and then by the war and the Occupation, a number of conditions had to be fulfilled, some material, some psychological. . . . It was no longer a question of catching up with the other developed countries, it had become necessary to reconstruct a country partly destroyed by the war, to modernize its plant made obsolete by the depression crisis and enemy occupation, to invest on an unprecedented scale when the nation would be clamoring for rapid satisfaction of consumer wants. In short, a plan was needed that would give priority to investment in general, and more particularly to capital expenditure that would lead the economy's development and make it possible to attain, after an initial phase of relative austerity, a level of consumption the French had never known. . . . [It had to begin with reconstruction because] the damage sustained by France in World War Two was more than double what she suffered in World War One; but most important [there had to be] a renewal of the nation's capital stock, which had been destroyed, depleted or reduced to obsolescence.[14]

By early December 1945, Monnet and his colleagues had delineated a concept and procedure for producing a plan. On December 6, 1945, Monnet sent de Gaulle their recommendations, entitled "Proposals for a Modernization and Investment Plan." In these proposals the team argued that France must pursue reconstruction and modernization simultaneously if it wished to raise its standard of living and recover its place in world affairs. This meant increasing productivity in both agriculture and industry by introducing the latest production methods and machinery. Only through increased production at competitive costs could France raise its exports to the level where it could pay for the massive imports of necessary raw materials such as coal and equipment. Monnet's team stressed that the pace of modernization depended on the ease with which France obtained foreign credit to buy equipment. They stressed the need for a long-term production plan that would coordinate and prioritize the numerous demands competing for scarce resources.[15]

Following Hirsch's advice, the team recommended the creation of committees or modernization commissions that brought together representatives involved in each level of a sector's production. Hirsch had observed the British Labour government's experiment with industrial working groups created in 1945 to conduct a self-examination of certain flagging industries. These groups included individuals from labor and management as well as trade union leaders, civil servants, businessmen, government officials, and consumers. Monnet's team advised the establishment of such commissions for coal, power, steel building, public works, building materials, and agricultural products and machinery. Monnet's team recommended the adoption of this consultative approach, called *économie concertée*, an "orchestrated" or collaborative economic effort, because the overall plans formulated by these groups for each sector would more likely be enforced and followed. Also, they proposed the appointment of a planning commissioner to supervise and synthesize the recommendations made by the commissions and the drafting of a plan to modernize production (Plan de Modernisation et d'Equipement). They proposed that the final plan be submitted first to a planning council of thirty members representing both the ministries and business and then to the government for approval.[16] Pierre Massé, economist, business leader, and later government official, echoed his support for this effort: "We all knew we had two choices at the end of the war: modernization or decadence, and we unanimously supported the former."[17]

Monnet's plan won de Gaulle's support because it was a pragmatic way of meeting the crisis created by the termination of Lend-Lease. Moreover, both men shared the same goals for their nation. Each understood the need to renovate their war-torn economy in order to enhance French security and restore France to a position of influence and leadership in Europe. The general understood that economic modernization was essential to furthering his foreign policy goals—the pursuit of greatness and national independence for France. The full cabinet adopted Monnet's proposals and issued a government decree on January 3, 1946, creating the Planning Commission and the Planning Council, which were attached to the head of the government, not a ministry. Monnet had insisted that the planning unit be outside of any ministry's control in order to avoid jurisdictional struggles, political battles, and parliamentary supervision. De Gaulle appointed Monnet the new planning commissioner and issued him instructions, which were quoted almost verbatim from a memorandum Monnet's group had drafted.[18] In January 1946, the French Provisional Government agreed to negotiate the US request that France reduce customs barriers in return for large-scale US credits needed to finance the rebuilding of the economy.[19]

While Monnet himself was neither technician nor politician, his ability to attract an extremely able team to help him design the plan proved a key factor in its success. In addition to Marjolin, Gaillard, and Hirsch, who was responsible for the individual sectors of industry, he added Pierre Uri, a brilliant Princeton-trained economist, and Jean Fourastié and Jacques Dumontier, statisticians who served as heads of the economic and statistical division. Jacques Van Helmont, an astute French analyst; François Fontaine, a writer; Jean-Paul Delcourt, a young economist; Albert Sauvy, an economic expert; and Jean Vergeot, a senior official from the Ministry of Economic Affairs, also joined the team. "Monsieur Vergeot, as we called him out of a mixture of respect and friendship," recalled Monnet, "was meticulous about everything, with a precision of mind and expression that made him a remarkable expositor of our ideas. . . . The Plan . . . owes to him the fact that it was read and understood by so many of his compatriots."[20]

Monnet also chose Paul Delouvrier, a young intellectual who had played an active role in the resistance and was an inspector of finance. This well-educated Frenchman had met Monnet in 1944 at the Ministry of Finance when the man from Cognac was traveling back and forth to Paris negotiating loans from Washington. When Monnet invited Delouvrier to be in charge of financial affairs, to help him understand French financial problems, and to collect the needed funds, "I didn't hesitate to join his team," recalled Delouvrier. "Monnet had a special relationship with his collaborators, a capacity to seduce people, a special nature that endeared him to those with whom he worked. His mind was like a trapeze and there was a total absence of vanity."[21]

These men formed what was probably the most creative team in Paris. Envied by established ministries, they worked unostentatiously in their new but cramped quarters of a small townhouse at 18 rue de Martignac around the corner from the Matignon, the prime minister's office. Seated around a large wooden trestle table, which served as Monnet's desk, these men, who had direct access to ministers, would discuss draft upon draft, rewrite, and debate knowing they were tackling important issues. Monnet's chief of staff, Jacques Rabier, spoke of Monnet's rich imagination and "how determined he was to finish anything he started. He did not have subordinates but members of a team."[22] Hirsch stated that it was "a true team effort where each member was called upon to participate in all the decisions."[23] Delouvrier also noted Monnet's ability to lead the group effectively and said, "he barely had a school certificate and dominated the lot of us."[24]

Marjolin, Monnet's deputy, recalled how the team worked.

> The division of labor . . . was effected without difficulty. Monnet relied on me for the overall design and general balance of the system we were trying to set up. . . . Of course, Monnet did not accept my conclusions without our having discussed them at length, and, in some cases, my having been talked into amending them. As is the way with all strong minds, he appreciated resistance, even if it sometimes irritated him. I remember . . . a discussion that lasted a whole afternoon . . . about the Plan's targets. The discussion had become . . . a passage of arms between Monnet and myself . . . the others . . . having reached the end of their arguments. Late in the evening, when we were all exhausted, Monnet wound up the discussion with these words: "Marjolin, the trouble with you is that you're an intellectual. All right, I give in, but I want you to know that if I do it is not because you have been so insistent, but because I have convinced myself, in spite of your cussedness, that you were right." [Marjolin wrote that he mentioned this incident because it illustrated] the kind of relationship that had developed between Jean Monnet and me, the fighting spirit we showed, he and I, in our search for the truth, the great objectivity he was capable of demonstrating. Needless to say, the situation was frequently reversed; I too knew how to give in when his practical sense, which

was nothing short of genius, enabled him to identify clearly the goal to be attained.[25]

Monnet's inspiration for his plan grew out of ideas prevalent during the war years when, as Stanley Hoffmann argues, both the Vichy government and the resistance movements advocated the need for state intervention and planning.[26] Philippe Mioche asserts that Monnet was influenced by the changes in the French mentality and that a compatibility existed between liberal economic ideas and indicative planning, central economic planning implemented by the state, after the war.[27] Monnet's design of the plan also owed much to the Anglo-American example, especially to the Americans and their expansionist economic philosophy. Fascinated by the US economic model and the willingness of its people to innovate constantly, he believed that nation had found the way to prosperity and power and wished to sell it to his countrymen. He was convinced that productivity and growth were solutions to France's economic and social problems, that they would end an economy of scarcity, quarrels over distribution, and economic weakness that had undermined his nation's capacity to act in the world in the past. To change French thinking about economic growth became one of his goals. He and the planners repeatedly said it was less important for the French farmer to have a new tractor than to think differently about output. Having worked with the small group directing US war mobilization in Washington, Monnet learned that fundamental decisions could be made more efficiently and speedily by a small group of key players and that the obstructive, meddling procedures of civil servants in bureaucracies should be avoided.[28] But the planners as well as French political leaders understood the need for the state to play a strong role in the economy. "It was not a question of ideology but of necessity," Uri remarked. "The state was needed to solve financial problems. It was the only way to transfer whatever savings there were into the current investment that France needed. Since we had no other resources, the state had to play a role in our reconstruction and modernization."[29]

## Setting Ambitious Goals

Monnet's team designed an investment plan as a means of securing US aid and established pragmatic, limited goals for the 1947–1950 period. These included developing national production and foreign trade, particularly in the fields where France was most favorably placed; increasing productivity; ensuring full employment; and raising the standard of living and improving the conditions of national life. Their production target was to be a quarter larger in 1950 than that of 1929 and 50 percent larger than that of 1938. Since the French economy had generated virtually no investment to renew equipment since 1930, these goals were ambitious.

The planners delineated clear priorities for the allocation of scarce resources by selecting six basic activities, that is, industries or sectors, for investment priority. They were (1) coal mining; (2) electricity; (3) transport such as railways; (4) iron and steel; (5) cement works; and (6) fertilizer, tractors, and other agricultural machinery. "These were the strategic productions," noted Uri, "or the key sectors of the economy on which the increase in all other forms of an industrial output was believed to depend."[30] Monnet's team understood that selecting priorities also required certain sacrifices. This meant that manufacturing, consumer goods industries, and housing construction had to be postponed. "We first had to put the railways in order or recovery would have been impossible," recalled Uri. "At the end of the war, we didn't have even 30 miles of track. We had to repair all of them quickly and eliminate the bottlenecks. We solved agricultural problems by reviving the industries that worked for agriculture. The great decision was to get industry on its feet before anything else—it was a great political achievement."[31] The planners, noted historian Richard Kuisel, "chose investment over consumption, modernization over reconstruction, and the future over the present."[32]

Monnet's team favored heavy industry. They agreed that France had to make this sector more competitive, especially in relation to Germany, and viewed a strong base in energy and steel as the foundation of industrial might. France's steel industry, generally uncompetitive during the 1920s and 1930s, was shattered by the war. Its most modern steel plant had been built in 1906, and almost no new investment had been made in this industry between 1940 and 1945. The planners outlined three goals for the steel industry: (1) to revive and modernize it as the key to industrial power and their plan's success; (2) to open it up to foreign competition by making exports competitive with Germany; and (3) to supply the home market at competitive prices. Since the strength of French steel depended upon German coke,[33] they needed to secure access to coke and coal supplies from Germany's Ruhr Valley. That area symbolized to the French mind the rise of Nazism and militarism and conjured up memories of horror, bloodshed, and the humiliating occupation.

Some have argued that the Monnet Plan sought French economic recovery at the expense of an economically weakened Germany. And because of this, they argued, Monnet based his plan on the assumption that the French would have unlimited access to Ruhr coal and that they could exploit markets previously filled by German producers. The argument was that since French steel was the key to industrial power, it must expand by using Ruhr coke until it largely replaced German steel.[34] There is no evidence that Monnet or his planning team wished to turn France into the center of Western European manufacturing.[35] The plan's goal to revive the flagging steel industry did not represent an attempt to seize German resources and capture its markets nor did it aim at replacing Germany in heavy industry or treat Ruhr resources as its own. Although some members of the foreign ministry harbored such goals, the planners actually favored internationalization of that Ruhr region to guarantee their access. They believed international oversight was the best way to restrict German sovereignty there and to prevent Ruhr mine owners from controlling French steel production by regulating the supply of coke exported to France. As French security depended on continued access to the Ruhr, Monnet warned that if the Ruhr mine owners decided to control French steel production by regulating the supply of coke, "it could lead only to subordination or conflict."[36] The planners knew that economic modernization could not occur without a resolution of the Ruhr problem. Their goal was to revive and make the French steel industry competitive, not to subordinate or supplant the Ruhr.[37]

The desire for self-sufficiency meant the plan emphasized France's own resources, coal and hydroelectric power, rather than imported oil and gas. But acute coal shortages and the terrible condition of the coal mines right after the war meant greater dependence on foreign sources.[38] The coal-rich German province of Saar had been placed under French economic control in 1945, and some in the French government fostered hopes of integrating it economically with their nation. But Monnet's position on the Saar was that it also should be internationalized under a body with joint control. In June 1945, Monnet suggested to Clayton that a "dictator" of German coal should be established under three Western Allied governments.[39]

## Seeking a US Loan

The strong popular support of de Gaulle's provisional government didn't last long as sharp conflict developed over policy issues and the character of the new constitution. And much to everyone's surprise, de Gaulle abruptly resigned in January 1946. A broad left-wing coalition led by Socialist Félix Gouin headed the provisional government until the new constitution was ratified and promulgated the following October. Gouin sent a strong delegation to Washington in March 1946 to negotiate credits for economic recovery, settle French war debts, and delineate trade policy. Léon Blum, former Socialist premier of the Popular Front Government of 1936, led the group, which included Monnet and Emmanuel Monick, governor of the Bank of France, as the chief negotiators.[40]

Carrying a draft of the plan for use in the negotiations, Monnet hoped to obtain a loan to sustain his plan for five years. He had told Clayton that since France was as important to Europe as Britain, he wished to have a US loan comparable to its $3.75 billion loan to the British. To convince the Americans of the seriousness of their effort to rebuild their economy, the planners had prepared a quantitative analysis of the French economy. They hoped that it would demonstrate that France's economic plight was caused by the devastation of two wars and inadequate long-term capital investment. They also argued that

France could not itself generate the necessary investments or pay for the large foreign exchange debt.[41]

The French found American officials somewhat hostile, demanding, and unwilling to meet their full requests. In large part, this attitude was due to a division in Washington on how to deal with these loan negotiations. The War Department advised that they be used to punish the French for their lack of cooperation with US policies to reconstruct Germany. But the State Department agreed with Jefferson Caffrey, the US ambassador in Paris, who urged that generous credit should be given on political rather than financial grounds. Some harbored the earlier US views of Blum as a radical socialist. Others worried that a loan made in the interest of strengthening capitalist France might paradoxically work to benefit a Communist regime should it come to power there. But the complex negotiations revealed that the Americans didn't feel the sense of urgency that had surrounded the earlier Lend-Lease to France. US officials asserted that the British loan was unique because Britain had been a wartime partner, and its sterling was an international currency. In addition, they explained that Congress was hostile to more foreign aid loans and enumerated their considerable demands that France liberalize its trade policy, devalue the franc, end its restrictive trade practices, and enact a more liberal policy on US investment. They also believed the proposed French reconstruction plan would be inflationary and that political stability required more funding for consumption and housing.[42]

The final Blum-Byrnes Agreement, signed May 28, 1946, by Secretary of State James Byrnes, provided approximately $650 million of new money in a loan from the Export-Import Bank instead of the $2 billion requested. While cancelling $2.8 billion of Lend-Lease obligations, the Truman administration consolidated the cost of all deliveries in the pipeline to France into a new loan of $420 million, added another $300 million to pay for US surplus goods left in France, and promised to support a loan of $500 million from the World Bank the following year. The Americans were convinced that the French were serious about rebuilding their economy. They also justified the loan as a means of supporting the anti-Communist factions in France and ensuring that pro-American leaders like Blum did not feel abandoned. And while US officials did not endorse the French plan, they suggested no major modifications.[43]

France did not receive the means to finance the plan, despite Monnet's assertions later that the loan was predicated on it. Although disappointed in the result, the French delegation provided assurances about trade liberalization and promised free access to French markets for US products. But Monnet remained undaunted by this financial setback. Irwin Wall asserts:

> Monnet's genius as a statesman was to look beyond momentary failure and to perceive reality over the long term. His immediate reaction to Blum-Byrnes was to revise downward the investment projections of the plan and

separate the year 1947 from its long-term goals. Monnet could see the crisis of 1947 looming, but he retained the conviction that the Americans would come to see that the reconstruction of Europe and its insertion into the world economy, under the leadership of a resurgent and modernized France, was in their own interest as well as the interest of Europe.[44]

Moreover, Monnet stressed to his government's ministers what he wanted them to believe—that the US loan was tied morally, if not legally, to the plan.[45]

## Finalizing the Monnet Plan

In 1946, Monnet's team acted as the innovators and coordinators of French economic policy. Faced with less funds from their government and the United States than anticipated, Monnet and his team readjusted the plan's goals. They separated the year 1947 from its long-term goals and reaffirmed their priorities but concentrated funds more narrowly on the six priority sectors. They reduced the investment projections of the plan, made no attempt to influence short-term policy, and accepted inflation as a consequence of the heavy investment program. The allocation of investment resources and imposition of restrictions on access to capital markets favored producer industries while private industry, especially for consumer goods, was accorded a low priority.[46]

The planners used the twenty-four modernization commissions they established to formulate sectoral plans, strategize collectively, and set goals and production targets for the individual sectors. Monnet believed it was critical to get labor on his side and chose respected men of standing in both industries and unions to serve on the commissions. By picking the key people, the planners helped maintain their position as referees among groups in the sectors. Monnet won the support of the Communists in 1947 and praise from both Communist leader François Billoux and labor leader Benoit Frachon for being practical. Viewing the process of planning as a collaborative endeavor of all economic groups, Monnet wrote, "Our action had to be at once less dictatorial and more specific: we had to persuade, not compel, private enterprise to act in accordance with public needs. The best way . . . was to . . . jointly seek the common interest which no one of them could determine alone, but in which all of them had a share." Monnet added, "We were putting into administrative practice the notion of interdependence which is fundamental in the world of business."[47] Economist Pierre Massé argued, "Monnet created a Plan that was made by men discussing around a table and that obligated no one." He ordered drafts be rewritten multiple times so the priorities of the plan could be "explained to the politicians and public opinion in ways they can understand."[48]

Monnet tapped his friend Robert Nathan, the American economist, to advise him in designing the final draft of the plan. After analyzing the first ver-

*Courtesy of Fondation Jean Monnet pour l'Europe. © European Union, 2011.*

*Jean Monnet and his team of collaborators at the Monnet Plan office, rue de Martignac, Paris, 1946 or 1947. From left to right: Paul Delouvrier, Jean-Paul Delcourt, Robert Marjolin, Jean Monnet, Etienne Hirsch, unknown, Jean Vergeot, François Valéry.*

sion in March 1946, when Monnet was in Washington, Nathan explained how the US experience of mobilizing its economy for war might be applicable to the French goal of reconstruction. Nathan argued that France needed statistical data analysis as a basis for economic and business planning. He recommended that a central group in the French government be established to collect, disseminate, and analyze essential and accurate data on each industrial activity. After traveling to Paris to review successive drafts with the planners in August, Nathan emphasized that a sound plan must be based on realistic estimates and objectives, underscored the need for the scheduling of investments as well as production of consumer goods and services, and stressed that annual schedules had to be based on both needs and feasibility. Since manpower was the most important limiting factor in the expansion of its economy, he argued that the French government must allocate labor to economic areas important to the country, increase the workweek from forty to forty-eight hours, and import extra labor. He also stressed the importance of fiscal policies and vigorous efforts to reduce nonessential governmental expenditures as well as the need to balance the budget and control inflation. Since it was critical to gain public support of the plan, Nathan recommended a general media campaign to educate the government as well as the public.[49]

Completed in November 1946, the Monnet Plan was adopted on January 14, 1947, by the new Blum cabinet and launched by government decree creating the Planning Commission (Commissariat du Plan). Appointed the planning commissioner (*commissaire général au plan*), Monnet was awarded the task of executing the plan under the conditions he had personally requested. The planning unit under his control was to be a small, apolitical staff of skilled planners not attached to or controlled by any ministry but directly responsible to the head of government. As a result, no separate vote of the legislature was required for the allocation of funds to it. The plan's budget in subsequent years was included as part of the administration's overall budget, which was voted on as an entity. This helped to minimize political and jurisdictional battles that Monnet had worked so hard to avoid. As head of the Planning Commission, Monnet was not a member of government, and, at his insistence, this first plan was never submitted to parliament for approval.[50]

## Implementing the Plan

From 1947 to 1950, the members of the Planning Commission under the direction of Monnet largely determined France's economic policy and implemented the nation's first economic plan. By acting as a unit, the planners provided stability and consistency in economic policy for a nation that experienced a flurry of cabinets and prime ministers. This small group of creative thinkers and problem solvers shaped many of the key economic decisions because the rapid turnover of weak governments meant the elected politicians were not in power long enough to make any major changes in the plan's long-term policies and goals. Marjolin, Hirsch, Uri, and Monnet met with business and labor leaders, managed the reconstruction, allocated credits, and enforced decisions. They used the power given them under the plan to levy taxes to encourage or even coerce reluctant industrialists to cooperate. But they had less direct impact on sectors outside the basic activities and investment industries: "We used saliva and taxes," Hirsch claimed. "We commissioners were the continuity. With each change in cabinet, it took a lot of saliva to explain our policies over and over again." But he added, "The politicians never stopped anything that had been started, and they were never in power long enough to start something new that was dangerous. If so, I could always delay implementation until there was a new government."[51]

Monnet and his team avoided ideological and bureaucratic battles, cultivated senior officials in the Ministry of Finance, and worked outside of the other powerful ministries. The team operated as policy commandoes and troubleshooters but did not win all the battles.[52] Monnet energetically fought to maintain his independence and access to the top by repelling any efforts by ministries to control him and by threatening to resign. Not seeking higher office and careful not to tread on other jurisdictions, he concentrated on key issues. He relied on his powers of persuasion, not his title or power, to get the information he needed from the ministers. His unit created some jealousies such as with Minister of Industry Robert Lacoste, but Monnet had good relations with his old friends René Mayer and Henri Queuille, successive ministers of finance. One of his loyal supporters and key allies was François Bloch-Lainé, director of the treasury from 1947 to 1953, who believed Monnet's team was tackling a vital issue and deserved support.[53]

## Facing the Obstacles

Between 1947 and 1949, many obstacles impeded the execution of Monnet's plan. Tackling inflation and financing the plan became two of the most important challenges. Unsuccessful harvests caused food prices to double between August 1946 and May 1947 and brought a flood of imports as well as a drop in foreign exchange reserves. The scarcity of dollars became increasingly serious. Coal, electricity, and labor shortages had produced an energy crisis in 1946 as production declined and industrial prices soared. Sporadic strikes plagued the Renault car plant during 1947, and in May the government expelled its Communist members. France along with most of Western Europe faced a critical situation in external payments by mid-1947. "Monnet at first was not interested in the problem of inflation," explained Uri, "but it was exploding—it had been 60 percent under de Gaulle but was still 45 percent in 1947—and he realized the risk of dislocation." It became a serious problem for the whole government because it affected every segment of society.[54]

By July 1947, France faced an economic crisis. Monnet's team realized it had overestimated the government's ability to stabilize prices and wages and control inflation. In addition, they had misjudged the time needed for the recovery of exports. They feared the plan would be jeopardized without further assistance from the United States and an effective stabilization program from the government. Monnet began working in the summer of 1947 to persuade the national government run by Socialist Premier Paul Ramadier to tackle the emergency. Bombarding the Ministry of Finance with proposals to combat inflation, he urged the development of an effective long-term, nonpartisan stabilization program. Ramadier accepted Monnet's advice, and in October ordered him to establish a special commission to analyze and solve the problem. Monnet created and chaired the National Balance-Sheet Commission and appointed Uri as chief economist and drafter of its report. According to Uri, the source of the idea for the commission was Edward Bernstein, a former US Treasury official and then chief economist at the International Monetary Fund. Monnet also consulted the British economist Nicholas Caldor for advice. Among the commission members appointed by Monnet were prominent officials, such as Bloch-Lainé and Pierre Lebrun, Communist leader and head of the labor union General Confederation of Labor (Confédération Générale du Travail).[55]

This macroeconomic policy initiative would have normally been assigned to the finance ministry, but was given to Monnet because he was respected and influential among policymakers. Known to have good advisers, he had been the first to present ideas on how to tackle inflation. Pierre Pflimlin, who was a member of several postwar cabinets, later recalled an incident in 1947–1948 when he was minister of agriculture:

> I rapidly realized I had to convince Jean Monnet, who was the key man. Without participating in government, he inspired its decisions in the economic domain. . . . I soon discovered he was a powerful personality with a clear-sighted mind who quickly went to the heart of problems. . . . What was remarkable was the authority that Jean Monnet exercised over his planning commission composed of men with different expertise. His ideas were so clear, so sensible that his initiatives were often adopted without discussion. . . . he ranks at the top of those who have made history in our epoch.[56]

The commission's report, written by Uri and completed in December 1947, persuaded the government to take exceptional measures to reduce inflation. These included imposing a levy on higher-income groups and taxing those benefiting from inflation such as shopkeepers whose income rose as a result of inflation. Monnet had argued that unless such excess disposable income was absorbed by new taxes, wage increases given to the striking workers in the fall of 1947 would further fuel inflation. The finance minister took Uri's word that a heavy levy on farmers was also necessary. Monnet had also argued that segments of this tax should be utilized for investment and reconstruction in the basic sectors.[57] As Uri, not known for his humility, recalled, "We worked night and day and produced a report in two months that Monnet adopted. It was a fantastic success."[58]

The stabilization program implemented by the national government in late 1947 and 1948 brought economic stability to France within two years. Its successive measures reduced inflation from 45 percent to zero by 1949, even though some of these measures were negated by strikes and political instability in the summer of 1948. Uri and Monnet were successful in persuading the trade unions to accept the economic policies of the government, including two key decisions that helped turn the economy around: to make the forty-hour week more flexible and to accept overtime for 25 percent in additional wages.[59] "Monnet persuaded the trade unionists to start with tools rather than houses," noted Uri. The economist noted that, beginning in mid-1948, "France experienced three years of stability without any encroachment on the rate of growth."[60]

Financing their program became a critical challenge for the planners between 1947 and 1949 because they had failed to obtain adequate funding for it. The lack of domestic French capital coupled with inflation diminished private investment and forced Monnet's team to rely more heavily on public funding. However, these funds were subject to annual parliamentary votes as well as monthly ministerial allocations. Moreover, in the fall of 1947, parliament cut the budget in the basic sectors by 20 percent. At the end of 1947, at the height of his influence with government decisionmakers, Monnet argued strongly for an autonomous fund for the Planning Commission. In January 1948, he persuaded the Schuman-Mayer government to authorize new equipment funds. While this partial funding for the basic sectors was a considerable victory, it was insufficient for the Monnet Plan's needs. In the spring of 1947, Monnet had recognized that external aid was vital if the plan's targets of growth in output and modernization—which required massive imports—were to be met without seriously compromising the future. By the summer of 1947, only $240 million remained from previous loans that were needed to meet an estimated $450 million deficit for imported grain, coal, gasoline, and raw materials.[61]

## Assistance from the Marshall Aid Program

A deteriorating European economy and threats of continued Soviet expansion in Western Europe in 1946 and early 1947 persuaded the Truman administration to provide reconstruction aid to European nations. Since the end of the war, US policymakers believed that a revitalized Western Europe would contain the Soviet Union and encourage political stability in these war-torn nations. When Greece and Turkey were threatened by increased Soviet influence, the president announced in March a $400 million program of military and economic assistance to those countries. In what became known as the Truman Doctrine, he pledged to assist other nations threatened by Communist intimidation, internal subversion, or external aggression. Historian John Gaddis asserts that this policy of containment of the Soviet Union provided a rationale for continued US activism in Europe and paved the way for the Marshall Plan.[62]

Western Europe's worsening economic situation alarmed Washington. Growing shortages of food, coal, fertilizer, and agricultural machinery combined in 1946–1947 with one of the harshest winters on record to limit spring harvests and production severely. Governments had difficulty financing food imports, and US loans and other aid to France, Italy, and Britain had dried up. US Secretary of State George Marshall, convinced that the Soviets were trying to force an economic breakdown in Europe, announced his grand strategy for reversing the desperate conditions through a long-term plan to assist Europe economically and to help these countries rebuild their economies.[63] In his June 5, 1947, speech, Marshall stressed the initiative for recovery had to come from the European nations themselves, and they would be expected to join in a cooperative effort to restore their collective economic health. This news brought Europeans a sense of profound relief. British Foreign Secretary Ernest Bevin later characterized it as "a lifeline to sinking men. It seemed to bring hope where there was none. . . . I think you can understand why we grabbed the lifeline with both hands."[64]

The Marshall Plan legislation, the Foreign Assistance Act of 1948, officially known as the Economic Cooperation Act, passed Congress on March 30 and was signed by President Truman on April 1, 1948.[65] The Marshall Plan consisted of economic assistance to France, Germany, Belgium, the Netherlands, and twelve other Western European nations. The terms of the program required that nations receiving aid design an equitable method for its distribution and to plan their economic activities collectively. US officials invited the Soviet Union to participate in the program but it refused the terms, rejected the offer, and did not permit any Eastern European nation to join. In April 1948, representatives from each of the countries receiving Marshall Plan aid created the Organization for European Economic Cooperation (OEEC). Though the OEEC failed to develop a comprehensive European recovery program, as US officials had hoped, it furthered US policy goals because it encouraged the liberalization of trade and fostered new modes of thinking about ways to achieve closer integration of their economies.[66]

Washington's implementation of the Marshall Aid Program and Monnet's influential role in shaping French economic policy from 1946 on enabled him to ensure that a large share of those funds allotted to France was used to finance the Monnet Plan. The Marshall Program also gave him the opportunity to exploit US government pressure on his own government's officials in two important ways. He used it to urge them to take the lead in support of the US policy encouraging European cooperation and to implement concrete measures to achieve financial stability and thereby combat inflation in France. In a July 24, 1947, memorandum to Foreign Minister Georges Bidault, Monnet urged him to seize the initiative and present the "outlines" of a sound program for rebuilding Europe, as required in order to continue to receive US aid. Monnet also emphasized the urgency of revising France's policy toward Germany. He argued that France must discuss the German problem and the status of the Ruhr with Great Britain and the United States, and this must be incorporated into a European program. To achieve his aim of modernizing the economy and establishing a satisfactory German peace settlement that was nonthreatening to France, he believed his government had to lead Europe in promoting the US desire for European cooperation. This, he said, would bring France the benefits of US goodwill along with the essential aid. He asserted his modernization plan "represents hope" and is "in fact the guarantee of French economic independence." Monnet continued,

> Accordingly, this Plan (whose implementation is obviously made easier by
> foreign financing, but not determined by it, since implementation depends
> first of all on the effort put forth by the French) puts the funds proposed by
> General Marshall in their true perspective: that is, temporary assistance that
> will enable us subsequently to stop contracting debt—productive assistance
> that will promote our own production programs and prevent us from spong-
> ing off of the United States.[67]

Bidault agreed with Monnet and helped convince the Americans that the
French attitudes were at least constructive toward trade liberalization and economic cooperation.

The United States created the Economic Cooperation Administration
(ECA) to administer the national Marshall Plan Aid Programs. It also established a Marshall Aid Mission of officials located in each recipient nation
whose function was the supervision of expenditures of counterpart funds.
These were the monies accumulated by governments as a result of selling
goods delivered and paid for by the US government through the Marshall Plan.
The bilateral Franco-American agreement on Marshall aid of June 28, 1948,
gave the US mission officials in Paris control of the counterpart fund expen-
diture. As a result, it became a critically important pressure group in French
economic policy with political influence and became a parallel and sometimes
rival service to the State Department. Washington hoped to control the release
of counterpart funds as a way of preventing inflation and achieving financial
stability in France. In implementing this policy, the US embassy also agreed
to release 25 billion francs of counterpart funds in exchange for further French
promises to refrain from inflationary forms of financing.[68]

The use of the US funds to influence economic policy aroused resentment
in some French political circles. But others, like Henri Bonnet, French ambassador to the United States, believed that his countrymen must be educated to
understand that the counterpart funds were necessary to enable the objectives
of the Monnet Plan to be fulfilled, which in turn would lead to the reestablish-
ment of French independence. Pondering France's future realistically and its
important relationship with the United States, Monnet made the same point to
Bidault: "We are to a great extent going to depend on this country [the United
States] as much for the maintenance of our economic life as for our national
security. This situation cannot continue without great danger. . . . We must
transform this situation quickly into one of independence and collaboration."[69]

## Forming an Influential Triumvirate

Two US officials worked closely with Monnet to bring increased financial and
economic stability to France and implement the Monnet Plan. The twenty-nine-
year-old William Tomlinson from Boise, Idaho, established a close friendship

with the fifty-nine-year-old Monnet soon after being sent to Paris in 1947 as the US embassy's treasury representative and financial attaché. Meeting during the financial negotiations for US aid, the two had a relationship that gradually grew into a trusting friendship and closeness of father and son. Tommy, as this graduate of Brown University was affectionately called, developed a respect for Monnet and his goal to unite Europe to prevent another war. "Both had a fire burning in them to change the world," remarked a colleague of Tomlinson, "and the chemistry worked for both of them."[70] The young American became an informal member of Monnet's team that met almost daily to thrash out ways to implement the Monnet Plan. As a result, Tomlinson gained an understanding of the difficult economic problems facing France.[71] He came to believe, under the tutelage of Monnet and his team, how critical economic recovery was not only for France's security in Europe but for that nation's role in European integration. As Stanley Cleveland, an embassy official who worked for Tomlinson in Paris, recalled, "Tomlinson shared a common trait with Monnet, one reason they got on so well together, which was that Tomlinson had a capacity for working with people for a singular objective regardless of . . . what government they were working for."[72] Jacques Van Helmont, a valued member of Monnet's team, stated, "Tommy . . . worked closely with Monnet without regard to rank or nationality. . . . [H]e spent so much time with us around the table that he learned the division of labor between Monnet and his close associates."[73]

Introduced by Monnet to many of the key officials in the Ministry of Finance, Tomlinson quickly developed a reputation among both Americans and the French as a brilliant and penetrating mind and an effective, trusted negotiator. To Arthur Hartman, a young diplomat and economist who worked with Tomlinson in Paris, he was one of the most extraordinary men he ever knew. Hartman, who later became US ambassador to both France and the Soviet Union, declared that Tomlinson had analytical abilities that did not come from graduate school training nor did he use the techniques employed by other economists. "He had an instinctive way of analyzing an economic situation . . . and came to the same conclusions as the other economists but in half the time."[74]

Tomlinson's responsibilities increased when David Bruce became the first head of the Marshall Plan mission in Paris in 1948. This elegant, handsome Virginia country gentleman and lawyer, who had run the Office of Strategic Services (OSS) in London during the war, soon became a trusted friend and collaborator of Tomlinson. Bruce made Tomlinson director of financial and trade affairs for the ECA mission to France. Recognizing the need for improved coordination among US officials, Bruce also created a tripartite group, a combined State Department, Treasury, and ECA nucleus, which was located in the annex of the US embassy. With US Treasury Secretary John Snyder's approval, Bruce appointed Tomlinson as its director. Tomlinson's dual treasury and Marshall Plan roles gained him unusual access to the French bureaucracy and made him especially effective at pressuring that government to make needed reforms. Cleveland, who was working for Tomlinson, recalled,

> Tommy was an extraordinary man. He was the only authentic genius I've ever known, an incredible fellow who at the age of about 34 was one of the most important American officials in Europe. It was a position he had earned . . . for the way he manipulated the French situation during the Marshall Plan period. . . . He had done this by a combination of using the external pressures of the U.S. government combined with an extraordinary penetration of the French bureaucracy. This included both the Ministry of Finance and Monnet's Plan. These were the real economic power centers in the French government. They were very hostile to each other yet Tommy got on well with both of them.[75]

As Hartman asserted, Tomlinson and Monnet "were so central to the aid allocations, the special terms, the bilateral negotiations, everything else, that everyone watched with a mixture of envy, admiration and disconcertment. . . . The U.S. bureaucratic structure . . . made people like that terribly powerful in policy-making."[76]

Through Tomlinson, Bruce soon met and became friends with Monnet, and this triumvirate worked together and with their governments to stabilize the French economy.[77] They employed the leverage of the aid mission and its control over the release of counterpart funds to pressure French leaders to enact reforms to reduce inflation in mid-1948 and to tighten credit for the rest of the year. When Prime Minister Henri Queuille requested on September 15, 1948, assurances from the Americans that they would release counterpart funds through November, Bruce fought hard. He won assurance from Washington that the funds would indeed be released if Queuille adopted responsible fiscal policies. Tomlinson and Bruce met with the prime minister on November 15 and were told a week later the French government would undertake the necessary reforms. Bruce sent a strongly worded letter to the prime minister stating that unless the French made a greater effort in creating financial stability and restoring confidence in the French franc, the success of Western European recovery would be jeopardized. Many prominent French politicians and officials supported the need for drastic reforms. They were relieved when the Queuille government introduced a promising program of stabilization for the following year. When Queuille outlined this program in his December 27, 1948, letter to Bruce and stated that the promised fiscal programs of stabilization were in place, he asked that 25 billion francs of counterpart funds be released in order to lower the ceilings of advances from the Bank of France. His request was quickly granted.[78]

The triumvirate had formed an alliance with some key officials in the finance ministry, especially Bloch-Lainé. Together they ensured that Marshall aid was used directly or indirectly to maintain basic investment in the Monnet Plan. In May 1949, when Bruce became the new ambassador to France, he appointed Tomlinson his deputy in charge of all economic matters at the embassy and his financial and trade adviser. The status of these three men had risen on both sides of the Atlantic. According to Hartman, "The deal struck between Monnet and Tomlinson was that the Americans would not give their approval to any proposal which Monnet didn't feel fitted in with his plans. . . . People in the French Treasury were aware of it, and also used it to make sure that the funds were not used in a way they did not approve of. . . . We would insist on those conditions and in effect force the politicians to accept them."[79]

Monnet won the battle with the French and US governments to secure counterpart funds to finance the basic six designated sectors of the Monnet Plan. Reflecting the financial conservatism of the businessmen and industrialists who administered the Marshall Aid Program in Europe, the ECA in Washington pressed for higher taxes, restraint on wages, and fiscal conservatism in France in order to prevent inflation, which they regarded as the source of French political instability. Therefore Washington denied aid for any action it deemed inflationary.[80] Bruce and Tomlinson helped Monnet convince Washington that investing funds in the Monnet Plan was not inflationary and were able to obtain much of what they wanted for France. Tomlinson's ability to manipulate Treasury and State Department officials aided this endeavor. He would send lengthy complicated telegrams detailing French requests and include so many items requiring responses that it took Washington a long time to reply. And by the time it did, decisions had already been made by the triumvirate. Tomlinson would fire back another lengthy epistle to the State Department with more questions and state that circumstances had changed. This meant the bureaucrats' replies with instructions or comments were always outdated, superseded, or ultimately irrelevant.[81] Cleveland asserted that Monnet knew

> he needed Tommy and the Americans as much as the American group needed him, in a sense, perhaps more. He knew he had to keep the Americans close and supportive. The only way he could do this was to make sure that he took account of their concerns. He knew that Tommy had the ability to be both imaginative in terms of the substance of the problem and at the same time to know how to package things for the U.S. government.
>
> And he knew how to manipulate the U.S. government because he had done it most effectively in connection with the Marshall Plan. Monnet had watched that process. So he knew he had in Tommy not only a collaborator in the intellectual sense but also somebody who had the confidence of Bruce and McCloy and one who was peculiarly able to manipulate the U.S. bureaucracy. . . . [Monnet] had a sense of where power lay, and he understood very well the realities of power as distinguished from the appearances of power. He knew how to use people, no question. . . . I count myself . . . proudly among them [people who allowed themselves to be used by Monnet].[82]

Sensitivity and resentment at dictates from Washington and Tomlinson's harsh demands often rankled French officials in ministry circles and at the Bank of France. But Monnet, with the help of Bloch-Lainé, persuaded the French ministers that their country should not lose this opportunity to use these funds to meet the goals of the Monnet Plan and hence should meet US demands. If the government failed to do so, the planners argued, France would remain economically backward.

As a result of continual negotiation during 1949–1950, with the help of Tomlinson and Bruce, Monnet achieved much of what they and many French officials wanted for France. They gained greater mission control over the funds; regularized quarterly releases of the funds as opposed to a project-by-project basis, which the Americans wanted to control; and secured ECA's commitment of most of the counterpart funds for the Monnet Plan. Because of Monnet's persuasion backed by US pressure, the French cabinet consented to allocate these funds to the industries designated under the plan. This success made a critical difference in its implementation.[83] While Marshall funds constituted only 20 percent of French investment from 1948 to 1952, "it was a crucial margin," argues François Duchêne. In 1949, Marshall aid comprised a large portion of the state funding for France's manufacture of investment goods, which was about one-quarter of the country's industrial output. The aid "loosened France's main external bottleneck, the inability to earn dollars." Duchêne asserts it also enabled the modernization of some of the large-capacity steel-rolling mills, and aided coal production, the electricity industry, and railway construction. He concludes, "Without Marshall aid, the French, starved of dollars, could probably not have carried their intentions through."[84] As Jean-Pierre Rioux asserts, "With industrial output rising and trade reviving, the closing of the 'dollar gap,' and the modernization of production, the economic benefits directly attributable to Marshal Aid were incontestable."[85]

Paying tribute to his American friends, Monnet wrote,

> In 1948, without the help of Bruce and Tomlinson, I should never have succeeded in persuading the U.S. Administration to allow hundreds of billions of francs' worth of counterpart funds to be used by the French Government; and I should have found it hard to persuade the latter to allocate them to the Plan. . . . [T]he certainty that so prolonged an effort could be financed without fail gave a sense of confidence to the whole French economy. . . . It was the necessary basis for national independence and preservation of democracy.[86]

Praising both Monnet and his US colleagues, Uri exclaimed, "They conducted a fantastic piece of diplomacy."[87]

The French planners also owed a debt of gratitude to another important American, George Ball. Monnet met this young lawyer when he was an associate general counsel of the Lend-Lease Administration in the early 1940s. At the end of 1945, Ball became a partner in the law firm of Cleary, Gottlieb,

Steen, and Hamilton as a specialist in international law and commercial relations, and Monnet retained his services for the French Supply Council. Once Monnet assembled his team of planners, he asked Ball to give them legal and political advice. Between 1945 and 1954, when Ball traveled to his firm's Brussels and Paris offices, he would often stop by to see Monnet and his colleagues and worked sporadically out of Monnet's small office at 18 rue de Martignac. Ball's political contacts in Washington and his extraordinary abilities as an attorney benefited Monnet's efforts to prudently frame France's request for credit and technical assistance. He drafted the specialized language required for commercial and legal documents that would inevitably be scrutinized by US legislators and bureaucrats. When Ball was in Washington, Monnet would often call him, making use of the new transatlantic cable, an instrument to which Monnet became addicted. The Frenchman did not hesitate to ring up Ball in the early hours of the morning or night and summon him to the next day's discussion. "Catch the night plane for Paris," he would plead. And Ball most often complied. When in France, Ball would often spend the night at the Monnets' home in Houjarray and be summoned to join his host on Monnet's routine early morning walks in the surrounding woods. In a very short time Ball became a de facto political agent of the Fourth Republic, an important part of Monnet's US lobby, which the Frenchman called his "well informed friends."[88]

During the years 1945–1961, these two men developed a close, constructive friendship and professional association and earned each other's unconditional respect. "Powerfully built, he exuded strength and level-headedness," wrote Monnet about Ball, and his "massive appearance" matched his "intellectual resources." Ball gave "excellent advice and I profited greatly from his talents as a lawyer, blending the most concrete practicality with the very broadest concern for the general interest."[89] Monnet recalled that this young American "helped me to clarify the problem we had to deal with. He had an intellectual mechanism which I think functions quickly without any prejudice . . . he viewed problems simply." Monnet described their friendship as "a creative relationship, an exchange, a collaboration, and if he learned from me I certainly did learn from him, a great deal."[90] Monnet found in Ball the ability, rare among Americans, to comprehend European mentalities. Historian David DiLeo writes that Monnet often complained that "strong Americans are too simple; they don't see things in their complexity." But he found Ball was "a spirit who weighs things," had real judgment, and was well-balanced and loyal.[91] As a friend, DiLeo said that Ball "helped Monnet think."[92]

For the young lawyer, "it was reciprocal and a mutually nourishing association." Ball discovered that Monnet's real interest in having him around was to be "a kind of intellectual punching bag, someone he could keep throwing ideas at" and debate the responses that followed. He added, "While Monnet profited by what I called our 'collective spiral cognition,' I learned much from helping a wise man shape ideas like a sculptor with a knife. My role was essential, for Monnet himself was no writer. . . . [H]e evolved letters, papers, plans, proposals, memoranda of all kinds by bouncing ideas against another individual."[93] Ball often expressed his deep admiration for and great debt to his French friend.

He soon adopted the fundamental assumption of Monnet that if French recovery was to be sustained, it had to occur within the context of general European reconstruction, which required the creation of a united Europe as a commercial and political entity. In a letter to Silvia and Jean in 1976 after his Thanksgiving visit with them, he wrote, "I was grateful, as always, for your sound advice and wisdom that informed your conversations. Although I have not always been an apt pupil, Jean has been a magnificent teacher, and I think I have learned more from you, Jean, than from anyone else."[94]

## Achievements and Shortcomings of the Plan

The Monnet Plan succeeded in changing the structure of the French economy and launching postwar recovery. From 1948 on, the economy overall grew 5 percent a year, and, by 1949 and early 1950, helped by favorable international economic conditions, it stabilized. The plan succeeded in rebuilding the country's infrastructure, eliminating obstacles to growth, distributing limited resources, and establishing the foundation for a more modern competitive economy. The planners' industrial strategy of selecting the six basic sectors for priority investment and setting limited goals proved successful, particularly in the nationalized enterprises like railroads. These industries, including energy, expanded and increased their level of production and capital formation and, by 1952, were benefiting from large investment programs, some reorganization, and modernization programs. Many segments of the French economy, including agriculture, experienced sustained growth in productivity by 1952. The plan reshaped the steel sector by providing money and an investment strategy, and crude steel production, which was 4.4 million tons in 1946, more than doubled by 1949. The planners' 1929 target of 10 million tons was reached in 1951, and the modernization goals, with many new installations, were met in 1953.[95]

Through the plan, Monnet and his colleagues propagated and nourished the idea that economic modernization was an important national goal for France and was intrinsically linked with French security. Most important, they planted the seeds of a consensus that held reconstruction and economic growth were top priorities for France and that all elements of society must work together to achieve these goals. The Monnet Plan encouraged this change in attitude by favoring an expansionary mentality among politicians, laborers, and businessmen, as historian Richard Kuisel contends, at a time when France could take advantage of the international postwar economic boom. That consensus grew and flourished in the postwar period.[96] The plan helped change the French image of their nation from a "moth-eaten great power" to one of a medium-sized but ambitious economy, argues Duchêne, and "fixed its slogan of 'modernization or decadence' in the French consciousness."[97] Marjolin stated, "It crystallized the urge that everyone felt to go forward to build."[98] For Hirsch, "the most important result of the plan was that it changed the French mentality and encouraged people to take risks and to invest."[99]

The plan aimed at reestablishing private enterprise and the market, argues Kuisel, and spurred a growth in productivity and competitiveness. It directly and indirectly aided private endeavors because the state permitted enterprises to do what they were capable of doing. It facilitated the exchange of information between public and private sectors to their mutual benefit and contributed to a rise in the standard of living. In the 1950s, Monnet's plan stimulated private investment in industry, facilitated collective decisionmaking and problem-solving, and promoted the creation of government institutions to perform statistical analysis and forecasting. It became "an agent of economic growth in France rather than a step towards socialism." The plan also facilitated the negotiations for US aid without which the French recovery would not have been so rapid or comprehensive.[100] Massé concluded, "Monnet played a very great role and the success of the plan was in large part due to his personality. We could not have succeeded without the Marshall Plan. It was one of the greatest historic acts of our time."[101]

The Monnet Plan nonetheless fell short of some of its ambitious goals. It wasted money, erred in forecasting demand in some sectors, and contributed to inflation. While investment under the plan approved in 1947 was predicted to be at a rate of 23 to 25 percent of GNP a year, it proved to be only 18 to 20 percent a year. The planners mistakenly assumed that investment capital was readily available, and as a result had to rely more than they had anticipated on loans, treasury advances, and the state. While production targets were almost met in electric power and railways, the sectors of coal, cement, and tractors fell short of their targets.[102] The coal industry, for which they had harbored unrealistic assumptions about demand and costs, did not fare as well as they hoped despite the planners' successful efforts at increasing investment in the coal mines. Moreover, coal production did not increase to the expected level in 1949. The French coal shortages in the 1940s, asserts historian John Gillingham, were due more to the failure of the British to export and the failure of the Allies to raise output in the Ruhr than to the plan's limits. But energy goals were basically achieved in part because oil became widely used.[103]

The Communists and labor proved difficult for Monnet as well as for the French government and Americans. While he had won the support of the labor movement and trade unions in 1946–1947, the Communists and labor abandoned him by 1948 because they became the most determined opponents of

the Marshall Plan and, by extension, of Monnet's plan. The Communists complained loudly about the "Marshallisation" of France.[104] In the context of the
Cold War, Marshall aid was viewed by these opponents as blatantly anti-Communist. Since many French and US supporters of the Monnet Plan did indeed
believe economic reconstruction was an effective way to curb communism in
the labor movement, this opposition to the Monnet Plan was troublesome.
Monnet never wanted to confront the labor unions directly, but they became
an obstacle in the coal miners' strikes in 1948 and attacked everyone who was
"working for the Americans."[105]

The creation of France's first plan and its implementation demonstrated to
leaders in France as well as the United States that Monnet possessed an
unusual combination of talents. It proved once again that he was a visionary
who pondered the future and understood what France had to do to restore itself
to a position of leadership in Europe. A creative thinker who designed a pragmatic strategy for France's economic woes, he showed he could be an
assertive leader who, with the help of his team, could implement his own plan
by using strategic tactics and constructive dealings with bureaucrats. He
demonstrated his innovative diplomatic and political skills throughout negotiations, especially in dealing with de Gaulle, securing US funds for the plan,
and using the US government to pressure France to reform fiscal policy. His
manipulative powers were evident in his relations with de Gaulle. He persuaded the general that for France to have a say in the world, it must modernize its economy. To do so, he argued, required US aid. But as US funds were
contingent upon France having a plan for postwar economic development, he
secured from de Gaulle a commitment to economic planning and made it
likely he would be named the planning commissioner. Along with his team, he
fought to establish investment as a priority in the French system. He succeeded
in persuading Bidault to make France the leading supporter of US policy,
which demanded economic cooperation among the nations receiving Marshall
dollars in return for the assurance of Marshall Plan aid and influence on US
policy toward Germany.

From 1947 to 1950, Monnet's team shaped overall economic policies and
provided some stability and continuity in an area that was absent in the political sphere. His pragmatism and apolitical style were central to his success.
His party preferences were not known as he was able to work with socialists
like Blum as well as conservatives like Mayer and Bidault. Without being ideological or doctrinaire, he was able to bring diverse groups, parties, and politicians together to support his efforts and to use US aid, despite the strong anti-
Americanism in France during this period. Moreover, he was willing to use
planning, nationalized and private enterprise, and the market to secure economic growth for France.[106] As French statesman François Bloch-Lainé
recalled,

> The genius of [Monnet] and his lieutenants was to avoid ideology at the polit-
> ical and theoretical levels and demarcation disputes at the bureaucratic one;
> then to produce good papers and have good conversations to present their
> view and convince people. . . . There was of course an obvious need. Nothing
> less could have brought aboard such a motley crew as the U.S. government,
> the Communists, the Third Force parties of the regime, the nationalists behind
> de Gaulle, and the Labor Unions. The fact remained that others besides Mon-
> net had tried and failed. It was he who gradually mobilized a political coali-
> tion on both sides of the Atlantic behind investment in France.[107]

Historian Irwin Wall points out that planning was not new in France, as
such ideas had proliferated among unions as well as resistance groups during
the war. But he argues that "Monnet's genius was to propose a politically
acceptable vehicle for reconstruction of a neo-liberal capitalism through the
use of the state. This enabled him to gain a political consensus around the plan
as that all could see in it what they wished."[108] Ernest May asserts, "This kind
of planning had been previously associated with totalitarian governments,
such as the Soviet Union, and it was very daring and original of Monnet to
propose that a capitalist state adopt the practice."[109]

Monnet's successful design and implementation of his plan owed a considerable debt to his US connections. Nathan and Ball were especially helpful
as advisers in designing the plan, and Tomlinson and Bruce were crucial in
securing funds for its implementation. The young diplomats who worked at
the Marshall Plan Aid Mission and the embassy, such as Hartman, Cleveland,
and Donald McGrew, were each captivated by this charismatic Frenchman and
worked hard to implement his goal of modernizing the French economy with
the help of US funds. Bruce and Tomlinson played critical roles in persuading
the US government to allow the counterpart funds to be allocated to the Monnet Plan and in pressuring the French government to implement the necessary
fiscal reforms to gain US aid. Without the help and influence of these important American friends and Marshall aid, Monnet's plan might not have revitalized the French economy as effectively or as fast as it did in the 1945 to 1950
period.

The US economic model also played a role in shaping the plan. Monnet
was quite taken with the competitive spirit of US capitalism and was one of its
champions. He really believed the Americans had found the way to prosperity
and power, and he was intent on selling it to his countrymen. In addition, he
was convinced that productivity and growth were solutions to France's economic, social, and political problems and that such measures would end an
economy of scarcity, quarrels over distribution, and economic weakness that
undermined his nation's capacity to act in the world.[110]

Monnet's creation and implementation of his plan clearly delineate his
method of operation. He purposefully worked outside the political party system

and had no political base. He made sure that he and his planning staff were responsible to the head of the government so they could bypass formal channels and parliament, skirt entanglement in the bureaucracies of the ministries, and not be hampered by the rapid changeover in the governments. He relied on his own personal powers of persuasion and developed relationships with key ministry leaders when he needed them, carefully avoiding the appearance of being a competitor. But despite his talents for working friendships and alliances, he would find in the future that, as an outsider, there were limits to his personal influence.[111]

His plan was not only one of Monnet's most important achievements and contributions to France but also a key initial stepping-stone in achieving his goal to integrate Europe and thereby establish peace. By placing his nation on the road to economic recovery, Monnet expanded the range of options open to future French leaders. The plan increased his influence and prominence in government circles as well as in European capitals. Without this new power and stature, he would not have been able to initiate, create, and gain support for his next constructive concept, which he hoped would be an important step toward achieving Franco-German reconciliation.[112]

## Notes

1. Richard Kuisel, *Capitalism and the State in Modern France* (Cambridge, UK: Cambridge University Press, 1981), pp. 187–202; Stephen Cohen, S. Halimi, and John Zysman, "Institutions, Politics, and Industrial Policy in France," in *The Politics of Industrial Policy,* ed. C. E. Barfield and W. W. Schambra (Washington, DC: American Enterprise Institute, 1986), pp. 107–112; interviews by the author with Pierre Massé, May 23, 1984; Pierre Uri, May 29, 1984; Etienne Hirsch, June 21, 1984; and Robert Marjolin, June 13, 1984.

2. Marjolin, interview.

3. François Duchêne, *Jean Monnet: The First Statesman of Interdependence* (New York: W. W. Norton, 1994), p. 145.

4. Gordon Wright, *France in Modern Times, 1760 to the Present* (Chicago: Rand McNally, 1966), pp. 527–531.

5. *FRUS*, 1945, vol. 4, pp. 707–711.

6. Jean Monnet, *Memoirs* (New York: Doubleday, 1978), p. 228.

7. Ibid.

8. Duchêne, *Jean Monnet*, p. 145; Kuisel, *Capitalism*, pp. 221–222.

9. Kuisel, *Capitalism*, p. 222.

10. Monnet, *Memoirs,* pp. 232–234.

11. *FRUS*, 1945, vol. 4, pp. 757–774; *FRUS*, 1946, vol. 5, pp. 399–400.

12. Clifford Hackett, *A Jean Monnet Chronology* (Washington, DC: Jean Monnet Council, 2008), p. 205.

13. Eric Roussel, *Jean Monnet* (Paris: Fayard, 1996), p. 454.

14. Robert Marjolin, *Architect of European Unity: Memoirs, 1911–1986* (London: Weidenfeld and Nicolson, 1989), pp. 160–161.

15. Duchêne, *Jean Monnet*, 148; Kuisel, *Capitalism*, pp. 222–223.

16. Kuisel, *Capitalism*, pp. 222–227; Hirsch, interview.

17. Massé, interview.

18. Kuisel, *Capitalism*, pp. 222–230.

19. *FRUS*, 1945, vol. 4, pp. 757–774; *FRUS*, 1946, vol. 5, pp. 399–400.

20. Monnet, *Memoirs*, pp. 242–243.

21. Paul Delouvrier, interview by Antoine Marès, June 3, 1981, Fondation Jean Monnet pour l'Europe Centre de recherches européennes, Lausanne, Switzerland.

22. Duchêne, *Jean Monnet*, pp. 153–154; Kuisel, *Capitalism*, p. 224.

23. Etienne Hirsch, "Témoignage de Etienne Hirsch," in *Témoignages à la mémoire de Jean Monnet* (Lausanne, Switzerland: Fondation Jean Monnet, 1989), p. 278.

24. Delouvrier, interview.

25. Marjolin, *Memoirs*, p. 164.

26. Stanley Hoffmann, "The Effects of World War II on French Society and Politics," *French Historical Studies* 2 (Spring 1961), pp. 30–31.

27. Philippe Mioche, "L'Invention du Plan Monnet," in *Modernisation ou décadence*, ed. Bernard Cazes and Philippe Mioche (Aix-en-Provence, France: Presses Universitaires de Provence, 1990), pp. 15–24.

28. Kuisel, *Capitalism*, p. 224; Richard F. Kuisel, "The Marshall Plan in Action: Politics, Labor, Industry, and the Program of Technical Assistance in France," in *Le Plan Marshall et le relèvement économique de l'Europe* (Paris: Comité pour l'histoire économique et financière, Ministère des Finances, 1993), pp. 336–337; John Gillingham, *Coal, Steel, and the Rebirth of Europe, 1945–1955* (Cambridge, UK: Cambridge University Press, 1991), pp. 137–138.

29. Uri, interview.

30. Ibid.; Kuisel, *Capitalism*, pp. 224–225; Sherrill Brown Wells, *French Industrial Policy: A History, 1945–1981* (Washington, DC: Department of State, 1991), pp. 12–22; Monnet, *Memoirs*, p. 240; Duchêne, *Jean Monnet*, pp. 157–160.

31. Uri, interview.

32. Kuisel, *Capitalism*, p. 225.

33. Duchêne, *Jean Monnet*, pp. 157–160, 164–165; Kuisel, *Capitalism*, p. 222; Irwin Wall, "Jean Monnet, the United States and the French Economic Plan," in *Jean Monnet: The Path to European Unity*, ed. Douglas Brinkley and Clifford Hackett (New York: St. Martin's Press, 1991), pp. 103–104.

34. Alan Milward, *The Reconstruction of Western Europe, 1945–51* (Berkeley: University of California Press, 1984), pp. 129–130; Frances Lynch, "The Political and Economic Reconstruction of France, 1944–1947, in Its International Context" (Ph.D. thesis, University of Manchester, 1981), p. 275; Desmond Dinan, *Europe Recast* (Boulder, CO: Lynne Rienner Publishers, 2004), p. 32.

35. Richard Kuisel, interview by the author, September 23, 2001; Duchêne, *Jean Monnet*, p. 164.

36. Monnet, *Memoirs*, pp. 351–352.

37. Kuisel, interview.

38. Gillingham, *Coal, Steel, and the Rebirth*, pp. 138–142.

39. Gérard Bossuat, *La France, l'aide américane and la construction européenne, 1944–1954*, vol. 1 (Paris: Comité pour l'histoire économique et financière de la France, 1992), p. 56.

40. Kuisel, *Capitalism*, pp. 230–231; Wells, *French Industrial Policy*, pp. 16, 22–23.

41. Kuisel, *Capitalism*, pp. 231–232; Wells, *French Industrial Policy*, pp. 22–23.

42. Irwin Wall, *The United States and the Making of Postwar France, 1945–1954* (Cambridge, UK: Cambridge University Press, 1991), pp. 49–62.

43. Wall, *United States*, pp. 49–55; Duchêne, *Jean Monnet*, pp. 158–60; Wall, "Jean Monnet," pp. 86–96; *FRUS*, 1946, vol. 5, pp. 46, 435–436, 459–464; Wells, *Industrial Policy*, p. 23; Kuisel, *Capitalism*, pp. 231–232.

44. Wall, "Jean Monnet," p. 96.

45. Wall, *United States*, p. 55.

46. Duchêne, *Jean Monnet*, p. 160; John Sheahan, *Promotion and Control of Industry in Postwar France* (Cambridge, MA: Harvard University Press, 1963), pp. 37–38; Geoffrey Denton et al., *Economic Planning and Policies in Britain, France, and Germany* (New York: Praeger, 1968), pp. 80–82.

47. Monnet, *Memoirs*, pp. 236, 239–240.

48. Massé, interview; Kuisel, *Capitalism*, pp. 222–227; Duchêne, *Jean Monnet*, pp. 157–160.

49. Robert Nathan, "Inflation and Fiscal Policy," August, 17, 1946, AMF 5/3/18. Also by Nathan, "Strategy of Presentation," August 13, 1946; "Broad Philosophy and General Objectives of the Plan," August 16, 1946; and other studies by him, Nathan Papers, Fondation Jean Monnet.

50. Duchêne, *Jean Monnet*, p. 166; Kuisel, *Capitalism*, pp. 228–230.

51. Hirsch, interview.

52. Duchêne, *Jean Monnet*, p. 154.

53. Ibid., pp. 150–155; Kuisel, *Capitalism*, pp. 237–239.

54. Uri, interview; Kuisel, *Capitalism*, pp. 237–238.

55. Kuisel, *Capitalism*, pp. 237–238; Duchêne, *Jean Monnet*, p. 166.

56. Pierre Pflimlin, "Jean Monnet que j'ai connu," in *Témoignages à la mémoire de Jean Monnet* (Lausanne, Switzerland: Fondation Jean Monnet, 1989), pp. 385–387.

57. Duchêne, *Jean Monnet*, pp. 170–171.

58. Uri, interview.

59. Duchêne, *Jean Monnet*, pp. 170–171.

60. Uri, interview.

61. Kuisel, *Capitalism*, pp. 239–240; Jean–Pierre Rioux, *The Fourth Republic, 1944–1958* (Cambridge, UK: Cambridge University Press, 1987), pp. 114–115.

62. John L. Gaddis, *We Now Know: Rethinking Cold War History* (Oxford, UK: Clarendon Press, 1997), pp. 1–53, 113–129; Charles S. Maier, "The Politics of Productivity: Foundations of American International Economic Policy After World War II," in *The Cold War in Europe: End of a Divided Continent*, 3rd ed., ed. Charles S. Maier (New York: Markus Wiener, 1996), pp. 169–201; Robert Pollard, *Economic Security and the Origins of the Cold War, 1945–1950* (New York: Columbia University Press, 1985), pp. 33–132.

63. John L. Gaddis, *The Cold War: A New History* (New York: Penguin Press, 2005), pp. 30–32.

64. *New York Times*, April 2, 1949, p. 4; *FRUS*, 1947, vol. 3, pp. 237–239; Bossuat, *La France, l' aide américaine*, pp. 141–148.

65. Michael Hogan, *The Marshall Plan: America, Britain, and the Reconstruction of Western Europe, 1947–1952* (Cambridge, UK: Cambridge University Press, 1987), pp. 18–134; Gérard Bossuat, *L'Europe occidentale à l'heure Américaine, 1945–52* (Paris: Editions Complexe, 1992); Gérard Bossuat, *L'Aide américaine et la construction européene, 1944–1954*, 2 vols. (Paris: Comité pour l'Histoire économique et financière de la France, 1992).

66. Mark Gilbert, *Surpassing Realism: The Politics of European Integration Since 1945* (Lanham, MD: Rowman and Littlefield Publishers, 2003), pp. 15–25.

67. Monnet to Georges Bidault, secret memorandum, July 24, 1947, *Un change-ment d'espérance: La Déclaration du 9 mai 1950, Jean Monnet–Robert Schuman* (Lausanne, Switzerland: Fondation Jean Monnet pour l'Europe, 2000), pp. 53–64; Gillingham, *Coal, Steel, and the Rebirth,* pp. 144–5; Monnet, "Projet de memoran-dum," 30 August 1947, AMF 14/1/3, Fondation Jean Monnet; *FRUS,* 1948, vol. 3, p. 401; Monnet, *Memoirs,* pp. 271–272.

68. Wall, *United States,* pp. 159–161; Kuisel, *Capitalism,* pp. 239–240.

69. Monnet to Bidault, letter, *Un changement,* April 18, 1948, pp. 65–67; Wall, *United States,* 165.

70. Donald McGrew, interview by the author, May 29, 1991.

71. Sherrill Brown Wells, "Monnet and 'The Insiders: Nathan, Tomlinson, Bowie, and Schaetzel,'" in *Monnet and the Americans,* ed. Clifford Hackett (Washington, DC: Jean Monnet Council, 1995), pp. 204–211; interviews by the author with Uri, Hirsch, and Duchêne, September 13, 2002.

72. Stanley Cleveland, interview by Leonard Tennyson, June 12, 1981, Fondation Jean Monnet.

73. Jacques Van Helmont, interview by Cliffort Hackett, February 11, 1990, Fon-dation Jean Monnet.

74. Arthur Hartman, interview by the author, October 15, 1990.

75. Stanley Cleveland, interview.

76. Hartman, interview; Wells, "Insiders," pp. 206–207.

77. Hartman, Cleveland, and Uri interviews; Wells, "Insiders," pp. 206–207; Kuisel, *Capitalism,* pp. 238–241; Duchêne, *Jean Monnet,* p. 172.

78. Wells, "Insiders," pp. 206–207; Wall, *United States,* pp. 158–172.

79. Hartman and McGrew, interviews; Wells, "Insiders," pp. 206–207.

80. Wall, *United States,* pp. 158–167.

81. McGrew, interview.

82. Cleveland, interview.

83. Hartman and McGrew, interviews; Kuisel, *Capitalism,* pp. 237–244; Wall, *United States,* pp. 237–242.

84. Duchêne, *Jean Monnet,* p. 173.

85. Rioux, *Fourth Republic,* p. 134.

86. Monnet, *Memoirs,* p. 270.

87. Uri, interview.

88. George W. Ball, interview by Leonard Tennyson, July 15, 1981, Fondation Jean Monnet; David DiLeo, "Catch the Night Plane for Paris: George Ball and Jean Monnet," in *Monnet and the Americans,* ed. Clifford Hackett (Washington, DC: Jean Monnet Council, 1995), pp. 141–146.

89. Monnet, *Memoirs,* p. 227.

90. DiLeo, "Catch the Night Plane," p. 146.

91. Ibid., p. 165.

92. Ibid., p. 146.

93. George W. Ball, *The Past Has Another Pattern: Memoirs* (New York: W. W. Norton, 1982), p. 73.

94. DiLeo, "Catch the Night Plane," pp. 145, 165; Letter from George Ball to Sil-via and Jean Monnet, December 14, 1976, Box I, 70, George Ball Papers, Princeton Library.

95. Christian Stoffaës, *Politique industrielle* (Paris: Les Cours de droit, 1984), p. 87; Sheahan, *Promotion and Control,* pp. 66–88; Kuisel, "The Marshall Plan," pp. 352–357; Gillingham, *Coal, Steel, and the Rebirth,* pp. 142–143.

96. Richard Kuisel, "La Planification," in *Modernisation ou décadence*, ed. Bernard Cazes and Philippe Mioche (Aix-en-Provence, France: Presses Universitaires de Provence, 1990), pp. 117–143.

97. Duchêne, *Jean Monnet*, 178.

98. Marjolin, interview.

99. Hirsch, interview.

100. Kuisel, "La Planification," pp. 118–130; Kuisel, *Capitalism,* pp. 246–247.

101. Massé, interview.

102. Kuisel, *Capitalism*, pp. 245–247; Duchêne, *Jean Monnet*, p. 177.

103. Gillingham, *Coal, Steel, and the Rebirth*, pp. 141–142.

104. Michel Margairaz, "La Mise en oeuvre du Plan Monnet (1947–1952)," in *Modernisation ou décadence*, ed. Bernard Cazes and Philippe Mioche, pp. 50–51.

105. Kuisel, interview.

106. Ibid.

107. Duchêne, *Jean Monnet*, p. 178.

108. Wall, "Jean Monnet," p. 88.

109. Ernest May to the author, letter, December 19, 2003.

110. Kuisel, interview.

111. François Duchêne, "Jean Monnet's Methods," in *Jean Monnet: The Path to European Unity*, ed. Douglas Brinkley and Clifford Hackett (New York: St. Martin's Press, 1991), pp. 184–209.

112. Duchêne, *Jean Monnet*, pp. 178–180.

# 5

# Creation of the Coal and Steel
# Community, 1950–1952

The Schuman Plan, which created the European Coal and Steel Community (ECSC), stands as Jean Monnet's most significant contribution to European peace and integration. It stemmed from the critical nature of Franco-German relations in 1949 and early 1950 as tension between the Western powers and the Soviet Union gradually increased. In April 1947, the negotiations between the tripartite powers (Britain, France, and the United States) and Moscow concerning the Allied occupation of Germany had broken down. A Communist coup in February 1948 ousted the government in Prague, and the Soviet Union blockaded Berlin that following summer. Moreover, the revelation of the first Soviet atomic bomb test in September 1949 and repeated threats from the Kremlin compounded its strained relations with the West. The intensification of the Cold War strengthened Washington's belief that West Germany's economic potential had to be at the disposal of the West. As a result, the status of Germany became a major stake in East-West rivalry. From the Marshall Plan onward, the United States came to view the economic recovery and rearmament of West Germany as vital for European as well as world power balance. The challenge for US policymakers was how to revive West Germany without alienating France because a revitalized Germany fueled French security concerns. For Dean Acheson, who became secretary of state in January 1949, the restoration of political and economic stability to Europe was his top foreign policy priority. Accordingly, in September 1949, he put pressure on Robert Schuman, the French foreign minister in ten successive governments from July 1948 to December 1952, to develop a policy that would reintegrate Germany into the Western concert.[1]

Difficult issues remaining from three wars fought between France and Germany confronted Schuman and the new West German Chancellor Konrad

Adenauer, leader of the Christian Democratic Union Party, who took office in September 1949. These leaders were acutely aware of the two central problems in Franco-German relations after World War II: security and the status of the coal-rich Saar region. As a patriotic native of the Rhineland, Adenauer adamantly opposed France's economic annexation of that region, which was administered by France after the war. The French hoped to establish a virtual protectorate over the Saar, with extensive rights over the railways, and to anchor the special status of that region in international law. On his first official trip to Bonn in January 1950, Schuman demanded that West Germany cede France a fifty-year lease over the disputed territory in return for future concessions. But Adenauer refused and abruptly ended the discussions. He knew the Saar issue was "political dynamite" for his people, who demanded the region's return to Germany. Fearing the issue might destroy the domestic political basis of his entire policy toward the West, his tactics were to gain time and prevent a final, unfavorable settlement.[2] For Schuman, his visit dramatized the need for a change in French postwar policy toward its former enemy. French policy at the time depended upon West Germany remaining weak as well as on US support, a combination that fueled Franco-German animosity.[3]

## Monnet's Conceptual Breakthrough

Because Monnet realized that France's economic recovery and its security required a new approach, he developed a novel strategy toward a revitalized West Germany. With growing anxiety in 1949, he recalled that French policy toward their former enemy was "beginning to slip back into its old ways." He observed, "in varying degrees all shades of public opinion, all public authorities, and all private interests in France were supporting our diplomatic rearguard action against Germany's inevitable rehabilitation."[4] Monnet was also deeply worried about West Germany becoming the centerpiece in the Cold War. He understood that its rapidly growing industrial might was a potential rival to his country and that France's steel production depended on German coking coal. Above all, he feared the possibility of a renewed arms race and the specter of war. "In the confused state of Franco-German relations, the neurosis of the vanquished seemed to be shifting to the victor," he wrote.

> France was beginning to feel inferior again as she realized that attempts to limit West Germany's dynamism were bound to fail. . . . If only the French could lose their fear of German industrial domination, then the greatest obstacle to a united Europe would be removed. A solution which would put French industry on the same footing as German industry, while freeing the latter from the discrimination born of defeat—that would restore the economic and political preconditions for the natural understanding so vital to Europe as a whole.

Only then, Monnet reasoned, would the vital economic and political foundations be laid for an understanding, which might be a springboard for European
unity. Monnet underlined, "Coal and steel were at once the key to economic
power and the raw materials for forging weapons of war. . . . To pool them
across frontiers would reduce their malign prestige and turn them instead into
a guarantee of peace."[5]

Monnet developed his idea in March 1950 while on a meditative walking
holiday in the Alps. Once back in Paris, he produced with his closest French
colleagues nine drafts of his proposal: that France and Germany enter into
negotiations to "pool" or "fuse" their coal and steel resources and markets in
order to create a common market in coal and steel. Monnet sent a copy of this
plan on April 20 to Prime Minister Georges Bidault. After getting no response,
he arranged to have it delivered personally to Schuman by the foreign minister's chef de cabinet, Bernard Clappier, on April 28. Schuman read it that
weekend at his home in Lorraine.[6]

Monnet's close relationship with his American friend, John McCloy,
proved especially useful in gaining US and French support for his plan. In the
last six months of 1949, Monnet had discussed his ideas and concerns with this
prominent Wall Street Republican lawyer. A former secretary of war and head
of the World Bank, McCloy had been appointed US high commissioner in
West Germany in the spring of 1950 by President Truman. Arriving in Bonn
in July of that year, he replaced General Lucius Clay, head of the US military
government, which managed the US zone of occupied West Germany. The
Allied High Commission, created by a joint Allied decision at the Washington
Conference of April 1949, demonstrated the West's decision to move away
from a four-power approach to the German question because of the Soviets'
hostile actions. The Commission, composed of civilian representatives of
Britain, France, and the United States, was designed to police the democratic
development of the new German government. These three nations agreed on a
short Occupation Statute, which retained for the Allies extensive and final
authority over many broadly defined areas, including foreign affairs, demilitarization, controls on the Ruhr, reparations, decartelization (reduction or elimination of German cartels), deconcentration (reduction of the size and number
of the coal and steel firms), foreign trade and exchange, war criminals, and
other key issues facing postwar Germans. The Occupation Statute was part of
a larger bargain, which included the North Atlantic Treaty signed in April 1949
(which created NATO),[7] to give the French security against Germany. The
British and Americans also agreed to the French demands for a Military Security Board to be created in the future to supervise German demilitarization and
for an international authority for the Ruhr to guarantee France had adequate
supplies of Ruhr coal for its steel industry. In return, the French finally agreed
to the establishment of the West German state, a reduction in their demands
concerning the dismantling of German industries, and majority voting within

the Allied High Commission. McCloy was a strong proponent of European solutions to the postwar problems and had come to believe that the integration of Western European economies might be part of the answer. During his first year, as high commissioner he strongly promoted the rehabilitation of Germany through its integration into Western Europe.[8]

Monnet used US support to gain Schuman's approval of the plan for a common coal and steel market. From McCloy, Monnet had earlier learned that the Americans might support a proposal to achieve France's objective of internationalizing the industrial Ruhr Valley if it were accompanied by a clear promise of greater efforts toward European unity. McCloy had urged Secretary of State Acheson to let the French know how vital a European federation was to US policymakers and that the principal barrier was the French attitude toward Germany. McCloy also made it clear that, if necessary, the Americans would proceed with Germany's rehabilitation without France. In his message to Schuman, therefore, Monnet used McCloy's two arguments—support for a concrete step toward European unity and the US determination to revive West Germany—to persuade Schuman to adopt his plan. Monnet stressed that his plan served and benefited France's national interest. The West Germans were demanding an increase in their steel quota, which he argued the French "would refuse, but Americans will insist . . . [and] we shall give in."[9] Monnet also knew that Acheson had conveyed to Schuman in a secret message that the United States was prepared to allow a freely elected West German government to decide the question of ownership of its heavy industry.[10]

Monnet's persuasion worked because Schuman understood this bold initiative had enormous diplomatic value and that France would benefit if it exploited the crisis in this way.[11] Therefore Schuman adopted Monnet's plan, took charge of it, and conducted the whole operation with secrecy, discretion, and speed. As a result, he successfully bypassed much of the possible official and industrial opposition. He quickly secured the consent of Bidault, side-stepped officials of the Quai d'Orsay and the industries involved, avoided consulting parliament, and ignored the British. He obtained Acheson's approval on May 7, despite the secretary of state's negative initial reaction to Monnet's scheme. Acheson had declared it sounded like "the damnedest cartel I have ever heard in my life."[12] After receiving Adenauer's backing, Schuman won cabinet approval the morning of May 9. After being briefed by Monnet, Ministers René Pleven, René Mayer, and Antoine Pinay voted to support it. Schuman announced this bold plan to the public at a crowded press conference at the Quai d'Orsay late that afternoon. It was timed to preempt the May 10 opening of the tripartite foreign ministers' conference in London where the Americans planned to demand an accelerated phase-out of Allied occupation of Germany.[13]

Schuman announced France was willing to sacrifice national sovereignty for the benefit of Europe and asked its neighbors to join his nation in an

*Robert Schuman announced the Schuman Plan in the Salon de l'Horloge, Quai d'Orsay, Paris, May 9, 1950. Schuman is at the microphone with Jean Monnet (seated, left), among others, in attendance.*

unprecedented undertaking to prevent war. Following Monnet's plan, the foreign minister proposed that France and Germany enter into negotiations to create a common market of their coal and steel resources. This pool would be directed by a supranational institution, a single "high authority" composed of independent individuals and appointed by the participating governments, that would regulate these sectors by executive decisions. An idea that had circulated among political circles in Europe prior to World War II, supranationalism refers to a process by which national governments share sovereignty with transnational institutions whose laws and policies are binding on those governments.[14] Unencumbered by customs duties, the proposed common market for these two major products would favor modernization and eliminate unprofitable and inefficient producers, Schuman stated. He invited any democratic European country to join this effort, provided it was willing to accept these principles and to sacrifice national sovereignty for the common good. It was, Schuman declared, an opportunity to discard old rivalries and begin negotiations in the spirit of equality. He proclaimed that the ensuing solidarity would make any war between France and West Germany "not merely unthinkable but materially impossible." Using Monnet's phrases, Schuman stated it would be a first step toward the federation of Europe. It would result, he argued, in the "fusion of interests which is indispensable to the establishment of a common economic system." This in turn would be "the leaven from which may grow a wider and deeper community between countries long opposed to one another."[15]

Schuman seized Monnet's audacious idea because he viewed it as an opportunity to advance his personal goal of promoting reconciliation between France and Germany in a manner that served his nation's national interest. A devout Roman Catholic, distinguished jurist, and passionate advocate of democracy, this tall, gray-haired Frenchman with a distinctive nose was raised by his French parents in the German-occupied province of Lorraine. Educated under the German system, Schuman served in the German army during World War I. As a French parliamentarian in the 1920s and 1930s, he had specialized in German problems raised by the return of the Alsace-Lorraine region to France at Versailles in 1919. He believed moral rehabilitation was required to help Germany become genuinely democratic. Convinced the Germanophobia of the Third Republic was anachronistic, he believed that France must be ready to cooperate on an equal footing with its traditional enemy. He thought Monnet's plan tackled the essence of the political problem they faced: the need to remove the bitterness from relations between France and West Germany in order to guarantee peace and create a climate of cooperation in Europe.

Moreover, he had felt Acheson's pressure intensely. As Clappier recalled, Schuman had consulted many individuals in his search for a solution after his September 1949 meeting with Acheson. He knew France had to take the lead and West Germany had to be trusted and treated as an equal. He also believed foundations had to be laid for common interests to link West Germany to France. He was persuaded by Monnet's reasoning and agreed that this plan to pool their coal and steel resources clearly served French long-term national interest. He also understood it might provide the necessary framework for the integration of Germany into the West. On the economic side, the foreign minister also agreed with Monnet that France's economic recovery could not continue unless the problem of West German industrial output and its competitive capacity were settled.[16]

In the spring of 1950, political and international factors also stimulated Schuman to reexamine French policy. On the domestic side, the socialists had left the government in February. Social tension was high, and a crisis of steel overproduction loomed large as European producers stubbornly adhered to cartel practices. On an international level, he personally felt the pressure from Acheson not only to reintegrate Germany into Europe but to show that Europe was willing to take collective steps to overcome some of its problems. The US policy of containment of the Soviet Union dictated that the new West German state be integrated within Western Europe so it could no longer be a pawn between East and West. The foreign ministers of the Western occupying powers—Acheson, British Foreign Secretary Ernest Bevin, and Schuman—had begun to meet every few months after NATO was created in 1949. In addition, there was hope in some circles that a demonstration of European unity

and dynamism might ease international tension. While many French politicians were initially shocked by the reversal of their government's policy,
French opinion began to swing in favor of an economic accord with West Germany because the public understood that such economic ties served French
national interests. Schuman's surprise tactics helped ensure that the plan could
not be defeated before it had taken hold.[17]

## Adenauer's Positive Response

Konrad Adenauer responded enthusiastically to Schuman's proposal. This
prominent, spirited Catholic politician and former mayor of Cologne had suffered arrests by the Nazis and had courageously escaped from imprisonment.
Resolutely anti-Communist, he rejected a nationalistic foreign policy and had a
genuine personal yearning for Franco-German reconciliation. He was aware of
the deep French distrust of Germany and believed that the only way his nation
could regain some respectability in the international community was through
reconciliation and cooperation with France. Believing progress would result
from concrete steps and that the Franco-German core was essential for Europe
to evolve, he realized that only by integrating closely with neighboring European countries could West Germany hope to remove the remaining controls by
the Western powers on its domestic and foreign policy. In early 1950, Adenauer
signaled his receptiveness to a proposal for integration by floating the idea of
an organization based on international cooperation in areas of coal and steel.[18]

    In his May 7 letter to the chancellor, Schuman had written he was about
to propose that his government take an important decision for "the future of
Franco-German relations, of Europe, and of peace" and would be asking Adenauer's government "to accept and publish" a declaration. Repeating Monnet's
words, Schuman explained the "spirit in which I have written this declaration." He wrote,

> World peace cannot be guaranteed without creative efforts proportional to the
> dangers that threaten it. The contribution which an organized and living
> Europe can make to civilization is indispensable for the maintenance of
> peaceful relations. Europe will not develop at a stroke or as a common con-
> struction. It will develop when concrete achievements create a first tangible
> solidarity. The gathering together of the European nations demands first of
> all the elimination of the centuries-old opposition between France and Ger-
> many. . . . You yourself have emphasized . . . your full agreement with such
> an intention . . . [and] have proposed the establishment of an economic union
> between our two countries.

Schuman stressed that since the French government viewed the time as ripe to
adopt such a course, it wished to take the initiative in a limited but vital area

of coal and steel production. He emphasized that the ownership of businesses involved would not be affected and that the responsibilities of the International Ruhr Authority, established in April 1949, would have to be taken into account "in so far as these will continue to exist." Schuman expressed his confidence that the French Council of Ministers would be receptive to the call for "peaceful cooperation" and establishment of the "foundations of a European economic organism."[19]

Adenauer responded positively to Schuman's proposal in a personal letter the next day because it reflected his own thinking. The chancellor was convinced that this initiative could create an entirely new situation in Europe and believed there needed to be an alternative to the nation-state. As a statesman with a keen sense of history, he believed West Germans had to reorient their thinking. This proposal could also create the support Adenauer needed to gain his country's acceptance in the Council of Europe, the first political postwar organization founded to unify the continent. He expressed his pleasure that the plan gave Franco-German relations, "which threatened to be paralyzed by mistrust and reserve, a fresh impetus towards constructive cooperation" and used the term "equality," which Schuman had not employed. He believed West German public opinion would respond positively because, for the first time since the catastrophe of 1945, West Germany and France would be working with equal rights on a common task.

The West German chancellor's official response demonstrated he was innately cautious. He wrote he welcomed ideas proposed by the French "as a vital step towards a close association" between their two countries and "thus to a new order in Europe built on the basis of peaceful cooperation." His government would give thorough consideration to the French plan as soon as its details were known. However, he said he could "declare West Germany's readiness to take part in the scrutiny of the plan and in preparing the organizational measures that will be needed in the future." The letters were hand carried to Schuman in Paris on May 8. Two hours after Schuman's 6 p.m. announcement on May 9, Adenauer held a press conference in Bonn to relay the news of his cabinet's decision to join the Council of Europe and praised Schuman's plan as being of the "greatest conceivable significance." He stated, "I have had this goal in mind for more than twenty-five years."[20]

While the idea of pooling the coal and steel resources of France and Germany had been discussed for years in political and intellectual circles, Monnet had creatively crafted it into a pragmatic plan in 1950 that dramatically departed from France's conventional policy. Although he had pondered a somewhat similar scheme in 1943, he refined it at this time to solve a looming crisis. Furthermore, he believed the circumstances were right. His plan was based on the principle of equality of the participants before laws jointly made, as he had insisted on equal competitive conditions. Monnet was shrewd in not asking for French quotas or guarantees in the Ruhr. The plan focused on specific, concrete goals in two sectors, not the whole economy, and hence was deemed manageable and achievable. It moved beyond the recent history of Franco-German relations by taking a bold step toward reconciliation with West Germany. This new departure by Monnet and Schuman was attractive to their neighbors because it signaled that the French government was serious about finding a way to reduce Franco-German tensions and offered modest integration through the economy.[21]

Most European countries received the news of the Schuman Plan quite favorably, while Great Britain and the Soviet Union immediately condemned it. Monnet worked hard to get the British to join because he felt their membership was essential. But they refused to be a part of any supranational body within Europe and had no interest in reordering their policies toward Germany. British officials assumed that too close an involvement in the process of European integration would jeopardize London's strong political and economic orientation toward its declining empire and emerging commonwealth. And since Bevin resented not being consulted by France prior to Schuman's announcement, his government did not carefully assess the plan. So Monnet pressed forward without the support that he wanted from the United Kingdom.

While the Schuman proposal was popular with the French public, it made some politicians nervous. Charles de Gaulle denounced it because of its supranational character, while the socialists gave it some support and Schuman's party wholeheartedly endorsed it. But the Communists and the trade union federation, Confédération Générale du Travail, regarded it as an anti-Soviet initiative. Stiff opposition came from the iron and steel producers because they had hoped to organize their own cartels. But the backing of the nationalized industries that consumed steel allowed Schuman to overcome this opposition.[22]

## US Support for Schuman Plan

Despite some opposition at the Treasury and Justice departments and skepticism in other circles, the Truman administration and the US press on the whole enthusiastically supported the Schuman Plan. To the top State Department officials, this scheme appeared to be an important mechanism for the integration of Germany into Western Europe. It served as a way to remove a main obstacle to German reconstruction, which was deemed necessary for Atlantic security and a step toward greater European unity, which the Americans had advocated since the end of the war. John Foster Dulles, then a US senator from New York, telegrammed "congratulations" to his close French friend on May 10 and wrote a letter to him on May 23 applauding the initiative. He wrote Monnet that "the political implications seem to me even more important than the economic." He noted a "genuine union of interest between Germany and France is an enormous insurance for a peaceful future. The proposal brings a new spirit into a western world which has so far not been able to imagine any-

thing better than going down the rather dreary road which in the past has usually led to war."[23] Averell Harriman, the US special representative in Europe,
described it as "the most important step toward economic progress and peace
since the original speech on European recovery."[24]

McCloy, who had come to Paris to discuss the proposal with Monnet,
reported enthusiastically to Acheson that the plan would work to increase production in both France and West Germany. Although Acheson had been dubi-
ous about the plan at first, he realized—once he learned more about it—that
Monnet's inspired scheme might be the solution to ending Germany's "pariah
status." In a cable to the president, the secretary stated he believed it important
that the French be given credit "for making a conscious and far-reaching effort
to advance Franco-German rapprochement and European integration generally."[25] Delighted by "Monnet's cunning and Schuman's nerve," Acheson
wrote, the genius of the Schuman-Monnet plan "lay in its practical, common
sense approach, its avoidance of limitations upon sovereignty and touchy
political problems. What could be more earthy than coal and steel, or more
desirable than pooling a common direction of France and Germany's coal and
steel industries?"[26]

The combined efforts of Schuman and Monnet succeeded in turning
Acheson into a believer in a united Europe. Originally, he was convinced
Europe had to set its own pace, without pressure from Washington, and
frowned on pan-Europeanists like Senator J. William Fulbright who echoed
Winston Churchill's call for a United States of Europe. Although the secretary
of state had grown to admire Schuman's postwar tenacity and developed a productive rapport with him, he never had the warm personal relationship with the
foreign minister that he had with Monnet. "Acheson saw Monnet as a citizen
of Europe, a man who thought in terms of what is best for Europe," writes historian Douglas Brinkley. He saw "Schuman as a Frenchman first and a European second." And while Acheson believed European unity would never
become a reality unless the French did something about their constitutional
system, "he was won over to the European integration movement partly,"
argues Brinkley, "because of his admiration for French ingenuity as exemplified by Jean Monnet and Robert Schuman." Although Acheson harbored some
ambivalence and believed France represented the inherent deep-seated weakness in the whole Western Alliance, he told a Princeton audience in 1953 that
"at the same time there is the greatest inventiveness and ingenuity coming out
of France" and that the Schuman Plan "was a brilliant idea."[27]

## Monnet's Visit to Adenauer

Schuman wisely appointed Monnet to lead the negotiations of the six participating nations: France, Germany, Italy, Belgium, the Netherlands, and Luxem-

bourg. Their representatives were assigned to prepare a detailed governing structure for this new economic community that would be embodied in a treaty. Leaving Monnet free to choose the French team, Schuman assumed responsibility for the difficult maneuvers over the Saar, carried the policy inside the government, and stood firm against the opposition of many of the steelmakers. The French government needed the consent of the Allied High Commission, headed by McCloy, for Germany's participation in the Schuman Plan talks on an equal footing with France. Once McCloy approved, Monnet, accompanied by Clappier, traveled to Bonn on May 23, 1950, to talk with Adenauer.

Before their meeting, Adenauer had reason to be uncertain and somewhat skeptical about whether this Frenchman could be trusted. Monnet was "a powerful and potentially dangerous" exponent of French self-interest, asserts historian Hans-Peter Schwarz, and his career embodied the cooperation of the Western democracies against Germany in two world wars. To persuade Bidault's cabinet to accept the plan, Monnet had warned in strong language that France would soon be exposed to the competition of German industry and that the Schuman Plan was designed to counter a "threatening German industrial preponderance." Monnet had stated the French desire was to "obtain a larger market area through the fusion of markets," which, in the short term, was bound to lead to a reduction in German coal and steel prices. Since this would inevitably result in adjustment difficulties for the German coal and steel industry, it appeared to Adenauer that Monnet aimed at control of Germany through a "modern concept designed to lead to a partnership and in the longer term to a European federation."[28]

Adenauer's fears diminished during the first two-hour meeting with Monnet as it produced remarkable results. After describing the project in convincing terms, Monnet made it clear he not only headed the negotiations but would also decide both the rules and identity of the players. While the United States, the high commissioners, and the Benelux nations (Belgium, the Netherlands, and Luxembourg) favored the project, he said the British were hesitating but might join later. He repeated his vision: the organization of heavy industry and the elimination of Franco-German enmity in order to achieve peaceful cooperation and the renewal of Europe's major role in the world. Monnet sensed Adenauer's concerns. He later wrote, "That was not a confident man but one who was curious about what I had to say and who found it difficult to free himself of a certain mistrust. Apparently he could not believe that we were really offering him equal rights, and the years of difficult negotiations and wounded pride still marked his attitude."

But after their discussion, Adenauer endorsed Monnet's essential requirements. These included granting the independent High Authority powers to make decisions that were binding for all participants. In addition, he agreed with Monnet that the delegates to the negotiations had to work on equal terms to create the framework for the political institutions needed to establish what would be called a coal and steel community. Adenauer understood that the final agreement would be embodied in a general treaty signed by the participating nations. Noting that the technical and economic issues would be ironed out at a later date by the "technicians," Monnet stressed the political nature of the enterprise and "that specific problems could be solved as long as they were approached with the great idea in mind."[29]

Adenauer also learned that the Frenchman was sincere about the Germans being treated as equals in the negotiations. In their discussions, the two men discovered they shared the same goals for Europe and each believed they had a "moral duty" to their people. They discovered they had similar approaches to solving problems: "first the big idea and then a complex negotiating process," which required tactical skills. While Adenauer understood that the West Germans would be forced to accept Monnet's decisions on major economic issues of production, quotas, prices, and markets, Adenauer viewed the Franco-German plan in a similar way. They both believed it to be primarily of a moral nature with technical details playing a secondary role. Adenauer had no real objections to experimenting with a coal and steel community. Like Monnet, he was convinced that European solutions would suit German interests. The chancellor also agreed to exclude occupation issues from the impending negotiations.[30] He was eager, writes Schwarz, "to confirm that the German federal government had no desire to achieve a new German supremacy" and, therefore, "these two experienced practitioners took their first steps towards the great venture of European reconciliation."[31]

As they parted, Adenauer assured Monnet he regarded "the French proposal as the most important task before me." He added, "Should I succeed in handling it well, I believe, I will not have lived in vain."[32] A few days later, Adenauer acknowledged that the Frenchman was "very clever, very well-meaning, very well-informed, calm, free of vanity." He believed Monnet genuinely wanted to bring about a political understanding between their two peoples. In a remark sometime later, Adenauer described Monnet as "a man endowed with a very great talent for economic organization, a real man of peace, and a charming negotiator. I continued to enjoy his friendship in later years."[33] Monnet had also been impressed with the West German leader and declared after that meeting, "We were friends for life."[34] The mutual respect and friendship that began at this first meeting proved invaluable to both countries in the subsequent years.

As a sign of their growing mutual trust and respect, Adenauer took the unusual step of discussing with Monnet the selection of the individual to head the West German delegation. After the Frenchman declined to approve some of his initial suggestions, the chancellor chose Walter Hallstein. A distinguished law professor from the University of Frankfurt, this German had also taught at Georgetown University and understood the US federal system and its antitrust laws. Monnet knew his expertise would be useful during the negotiations. Hallstein soon became a friend and confidant of Monnet, who described the German as "a man of action as well as a scholar" and someone who had a political vision. Monnet noted they "trusted each other from the first. . . . and it was great good fortune that he [Adenauer] placed his trust in Hallstein who was as eager as we were to push ahead and transform the situation by means of the Schuman Plan." Monnet added, "Agreement between France and Germany was a political necessity; but in this case necessity was greatly aided by the choice of men."[35]

## Beginning the Negotiations

Negotiations to create a single, community-wide area for the competitive sale of coal and steel products began on June 20, 1950, between France and the five other nations. All six nations accepted supranationality as their governing principle. Working closely with Schuman, who provided overall direction to their delegation, Monnet dominated the negotiations by organizing the conference, setting the agenda, and chairing the sessions. Deliberately excluding representatives of French ministries and producers from the talks, Monnet appointed members of his planning staff, including Etienne Hirsch and Pierre Uri, to the French delegation. In his able negotiating team he also included Clappier; Hervé Alphand; Paul Reuter, a legal adviser to the Foreign Ministry; and Maurice Lagrange, an eminent French jurist and member of the Conseil d'Etat, who played a key role in designing the institutions for the new community. Monnet divided the negotiations into three working groups: (1) lower-level officials who met frequently and hammered out details; (2) heads of delegations from foreign ministries meeting in restricted sessions; and (3) foreign ministers who were occasionally convened to solve difficult problems. The French delegation provided the delegates with a draft working document and position papers for the pooling of coal and steel, which served as the basis for negotiations. These papers reflected the US New Deal model because the new institutions the French negotiators planned to create reflected a strong executive authority and were, in their minds, to be agents of political reform.[36]

## US Pressure to Rearm Germany

The outbreak of the Korean War on June 25, 1950, just five days after the Schuman negotiations began, posed difficult and unexpected challenges for both American and European leaders. The invasion by Communist North Korea across the thirty-eighth parallel into the Republic of Korea in the south was widely assumed to be inspired by Moscow. Since US troops stationed in Korea immediately fought back after they were attacked, President Truman issued a declaration of war the next day. The Korean invasion heightened US and Western European leaders' concerns about increased Soviet military power and intentions, and they feared Stalin might be contemplating a possible attack in Europe. On July 14, Acheson reported to the cabinet that anxiety was sweeping across Europe and the situation was "one of gravest danger." He said the war in Korea indicated to the world that US forces could not both fight in Korea and counter the threat in Europe. "The feeling in Europe is changing," he said, "from one of elation that the United States has come into the Korean crisis to petrified fright."[37]

Acheson and European leaders knew Europe's defenses were clearly inadequate for any serious challenge from Soviet forces. Therefore, after extensive internal discussions as well as with the British and French, the Truman administration agreed on a plan to improve European defense. It stipulated that the United States would send four additional combat divisions to Europe, that a unified command structure for the NATO alliance would be created with an American Supreme Allied Commander Europe (SACEUR), and that an integrated NATO defense force would be established, which included German units. As a result, Washington asked the French to support West German rearmament to bolster the common defense of Europe against the Soviet armies.[38] But plans to rearm their former enemy greatly alarmed the French and forced officials in Paris to resist German rearmament at the same time they were negotiating over the Schuman Plan.[39] Moreover, Washington's readiness to commit significant additional forces to Europe failed to calm French fears. After France blocked the US request to integrate West German forces into NATO, the Federal Republic's defense contribution became a key issue of debate within the Western Alliance and in West German and French domestic politics.[40]

Adenauer had raised the question of his nation's defense role even before the North Korean invasion. He had feared not only an attack from the rapidly expanding "people's police"—Volkspolizei—in the Soviet-occupied Eastern Zone of Germany but also the possibility of major Soviet aggression. The Allied high commissioners had accepted the chancellor's proposal made in early June 1950 that German defense units should be established. In early August 1950, Adenauer sent his chief of staff to Paris to brief Monnet about his fears. Since Monnet had not understood until then the serious possibility and danger of such an invasion, he briefed his friend and now Prime Minister René Pleven, who agreed to urge the US and British governments to reinforce troops along the Elbe River, which formed part of the border between East and West Germany.[41]

## Proposing a European Army

George Ball records that Monnet realized the implication of the North Korean attack for France and the Schuman Plan negotiations "almost faster than

Washington." Monnet told him that "for Americans to intervene in Korea would not only jeopardize the Schuman Plan; it might well create panic in Europe and increase American insistence on a larger German role in the defense of the West."[42] As historian Jean-Pierre Rioux points out, "the dilemma faced by France was acute." Should it "bow to American pressure and abandon the hopes of the Liberation by accepting a German defense of Europe" or resist "and risk provoking a crisis within NATO" when the best French forces were in Indochina and when a generalized conflict in Europe "seemed imminent"?[43] Monnet believed France's refusal to accept the US proposal to put German troops under NATO threatened the delicate balance between France and Germany necessary for the Schuman negotiations to succeed.[44] He also feared the Germans, if rearmed, might try to provoke the Americans to undertake another war to recover the territory they lost in Eastern Europe. In a forceful letter to Pleven on September 3, 1950, Monnet urged the French government "to take the lead in providing what is needed, a universal political vision inspired by the same principle that informed the Schuman Plan: transform the existing state of affairs."[45]

Monnet realized the strong French opposition to the American demand for German rearmament disturbed US officials, especially McCloy. Since US support was needed for the Schuman Plan negotiations, Monnet devised a plan to solve this crisis. He and his team outlined a French proposal on rearmament that would deflect US pressure for a rearmed Germany and defuse the issue for French leaders.

Monnet took the idea of a European army, initially proposed by his American friends McCloy and Robert Bowie, and expanded it. A brilliant Harvard law professor whom McCloy recruited to serve as his general counsel, Bowie was an expert in antitrust law and was the high commissioners' most influential and important adviser. As he had served in the US Army in Europe as a commissioned officer during the war and worked under Clay in occupied Germany from 1945 until 1946, Bowie had firsthand knowledge of that country. After joining McCloy in Bonn, he met Monnet, who soon realized this American could be useful to him. Monnet's plan involved the creation of a new European supranational military community, modeled on the Schuman Plan, with a European army of about 100,000 men composed of small national fighting units. The army would be directed by a European minister of defense and controlled, in turn, by a European Assembly. The arms programs and military budget would be jointly controlled, and the national forces would be integrated at every level of command. This new plan avoided creating a new German military staff and division-sized units, which the French greatly feared. It would permit gradual German rearmament within the context of a larger European army and not put German troops under NATO. On September 16, 1950, Monnet warned Schuman and Pleven that since France had to respond to US pressure, they had only three options: (1) to do nothing, (2) to back German rearmament, or (3) to widen the Schuman Plan to include defense.[46] Pleven accepted Monnet's plan, and believed it would gain the French some time to recover the initiative and prevent the collapse of the Schuman Plan negotiations. On October 24, 1950, he proposed it to the National Assembly, which endorsed it by a vote of 343 to 220. Monnet's scheme became known as the Pleven Plan or the plan for a European Defense Community (EDC).[47]

Pleven accepted Monnet's plan for several reasons. French historian Philippe Vial argues that as the two men had worked together on several occasions since the 1920s and become friends, Monnet had Pleven's ear. And as this prime minister's main priority was the defense of his nation, he viewed France's contribution to the West's rearmament as very important. But for Pleven, states Vial, it was less a problem of German remilitarization than of the way in which France would implement its own rearmament. Like Monnet, he had been concerned about military expenses for the Indochina war getting out of control just as the French economy was stabilizing in 1950.[48] Moreover, Pleven agreed with Monnet's arguments that France had to lead in building Europe along the lines of the Schuman Plan and design the policy that would "contribute to a defense of Europe against outsiders." Monnet had also stressed in his letter to him that defending Europe against the real and immediate Soviet danger was more important than France's pursuit of an absurd policy in Indochina that claimed to "contain communism in South Asia" and was "doomed to failure."[49]

Following Monnet's advice, Pleven stipulated that the EDC could not be created until the Schuman Plan was completed and the political institutions of a united Europe were in place. Since these conditions signaled that implementation might be delayed indefinitely, the Americans were not pleased. European capitals reacted with genuine skepticism and suspicion.

Knowing that US support for the Pleven Plan also was essential, Monnet astutely worked to obtain it. He genuinely believed in some sort of European army, especially if France were leading it, argues Schwartz. But he also recognized that "if he channeled the American drive for 'doing something' to defend Europe into backing that proposal, he could save the Schuman Plan from being undermined by French resistance to German rearmament."[50] While the Schuman Plan negotiations continued, Monnet invited McCloy and Bowie to Paris in October 1950 to convince them that the French had made a "genuine effort" to solve the problem of German rearmament. Monnet believed his close friend McCloy could persuade Adenauer and Acheson to support the proposal. At a meeting he arranged of McCloy, Bowie, Schuman, and Pleven at his house in Houjarray, the three Frenchmen emphasized the defensive aspects of the plan. They argued that US support was a precondition for German participation and promised there would be discrimination against the Germans only in the transitional period. German recruiting would begin only under a European authority, they asserted, and they would complete the Schuman negotiations quickly if their new plan was adopted. McCloy came away convinced at least of French sincerity and told Adenauer the French were prepared to accept German equality within the European army. He urged Adenauer to understand the importance of reaching an agreement with the French and called the plan "an important contribution to European integration," a main objective of German policy. Acheson did not pressure Europeans to accept the idea of EDC but eventually supported it.[51]

Adenauer, however, reacted negatively to Monnet's new scheme. Convinced that French intentions were not honorable, he was afraid that the Quai d'Orsay's solution to the problem of security with Germany would be cooperation with the Soviet Union. Fearing US isolationism during the fall of 1950, he believed that if the United States withdrew from Europe, the French might be tempted to make an agreement with the Soviet Union. Moreover, he was concerned that if the four-power negotiations on the future of Germany appeared to be aimed at neutralizing Germany, along with the simultaneous withdrawal of the occupying troops, this would leave Americans uninvolved in Europe. Alternatively, it might lead them to keep minimal forces there while the Soviets maintained strong forces behind the Oder River, which formed part of the German border with Poland. Because he was convinced the United States was considering the option of a peripheral defense and an abandonment of Europe, Adenauer intensified his appeal to the Western Allies. He asked them to unite on German policy and transfer US troops to Europe so the German people could be convinced of the US will to resist the Soviets. He continued to press for a German defense contribution and a reorganization of German relations with Western powers as a way of keeping the United States involved in Europe.[52]

Monnet designed the Pleven Plan to achieve three goals: (1) to prevent the Schuman negotiations from being derailed, (2) to preserve French military power by counterbalancing the rearmament of Germany, and (3) to ensure Germany did not form a national army. It also aimed to enhance French security within a unified Europe under the jurisdiction of supranational institutions. "The scheme was ingenious, and with integrated recruitment, supranational logistics, and common defense objectives, it removed for a time the specter of a German army and organized the debate around a French initiative," argues Jean-Pierre Rioux. "Its fundamental weakness undoubtedly lay in the attempt to create a common European Army for a Europe whose political immaturity and disunity was obvious."[53] As Monnet admitted later, the idea of a European army was "at best premature."[54]

## Negotiations for the New Economic Community

While the debate raged in Paris and Bonn throughout the fall of 1950 over US defense requirements in Europe and the new French initiative, the Schuman

Plan negotiations continued. The delegates focused on the jurisdiction, institutions, and decisionmaking procedures of the proposed coal and steel community. The centerpiece of the new organization designed by the negotiators was the supranational institution called the "High Authority." In Monnet's mind, it was to be the institutional depository of shared national sovereignty over the coal and steel sectors. Monnet envisioned it as composed of capable public figures who would not seek instructions from their governments but who would make decisions based solely on the common interest and support decisions taken by a majority vote of the High Authority members. In the eyes of the French team, the High Authority would be responsible for formulating a common market in coal and steel. Monnet's idea was that it would regulate business through competition, pricing and investment pooling, and the supervision of wages but would not replace private enterprise. Its purpose, he declared, was to make real competition possible in a large market, thereby benefiting workers, producers, and consumers alike. It was to be a powerful directorate, with executive powers concentrated in a president who would enforce a code of industrial conduct. Monnet believed the High Authority could serve as an embryonic European federal government. As Robert Marjolin wrote in his memoirs, Monnet, as early as 1950, envisioned a Europe "endowed with efficient institutions resembling, even very remotely, the United States constitution."[55] While the time was "not yet ripe" for a grandiose proposal for a European economic or political confederation, Ball recalled, Schuman and Monnet set out "[to make] a decisive breakthrough at a narrow point [and not] undertake an assault on a wide front against entrenched concepts of sovereignty."[56]

The coal and steel community was structured so that the six national bureaucracies would have to cooperate closely with the High Authority to implement community legislation. A separate institution, the Court of Justice, was proposed to adjudicate disputes and ensure member states' compliance with the terms of the treaty. The Dutch delegation, headed by diplomat Dirk Spierenburg, angered Monnet because its representatives distrusted supranationalism and wished to limit the power of the High Authority. Fearful also of Franco-German domination and being forced to abide by decisions made by the larger powers, the Dutch and other negotiators forced Monnet to accept the creation of a council of ministers. This body of national representatives, slated to embody member states' interests, was to serve as an advisory and intermediary group to the High Authority. The final draft treaty also created a common assembly consisting of delegates of the national parliaments, which was intended to give the coal and steel community the component of direct democratic accountability. In the end, the negotiators created an organizational structure capable of a certain degree of *dirigisme*, or state interventionism, that overruled or dictated policy to the individual states.[57]

The negotiations proved extremely difficult as each country's delegation, especially the French and the German, pursued its own national interest.

Because Monnet had had no influence in the selection of the representatives from Italy, Luxembourg, Holland, or Belgium, he could not always enforce his will and he exploded in anger. The most difficult issues centered on the cartels: The French wanted to create their own, and the Germans wanted to preserve theirs. The contentious negotiations aroused fears in West Germany that Adenauer was sacrificing their most valuable German industries to foreign competition. The critical press printed a cartoon portraying Monnet sailing "a hyper-cartel" ship in front of the Americans under the flag of a ban on cartels. Other difficult issues discussed concerned the position of the Saar region in this new community, the future status of the Ruhr, the question of North African ore, the deconcentration and decartelization of the coal and steel industries, and the German industrialists' opposition to any restrictions or link between coal and steel.[58]

## US Assistance with Negotiations

The United States did not participate directly in the coal and steel treaty negotiations, but it monitored and constructively facilitated them through close contact with Monnet. The tireless, intense William "Tommy" Tomlinson, as chief economic and financial adviser to US Ambassador David Bruce, headed a special working group in the US embassy on the Schuman proposal. Embassy staff economists and specialists tracked the negotiations on a daily basis. Acting as unofficial advisers to Monnet, this group served as the link between Monnet and US policymakers in these negotiations. Because childhood rheumatic fever had left Tomlinson with a hole in his heart, he had been handicapped by poor health. In spite of doctors' warnings that his life would be shortened unless he took it easy, he continued to spend often seven days a week at his duties. He kept the same workaholic pace during the coal and steel negotiations as he had during his work on the Monnet and Marshall plans. This driven young man did not want his health to interfere with his effectiveness as a supporter and advocate of Monnet's goals. As an administrator, he always possessed a clear understanding of what should be done. The diplomats working under him experienced his demanding regimen of endless drafting and rewriting. Those who survived his system found him "formidable, exciting, and exacting but always fair"[59] and reported that he never asked anything of them that he did not ask of himself. Ball recalls that he "often found myself working with Tommy late into the night after which he would disappear to visit the nightspots, since he relaxed as vigorously as he worked."[60]

Other US officials, especially Allied High Commissioner McCloy and his general counsel Bowie, proved helpful in these negotiations. Bowie's "razor-sharp mind," his knowledge of antitrust law, and his negotiating skills proved valuable in surmounting the most difficult obstacles for the Germans: the number and power of the cartels in the German iron and coal industries.[61] Both Bowie and McCloy strongly supported Monnet's goal of linking Germany in a constructive way to the other major countries in Europe. Both US statesmen believed that helping to end Franco-German animosity was in the US national interest as it would help position a revitalized Europe to be a valuable partner for the United States. McCloy extolled the merits of the Schuman Plan to the German government, industrialists, and trade union officials. To the industrialists, McCloy argued that the Schuman Plan gave Europe "renewed hope" for peace, and that its success could diminish the fear of Germany in other European countries. This strong US backing reinforced Adenauer's support for it.[62]

Bowie worked closely with Monnet and Tomlinson in Paris on German issues arising from the Schuman Plan. Bowie had been given the responsibility of implementing Law 27, a ruling adopted by the Allied High Commission to deconcentrate or reduce the size of some of the largest companies in the German coal and steel industry. While being fair to German industry, their objective was to make sure that its units were comparable in size to the other European units. They wanted to prevent German industry from gaining an unfair advantage over the other nations' steel and coal plants in case of a shortage of coke or coal.[63]

In the summer of 1950, McCloy sent Bowie to Paris to figure out how to relate the Schuman Plan to Law 27 on cartels, and there he met Monnet. The American lawyer soon became a close friend of the whole Monnet family and was often a guest at their home. Shuttling by train from Bonn to Paris almost weekly from June 1950 until February 1951, Bowie met with Tomlinson, Uri, Hirsch, and Monnet, either at the embassy or at Monnet's office, to hammer out terms acceptable to both the French and Germans. Upon his return to Bonn, Bowie reported the details of his discussions in Paris to McCloy. Monnet's team relied on Bowie and McCloy to handle the Germans and the objections of German officials and industrialists. Bowie, along with Ball who was often in Paris, in turn encouraged the French to make the Schuman Plan "as unlike a cartel as possible" and, most importantly, to include strong antitrust provisions within the final treaty.[64]

Law 27 on cartels provoked a major struggle between the French and the Germans and confronted Bowie, Monnet, and McCloy with a difficult problem. Since the Ruhr coal was marketed through a common sales agency, the French believed this would give the Germans too much bargaining power within the common market for coal proposed by the treaty. The French also feared that failure to break up the steel monopolies would reinforce German dominance of the pool. McCloy took the lead in the negotiations with the German political authorities and the Ruhr industrialists as well as with the British and French authorities as the occupying powers. Respecting Bowie's sound judgment, Monnet used the latter's legal training in writing the treaty by having him draft provisions regarding restraint of trade and monopolies. Familiar with US antitrust legislation, Monnet insisted on strong provisions against cartels. Bowie's drafts were rewritten in a European idiom by the distinguished lawyer Maurice Lagrange who had the responsibility of giving Monnet's ideas formal legal expression. Monnet asked him to draft an agreement rigorous enough to last fifty years and serve as a model for future European treaties. "His contribution was invaluable," wrote Monnet about this tall, modest litigation counselor. As a result of Bowie's design and Lagrange's refinements, Articles 65 and 66 of the final treaty embodied the most advanced American antitrust thinking.[65]

Ball continued to serve as Monnet's unofficial legal adviser from 1950 to 1954 and spoke often with him by telephone. Ball first learned about the Schuman Plan from an article in the press. While acknowledging that he was personally disappointed not to have been involved in its creation, he expected to be summoned to Paris eventually. Monnet's call came on June 18, 1950, with the usual demand: "Be here tomorrow." Ball was relieved to be asked to help and immediately flew to Paris. Upon arrival, Monnet handed him a large sheaf of papers and said tersely, "Big things are happening. Read this." Once immersed in the drafts of the Schuman Plan, Ball soon understood the logic and magnitude of what was being done. To be helpful, he maneuvered himself into the center of the storm of activity at Monnet's headquarters on rue de Martignac and worked out of a small office under the stairs. Writing draft documents used in the negotiations, he strove to provide his client with the simplest formulations of the complex ideas. These proved useful to the team at headquarters as well as to the negotiators. For example, Ball wrote, "The Single Market is an indispensable principle of the Schuman Plan." And he captured the radical nature of the proposal when he wrote, "The Schuman Plan involves a revolutionary change in the production and distribution of coal and steel. This implies not only a change in the legislation which now controls the operation of these industries, but a change in the habits of thought of managers of the individual enterprises."[66]

According to Bowie, the consensus of the participants was that Monnet conducted these difficult negotiations expertly and pragmatically. The American lawyer described them as illustrative of the method of operation that Monnet always used to solve highly complex problems. "The negotiations were conducted in a very intimate, frank, straightforward and cooperative arrangement," noted Bowie. "All issues were treated as problems for joint solutions and were debated and discussed in the Monnet approach. This meant that the negotiators were placed on one side of the table and the problem on the other." Bowie stated that they collaborated as equals with each side influencing the other.[67] Spierenburg, the hard-headed Dutch representative who often challenged the Frenchman, described the atmosphere created by Monnet as one of consultation rather than negotiation. Many drafts were created for discussion and then replaced by another. Monnet knew, the Dutchman wrote, "how to organize working groups, hold bilateral talks on tricky points, and remind everyone that they were not up against each other but against the problems they must solve together." Monnet understood that he had to try to persuade the sixty delegates that "they were there to negotiate not for their own national interests but for the advantage of all."[68]

## Dealing with German Resistance

While the acrimonious debates continued in Paris and Bonn about the controversial Pleven Plan during the last months of 1950, the Schuman Plan negotiations concluded in December after nine months of hard bargaining and lengthy arguments. The process modified substantially some of Monnet's original ideas but produced a treaty, largely written by Uri and Lagrange, creating the European Coal and Steel Community. This agreement mandated a single market in coal and steel free of customs duties and other trade restrictions. Discriminatory practices were forbidden. Firms would be required to post prices, and fines would be levied for cheating. Foremost among the new institutions created to run the new community was the High Authority, a supranational body with executive power to enforce Europe's first strong anticartel law. The High Authority could contract and extend loans, aid adjustments of labor to technological change, and, with the Council of Ministers, the body composed of individuals representing each member nation and its interests, establish production quotas. The treaty also created a Court of Justice, to which High Authority decisions could be appealed, and a Common Assembly. True to Monnet's vision, this treaty delegated major powers to these new European institutions.[69] He fervently believed the new bodies were necessary to change the context in which individuals from different nations related to each other and, more importantly, their thinking.

The Germans, however, refused to decartelize the Ruhr, a condition set by the French and the Americans to break up or dissolve the cartels, and this delayed the signing of the treaty. West German industrialists refused to abandon the practice that had allowed them for decades to control prices and regulate output. On most occasions, Monnet was open to consider "a better idea," noted Max Kohnstamm, a member of the Dutch delegation. For example, after negotiations pertaining to the shape of the High Authority had concluded, Monnet willingly agreed to modify a clause that Adenauer asked him to change.[70] But on key issues like decartelization, Monnet remained adamant. As the ongoing negotiations for the EDC had given the Germans more influence and leverage because the French wanted German agreement to the EDC provisions and the United States wanted to rearm West Germany, the Germans remained firm. And, as the Americans also stressed the importance of a strong West German state in the free world, they enabled the Germans to resist some of the other tough French demands. But the French and Americans agreed that deconcentration was necessary and insisted the Bonn government propose the final settlement itself.

Ludwig Erhard, minister for economic affairs, and Adenauer held discussions with German industrialists in February 1951, while McCloy and Bowie worked hard to gain German support for Law 27. After bargaining, they gave German steel companies 75 percent of their coking coal supplies, not their requested 100 percent, because that was Monnet's precondition for French approval of the Schuman Plan. McCloy helped Adenauer by agreeing to meet individually with groups of German industrialists and trade unionists to explain why Washington insisted on Law 27. McCloy stressed to them the political significance of the Schuman Plan for Europe and argued that its approval would greatly affect European attitudes toward the Federal Republic. He stated that German adoption of the plan would eventually mean a lifting of most of the controls on German economic development. After getting Monnet's approval, McCloy made one compromise for the trade unionists and agreed that the Deutscher Kohlen-Verkauf, the Ruhr's coal sales organization, be phased out after a three-year period, not immediately, to avoid unemployment at marginal mines. Monnet finally agreed because he was eager to obtain German trade union support for the Schuman Plan. Kohnstamm gave Monnet much credit for winning over members of the Social Democratic Party of Germany and gaining their backing of the coal and steel community.[71]

The German industrialists' firm opposition to the treaty's terms had forced McCloy to get tough. He broke the impasse by making it clear that without a German signature on the ECSC Treaty signifying agreement to all its provisions, there would be no general treaty amending the Occupation Statute or any freedom of maneuver for Bonn in the field of foreign policy. Because of this threat, the Germans reluctantly succumbed to US pressure. On March 14, 1951, Adenauer agreed to accept the American compromise, make Law 27 his own proposal, and sign the treaty. Later acknowledging the importance of McCloy's role, Monnet said the treaty would never have been signed without the firm assistance of the United States and "Mr. McCloy's support."[72]

In an October 3, 1965, speech given on the occasion of a commemorative plaque placed on Schuman's house, Monnet paid tribute to the French minister who had died in 1963. "To Robert Schuman must go the great merit of having committed his own responsibility as Minister of Foreign Affairs in favor of a proposal whose aim was not only to reconcile France and Germany but also gradually to establish a new form of relationship between European countries," Monnet declared. "I can still hear his voice at the end of the negotiation which led to the ECSC Treaty: 'It is the first time,' Schuman said, 'that I have ever seen talks of this kind—this is not a negotiation in which everyone merely seeks to defend his own interests: it is a joint attempt to secure the interest of all.'"[73]

The Treaty of Paris, initialed on March 19, 1951, by the six delegations and signed at the Conference of the Six Foreign Ministers in Paris April 18, 1951, established the European Coal and Steel Community for fifty years. After Monnet's April 4–6, 1951, visit to Bonn, Adenauer had accepted the Frenchman's proposal that France and Germany should have equal representation in all ECSC bodies irrespective of the status of the Saar region or of German reunification. A compromise was reached on the membership of the High Authority: Its nine members were to be nominees of national governments for terms of six years. While all states would be represented, not more than two members could come from any one state. In practice the two largest states, France and Germany, were to have two representatives each, the others only one, with the ninth member elected by the other eight. The Germans wanted the presidency to rotate among the members on an annual basis to prevent the French from remaining in that position over a lengthy period. But they compromised and agreed that both the president and vice president would be appointed for two-year renewable terms, thereby permitting rotation. Decisions were to be taken by majority voting in the High Authority, a requirement insisted upon by Monnet. Difficult negotiations also ensued over the voting system for the Council of Ministers, as the French and the Germans called for a double vote. This was challenged by the Italians, who felt disadvantaged, and the Belgians, who argued they deserved more influence than the Netherlands and Luxembourg. But to break the stalemate, the six nations compromised on weighted voting, with France and Germany each getting two votes, the other countries just one.

Further restraint on the High Authority was to be provided by the Common Assembly, the first international assembly in Europe with legally guaranteed powers. Battles ensued over the composition and the appointment of members to the Assembly because the Benelux countries were trying to guard against Franco-German domination. France, supported by Adenauer, proposed election by direct universal suffrage, but the Benelux rejected that proposal as politically premature. It was decided that each state could decide whether members should be appointed by their parliaments or directly elected to the Assembly and that there would be seventy-eight members: eighteen each from Germany, France, and Italy; ten each from Belgium and the Netherlands; and four from Luxembourg.

These governments also decided that the Court of Justice would be composed of seven judges drawn from each of the six national judiciaries and chosen for their qualities of independence and competence, with renewable six-year terms. For Monnet, this institution was of critical importance because it rooted the whole ECSC structure in the rule of law. The Court of Justice had the power to rule on the legality of any decision of the High Authority and overrule it. As this body could also adjudicate complaints submitted by national governments or enterprises, it also served as a check on actions by individual governments. And as the Court's decisions were final, there could be no appeal. Because of the introduction of the concept of the rule of law in this new community, it became an important principle embedded in the whole integration process.[74]

## Vital US Support for Pleven Plan

Throughout the Schuman Plan talks, intense debate had continued about the future of the proposed European Defense Community. The tense, difficult EDC negotiations, begun in February 1951, led to many serious disagreements, especially over the size of the integrated units and the degree of supranationality. In France, the Gaullists and Communists roundly opposed this scheme of Monnet's, just as they had denounced the Schuman Plan, and all shades of political opinion were united in their resistance to the reconstruction of a German army and a general staff. De Gaulle derided it as a "stateless melting pot" and condemned the idea of merging the French army, of which he was a prominent member, into a European force.[75]

The White House, State Department, Pentagon, and NATO all proclaimed Monnet's EDC plan militarily unfeasible. But since the French rejected any alternative proposals, Washington was forced to consider the Pleven Plan as the only workable solution to the problem of how to rearm Germany without arousing French fears.[76] McCloy and Bruce, its strongest proponents, argued it would, in some form, win acceptance in France and that the debates about it might lead to a modified and more practical scheme. Since McCloy believed that close links with the West were the best way to stabilize the new German democracy, he tried to persuade Washington of the need to offer Germany considerable equality within the Western Alliance. Arguing that a European framework for rearmament would be best, he pushed for a merger of the Petersburg discussions, which concerned the contractual agreements to end the occupation and to grant Germany's political sovereignty, with the ongoing EDC talks. McCloy firmly rejected Adenauer's proposed interim and provisional solutions to German rearmament, reassured Monnet of US support, and worked to find a solution within the framework of the Pleven Plan.[77]

At Bowie's suggestion, McCloy arranged for General Dwight Eisenhower, the new NATO Supreme Allied Commander Europe, to meet with Monnet in hopes that the European army concept would be more enthusiastically supported if it could be shown to be effective from a military point of view. Eisenhower initially opposed the Pleven Plan as militarily unsound and ineffective and believed it would most likely encourage division rather than unity in Western Europe. He also knew his military colleagues preferred German rearmament within NATO. But he agreed to talk with Monnet, whom he had met in Algiers in 1943.[78]

Charming and persuasive, the Frenchman quite brilliantly convinced Eisenhower over lunch in Paris on June 21, 1951, that the EDC would foster both European security and unity. Repeating the arguments used to sell the Schuman Plan, Monnet asserted that "Europe would become responsible and strong only if it were united." A short-term Allied plan, which sought to "rush into raising a few German divisions on a national basis, at the cost of reviving enmity between peoples," he cleverly argued to the general, "would be catastrophic for the very security of Europe that such a step would be intended to ensure." A European army would give France, Germany, and their neighbors "common resources to exploit and defend" and would, he believed, help Europe "to recover the will to resist." But he added that the critical issue was not the size of the divisions but the creation of a common outlook, which in turn would foster a common interest and common spirit. Besides, he argued, the essence of the matter was not so much military effectiveness as political soundness.[79] Eisenhower had come to believe that a united Europe was essential for European security and therefore found Monnet's arguments appealing. At the end of their conversation, Monnet had gained an important ally.[80] Having first convinced Pleven to adopt his EDC proposal, he was also successful in persuading this prominent, influential US military leader to view it favorably.[81]

Eisenhower's support of Monnet's plan helped dispel some of the military's objections and swing official US opinion in favor of the EDC. In a July 3, 1951, speech in London, Eisenhower called for unity in Europe, which "could build adequate security and . . . continue the march of human betterment that has characterized western civilization." The general urged the European peoples to unite to secure their future against the Communist threat. He stressed the merits of European unity, stating it would result in a more efficient division of labor and resources and would increase the flow of trade among the European nations. "It would be difficult indeed to overstate the benefits," he stressed, "in these years of stress and tension, that would accrue to NATO if the free nations of Europe were truly a unit."[82] By midsummer of 1951, Washington favored Monnet's idea for a European army because there was no alternative proposal. Moreover, many American officials viewed this plan as a further step toward European integration. Monnet's discussions with Eisenhower and other US leaders had even persuaded him and Alphand, French ambassador to NATO, to transform their initial version of a European army into a broader proposal for an EDC. The French also acknowledged US concerns by agreeing to treat the West German contribution on the basis of equality and to integrate the proposed EDC within NATO.[83] As Schwartz argues, McCloy, Eisenhower, and Bruce optimistically hoped that "greater unity would also end the need for extensive American involvement before isolationist sentiments returned." For them, the EDC "seemed to solve so many problems—Soviet expansion, German nationalism, European weakness, [and] American isolationism." Further crises in NATO "threatened to undermine Western stability and encourage the Soviets," he notes, and the EDC "seemed the only way to 'square the circle' and guarantee both French security and German equality."[84] A united Europe for these three men, Schwartz writes, "had become 'the skeleton key' to unlocking the solutions to Europe's problems, from ending Franco-German enmity to containing the Soviet 'threat from the East.'" As Eisenhower declared, "joining Europe together is the key to the whole question."[85]

In the fall of 1951, Monnet used Eisenhower to lobby NATO allies and ask for their support of the EDC. The Frenchman had been chosen as one of the three wise men of the newly created Temporary Council Committee of NATO (TCC) along with Harriman, Truman's special adviser on foreign affairs, and Hugh Gaitskell, British chancellor of the exchequer. Their task was to analyze NATO's military needs compared with each member's economic capacities. Since he could not attend the TCC meeting when it reported to NATO on November 24 in Rome, Monnet met with Eisenhower beforehand and asked him to stress the need for "European amalgamation" at that meeting. The general agreed. In his speech two days later before the North Atlantic Council of NATO, Eisenhower emphasized the political, economic, and military advantages of Western European unification and declared his strong support for the creation of a European defense force. By the end of 1951, Monnet and the general had become friends.[86]

## Adenauer's Reluctant Acceptance of the Pleven Plan

Eisenhower's shift in position proved decisive in overcoming Acheson's skepticism and Truman's initial reservations about the Pleven Plan. Once Truman approved it on July 30, 1951, Adenauer saw no prospect for any other solution. In May 1952, after fifteen months, most of the serious obstacles in the contentious EDC negotiations were gradually overcome and the contractual negotiations regarding the terms that would end the occupation were completed. As a result, a treaty creating the EDC was signed on May 26–27, 1952, at Bonn and Paris by all six ECSC members. The common institutions of this supranational community were given limited powers—a Commissariat similar to the High Authority, a Council of Ministers, and a Court of Justice. The army units from each country, composed of 13,000 men, would be merged and under an integrated command. Recruitment, training, and control of the reserves remained the responsibility of each nation, and supplies and arms would be jointly controlled. Decisions would be binding, and the armed forces fused, not just coordinated, but the negotiators made it more of a coalition than real integration.[87]

US officials had worked hard to make this complicated EDC proposal acceptable to all six nations, especially to the Germans, while pressuring Adenauer to sign the treaty. The United States had agreed to incorporate the German defense contribution into the complex framework of the EDC, abolish the rearmament ban imposed by the Allies, and envisage full German membership of NATO. Moreover, it declared it would end Allied occupation when the treaty was signed, thereby restoring German sovereignty over domestic and foreign affairs. But the entry into force of these contractual agreements depended on the creation of the EDC. McCloy stressed to Adenauer that the plan was an important contribution to European integration, a main objective of German policy. Adenauer preferred German membership in NATO, had doubts about French intentions, and feared Paris would delay the EDC ratification and thereby the elimination of the Occupation Statute. But because he had no other choice, he finally consented. He was forced to defend his decision to sign the EDC Treaty against attacks by his cabinet and backbenchers by persuasively pointing out the negative consequences of not ratifying it. He argued that if the Bundestag voted against the treaty, the Occupation Statute would be reimposed in full. He stressed that if Germany were excluded from the defense of the West, the NATO defensive concept could not be sustained and Germany would be a battleground if war broke out. He pointed out that negative sentiment toward Germany remained strong abroad, except among Americans, but if the treaties were not ratified, the US president could reverse policy and withdraw from Europe. The close relationship between Monnet and McCloy had helped sustain US and European cooperation in the EDC discussions, but without the US administration's strong pressure exerted by McCloy on him, Adenauer would not have agreed to the creation of the EDC.[88]

The French government signed the complex EDC Treaty on the tacit condition that there would be no attempt for parliament to ratify it. Many French officials considered the treaty unsatisfactory because of its many contradictions, defects, and ambiguities. Despite the rhetoric in the treaty language, the twelve German units, compared to the fourteen for France, in fact created a German army. They believed the shared structures of the European military community were weak and unworkable. Moreover, the proposal for a common defense minister had been eliminated, and the British and US forces' length of stay in Europe was not specified. A central condition of the treaty was that West German sovereignty would not be restored until the EDC's ratification by all signatories. While West Germany and the Benelux states had ratified the treaty by early 1954, the great fear of German rearmament and party conflicts meant that no French government dared to bring this treaty before parliament. As a result, Rioux writes, the weak EDC, which was "firmly installed under the shelter of the American umbrella" and appeared "likely to become a simple tool of American policy," remained at a parliamentary and diplomatic standstill for the next two years.[89]

## Ratification of the ECSC Treaty

While the EDC Treaty remained in limbo, all six nations had ratified the ECSC Treaty, which created the European Coal and Steel Community, by mid-June

1952. These ratification debates provided some political circles the opportunity to express their hostility to the High Authority. In France, opposition from the Communists and Gaullists was countered by support from the independents. Monnet's group argued that French industry could compete with Germany and that the ECSC would help by guaranteeing coking coal supplies at competitive prices. To the surprise of Monnet and Schuman, the steel interests in France failed to negatively influence the French assembly, which voted on December 13, 1951, to pass the treaty by 377 to 233 votes. The steel association complained loudly about being left out of the negotiations and about increased competition and loss of power, although a minority of the steel masters backed the Schuman Plan. In the Benelux countries, many voiced opposition but only the Communists voted against the treaty. In Germany, the socialists and those who wanted more Ruhr concessions voiced opposition, but on January 11, 1952, a Bundestag majority of 232 to 143 voted for it. Agreement was reached over lingering details between the French government and the Germans in July 1952.[90] The ECSC came into being on August 10, 1952, with Monnet installed as the High Authority's first president.

Monnet's US connections and their diplomatic skills played a decisive role in the creation of the ECSC. Bowie, Tomlinson, Ball, and, most importantly, McCloy enabled the United States to facilitate this bold French initiative constructively by working closely with Monnet and Adenauer. Bowie and McCloy played an important role in moving the negotiations forward through effective shuttle diplomacy between Paris and Bonn. Acheson supported the initiative, firmly told the British not to interfere in the negotiations, and helped counter the Dutch concern about the powers of the High Authority.[91] By hammering out possible solutions to problems between the Germans and the French and leveraging US power as the principal occupier of West Germany, these officials furthered the goal of the United States and Monnet to link Germany in a concrete endeavor to other major countries in Europe.

The US government played a determining role in the completion and passage of both the ECSC Treaty, which implemented the Schuman Plan, and the EDC Treaty. Monnet astutely used his influential American friends, especially McCloy, to force Adenauer to accept all the provisions of the ECSC Treaty demanded by the French and the Americans. If the German leader had refused to bow to US demands, the Schuman Plan might never have been adopted. If Washington officials had not pressured the French and German governments to iron out and accept the provisions of the EDC Treaty, the Schuman Plan negotiations might have been derailed. Thomas Schwartz argues that Monnet had the most influence on US policy toward integration in the period when McCloy was high commissioner. Their close relationship symbolized the critical "transnational partnership" they created between the United States and Europe.[92]

In 1950, Monnet designed two plans to meet two separate crises and used his influence with his powerful American government officials to gain the acceptance and passage of them both. That year he was a powerful influence on French foreign policy because he had the ear of both Schuman and Pleven. But his close relationships and his links to the Americans engendered distrust and resentment in French political circles in the late 1940s and early 1950s. The Gaullists and other rightist groups believed that he was more American than French and harbored suspicions of possible secret deals he had made with Washington. The Right berated him for being an internationalist with close ties to Washington and for not looking after what they claimed were French interests.

Both Presidents Truman and Eisenhower viewed the Schuman Plan as very much in the interest of the United States because it represented a profound shift in US policy toward West Germany: from constraining Germany to integrating it economically into a community with other nations, as Bowie noted.[93] McCloy and the other US representatives were convinced the plan was a positive and pragmatic way to deal with that defeated power, and McCloy was relieved that the leaders of France and Germany were finally attempting to end a long European civil war.[94] For historian John Gillingham, the ECSC was significant because it "substituted for a peace treaty with Germany."[95] And for Ernest May, it was a way of "knitting Germany to France" and both to the rest of Europe.[96]

The creation of the ECSC stands as Monnet's greatest achievement. It was a major first step on the way to achieving his main goal of establishing a lasting peace in Europe. A response to a perceived resurgence of Germany, he saw it as a pragmatic way to link age-old enemies and engage the two nations in practical, limited economic endeavor that was in their mutual interest. Monnet knew that the ECSC represented a breakthrough in Franco-German relations and in German foreign policy, for it signaled French acquiescence to Germany's economic recovery. It was also an essential building block of Germany's policy of rapprochement with France and its full integration into the West. Most importantly for him, it served French national interest and symbolized a reassertion of French leadership on the continent.

Monnet's proposals were also revolutionary and a positive development in his own grand strategy for bringing peace to Europe. Monnet believed that European nationalism could only be contained by some framework involving political or economic unity and that new institutions were required to achieve this. He believed that by creating a set of institutions that could manage a limited portion of the economy—two sectors that had helped create the wars between these rivals—he could harness the productivity of countries and steer them to a joint and peaceful endeavor. Monnet asserts that the participating nations had to share their sovereignty in this limited area through "a supranational regime. . . . The indispensable first principle of these proposals is the abnegation of sovereignty in a limited but decisive field."[97] Allowing the Germans to be equal partners at the negotiating table was pragmatic and visionary. His scheme also served his nation's national interest and security as he knew France's future role in Europe depended upon some accommodation with the Germans and continued access to the Ruhr's German coke. The plan's promised equality also helped to allay French fears that the oligarchy controlling German steel and coal might dominate Western Europe.

Monnet's timing was critical. His proposal to pool the coal and steel sectors of these two enemies was a creative response to the special circumstances of the time—the serious crisis in Franco-German relations in 1949–1950. As his influence in France and in Europe was at an all-time high, he had the political clout to make it a reality. Having earned the reputation in Washington as its most trusted European, he took advantage of the US government's vision for an integrated Europe and helped channel that vision to his nation's benefit. In 1950 and 1951, he was surrounded by several of his closest friends in Paris and in Bonn, who were in positions of influence and who enthusiastically supported his efforts. As a skilled negotiator, he shrewdly leveraged US pressure through his American connections and utilized the power it gave him in Paris and in Bonn. That pressure and power were initially useful in persuading Schuman to accept his idea and effective later in convincing Adenauer of the need to sign the treaty establishing the ECSC.

Monnet's idea would have come to nothing had Schuman not accepted it and Adenauer not supported it. It was fortunate that men such as Schuman and Adenauer, who understood the need for such an initiative to improve Franco-German relations, were in positions of power. Monnet and Schuman exploited the crisis to create a new strategy and long-term policy for France. And it was Schuman, the experienced parliamentarian and statesman, who forced it on the French government. Without Schuman's ability to ram it through, this experimental community would not have been established. And without the capable and farsighted statesmanship of Adenauer, who believed creative thinking was needed in Europe, it would have come to naught. Because these two leaders, along with Monnet, shared a vision of a peaceful Europe and were willing to take political risks to support the plan, they together helped change the course of European history.

Most significantly, the ECSC's great strength lay in its offer of the modest but concrete integration of two sectors of the economy. It began the process of the six nations negotiating together about an issue of deep mutual concern. As Monnet's text asserted prophetically, it established "the first solid bases for the European federation essential for the preservation of peace." Desmond Dinan argues that Monnet was "more imaginative and astute than most" and that the ideal of a High Authority "as the supranational instrument of sectoral integration was novel and timely."[98] While Rioux states that the Schuman Plan negotiations were "expertly conducted by Jean Monnet," he asserts that "the realization of the French project was a considerable personal victory for Robert Schuman and an important contribution to the cause of European unity."[99] This federal experiment, argues François Duchêne, addressed the fragmentation of authority of nation-states that had led to war as no other international body had done. It was an important "breakthrough which laid the cornerstone of today's European Union."[100] Through this process of negotiation, these men created institutions that would form the structure of a united Europe. And it was through these new institutions that Monnet changed the context and the conditions under which Europeans interacted with one another. As Monnet later wrote in hindsight, this new experimental community was indeed the "pathfinder."

## Notes

1. Jean-Pierre Rioux, *The Fourth Republic, 1944–1958* (Cambridge, UK: Cambridge University Press, 1987), pp. 142–145; Desmond Dinan, *Europe Recast* (Boulder, CO: Lynne Rienner Publishers, 2006), pp. 32–34; François Duchêne, *Jean Monnet: The First Statesman of Interdependence* (New York: W. W. Norton, 1994), pp. 182–190; Bernard Clappier, interview by Robert Massip, November 11, 1980, Fondation Jean Monnet pour l'Europe Centre de recherches européennes, Lausanne, Switzerland; Clappier, Robert Schuman's chef de cabinet, describes Schuman's discussions with Dean Acheson in Washington, September 15, 1949.

2. Hans-Peter Schwarz, *Konrad Adenauer,* vol. 1 (Providence, RI: Berghahn Books, 1995), pp. 488–491.

3. Thomas Schwartz, "The Transnational Partnership: Jean Monnet and Jack McCloy," in *Monnet and the Americans,* ed. Clifford Hackett (Washington, DC: Jean Monnet Council, 1995), p. 181; Duchêne, *Jean Monnet,* pp. 182–206.

4. Jean Monnet, *Memoirs* (New York: Doubleday, 1978), p. 274.

5. Ibid., pp. 292–293.

6. *Un changement d'espérance: La Déclaration du 9 mai 1950, Jean Monnet–Robert Schuman* (Lausanne, Switzerland: Fondation Jean Monnet pour l'Europe, 2000), pp. 77–153.

7. The North Atlantic Treaty Organization (NATO), created by the North Atlantic Treaty signed on April 4, 1949, was a collective defense alliance composed of twelve member states to defend against attack from an outside power. West Germany joined after sustained negotiations in May 1955.

8. Thomas A. Schwartz, *America's Germany: John J. McCloy and the Federal Republic of Germany* (Cambridge, MA: Harvard University Press, 1991), pp. 28–45, 78.

9. Monnet, *Memoirs,* p. 292.

10. Schwartz, "Transnational Partnership," p. 182.

11. Rioux, *Fourth Republic,* p. 142.

12. Douglas Brinkley, "Dean Acheson and Jean Monnet: On the Path to Atlantic Partnership," in *Monnet and the Americans,* ed. Clifford Hackett (Washington, DC: Jean Monnet Council, 1995), p. 83.

13. Rioux, *The Fourth Republic,* p. 142; Duchêne, *Jean Monnet,* pp. 190–202; Monnet, *Memoirs,* pp. 302–306.

14. Desmond Dinan, ed., *Encyclopedia of the European Union* (Boulder, CO: Lynne Rienner Publishers, 1998), p. 441. Decisions by the national governments are made by majority voting.

15. *Un changement d'espérance,* pp. 175–183.

16. Rioux, *Fourth Republic*, p. 142; Clappier, interview; see also Raymond Poidevin, *Robert Schuman: Homme de 'Etat, 1886–1963* (Paris: Imprimérie Nationale, 1986).

17. Schwartz, "Transnational Partnership," p. 181; Duchêne, *Jean Monnet,* pp. 190–201.

18. Schwarz, *Adenauer*, vol. 1, pp. 503–506.

19. Robert Schuman to Konrad Adenauer, letter, May 7, 1950, *Un changement,* pp. 159–161; Schwarz, *Adenauer*, vol. 1, pp. 503–504.

20. Adenauer to Schuman, two letters of May 8, 1950, *Un changement,* pp. 162–164, 185–193; Schwarz, *Adenauer*, pp. 504–507.

21. Duchêne, *Jean Monnet*, p. 202; Rioux, *Fourth Republic*, p. 142.

22. Rioux, *Fourth Republic*, p. 143; Duchêne, *Jean Monnet,* pp. 203–209; François Duchêne, interview by the author, September 13, 2002; Eric Roussel, *Jean Monnet* (Paris: Librairie Artheme Fayard, 1996), pp. 540–50; Edmund Dell, *The Schuman Plan and the British Abdication of Leadership in Europe* (Oxford, UK: Oxford University Press, 1995), p. 4.

23. John Foster Dulles to Monnet, telegram, May 10, 1950, and Dulles to Monnet, letter, May 23, 1950, Box 54, DP-PL, Dulles Papers, Princeton University.

24. Averell Harriman to Dean Acheson, letter, May 20, 1950; *FRUS*, 1950, vol. 3, pp. 702–704.

25. *FRUS*, 1950, vol. 3, pp. 694–695.

26. Dean Acheson, *Present at the Creation* (New York: W. W. Norton, 1969), p. 304; see also Brinkley, "Dean Acheson and Jean Monnet," pp. 83–84; John Gillingham, "Jean Monnet and the European Coal and Steel Community: A Preliminary Appraisal," in *Jean Monnet: The Path to European Unity,* ed. Douglas Brinkley and Clifford Hackett (New York: St. Martin's Press, 1991), p. 138.

27. Brinkley, "Dean Acheson and Jean Monnet," pp. 83–84.

28. Schwarz, *Adenauer*, vol. 1, pp. 508–512; Duchêne, *Jean Monnet*, p. 207.

29. French summary of Monnet's May 23, 1950, meeting with Adenauer, AMG 2/3/11, Fondation Jean Monnet; Monnet, *Memoirs*, pp. 309–311; Schwarz, *Adenauer*, vol. 1, p. 512.

30. French summary of Monnet's May 23, 1950, meeting with Adenauer.

31. Schwarz, *Adenauer*, vol. 1, p. 513.

32. French summary of Monnet's May 23, 1950, meeting with Adenauer. For the German summary of this meeting by Herbert Blankenhorn, German ambassador in Paris, see *Akten zur auswärtigen Politik der Bundesrepublik Deutschland,* ed. Hans-Peter Schwartz (Munich: R. Oldenbourg Verlag, 1997), pp. 154–159.

33. Konrad Adenauer, *Memoirs, 1945–53* (London: Weidenfeld and Nicolson, 1965), p. 263.

34. Monnet, *Memoirs*, p. 311.

35. Ibid., p. 320.

36. Rioux, *Jean Monnet,* pp. 553–560; John Gillingham, "Jean Monnet and the European Coal and Steel Community," in *Jean Monnet: The Path to European Unity,* ed. Douglas Brinkley and Clifford Hackett (NewYork: St. Martin's Press, 1991), pp. 139–140; Monnet, *Memoirs*, pp. 294–298.

37. Charles E. Bohlen, memorandum, July 13, 1950, and Dean Acheson, memorandum of conversation, July 14, *Foreign Relations*, 1950, vol. 1, pp. 342–345.

38. Samuel F. Wells, Jr., "The Korean War: Miscalculation and Alliance Transformation," in *The Routledge Handbook of Transatlantic Security*, ed. Basil Germond, Jussi M. Hanhimaki, and Georges-Henri Soutou (London: Routledge, 2010), pp. 17–19.

39. Ernest R. May, "The American Commitment to Germany, 1949–1955," in *American Historians and the Atlantic Alliance*, ed. L. S. Kaplan (Kent, OH: Kent State University Press, 1991), pp. 52– 65; Schwarz, *Adenauer*, vol. 1, pp. 516–551.

40. Schwarz, *Adenauer,* vol. 1, pp. 516–551; Duchêne, *Jean Monnet*, p. 227; Rioux, *Fourth Republic*, p. 144.

41. Schwarz, *Adenauer,* vol. 1, pp. 516–551.

42. Schwartz, "Transnational Partnership," p. 184; Duchêne, *Jean Monnet*, pp. 228–229.

43. Rioux, *Fourth Republic*, p. 144.

44. Schwartz, "Transnational Partnership," p. 184.

45. Monnet to René Pleven, letter, September 3, 1950, AMI 4/3/6, Fondation Jean Monnet. Max Kohnstamm, the Dutch diplomat who was a member of his nation's Schuman Plan negotiating team, called this a brilliant letter. Max Kohnstamm, interview by the author, November 19, 2005.

46. Identical letters from Jean Monnet to René Pleven and Robert Schuman, September 16, 1950, *Jean Monnet–Robert Schuman correspondance, 1947–1953* (Fondation Jean Monnet, 1986), p. 57; Monnet to Robert Schuman, memorandum, September 16, 1950, in *Jean Monnet–Robert Schuman correspondance,* pp. 58–59. An identical copy was sent to Pleven.

47. Schwartz, "Transnational Partnership," pp. 188–190; Rioux, *Fourth Republic*, p. 144.

48. Philippe Vial, "De la surenchère atlantiste a l'option européenne: Monnet et les problèmes du réarmament occidental durant l'été 1950," in *Jean Monnet, l'Europe et les chemins de la paix*, ed. Gérard Bossuat and Andreas Wilkens (Paris: Publications de la Sorbonne, 1999), pp. 307–342.

49. Monnet to Pleven, letter, September 3, 1950.

50. Thomas A. Schwartz, interview by the author, April 2, 2011.

51. Schwartz, "Transnational Partnership," pp. 186–187.

52. Schwarz, *Adenauer*, vol. 1, pp. 589–599.

53. Rioux, *Fourth Republic*, p. 144; see also Irwin Wall, *The United States and the Making of Postwar France, 1945–1954* (Cambridge, UK: Cambridge University Press, 1991), pp. 189–220.

54. Schwartz, "Transnational Partnership," pp. 184–185; Duchêne, *Jean Monnet*, p. 229; Monnet, *Memoirs*, pp. 345–350.

55. Robert Marjolin, *Architect of European Unity: Memoirs, 1911–1986* (London: Weidenfeld and Nicolson, 1989), p. 270.

56. David DiLeo, "Catch the Night Plane for Paris: George Ball and Jean Monnet," in *Monnet and the Americans*, ed. Clifford Hackett (Washington, DC: Jean Monnet Council, 1995), p. 150; see also Dirk Spierenburg and Raymond Poidevin, *The History of the High Authority of the European Coal and Steel Community* (London: Weidenfeld and Nicolson, 1994), p. 10.

57. Spierenburg and Poidevin, *High Authority*, pp. 17–18.

58. Schwarz, *Adenauer,* vol. 1, p. 608; Duchêne, *Jean Monnet,* pp. 207–215; Robert Bowie, interview by the author, September 19, 1990. Cartels are organizations of industrial or commercial producers of a commodity that have united to control production and prices. Many French and German businessmen wanted to require this form of organization in order to control markets and manage profits.

59. Donald McGrew, interview by the author, May 29, 1991; Arthur Hartman, interview by the author, October 15, 1990.

60. George W. Ball, *The Past Has Another Pattern: Memoirs* (New York: W. W. Norton, 1982), pp. 89–90.

61. Schwartz, *America's Germany*, p. 43.

62. Robert R. Bowie, interview by Francois Duchêne, May 17, 1987 Fondation Jean Monnet; Bowie, interview by the author, September 19, 1990; Sherrill Brown Wells, "Monnet and 'The Insiders': Nathan, Tomlinson, Bowie, and Schaetzel," in *Monnet and the Americans,* ed. Clifford Hackett (Washington, DC: Jean Monnet Council, 1995), pp. 211–214.

63. Wells, "Insiders," pp. 209–212; Robert Bowie, interview with the author, August 15, 1990; Gillingham, *Coal, Steel,* pp. 235–236; Gillingham, "Jean Monnet and the European Coal and Steel Community," pp. 138–139.

64. Schwartz, "Transnational Partnership," p. 184; Wells, "Insiders," p. 212.

65. Wells, "Insiders," p. 213; Bowie, interview by the author, August 15, 1990; Maurice Lagrange, interview by Antoine Marès, September 28, 1980, Fondation Jean Monnet; Monnet, *Memoirs*, p. 352.

66. DiLeo, "Catch the Night Plane," pp. 148–150.

67. Bowie, interview by the author, August 15, 1990.

68. Spierenburg and Poidevin, *High Authority*, p. 14; Monnet, *Memoirs*, p. 378.

69. Duchêne, *Jean Monnet*, p. 214.

70. Max Kohnstamm, interview by the author, November 19, 2005. Kohnstamm reported that after lengthy negotiations about the High Authority had concluded with all parties in agreement, Adenauer called Monnet. Franz Etzel said there could be no change, but Monnet said they would change if the chancellor had a good idea.

71. Duchêne, *Jean Monnet*, p. 217; Schwartz, "Transnational Partnership," p. 188; Kohnstamm, interview.

72. Duchêne, *Jean Monnet*, p. 217.

73. Jean Monnet, speech in Scy-Chazelles, October 3, 1965, Ball Papers, Box I, 70, Princeton University Library.

74. Duchêne, *Jean Monnet*, p. 219; Spierenburg and Poidevin, *High Authority,* pp. 24–25; Derek Urwin, *The Community of Europe* (London: Longman Group, 1991), pp. 47–51. Dulles mailed Monnet a brief note of congratulations on the initialing of the ECSC Treaty; Dulles to Monnet, letter, March 21, 1951, Box 54, Dulles Papers. For a concise list of the components of the rule of law, see Barry M. Hager, *The Rule of Law: A Lexicon for Policy Makers*, 2nd ed. (Washington, DC: Mansfield Center for Pacific Affairs, 2000).

75. Schwartz, *America's Germany,* p. 232.

76. Rioux, *Fourth Republic*, p. 144.

77. Schwartz, *America's Germany*, pp. 217–233.

78. Schwartz, *America's Germany*, pp. 135–145; Duchêne, *Jean Monnet,* pp. 231–233; Ernest R. May, "The American Commitment to Germany, 1949–1955," in *American Historians*, Kaplan, p. 70; Schwarz, *Konrad Adenauer,* vol. 1, pp. 598–599.

79. Monnet, *Memoirs*, pp. 358–360.

80. Duchêne, *Jean Monnet,* pp. 231–233; May, "Commitment," p. 70; Schwartz, "Transnational Partnership," pp. 189–190; Schwarz, *Adenauer*, pp. 622–623.

81. Pascaline Winand, *Eisenhower, Kennedy, and the United States of Europe* (New York: St Martin's Press, 1993), pp. 27–29.

82. Dwight Eisenhower, *Vital Speeches of the Day* 17, no. 20 (August 1, 1951), pp. 613–614.

83. Pascaline Winand, "Eisenhower, Dulles, Monnet, and the Uniting of Europe," in *Monnet and the Americans*, ed. Clifford Hackett (Washington, DC: Jean Monnet Council, 1995), pp. 106–107.

84. Schwartz, "Transnational Partnership," p. 190.

85. Schwartz, *America's Germany*, p. 224; see also pp. 217–234.

86. Winand, "Eisenhower, Dulles, Monnet," pp. 106–107.

87. Rioux, *Fourth Republic*, p. 145.

88. Schwartz, "Transnational Partnership," pp. 188–191; Schwarz, *Adenauer*, pp. 622–624, 671–683; Schwartz, *McCloy*, p. 303. Winand, "Eisenhower, Dulles, Monnet," pp. 105–107.

89. Rioux, *Fourth Republic*, p. 145.

90. Spierenburg and Poidevin, *High Authority*, pp. 32–34; Duchêne, *Jean Monnet*, pp. 207–210, 221–223.

91. Spierenburg and Poidevin, *High Authority*, pp. 26–27.

92. Schwartz, "Transnational Partnership," pp. 180–195.

93. Bowie, interview by the author, September 19, 1990.

94. Schwartz, *America's Germany*, p. 112.

95. Gillingham, "Jean Monnet and the European Coal and Steel Community," p. 156.

96. May, "Commitment," p. 71.

97. Monnet, *Memoirs*, p. 316.

98. Dinan, *Europe Recast*, p. 38.

99. Rioux, *Fourth Republic*, p. 143.

100. Duchêne, *Jean Monnet*, pp. 181–182.

# 6

# Losing the Battle for a European Defense Community, 1952–1954

Jean Monnet faced one of his greatest challenges when he began his term as president of the High Authority of the European Coal and Steel Community (ECSC) in August 1952. While the heated European Defense Community (EDC) debate continued in Paris, Monnet inaugurated the High Authority with an opening speech on August 10 in Luxembourg's stately Town Hall. In a spirited endorsement of the new experiment, he declared that the six member nations had willingly established the first European community. They accomplished this by merging some of its members' sovereignty and subordinating it to their common interest. Pledging to "carry out our tasks in full independence, in the general interest of the Community," he declared, "we shall neither solicit nor accept instructions from any government or any other body." He promised the six nations would "refrain from any action incompatible with the supranational character of our tasks."[1]

Monnet's prestige and reputation in Europe made it an opportune time for him to fulfill his dream of creating a new community that would bring enemy nations together in a joint project. While his ally Robert Schuman, the French foreign minister, was losing influence in France, Monnet had become the authoritative voice of many high-ranking European officials. "He was very powerful," wrote Jelle Zijlstra, minister of finance and later prime minister of the Netherlands. The Frenchman's experience, imagination, tenacity, and capacity for work as well as his ability to surround himself with able men of proven loyalty earned him widespread respect. Monnet approached the daunting challenge of building the institutions of this new community with excitement and confidence. He knew he was charting new waters with his experiment in supranationality. As no model existed, his team, along with the delegations of the six member countries, had designed the new components or

163

institutions that would govern the ECSC. He hoped that by working together for a common goal, the representatives from the six nations would change their minds about each other. He believed that changing perceptions of statesmen and officials could lead to changes in relations among leaders and ultimately states. But he also understood that such a process would be slow and take time. Moreover, the translation of the supranational concept into reality and the transformation of the experimental community into a working organization would be difficult. Yet Monnet believed he should start the process, which would evolve, be gradually amended, and undoubtedly improved over time.[2]

## Launching the New Community

The nine members of the High Authority met collectively for the first time in August 1952. Appointed by their governments, these men knew they faced a daunting task: to make this first European organization operational. They shared a commitment to a new Europe and a willingness to work with Monnet while forbidden to accept instructions from their governments or any lobby. Representing diverse professional backgrounds, the group included three career politicians, two trade unionists, one diplomat, one government official, and one steel company executive. Fifty-year-old Franz Etzel, close friend of West German Chancellor Konrad Adenauer and one of the founders of the Christian Democratic Union, came from a working-class background. He had studied law, politics, and economics, and fought in the war before being captured by the Americans in Lorraine. Having risen in this party to the chairmanship of the Bundestag Economic Policy Committee, he served as first vice president of the High Authority. Monnet viewed Etzel's direct access to Adenauer as advantageous in increasing Franco-German cooperation. But this German politician's friendships with Ruhr officials also meant he sought compromises. Belgian Albert Coppé, a forty-one-year-old, well-connected Flemish economist who had been a professor of economics at the University of Louvain, became second vice president of the High Authority. He worked hard to prevent Monnet from assuming too much power and strongly opposed his authoritarian methods. As a Christian Socialist, he supported European integration but was less supranational than the others. He proved to be a forceful defender of the views of the smaller countries by opposing Franco-German dominance in the organization. When Coppé heard that Etzel and Monnet met separately on occasion without including the other nine, he responded by having similar meetings with members from the smaller countries. But he remained an ardent supporter of the treaty and of majority rule.[3]

Enzo Giacchero, the forty-year-old Italian Christian Democrat who had lost a leg fighting the Fascists during the war, was known for his strong advocacy of European federalism as was his close friend, the Italian militant activist Altiero Spinelli. A brilliant analyst and good speaker, Giacchero proved capable of taking an independent line from Rome. The conservative Belgian labor leader Paul Finet, a fifty-five-year-old former metalworker and president of the International Confederation of Free Trade Unions, had met Monnet in October 1950. Having gained Monnet's confidence as a farsighted thinker and man of discretion, he was someone the High Authority's president always wanted on his side. The second trade unionist, the German Heinz Potthoff, a forty-eight-year-old Social Democrat with a receding hairline, had escaped to Switzerland to study economics in order to avoid being drafted by the Nazis. He was a member of the German Federation of Trade Unions, serving as spokesman for this group, and was sensitive to pressure from his own country. Industrialists viewed him as their ally and continually besieged him with their grievances. Dirk Spierenburg, the forty-three-year-old high-ranking Dutch diplomat and Europeanist, had been director general for external economic relations in the Foreign Ministry and the Dutch government's deputy commissioner for the Marshall Plan since 1947. As head of his nation's delegation to the Schuman Plan conference, he had often been Monnet's main opponent. He also served as a vice president of the High Authority. Albert Wehrer, a sixty-two-year-old Luxembourg diplomat who headed his nation's delegation in the Schuman talks, had been posted in both Germany and France. A cultured and experienced European, he often opposed Monnet in his defense of the Luxembourg steel industry. The second Frenchman, the distinguished, sixty-five-year-old engineer Leon Daum, had married former President and Prime Minister Raymond Poincaré's niece in 1923 after joining a large steel company at the end of World War I. He became a prominent representative of the steel industry but demonstrated he was independent of any group. As a result, he quickly won Monnet's confidence. Daum's "moral prestige," wrote Spierenburg, "helped to make the High Authority a cohesive body and promoted its image to the world at large."[4] While a few had known each other before joining the High Authority, the majority of these nine men had not previously met, and only Finet, Spierenburg, Etzel, and Wehrer had previously known Monnet.[5]

During the month of August, the nine members met daily to tackle the gargantuan task of creating the High Authority's administrative structure. They established departments, allocated duties, adopted rules of procedure, provided budget estimates, determined how to collect levies for administrative expenditures, and decided to have four official languages: French, German, Dutch, and Italian. They discussed ways to prepare for the opening of the common market, such as harmonization measures needed for it to function properly. Despite power struggles, hot tempers, genuine disagreements, and disputes over who got offices with a view, many decisions were made. They prepared for consultations with governments on price ranges, debated ways to ensure that certain

*Jean Monnet (left) and Konrad Adenauer in Strasbourg, attending the first meeting (September 10–11, 1952) of the Common Assembly of the European Coal and Steel Community.*

legal or regulatory provisions did not distort competition, and outlined many other policies, including plans to eliminate monopoly practices.[6]

The inaugural meeting of the Council of Ministers, the individuals representing each member nation and its interests, brought foreign affairs and economic ministers together September 8–10, 1952, with two heads of government, Adenauer and Italian Prime Minister Alcide de Gasperi. In his opening speech, the German chancellor stressed the weighty responsibilities of the council, the "federative body of the Community," charged to protect national interests. He pointed out that the harmonization role was difficult since the Council was the "meeting point between two different forms of sovereignty, one supranational and one national." He underscored the Council's main task as promoting the interests of the ECSC and permitting the High Authority "the freedom to develop." In his response, Monnet optimistically asserted that old habits could be broken, and everyone would quickly realize that the best interests of each country would be "in the end only served if they were subsumed into the common interest." The Council would not, therefore, have to seek a compromise between private interests but would "define a common point of view." He promised to maintain close ties with the governments and to consult the Council frequently while emphasizing that the High Authority was also accountable to the Assembly.[7]

On September 9, the Council adopted its rules of procedure. This body could take action by a majority vote, but in certain exceptions, a two-thirds, five-sixths, majority, or unanimous vote was required. These rules were complicated by weighting principles: Out of seventy-eight votes, France, Germany, and Italy each had eighteen votes; Belgium and the Netherlands ten; and Luxembourg four. In some cases the Council could oppose the High Authority's decisions if the vote was unanimous. In the event of a stalemate, the weighted voting system would prevent small countries from outvoting the larger ones and would stop Franco-German interests from dominating.[8]

The inaugural meeting of the Common Assembly, composed of national parliamentarians nominated by their governments, took place in Strasbourg, France, on September 10–13, 1952. For this body, a vote by the two-thirds majority of the members present was required to force the resignation of the entire High Authority.[9]

The Court of Justice, the highest body of appeal, embodied two of the principles deemed most important by Monnet: the rule of law and the right of appeal. Member states, enterprises, and associations had the right to appeal decisions of the High Authority to this court and have them declared void. This body was composed of one judge per member state plus one additional member and two advocates general. Each judge was to be independent of his government and appointed for a renewable term of six years in staggered three-year cycles. The seven members elected one of their number to become its president. The exception to that rule was the appointment in 1952 of Massimo Pilotti, a prominent Italian lawyer who presided over the first Court, set up in December 1952. Another body created by the ECSC Treaty, the Consultative Committee, resembled the Monnet Plan's Mobilization committees and represented economic and social interests such as producers, workers, and consumers.[10]

The ECSC attracted many qualified applicants from the six member countries for the available staff positions. Some yearned to be part of this new international experiment and were driven by the spirit of adventure. Others were idealistic, while some were attracted by the high salaries. Monnet also brought several members of his own team with him—Pierre Uri, Jacques Van Helmont, and novelist François Fontaine—and invited the High Authority members to invite other high-ranking European officials to join them.[11] Max Kohnstamm, an intellectual Dutch diplomat who had been Spierenburg's deputy in the Schuman Plan negotiations, became secretary of the High Authority. This Dutchman, who spoke four languages including fluent German, became one of Monnet's most valued and trusted colleagues as well as a close lifelong friend. Since Monnet had to work with those chosen by their governments, he soon learned the most the High Authority could hope for was to influence the decisionmaking process in the new community.[12]

Monnet had invited Altiero Spinelli, one of the leading figures in the movement for European integration, to prepare some remarks that the Frenchman could use in his opening speech of the High Authority in the summer of 1952. Monnet also offered Spinelli the opportunity to head the High Authority's bureau of the press and information. The Italian had founded the European Federalist Movement in 1943 but was unsuccessful in gaining Monnet's active support for that movement when they first met on July 5, 1951, in Paris.[13] Spinelli declined both of Monnet's offers to be part of the ECSC as he wished to collaborate with Monnet and have the Frenchman's public support but remain independent and not work for him as a European "functionary" or official.[14] In fact, Spinelli immodestly considered himself, along with Belgian Prime Minister Paul-Henri Spaak and Monnet, as one of the trio of most important Europeanists.[15]

## US Support of the New Community

John Foster Dulles, chosen to be secretary of state by newly elected President Dwight Eisenhower, flew to Luxembourg to commemorate the official opening of the European Coal and Steel Community on February 11, 1953. Monnet was pleased that his old friend was willing to honor him in this way and deliver the keynote address. Dulles spoke of the strong US support for the new community, which his presence at the ceremony clearly symbolized. In Monnet's mind, US support for the ECSC was necessary not only for its success but also for the advancement of European unity.[16] Responding to Dulles's speech, Monnet optimistically hailed the special significance of this community as "the beginning of this union of the peoples of Europe who, renouncing at last their age-old divisions, will soon unite in a strong, prosperous, and peaceful community to the benefit of their populations, free peoples, and civilization as a whole."[17]

Monnet had sent Dulles a congratulatory telegram on his new appointment after the presidential elections in November 1952. In his November 26 reply, Dulles wrote that he looked forward to their continued association and declared, "I share your conviction that it is of the utmost importance promptly to create greater unity politically, economically, and militarily in Europe. This as you know has been my conviction for many years."[18] Because of his deep concern about European economic and political security, especially the German problem, Dulles reassured his French friend that he was a strong supporter of the Schuman Plan. The new secretary of state viewed the ECSC as a logical way to integrate Germany into a unified Europe.

While Dulles was in Luxembourg, Monnet pressured his Republican friend to appoint David Bruce as US ambassador to the ECSC. Monnet believed that his new community would fail if the United States did not continue to demonstrate strong backing and felt he needed a special US representative to make that case in Washington. Alfred Gruenther, Eisenhower's former chief of staff and a good friend of Monnet, had already suggested the appointment of Bruce to the president. Not willing to leave this matter to chance, Monnet telephoned Gruenther the day after Dulles's departure, knowing he was an ally, and asked him to write Douglas MacArthur II, a confidant of Eisenhower and Dulles. Would MacArthur please ask the president to put pressure on Dulles to appoint Bruce? Dulles was initially reluctant because he feared vicious attacks by the isolationist wing of the Republican Party if he appointed a liberal Democrat like Bruce. But Dulles finally gave in to the strong pressure exerted by his French friend.

Bruce willingly served as US representative to the ECSC until he resigned in January 1955. At Dulles's suggestion, the president gave Bruce the added title of US observer to the European Defense Community Interim Committee. His appointment delighted Monnet and William Tomlinson, who headed the US embassy group in Paris in charge of relating to the ECSC.[19] The close-knit trio of Bruce, "Tommy," and Monnet, who had been so successful in steering Marshall Funds to the Monnet Plan, strove once again to further cement the transatlantic relationship.

Monnet had secured many privileged channels of communication to the influential men in Washington, New York, and the Republican administration. His most important contact and friend was Dulles and they functioned "as associates" during the Eisenhower years, asserts historian Pascaline Winand.[20] Other friends and sympathizers included John McCloy, then chairman of the Chase National Bank of New York; George Ball, practicing law in Washington; Robert Murphy, undersecretary of state for United Nations affairs; Livingston Merchant, deputy to the special representative in Europe; William Draper, assistant secretary of state for European affairs; Robert Bowie, head of the Policy Planning Staff at the State Department; and Walter Bedell Smith, Eisenhower's chief of staff during World War II and ex-director of the CIA, who was undersecretary of state.

A month after Dean Acheson's term as secretary of state ended, Monnet cabled his close American friend on February 11, 1953, to thank him for his help in making the reconstruction and integration of Europe a top priority of US foreign policy. Acheson replied a few weeks later. "You were more than kind to think of me on the day the common market went into effect. Certainly this step gives every indication of being the most significant, hopeful economic step in Europe in any of our memories," he wrote. "I hope it will have the environment to succeed and that it will succeed and lead to other developments as full of promise. It is good to look back on the work we engaged in together, and I am deeply touched that you should have sent me a cable including me in those who have had a hand in shaping this plan."[21]

## Setting a Brusque Tone

Monnet's strong, charismatic, yet demanding personality set the tone for the organization. François Duchêne writes that Monnet was "in many ways an inspiring leader who managed to impart a strong sense of service to a cause, even a pioneering spirit," to this diverse group. Duchêne had been hired by Monnet to be the ECSC's liaison to the Anglo-American press in 1953. Dutchman Edmond Wellenstein, who later succeeded Kohnstamm as secretary of the High Authority, stated that everyone agreed nothing Monnet did "was with his own career in mind or with France. . . . That really set the tone."[22] Monnet's preferred method was to attempt to gain a consensus on crucial issues, if possible, rather than risk confrontation or dictate a solution. Monnet often insisted on tact to get the voluntary consent of managers and used persuasion, for example, with labor unions to convince them of the rightness of a decision.[23] But when he believed he knew what had to be done and faced adamant opposition, he often became impatient, allowed his authoritarian streak to erupt, and demanded a certain course be taken.

Monnet idealistically viewed the High Authority as a forum for deliberations and discussions as well as a decisionmaking body that took action. The organization was divided into twelve divisions or departments—including transport service, financial affairs, investments, market production, social affairs, and statistics—with the heads of each working directly under the supervision of all nine members. Uri headed the Economics Division but his blustery personal style and close relationship to Monnet gave him more power than the other heads and thereby incurred resentment from the others. They claimed he acted like a tenth member. While Uri's French colleagues admired his brilliance, they bristled at his insensitivity to others.[24]

To facilitate deliberations, Monnet set up two scheduled meetings a week, one for the nine High Authority members only, which followed a prepared agenda, and the other for day-to-day matters with all department heads together with the nine. After consulting the Legal Service Division about a proposal, for example, a member had to convince the other members of its need and foresee the possible reaction of the Council of Ministers. When High Authority decisions were opposed by their own countries, the members found themselves subjected to heavy pressure.[25]

While they respected Monnet's goals and abilities, many High Authority officials chafed under his authoritarian style and incessant demands. Monnet's own established work habits influenced his staff and their schedules. Living in a nearby hotel before moving to a house in Bricherhof with his family on the outskirts of the city, he arose about 7 a.m., dressed casually, and took his early morning stroll through the Luxembourg countryside, which, he always claimed, rejuvenated his mind and soul. Upon his return, he dressed in a jacket and tie, ate a substantial breakfast, and sauntered down the road to his office

*Jean and Silvia Monnet at their home in Bricherhof, Luxembourg, 1953.*

about 10 a.m. Consuming a small late lunch after his morning meetings and discussions, he worked often until late in the evening. The atmosphere of permanent crisis he created at first generated a certain creative tension, which kept everyone on edge, but that soon dissipated. He disliked the restrictions imposed by a rigid organization, yet his own rigidities became obvious. He was strict about some things like working hours, and his own pattern of working late into the evening and Sundays especially annoyed those with families. His insistence that his colleagues be available at all times for discussions rankled others who became inured to his false claim that the discussion might take just "a little longer."[26] They tired of the rambling discussions and debate when he asked them to stand by while Uri put the ideas in writing.[27] For others accustomed to formal gatherings, his preference for informal meetings and ad hoc committees grated because he called on anyone he wished, regardless of rank or responsibility.

Monnet had been used to running fairly small organizations like the Planning Commission for the Monnet Plan where all the men were chosen by him, very loyal, and accustomed to his domineering style. In this larger organization, he had to tolerate more disagreement, rebellion, and rivalries. Coppé and Spierenburg, representing the Low Countries and fearing the strong Franco-German relationship, constantly protested that he tried to monopolize decision-making. They lamented he was far too involved "in the politics of Europe," a code name for the EDC debate, and not concerned enough about coal and steel. Spierenburg wrote that High Authority members worked under a "harsh regime," even though they could outvote him, and that "Monnet was no administrator." His high expectations, his belief that appointments and salaries were arbitrary, and the lack of coordination among divisions created a sense of disorder. By the time of his resignation in 1955, some pieces of the administrative machinery were not working as designed.[28] He later confessed he had never been a good manager.

## ECSC's Challenges and Limited Accomplishments

After working for six months to make it operational, the High Authority members began early in 1953 to create a single, community-wide area in which coal and steel products could be sold on a competitive basis. In general, the High Authority forged a good working relationship with the Council of Ministers and the permanent representatives of the member states. But the members soon found the goal of creating a genuine common market not only unrealistic but impossible to achieve. Coal and steel commerce had been regulated since the beginning of the century, and each nation's policies were dictated by national goals and vested interests. Power struggles arose on certain issues not only with industry but with governments reluctant to concede supranational power to the High Authority. It therefore remained powerless to alter producers' or government practices.[29]

The first challenge for this supranational body came with the opening of the common markets for the raw materials of coal, iron ore, and scrap on February 10, 1953, and for steel on April 10. Monnet realized his best hope was to persuade producers to adopt "nondiscriminatory" pricing policies since nationally mandated price controls, government subsidies, and artificial currency parities caused distortions in the market. As this meant, in practice, introducing price listing and imposing price reduction, Monnet envisioned the process as beginning with data collection of prices and production by producers. He believed that industrialists and High Authority representatives would thrash out a mutually acceptable policy through meetings. But that did not happen. Since producers or their governments controlled the prices, and marketing and fuel pricing were sensitive issues, the High Authority was powerless in the face of their opposition. As an alternative, the High Authority decided to begin by abolishing tariffs or customs duties, quotas, and discriminatory prices, a shrewd political action because tariffs did not exist for coal and were unimportant for steel. This action did eliminate some discriminatory practices such as export charges for Ruhr coal, which were about 10 percent above sales to Germans, and discriminatory freight rates, such as on iron ore from Lorraine to Belgium and on coke from the Ruhr to Lorraine.[30]

However, a common market in coal became nearly impossible to achieve because the High Authority lacked the power to confront the national cartels or the governments behind them. Production was subsidized, and the Ruhr was regulated by Allied occupation controls in effect until the common market opened. As the High Authority had little direct influence on Ruhr coal policy and the coal situation in France, the changes introduced by the opening of the common market in coal were inconsequential, and the officially removed barriers had little influence on the coal trade.[31]

Monnet soon understood that, as for coal, it would be impossible to also create a genuine common market for steel. Reassured by Daum's appointment as a member of the High Authority, relations between Monnet and the steelworkers changed during his presidency of the High Authority. Having been denounced by them after the announcement of the Schuman Plan, historian Philippe Mioche demonstrates that Monnet showed he could adapt to the times, change his attitude, and was able to seduce, even charm, the steelmakers into supporting the European goals of the ECSC. This community experience, argues Mioche, nourished their past European traditions.[32]

The ECSC's cartel policy also proved ineffective. Monnet had made the elimination of cartels one of his principal priorities and targeted the German Ruhr coal cartel, GEORG. But the High Authority failed to break it up. Its preparation for the common markets even accelerated the process of international cartel reformation and did not substantially change methods of sales. The steel industry continued to determine standards, sales areas for its products, and prices, which rose fairly steadily until Monnet left the High Authority in June 1955.[33] The High Authority adopted a "laissez faire" policy regarding concentration or mergers that promoted either efficiency or competitiveness. But one of the Ruhr steel masters reported that a tacit agreement existed among Monnet, Etzel, and the German firms that allowed the latter to reconcentrate gradually.[34]

The ECSC succeeded in setting up effective machinery to regulate European trade in scrap metal, often restraining national scrap cartels. It put its finances on a sound footing by finding an acceptable way to gain funds through a levy on coal and steel and a US loan. Monnet believed US funds were essential for the High Authority's capacity to govern. He thought such resources would enable him to direct the development of heavy industry, as he had done through the Monnet Plan, by making low-interest loans to influence investment decisions. The Frenchman had envisioned a large US loan as the precursor to flows of both public and private capital that could be channeled by the High Authority into the ECSC coal and steel interests. Monnet argued the funds would enhance the prestige of the High Authority in the minds of the producers, workers, and governments of the participating nations.[35]

However, Monnet's official trip to Washington in late May and early June 1953 at the invitation of Eisenhower produced a warm welcome but no loan.

*Jean Monnet at the White House meeting with President Dwight Eisenhower and Secretary of State John Foster Dulles, June 3, 1953. Seated, left to right: Monnet, Eisenhower, and Franz Etzel. Back row, left to right: Dulles, Dirk Spierenburg, David Bruce, and William Rand (deputy director of the US Mutual Security Agency).*

On his well-publicized trip to the United States the previous April–May 1952, he had been lauded by the *New York Times* as one of the architects of a new and unified Europe. He did not see Eisenhower but sent him a copy of his May 13, 1952, speech before the National Press Club where he proclaimed the unification of Europe "the most important political and economic undertaking of our time." He declared the six members of the ECSC were not creating a coalition of states but "a union among men."[36]

In the spring of 1953, Bruce had suggested to Dulles that Monnet be invited to present the merits of the ECSC to US steel industrialists and lawmakers. Monnet gladly accepted the invitation and arrived in early May, bringing Etzel and Spierenburg, his High Authority vice presidents, with him. Meeting with several key industrialists, he and Etzel, through "a masterful presentation of their version of the facts," succeeded in muting their skepticism and some of the outright opposition to their community, as historian Pascaline Winand asserts.[37] Enjoying social invitations from his New York friends, he also saw Bowie, Ball, and Felix Frankfurter in Washington.

After being awarded an honorary degree from Columbia University on June 2, Monnet met with Eisenhower the next day. The president called Monnet and his vice presidents, who accompanied him to the White House, representatives of the "new Europe." In the communiqué issued after the June 3 meeting, Eisenhower reaffirmed his support for European unity and for the efforts of the three men to implement the Schuman Plan.

Testifying before both the Senate and House Foreign Relations committees on June 4 and 5, "Mr. Europe," as he was hailed in the press, explained the goals of the ECSC. He tried to ease their doubts about the ratification of the EDC Treaty, in spite of Charles de Gaulle's opposition, and affirmed his faith in the development of a United States of Europe. In his meeting with the prominent senator from Arkansas, William Fulbright, he stressed the importance of a loan and hoped to convince him and the other lawmakers that the European movement was making progress. The three High Authority officials also met with Dulles several times as well as with other high-ranking policymakers, and to them all, the Europeans conveyed the same optimism about Europe's future. Monnet had Bowie draft a letter for Eisenhower, which the president willingly sent to the chairmen of both the Senate and House Foreign Relations committees, strongly recommending they provide financing for the ECSC.[38]

Monnet's May–June 1953 visit to the United States was successful in publicizing the merits of the Schuman Plan and garnering support both on Capitol Hill and in the administration. The White House and both houses of Congress "exchanged messages of support for the nascent Europe" but approved no funds. While Dulles and Eisenhower favored the loan to the ECSC, some Republicans declared they must cut the deficit, not add to it, and were opposed to aiding a European "cartel." But Monnet was not discouraged and continued to lobby each of these two influential political leaders by sending them letters, messages, and copies of his speeches.

Both Dulles and Eisenhower met with Monnet on his April 1954 trip to Washington when he once again asked Congress to grant a loan to the ECSC. On this visit, he spent a lot of time lobbying State Department officials, including Livingstone Merchant, then assistant secretary of state, who supported the request. Despite opposition from officials in Treasury, the State Department, the Foreign Operations Administration, and the Export-Import Bank, Monnet's persuasive personal diplomacy and the support of Dulles overrode them. As a result, the Frenchman secured a twenty-five-year loan of $100 million, giving the ECSC needed funds for modernization on generous terms: 3.875 percent interest with repayment to begin in 1958.[39] But the US loan did not prove as useful a lever in impacting industrial growth as Monnet had envisioned. Moreover, the ECSC never became an investment bank for coal and steel because both public and private lenders preferred to loan directly rather than through the High Authority. But the loan enabled the ECSC to become a lender and boost social programs such as subsidized housing and retraining assistance to unemployed workers.[40]

The crisis over the European Defense Community in France hampered Monnet's presidency of the High Authority. A mounting nationalist campaign in opposition to the idea of a European army began soon after the May 23, 1952, EDC Treaty was signed and continued unabated throughout that year and in 1953. It constantly distracted Monnet from his focus on ECSC initiatives and may explain his acquiescence to the merger policies that were so contrary to his rhetoric. Every major issue relating to the ECSC inevitably involved France and Germany, stoking French fears, and made them give great importance to their relationship with Germany. To deal with the German industrialists, the High Authority had to deal with Adenauer, and once McCloy left Bonn in June 1952, Adenauer relied on Monnet for advice. At one point, the chancellor warned his French friend that efforts to deal with Ruhr cartels could negatively affect the ratification of the EDC Treaty in the German parliament.[41]

## Critical Summer of 1954

The summer of 1954 proved a pivotal time for France, for Monnet, and for the High Authority. The sixty-five-year-old suffered a stroke but claimed it was only flu and left Luxembourg for the Swiss Alps, where he stayed much of the summer until the middle of August. As a result, he was unable to fulfill his duties at the High Authority or influence the EDC debates on the European army. But he had not been an important factor in these controversial discussions since Georges Bidault had replaced Schuman as foreign minister early in 1953. With Schuman's departure and Monnet away from Paris, Monnet was severed from French foreign policy for the first time in years. As a result, his stature plummeted in Paris.[42]

Coming to power a month after the May 1954 French defeat in Indochina, Prime Minister Pierre Mendès-France realized that EDC was a major obstacle to launching a new French foreign policy. Like his predecessors, he had been in favor of negotiating a new EDC Treaty. But, by August 1954, he concluded that a decision was necessary in order to break the EDC stalemate, to allow France to speak with greater authority within the Atlantic alliance, and to encourage fresh moves for European unity.[43] He decided not to submit the treaty to parliament before he had obtained additional provisions that would make its terms more favorable to France. At the final round of EDC negotiations conducted by the foreign ministers of the six nations in Brussels, August 19–23, the United States and the five member states rejected Mendès-France's request for five additional protocols that would amend the treaty. It had already become filled with annexes and protocols designed by the French to counter their fears of German rearmament and to delay the ratification by the French parliament.[44]

Tomlinson had worked tirelessly from 1952 to 1954 in his effort to persuade the French government to submit the EDC plan to parliament. He and

David Bruce had appealed to their own government to use all the weapons it could muster to exert pressure on the prime minister.[45] On August 21, Tomlinson went to Brussels with Arthur Hartman, the young American diplomat in the Paris embassy, to follow the negotiations. At 1:00 a.m. on August 22, long after the fiery debates had concluded, Tomlinson received a telephone call in his hotel from the French prime minister, who asked that the young American come to see him. In this early morning meeting, Mendès-France said he knew that Tomlinson was one of France's most loyal American friends. Because of that, he wanted to explain to him personally why he had decided to abandon the EDC and why the treaty would be defeated, and he asked Tomlinson to explain it to his government.

Much to Hartman's surprise, Tomlinson sauntered out of the lengthy meeting exhilarated instead of depressed. As the two young diplomats ambled arm in arm in the dark back to their hotel, Tomlinson exclaimed, "Who in their wildest dreams would have thought that a French prime minister would call in a young kid from Moscow, Idaho, and ask him to explain his actions to the U.S. Government?"[46] The next day, Tomlinson sent a lengthy telegram to the State Department detailing his long conversation with the prime minister and his counterarguments.[47] Instead of seeking parliament's vote on the EDC Treaty it had inherited, Mendès-France called on the National Assembly on August 30 to adopt "la question préalable," a procedural motion that effectively closed the highly charged session without a discussion. The vote of 319 to 264 in support of this motion killed the EDC.[48]

Having recovered completely from his stroke, Monnet had taken the train to Paris from his home in Houjarray and sat quietly in the public gallery of the National Assembly on August 30 listening to the debate. Monnet recognized the implicit criticism of himself and the ECSC in the prime minister's remarks to the National Assembly. After the vote, he quietly left the chamber.[49] Stooped by sadness and disappointment, the sixty-five-year-old ambled slowly down rue de l'Université, pondering the ramifications this defeat would have for France, Europe, integration, and peace.

The EDC's failure came to symbolize a defeat for integration and for Monnet. The untimely stroke and paralysis suffered by Tomlinson soon after the vote dramatically underscored this failure. This young American took the EDC's demise as a personal defeat that could have been avoided if he had worked harder. The following year, "Tommy," who loved both France and being a member of Monnet's team, died at the age of thirty-seven. Uri paid this young American a tribute seldom given to those who were not fellow countrymen, saying "Tommy was one of us."[50]

The failure of the French to ratify the EDC Treaty not only infuriated Acheson but deeply angered Dulles because it demonstrated a failure of a policy the United States had pursued on German rearmament and integrating that nation into the West. Since the secretary of state had argued that the objectives of NATO could not be realized without the EDC, it had become part of a package deal with that alliance. Dulles feared that EDC's failure meant that containment of the Soviet Union and communism in Europe, embodied in NATO, would be jeopardized. In the fall of 1953 and spring of 1954, the United States had aggressively lobbied the French government urging them to ratify the EDC Treaty. Using all diplomatic channels, including Eisenhower, in letters to Mendès-France's predecessor, French Prime Minister Joseph Laniel, US Ambassador to France Douglas Dillon, and the British government, the administration stressed the importance of the EDC as a way of securing a German contribution to the defense of Western Europe, tying Germany to those nations, and preventing a resurgence of German nationalism. In a private meeting with Bidault on October 18, 1953, at the French embassy in Washington, Dulles had stated that the United States believed that "the future of Europe and indeed Western Civilization depends upon whether we grasp the opportunity to integrate Germany with the West." He asserted that the United States had long hoped for European unity and "through the Marshall Plan and military aid has provided about $30 billion. Furthermore, our strategic planning [had] been based on [the] development of real strength in Europe through unification."[51]

At Bruce's suggestion, Dulles had traveled to London and Paris in April 1954 to play the Anglo-American card. He reassured his allies that the United States would maintain its fair share of military forces in Europe as long as the threat to Europe existed. When he learned about the French Assembly's failure to ratify the EDC Treaty on August 30, Dulles expressed his bitterness toward the French government in a lengthy statement the following day. "It is a tragedy that in one country nationalism, abetted by Communism, has asserted itself so as to endanger the whole of Europe," he wrote. "It would be unconscionable if the failure to realize the EDC through no fault of Germany's should now be used as an excuse for penalizing Germany. . . . The Federal German Republic should take its place as a free and equal member of the society of nations." But he added, "The United States stands ready to support the many in Western Europe who despite their valiant efforts are left in grave anxiety."[52]

The failure of this defense plan clearly demonstrated certain realities. It showed that many Frenchmen could not tolerate the rearmament of Germany under EDC's terms because it stirred up fears of a possible future war with that nation. Rioux argues that the "EDC quarrel helped to bring to the surface a past which had been dismissed, perhaps too hastily in 1945" and "focused attention on the recent nightmare." He contends that France since 1944 had "put its faith in the healing powers of collective amnesia yet which seemed to have lost none of its appetite for impassioned controversies. This stirring of the collective conscience," he adds, and "the revival of instincts of nationalism and self-preservation tended of course to inflame the quarrel over the EDC."[53] Moreover, the EDC failure also made it clear that Monnet's proposal, which embodied the idea of a possible federal or supranational "European Government," would not succeed. The "first Europe [ECSC] was in many ways a security Europe, not an economic one," Duchêne argues, as both the ECSC and the European army "were primarily addressed to German power." Yet paradoxically, "the EDC proved that it was dangerous, even impossible, to pursue further European union by direct security or political means."[54]

## Failures and Successes of ECSC

It had become clear very early in its operation that the European Coal and Steel Community failed as a supranational governing body to achieve its goal: the creation of a genuine common market in coal and steel. It found it was powerless to alter the long-held practices of producers or governments. And for some time, the European Defense Community debacle overshadowed the accomplishments of the ECSC. But Monnet's act of setting up the ECSC and converting it into a functioning international body proved significant for France, Germany, and European integration. Under Monnet in the first two years, the 200 representatives of six nations established an organization that gathered information, issued decrees, and attempted to enforce certain regulations. Monnet forged a team of men who most often looked beyond national boundaries. Though plagued by bureaucratic rivalry and resentment of Monnet's management style, the innovative High Authority of over 200 civil servants working together at the end of 1954 managed to create a new international political framework. This institution forced member states to negotiate with one another constantly and inhibited unilateral action by some states in certain areas on some occasions. Representatives made a habit of frequent consultation, and negotiation became a means of facilitating compromise. Moreover, many of the decisions and initiatives taken by majority vote on some issues were usually respected and enforced.

The creation of the ECSC and subsequent negotiations had the unintended consequence of solving the Ruhr problem. Historian John Gillingham claims that while Monnet intended to impose long-term controls on the German coal and steel industry, he succeeded "in liberating them from allied cooperation and restoring them to their traditionally dominant position in the economy of Western Europe." He points out that the ECSC negotiations bolstered the position of German heavy industry by generating spontaneous support for coal and steel throughout the German business community. Moreover, the anticartel campaign brought the Germans and French together in negotiations where they discovered previously unrecognized mutual benefits. Monnet's anticartel campaign furthered the process of "normalcy in Germany's foreign relations with France." The Americans supported this because they did not want to let decartelization and deconcentration jeopardize German rearmament and were committed to

restoring Ruhr industry to private ownership. Through new institutional arrangements, the Ruhr restoration occurred in the context of public control and social
responsibility, "inspired a new degree of confidence" between France and Germany, and set the stage "for more far-reaching integration."[55]

By establishing and running the High Authority, Monnet demonstrated
that supranational cooperation could serve as a brake on nationalism in some
specific, limited economic areas. By instituting the principle that High Authority decisions were made by majority vote, the ECSC showed that nations could
share some sovereignty and survive. It also demonstrated that some common
economic problems could be successfully dealt with by this community. In
addition, Monnet demonstrated his deeply held belief that institutions, based
on the rule of law, could serve as frameworks for changing patterns of thinking and behavior. By running Europe's "First Government" of international
civil servants from six different nations and institutionalizing cooperation, he
created a new transnational political elite, argues Schwartz, that "worked to
overcome the divisions of the interwar period and lay the foundation for a lasting and stable peace."[56] And this transnational organization made a significant
step toward Monnet's goal to unite Europe because he changed the context
within which the French and Germans, the wartime rivals, and other Europeans could think and work. As a result, he advanced Franco-German rapprochement and brought Europe closer to peace. The ECSC remains his greatest legacy. By making the newly created institutions function, however
imperfectly, he proved that Europeans could work together for a common
agenda within a new framework.

Monnet demonstrated once again that he was an innovator as well as a
pragmatic leader who had the ability to create a strategy to solve a crisis. As
in the Monnet Plan, he was able to transform his own concept for a European
Coal and Steel Community, designed with other Europeans, into a functioning
institution with himself at the helm. The very existence of the ECSC, which
focused on a practical, narrow goal, generated momentum to move European
leaders forward in their thinking. As a result, the ECSC became an important
step and served as a foundation upon which further integration was built. It
pushed European leaders to think positively about some additional concrete
forms of integration as a means of healing the wounds of war.

The failure of the European Defense Community scheme disappointed
but did not come as a total surprise to Monnet. Concocted under pressure, its
goals were unrealistic, and the institutional structure outlined in the treaty after
endless negotiations was flawed and unworkable. The EDC agreement lacked
the careful planning and attention to detail displayed in the Schuman Plan
negotiations. But Monnet's strategy of designing it as a solution to an immediate crisis—to satisfy the US call for German rearmament and save the Schuman Plan—was successful. For him, it was a matter of priorities. He had
known the idea of a European army would face firm opposition but was deter-

*Photo by Théo Mey. Courtesy of Fondation Jean Monnet pour l'Europe.*
*© Photothèque de la Ville de Luxembourg.*

*Jean Monnet (left) and Robert Schuman in Luxembourg on the third anniversary of the Schuman Plan, May 9, 1953. Etienne Hirsch is walking behind them at the left.*

mined that nothing should prevent the conclusion of the Schuman Plan negotiations and the ratification of its final treaty. And he had won the support of both his own and the US government. The EDC defeat was valuable and instructive. Through the EDC, the French government successfully slowed German recovery by delaying US attempts to rearm Germany. And while the EDC defeat discouraged integrationists in the short term, it was also a pivotal event because it generated constructive thinking about ways to continue the process.

Through the Monnet and Schuman plans and the EDC, Monnet played a key role in shaping France's postwar strategy of pursuing Western European consolidation and integration between 1945 and 1954. French leaders in positions of power and influence agreed with Monnet that European integration would serve French interests by enhancing economic recovery, containing Germany, and strengthening French influence in European affairs. He and his planners served French national interests by generating economic recovery and maintaining a degree of independence in executing the Monnet Plan by relying on US aid. Because France had recast Franco-German relations through the Schuman Plan, it created political goodwill between these rivals. And the EDC served French interests by postponing German rearmament until the positive and healing effects of the Schuman Plan could be experienced by both Germany and France and rearmament could be acceptably implemented under NATO. Despite institutional and political weakness, France had gained prominence from its political leadership in Europe and its economic growth, and de Gaulle was able to profit from this strength when he came to power in 1958.[57]

Monnet's American connections helped US policy maintain its support of French national interests and strengthen that nation's role as a leader in Europe. His friends played a major role in gaining White House support for his efforts to make the ECSC a viable international organization and sustain European cooperation for the EDC until 1954. McCloy, Acheson, Tomlinson, and Bruce, along with Eisenhower, persuaded Truman to support the Pleven Plan. Once Eisenhower became president, both he and Dulles strongly supported Monnet's request for a US loan to implement some High Authority programs. Ever since the Frenchman had met Eisenhower in July 1951 and ably convinced him that both the ECSC and the EDC would further European unity, Monnet wrote the president often while continuing his correspondence with Dulles. He knew these powerful Americans were both personal and official allies in his plans for European unity, and he wisely continued to lobby them to ensure their continued support. When McCloy left Bonn in June 1952, Adenauer lost an important supporter at his side in Germany but the prominent American lawyer remained a strong supporter of Adenauer and European integration from across the Atlantic. Bruce, Tomlinson, and Hartman continued to work closely with Monnet to help maintain US support for French initiatives that were aligned with the administration's goal of promoting political and economic security in Europe.

The EDC debacle greatly diminished Monnet's influence in Europe as well as France. Severely weakened because he symbolized the failed Pleven Plan, Monnet personally had become a lame-duck president of the High Authority and thought about resigning. He no longer had a voice in French foreign policy, since Schuman and Pleven had left office, and he suffered personal attacks because he was the embodiment of the "so-called failed federalism" and "supranationalism." De Gaulle continually attacked him without naming him, as the EDC replaced German rearmament as the real enemy among many political figures in France. These assaults made Monnet a controversial public figure,[58] and he never regained the influence and stature he had enjoyed when he embarked upon establishing the ECSC in the summer of 1952.

## Notes

1. Jean Monnet, *Memoirs* (New York: Doubleday, 1978), p. 375.
2. François Duchêne, *Jean Monnet: The First Statesman of Interdependence* (New York: W. W. Norton, 1994), pp. 238–239; Dirk Spierenburg and Raymond Poidevin,

*The History of the High Authority of the European Coal and Steel Community* (London: Weidenfeld and Nicolson, 1994), pp. 17, 55–56; Monnet, *Memoirs*, p. 375.

3. Spierenburg and Poidevin, *History of the High Authority,* pp. 50–52.

4. Ibid., p. 55.

5. Ibid., pp. 52–55.

6. Ibid., pp. 57–70; Duchêne, interview by the author, September 13, 2002.

7. Spierenburg and Poidevin, *History of the High Authority,* pp. 58–59.

8. Ibid., p. 59.

9. Ibid., p. 61.

10. Ibid., pp. 62–63.

11. Ibid., pp. 75–77.

12. John Gillingham, *Coal, Steel, and the Rebirth of Europe, 1945–1955* (Cambridge, UK: Cambridge University Press, 1991), p. 319.

13. Piero S. Graglia, interviews by the author, October 4, 2003, August 12, 2004, September 2, 2004, February 8, 2005, and October 30, 2010. See Piero S. Graglia, *Altiero Spinelli* (Bologna, Italy: Il Mulino, 2008).

14. Maria Grazia Melchionni, *Altiero Spinelli et Jean Monnet* (Lausanne, Switzerland: Fondation Jean Monnet pour l'Europe Centre de recherches européennes, 1993), pp. 31–41.

15. Melchionni, *Altiero Spinelli,* p. 41.

16. Pascaline Winand, "Eisenhower, Dulles, Monnet, and the Uniting of Europe," in *Monnet and the Americans,* ed. Clifford Hackett (Washington, DC: Jean Monnet Council, 1995), pp. 117–118.

17. Allocution de Jean Monnet, February 8, 1953, AMH 46/5/5, Fondation Jean Monnet.

18. Jean Monnet to John Foster Dulles, telegram, November 24, 1952, and Dulles to Monnet, telegram, November 26, 1952, Correspondence JM, Box 62, Dulles Papers, Princeton University Library.

19. Pascaline Winand, "Eisenhower, Dulles, Monnet," pp. 119–120.

20. Ibid., pp. 118–120.

21. Monnet to Dean Acheson, February 11, 1953, and Acheson to Monnet, March 4, 1953, Acheson Papers, Yale University Library.

22. Duchêne, *Jean Monnet*, p. 239.

23. Ibid.

24. Max Kohnstamm, interview by the author, November 19, 2005.

25. Spierenburg and Poidevin, *History of the High Authority*, pp. 71–74.

26. Kohnstamm, interview.

27. Ibid., pp. 56–57; Duchêne, *Jean Monnet*, p. 240.

28. Duchêne, *Jean Monnet*, pp. 239–240; Spierenburg and Poidevin, *History of the High Authority*, pp. 72–78.

29. Gillingham, *Coal, Steel*, pp. 319–322; Duchêne, *Jean Monnet*, pp. 241–242.

30. Gillingham, *Coal, Steel*, p. 321.

31. Ibid., pp. 322–325; Duchêne, *Jean Monnet*, pp. 241–242.

32. Philippe Mioche, "Jean Monnet et les sidérurgistes Européens," in *Jean Monnet, l'Europe et les chemins de la paix*, ed. Gérard Bossuat and Andreas Wilkens (Paris: Publications de la Sorbonne, 1999), pp. 297–306.

33. Gillingham, *Coal, Steel*, pp. 325–330.

34. Ibid., pp. 339–340; Duchêne, *Jean Monnet*, p. 249.

35. Gillingham, *Coal, Steel*, pp. 323–324.

36. *New York Times,* April 19, 1952; Jean Monnet, speech at the National Press Club, May 13, 1952, Pre-Presidential 1916–1952 Series, Principal File, Box 78, Eisen-

hower Papers; Jean Monnet, interview on *Meet the Press*, June 7, 1953, Cross-reference file, Jean Monnet, Box 2137, Eisenhower Papers; Pascaline Winand, *Eisenhower, Kennedy, and the United States of Europe* (New York: St. Martin's Press, 1993), pp. 43–46.

37. Winand, *Eisenhower, Kennedy,* p. 44.

38. Ibid., pp. 43–46. Monnet also reiterated these themes in his address to the Overseas Writers Club on June 5, 1953. A copy of this speech is in the George Ball Papers, Box I, 70, 14, Princeton University Library.

39. Winand, *Eisenhower, Kennedy*, pp. 52–54.

40. Duchêne, *Jean Monnet,* pp. 244–245; Gillingham, *Coal, Steel,* pp. 340–342; editorial note, *FRUS*, 1951, vol. 4, pp. 107–108; John Gillingham, "Solving the Ruhr Problem: German Heavy Industry and the Schuman Plan," in *The Beginnings of the Schuman Plan 1950–51*, ed. Klaus Schwabe (Baden-Baden, Germany: Nomos Verlagsgesellschaft, 1988), pp. 399–436.

41. Duchêne, *Jean Monnet*, pp. 249–250.

42. Ibid., pp. 249–254.

43. Jean-Pierre Rioux, *The Fourth Republic, 1944–1958* (Cambridge, MA: Cambridge University Press, 1987), pp. 228–229.

44. Ibid., 229.

45. David Bruce, diary entries, June to August 1954, Bruce Diaries, Virginia Historical Society; Sherrill Brown Wells, "Monnet and 'The Insiders': Nathan, Tomlinson, Bowie, and Schaetzel," in *Monnet and the Americans,* ed. Clifford Hackett (Washington, DC: Jean Monnet Council, 1995), pp. 210–211; Irwin M. Wall, *The United States and the Making of Postwar France, 1945–1954* (Cambridge, UK: Cambridge University Press, 1991), pp. 268–270.

46. Arthur Hartman, interview by the author, October 15, 1990; Wells, "Monnet and 'The Insiders,'" p. 210.

47. *FRUS*, 1952–1954, vol. 5, part 1, pp. 1064–1067.

48. Rioux, *Fourth Republic,* pp. 229–230; Eric Roussel, *Jean Monnet* (Paris: Fayard, 1996), pp. 669–675.

49. Duchêne, *Jean Monnet*, p. 256.

50. Pierre Uri, interview by the author, June 15, 1990.

51. *FRUS*, 1952–1954, vol. 5, part 1, pp. 826–828; Winand, *Eisenhower, Kennedy*, pp. 47–63.

52. *FRUS*, 1952–1954, vol. 5, part 2, pp. 1120–1122.

53. Rioux, *Fourth Republic,* p. 207.

54. Duchêne, *Jean Monnet*, p. 256.

55. Gillingham, "Solving the Ruhr Problem," pp. 434–436.

56. Thomas A. Schwartz, *America's Germany, John J. McCloy and the Federal Republic of Germany* (Cambridge, MA: Harvard University Press, 1991), p. 303.

57. William I. Hitchcock, *France Restored, Cold War Diplomacy and the Quest for Leadership in Europe, 1944–1954* (Chapel Hill: University of North Carolina Press, 1998), p. 203.

58. Duchêne, *Jean Monnet*, pp. 254–257.

# 7

# Regaining Momentum, 1954–1958

**In the fall of 1954,** the defeat of the European Defense Community (EDC) cast a shadow of gloom over many European leaders who favored integration. With Monnet discredited, the European Coal and Steel Community (ECSC) was weakened, and the forces of federalism and supranationalism were undermined. As Robert Marjolin noted, "The rejection of the EDC, was, by extension, that of all supranational institutions."[1] Monnet later called the EDC "a bad business." But discouraged and forlorn as he was, the sixty-six-year-old did not abandon his dream to bring peace through a unified Europe. Because Monnet had always believed that failures provided opportunities for reevaluation and learning, EDC's demise motivated him to think about additional paths to integration. Paul-Henri Spaak, then Belgian foreign minister, telephoned Monnet in early September 1954 and exclaimed, "Obviously it's a disaster. Can we do anything in the economic field?" Monnet replied, "We must try." As they both were ready to move forward, discussions in the following weeks led these men to decide to work together as a team to revive the momentum for European unity. Since integration in the security and political fields had been unsuccessful, they focused on the economic sphere. Because of Monnet's damaged stature, these two statesmen agreed that Monnet should prepare proposals and remain in the background while Spaak would take the lead in public and develop a diplomatic initiative.[2]

## Expansion of British and US Commitments to Germany

While Monnet and Spaak continued their discussions during the fall of 1954, British Foreign Secretary Anthony Eden proposed an alternative to the failed

EDC. He argued that, in light of the continued US insistence on adding German strength to European defenses, rearmament could easily be achieved within NATO. He pointed out that this defensive alliance could provide the necessary level of supervision of the West German army and thereby quell the worries of France. Bringing Germany into NATO, he declared, would also allow the Allies to formally end their occupation of West Germany and permit Allied governments to recognize its sovereignty. Eden proposed that a new framework for European defense cooperation be created, called the Western European Union (WEU), and be incorporated within NATO by amending and expanding the Brussels treaty. To achieve this, he recommended that West Germany and Italy become members of this mutual defense agreement, signed in 1948, by the three Benelux nations, France, and Britain. Because it facilitated the Federal Republic's membership in NATO, the other Alliance leaders consented. Eden therefore convened a conference in London of the five signatory members of the Brussels agreement, its new members Italy and West Germany, and the United States and Canada, which met September 28 to October 3, 1954. On its last day these nations adopted Eden's plan and agreed to establish the WEU.[3]

West German Chancellor Konrad Adenauer was happy to have achieved the NATO solution he wanted because he believed rearmament was an important part of his own Western-oriented policy of strength. He and the participants of the London Conference met again three weeks later in Paris. They negotiated the final details of the Occupation Statutes, the last provisions of the WEU, and the terms of the admission of the West Germany to NATO while Pierre Mendès-France and Adenauer had heated negotiations about the Saar. Agreements were finally reached and nine Western powers (France, the United Kingdom, Luxembourg, Belgium, the Netherlands, West Germany, Italy, Canada, and the United States) signed various protocols and declarations known as the Paris Accords (Paris Agreements) on October 23. They granted Germany a greater degree of sovereignty, secured a German agreement to end the Allied zones of occupation, created the WEU, and provided a plan to settle the future of the coal-rich Saar region by means of a referendum. The Federal Republic of Germany thus became an ally under NATO, with its forces placed under the Alliance's integrated command. To reassure France, the British gave the WEU a guarantee they had withheld from the EDC—that British troops would be stationed in West Germany unless a majority of NATO consented to their withdrawal.[4]

Adenauer viewed the Paris Accords as a success because he believed his nation's sovereignty was as important as NATO membership. More than ever before, the chancellor placed his faith in the United States as well as in Britain, which had linked itself permanently to the continent with its pledge to station British troops in West Germany. During the final negotiations in Paris, French Premier Pierre Mendès-France had pressured Adenauer to accept the French demand that a plebiscite be held in the Saar three months after its political freedom was established. Faced with the threat that the French would not otherwise sign the Paris Accords, the chancellor had finally assented. In his press conference in Paris, Adenauer claimed October 23, 1954, was "the day of reconciliation with France."[5]

The lengthy three-year EDC debate in France from 1951 to 1954 and that treaty's ultimate defeat impacted the US commitment to Germany and NATO. The sustained US efforts to persuade the French to adopt the EDC Treaty had affected Washington in several ways at a time when it was unusually open to European influence. It acclimated American officials and politicians to the idea of having US troops in Germany for the long term. It also made them aware that the British and US forces in Germany not only protected Europe against the Russians, whose offensive power seemed more ominous after events in Korea, but also afforded the Europeans protection against themselves. In addition, the peculiarities of the US political system, including fragmentation of the US national security apparatus, the bureaucratic rivalry and turf battles, and the competition among the individual military services, affected the climate in Washington. Ernest May argues that the system's "extraordinary openness to influence from sources outside the nation" enabled Monnet and some of his colleagues, Britons, and Adenauer to "become, at least temporarily, part of an organic federal system" and exert strong influence. US officials "embraced Britain and Western Europe" as if they "had become equal states in the American union" because of a combination of feelings of guilt and obligation toward Europeans as well as a belief that they needed US aid and protection. The need to reassure Europeans that isolation would not be revived and that the United States would not abandon them was a factor in the expansion of Washington's commitment. Moreover, the US adoption of NATO's strategic concept in December 1954 to defend the frontiers of NATO countries with its own forces greatly strengthened its commitment to Europe.[6]

By the end of 1954, the Paris Accords and the broadened US and British commitments to Germany helped provide increased security and stability to Europe. This new political climate enabled Europe's leaders to focus more on ways to continue with integration. The ECSC negotiations and the Council of Europe meetings fueled debates about European unity, which generated ideas for integration or cooperation on health matters, postal services, and transport and for an agricultural common market directed by a supranational institution. As many had concluded that shared national sovereignty over a single sector had not worked, others argued it was more logical to plan for the integration of whole economies. Some popular support for integration in general and for an initiative to counter the EDC's collapse convinced politicians to continue exploring further options. And, as political scientist Andrew Moravcsik argues, the history of the European Community began with the failure of the EDC.[7]

## Exploring New Initiatives

The fall of the Mendès-France government in February 1955 just before Monnet's scheduled departure from the ECSC's High Authority provided unexpected opportunities for him to push integration forward. After Monnet announced his retirement as High Authority president in November 1954, Spaak and Adenauer strongly urged him to stay in that position to further integration. When the February foreign ministers' meeting to choose his replacement was postponed, Monnet saw this as an opportunity to introduce new integration schemes. He told the German and Belgian leaders that he would remain High Authority president until a successor was named if they met his condition: that their governments commit themselves to negotiate treaties on new communities.[8]

Spaak and Monnet together successfully relaunched the integration process by convening a series of meetings between February and June 1955 of ECSC leaders to discuss Monnet's new proposals. Spaak circulated Monnet's ideas, developed with Etienne Hirsch, Pierre Uri, and Jacques Van Helmont, in a letter to the ECSC foreign ministers on April 4. Spaak proposed that a conference be convened to negotiate treaties to accomplish two goals: to extend the ECSC to create a further round of sectoral integration on the pattern of the Schuman Plan to cover all of energy and transport, and to create a new community for civil nuclear power (later to be called European Atomic Energy Community, or Euratom). Spaak wanted the conference chaired by Monnet, whom he believed could be persuaded to withdraw his resignation from the High Authority. Spaak and Monnet did not propose a general common market because they feared another EDC fiasco. As Monnet later explained, "We started with Euratom because we didn't dare go to a Common Market." Spaak added, "Our ambitions were modest. So were our hopes. It seemed important to us to advance on solid ground where we had real chances of success, leaving bigger plans till later. Above all, we had to avoid another rebuff."[9]

After discussing Monnet's proposals on April 23, 1955, Spaak and Johan Willem Beyen, foreign minister of the Netherlands, issued a joint memorandum that moved the integration discussions forward. In 1952, Beyen had announced that he believed sectoral integration was not sufficient to promote economic development and ultimately political union. Both Dirk Spierenburg and Max Kohnstamm had been part of a Dutch working group set up in 1949 with Beyen to consider measures needed to make economic integration work. They concluded the six nations should organize a single market and unify trade policy. Beyen asserted that a common market was needed because partial integration, like sectoral integration, did not reinforce the sense of solidarity and unity in Europe to the same degree as general economic integration. What was needed, he argued, was economic integration across the board. He asserted it must be supranational like the ECSC in order to function and must

*Jean Monnet (left) and Paul-Henri Spaak, September 10, 1952.*

include Germany in its framework. As a result, Spaak and Beyen decided to put forward two proposals—the "general" approach of Beyen and the "sectoral" approach of Monnet—and encapsulated them in what became known as the Benelux Memorandum. The sectoral approach was put in this diplomatic initiative, at Spaak's insistence, as a fall-back position should the general approach fail.[10]

The release of the Benelux Memorandum in mid-May 1955, just two weeks before the scheduled June 1–2 meeting of the foreign ministers of the six ECSC countries in the old Sicilian city of Messina, intensified political and business interest in the idea of a common market. And the prospect of a European conference for further integration forced the governments to define their positions. The leaders of the six had remained steadfastly supportive of new integration proposals throughout the spring of 1955, despite concerns about German rearmament and some clear opposition to European schemes and especially to Monnet. But finally the new French government under Prime Minister Edgar Faure ratified the 1954 Paris Accords on March 30, 1955. When these accords entered into force on May 8, 1955, Germany regained its sovereignty, began rearmament, and became a member of NATO.[11] Yet lingering anxiety about Germany helped the European leaders maintain their support for further steps that could harness that nation.

On May 21, 1955, Altiero Spinelli had dinner in Paris with Monnet who was preoccupied with discussions about the Benelux Memorandum. During the early 1950s, Spinelli had worked closely with Spaak and federalist leaders in an attempt to persuade European governments to adopt the federalist approach. The positive attitude of the US administration toward the EDC had encouraged some federalists to believe the EDC could create a kind of European military-political union and be a step closer to a federalist structure. But after the demise of the EDC, Spinelli's entry in his diary that day reveals how discouraged he was about the state of the federalist movement and his strong identification with Monnet.

> During this past year, we are dragging a cart like two stubborn donkeys. He [Monnet] is hoping to obtain a new initiative from governments; I am hoping to obtain a new surge from movements. Hope? To say the least. We are both deeply convinced that the world situation and the internal one of Europe no longer offers any fair possibility for the unity of Europe. We both feel a deep contempt for our contemporaries, both convinced that if we could seize power, we could do great things.[12]

Whatever Spinelli wished to believe, there was never a special relationship between the two men. But there was a mutual interest in maintaining contact, even though many of Spinelli's letters to the Frenchman continued to remain unanswered.[13]

## Relaunching of European Integration

At their meeting in Messina in June 1955, the foreign ministers of the six ECSC countries chose former French Prime Minister René Mayer to succeed Monnet at the High Authority and discussed the proposals for new European communities. Joseph Bech, premier of Luxembourg who chaired the meetings; Spaak; and Beyen were the driving forces in these complex, delicate negotiations that were pivotal in the integration process. Their goal, as stated in the Messina declaration, was to launch "a fresh advance towards the building of Europe" and create a market "free from all customs duties and all quantitative restrictions." The ministers drafted a joint proposal for the pooling of information and proposed they work on both the uses of nuclear energy and the establishment of a customs union that would lead to a common market. Reproducing much of the original Benelux position, they agreed to create an intergovernmental committee, headed by Spaak, that would consider, develop, and report back on the various proposals. In a private meeting with French Foreign Minister Antoine Pinay, who opposed the common market proposal, Spaak finally secured the latter's agreement to continuing exploratory talks on the implementation of the Benelux Memorandum. It was Spaak, despite general skepticism and the desire of most of the governments to proceed slowly, who turned the talks into a real *relance*.[14]

Monnet chose not to go to Messina because he knew that the current French government was hostile toward him. He also understood that, as Bech and Beyen thought him too controversial in France to be a positive force, the Benelux Memorandum had a better chance of succeeding if he stayed away. But accustomed to being at the center of key deliberations about Europe's future, it was hard for him to remain on the sidelines. He could not resist repeatedly phoning his close friend and colleague Kohnstamm, who was sent to Messina as an observer, and ordering him to deliver messages to Spaak and Walter Hallstein, state secretary of the West German Foreign Ministry. Driven mad by these constant directives, Kohnstamm finally shouted into the phone, "Mr. Monnet, please understand. They are not here to make Europe. They are here to *bury you*!"[15]

The Messina gathering succeeded in keeping the idea of European integration alive. By insisting on a nuclear-power community, these men gave the Europeanists in the French government, who supported some form of integration but opposed a common market, a chance to be involved in the process. At Messina, Spaak and Pinay agreed, if only tacitly, to allow Spaak, who was the most prominent integrationist next to Monnet, to explore the idea of a common market. Messina became a turning point because Beyen injected general economic integration through a common market into the process. Even though Monnet, the personification of the supranational, sectoral principle, was partially eclipsed, his ideas survived because the ministers accepted the sectoral grouping around nuclear power and confirmed "the institutional core of his approach," as developed in the Schuman Plan.[16]

After Monnet handed the presidency of the High Authority to René Mayer on June 10, 1955, he returned to France with his family after almost three years in Luxembourg. As their house in Houjarray was rented to another family through the end of that year, Silvia took the children to Cognac where they stayed with relatives. Happy to be back in France, Monnet moved in with his sister in Paris and set up an office in the large apartment of Silvia's brother, Alexandre de Bondini, at 83 avenue Foch, close to the Bois de Boulogne. It served as his place of work for the next twenty years. On entering the building, Monnet occasionally bumped into Prime Minister Edgar Faure, who lived on the floor below.[17]

After the meeting at Messina, Monnet developed with his colleagues a detailed plan for his proposal that a sectoral community be created to pool atomic energy resources for peaceful purposes. The Frenchman had become captivated by this idea after meeting American Max Isenbergh of the US Atomic Energy Commission (AEC) in November 1954. This young American lawyer and saxophone player was in Europe on a Rockefeller Senior Fellowship studying the control of civil nuclear power to prevent weapons proliferation. Because mutual friends Felix Frankfurter and Philip Graham had recommended the two meet, Monnet invited Isenbergh to have dinner with him in Luxembourg. "I suggested something which was obvious to me but sounded like pure poetry to him," recalled Isenbergh. "I suggested that cooperation among the six in the program for the peaceful development of atomic energy had a better prospect of bringing about integration than the Common army." Isenbergh said he presented it to Monnet "as a practical step. . . . Monnet was so excited that he kept me at his house until 2:30 a.m. Then in his imperious way, he insisted that I remain in Luxembourg . . . for the next ten days." In that period, "what was later called Euratom was born. . . . The original concept of Euratom was an organization for the peaceful development of atomic energy, with anti-proliferation as one of its central tenets."[18]

The concept appealed to Monnet primarily because he believed it would further European integration by achieving the immediate objective of the ECSC—to break down nationalism and channel energies into cooperative ventures benefiting the whole. After EDC's demise, he was anxious to try another experiment in supranationality, which he believed would promote European unity through a form of federalism. He was persuaded that a nuclear energy community had practical economic value because he believed nuclear energy could be a cheap source of electrical power for industrial use. For him, moreover, it had an important security dimension as he wanted France to gain the needed help to develop its nuclear energy program, which was inferior to the British, US, and Soviet programs. But he also strongly believed his own country should be constrained from developing atomic weapons for military purposes. Hoping to force Germany to channel its energies into this international sectoral endeavor, he envisioned a massive nuclear power program that not only would constrain Germany but would ensure Europe's energy security, unify Europe, and capture the popular imagination. He used the argument that a European atomic energy community would save Western Europe from political and economic decline.[19]

Monnet wrote, "The spearhead for the unification of Europe would have to be the peaceful atom . . . and only by integrating Europe's nuclear industries should we be able to guarantee that they were confined to strictly civilian use." It would be a "new industrial revolution" that would be uniquely European as no nation alone could achieve the results.[20] The idea of this new community seemed such an ideal way to fulfill so many of his cherished goals that he turned a blind eye to many of the difficult hurdles and harsh realities, such as disposal of fissionable materials, to be overcome if implemented.

Louis Armand, chairman of France's nationalized railways, worked closely with Monnet to develop the idea and promote Euratom from August 1955 through 1956. A man of influence as a board member of the French Atomic Energy Commission (CEA) and the Council of the Corps of Mining Engineers, Armand took it as his goal to promote a strong European industry.

As chairman of the Euratom Working Group of the Spaak Committee, he wrote a report on the community approach to these issues. He argued that large development costs could only be met by Europeans if they combined resources. Armand stressed that, to have effective policing, Euratom should control "the ownership and monopoly of the purchase and sale of all fissionable materials on the territory of the Six [nations]." Monnet harbored the unrealistic hope that Euratom would be free from direct US inspection or indirect UN inspection. Failing to see that the Americans would not permit it to be free from inspection, he optimistically proclaimed that Europeans were compelled to achieve atomic independence.[21]

## Creating the Action Committee for the United States of Europe

After months of deliberation and turning over the presidency of the High Authority to Mayer on June 10, 1955, Monnet focused on a way to build a political base from which he could further integration. Since he had no official position or title, he formed an international committee of political party and trade union leaders to lobby for European integration. In order to succeed in the effort to unite the six nations economically, he determined that the idea had to be publicized. For resolutions of his new group to have institutional force, both politicians and trade unions had to support them. He favored unions because they represented broad masses and, most likely, he rationalized, the general public interest. Visits in late 1954 and early 1955 from three German trade unionists—Heinrich Imig, head of the trade union for coal; Henrich Strater, head of the trade union for steel; and Walter Freitag, head of the German Federation of Trade Unions—had stimulated his thinking. These trade union leaders expressed their hope that integration would continue and their willingness to follow his lead. Strater told Monnet he enjoyed the confidence of the ECSC trade unionists, despite their fears his attitude was pro-French. He defined himself as a true European and expressed concern that Monnet's successor, Mayer, might not be equally European-minded. The three trade union leaders told Monnet they would commit themselves as delegates of their federations if he formed a new organization, with or without the German Social Democratic Party (SPD). Monnet's later two visits to Erich Ollenhauer, the SPD leader in Bonn, confirmed the SPD's readiness also to join his group.[22]

Monnet won the support for his new international committee from the French Socialist Party by cultivating a close relationship with its leader, Guy Mollet. The Socialists were willing to support European integration that focused on economic measures. They found Monnet's community for civil nuclear power appealing because it implied planning, a renunciation of weapons by the French, and nuclear controls on the Germans. As Monnet had wisely consulted Mollet about many of his drafts and ideas, these two men became close friends, and Monnet became Mollet's mentor on questions of European integration. With the Socialist leader's official backing, Monnet announced to the press on October 13, 1955, that thirty-three political and trade union leaders from all six ECSC countries had agreed to join in founding an Action Committee for the United States of Europe. Its purpose, as stated in its inaugural manifesto, was "to ensure that the Messina resolution . . . should be translated into a genuine step towards a United States of Europe."[23]

Monnet believed he was establishing "a new means of action," not a political party or another European movement.[24] He explained that he "always believed Europe would be built through crises and that it would be the sum of their solutions. But the solutions had to be proposed and applied."[25] He wrote that he "was not promising sensations but initiatives publicly explained and followed by action on the part of democratic organizations throughout Europe. Except through those organizations, the committee would have no means of action or influence."[26] He was convinced that his committee would become a strong political action group and a lobby for European integration in the six ECSC countries. It would be a way of turning the failure of the EDC into a positive movement toward unity and help counter the centrifugal forces of nationalism that threatened to prevent this union. Access to heads of government and a title are what he yearned for, and this committee provided both.

In the first three months of 1955, Monnet worked hard to meet and develop personal relationships with syndicalists and politicians in Germany, Belgium, the Netherlands, Italy, and Luxembourg in order to mobilize them in support of unity and democracy.[27] Because Kohnstamm spoke German and was an affable personality, he helped Monnet win bipartisan support for economic integration in Germany. Political parties and trade unions among the six countries that joined the committee were represented by their leaders, except for the Communists, Italian Nennie Socialists, and French Gaullists. Monnet's greatest challenge was his own nation's political leaders because the radicals and conservatives could not be counted on to be consistently pro-European. They not only disliked but distrusted him in part because they viewed him as an Atlanticist. His challenge was to persuade his countrymen to be in "a more European mood" and to accept both the common market idea and sectoral integration, a prospect that seemed remote in 1955.[28]

Even though Washington knew of Monnet's imminent departure from the High Authority in 1955 and that he no longer held an official office, his power to influence his American friends was not diminished. He persuaded John Foster Dulles, who in turn persuaded his State Department colleagues and President Eisenhower, to express their public recognition of the supranational approach just prior to the Messina conference. Monnet had also succeeded in persuading his friend Douglas Dillon, a Republican financier who was then the

*The first session of the Action Committee for the United States of Europe, Paris, January 17–18, 1956. Left to right: Jean Monnet, René Pleven, Erich Ollenhauer.*

Courtesy of Fondation Jean Monnet pour l'Europe.

US ambassador in Paris; Dulles; and President Eisenhower that his Action Committee was a new and positive development in bringing the European nations closer together.[29]

Monnet created the Action Committee at a time when improvement in the European and French economies fostered a more peaceful and optimistic climate in France on both the domestic and international fronts. The French government immediately accepted the result of the October 1955 Saar referendum, which produced an overwhelming vote in favor of a return of that territory to Germany. A June 1956 outline of an agreement on the Saar buried an issue that had plagued the two countries since 1919. As a result of the French legislative elections on January 2, 1956, five-sixths of the Gaullists in the National Assembly were defeated, breaking the deadlock between the pro- and anti-European forces, and giving the balance to the Socialist Party led by Mollet, who became prime minister on February 5. These developments strengthened French leaders' belief that a new era in international relations had been reached when peaceful coexistence and cooperation were seen as the most realistic policies for the nation.[30]

At its first session on January 18, 1956, the Action Committee adopted a resolution supporting the priorities of a civilian Euratom as outlined by Monnet and Armand. It welcomed non-ECSC members, such as Britain, which satisfied

Mollet, and declared that the resolutions in favor of Euratom would be introduced in each legislature of the six countries to pressure their respective governments. During the spring and summer of 1956, the committee's political parties accomplished this goal in all of the legislatures except Italy.[31]

## France's Nuclear Weapons Policy Jeopardizing Euratom

While Mollet had signed the Action Committee's resolution in support of Euratom, he was forced to change his position on weapons production after he became prime minister. Mollet and Monnet had been well aware of a belief among French officials that France would need its own nuclear force for reasons of both defense and prestige within the NATO alliance. On December 26, 1954, Mendès-France and forty officials had debated the merits of a French nuclear weapon but reached no formal conclusion. They decided to undertake the construction of a nuclear-powered submarine and to develop a nuclear energy infrastructure but delay the final decision on constructing an atomic bomb for a few more years. When Mollet announced to the National Assembly in January 1956 that all national nuclear programs would be taken over by Euratom and that member states would be forced to discontinue the construction of nuclear weapons, cries of outrage arose from the French Atomic Energy Commission (CEA), defense minister, members of parliament, and Gaullists, who all violently opposed renouncing the right to nuclear weapons. In July, Mollet was forced to change his position: France would not give up its right to construct an atomic bomb but would delay a definitive decision until 1961.[32]

Work on the bomb appeared even more critical to the French political establishment in 1956. Growing doubts about US willingness to use nuclear weapons against the Soviet Union, despite that power's continued nuclear progress, made France uneasy. Moreover, many of its leaders had felt abandoned by the Americans in the Suez Crisis created by Egypt's President Gamal Abdel Nasser's nationalization of that canal in July 1956. As a result, the idea of an integrated European nuclear force no longer looked so attractive. Many French politicians believed they needed their own nuclear capacity and sought a "trigger" in case the Americans hesitated to use nuclear weapons in defense of Europe. Even though French nuclear policy remained in transition, its primary objective was to make France a partner equal to Great Britain within, not independent of, the NATO alliance.[33]

While powerless to fight their nation's nuclear weapons policy, Monnet and Mollet worked hard to keep German support for Euratom. Mollet's January 1956 announcement that Euratom could not "preclude nuclear weapons" had infuriated the SPD and led German Foreign Minister Heinrich von Brentano to warn that the Bundestag would not ratify a treaty that discriminated against Germany. While Adenauer, the unions, and German Socialists in general supported Euratom, German industrialists believed they could gain better terms by dealing directly with the United States bilaterally on acquiring nuclear technology and supplies than by working through Euratom. Franz-Joseph Strauss, German minister of defense and atomic affairs, who was sympathetic to the industry's views, advocated freedom for his nation's private industry to own and freely dispose of fissionable materials subject to German government control. This view ran counter to Monnet's unrealistic view that the material should be sold to Euratom by the United States and subsequently leased to individual and public users, not to countries, and that Euratom should exercise any needed controls.[34] Monnet's enthusiasm continued to blind him to the hurdles facing his efforts to establish a civilian Euratom.

Fearing that an alliance among industry, Strauss, and the CEA would lobby against the Euratom Treaty, Monnet took action to quell growing opposition in Germany. He reassured the SPD through letters from Mollet to Ollenhauer, a member of the Action Committee, and stressed to Adenauer in Bonn on September 12, 1956, the priority of the Euratom Treaty over the common market treaty being negotiated by Spaak's committee. When Adenauer met Mollet on September 30, they agreed the treaties would be handled together, not separately. Just before another Mollet-Adenauer meeting on November 6, the US ambassador in Bonn, James B. Conant, was authorized by Dulles "to impress on Adenauer the importance of Euratom's monopoly ownership of fissionable materials and controls over use." Adenauer was convinced, overrode Strauss before meeting with Mollet, and saved Euratom from mounting German opposition. Monnet once again had used the US government to put pressure on Adenauer to gain his agreement.[35]

Monnet and Mollet continued to promote Euratom even after being forced to abandon the antiproliferation policy clause in the Euratom Treaty by the French establishment. This infuriated Isenbergh. The American lawyer who had given Monnet the idea of developing a program for the peaceful uses of atomic energy was so upset that it caused a rupture in his relations with Monnet. Isenbergh recalled,

> I think Monnet had . . . his goal—the integration of the six. He was indifferent to ways of getting there. He saw that somehow a program of peaceful development of atomic energy would help and that much he could embrace. But matters like proliferation of atomic bombs . . . didn't enter his mind affirmatively. . . . As soon as he discovered the French were against it, he realized that a provision for renunciation of weapon-making was a threat to his objectives. He didn't want to risk losing the French. He was therefore willing to go along with their desire for freedom to make atomic weapons. . . . He also, while affectionate in a touching way, could turn off affection completely. I experienced both sides of him. For a long period, he was very affectionate, considerate and thoughtful to me. When we broke on the proliferation issue, he became ruthless. . . . He made it known to my principals in the United

States, either in the Atomic Energy Commission, the State Department, or both that he regarded me as an obstacle to the integration of Europe. And that manifested itself in the communications I'd get from Washington.

The two men later became friends again, but Monnet's harsh treatment was not forgotten by Isenbergh.[36] Monnet treated some of his other colleagues badly, especially the younger ones, and had a reputation for ceasing to be friends with individuals who were no longer useful to him.[37]

Using the Action Committee, Monnet systematically and carefully pushed Euratom forward. The Suez Crisis exposed the dangers of Europe's dependence on Middle East oil and gave Euratom an unexpected boost. Mollet endorsed the Action Committee's proposal in its September 20, 1956, resolution that a "Wise Men's" group be formed to study nuclear-power production, define a program, specify targets, develop a realistic timetable for implementation, and thereby stimulate further political interest. On October 20–21, the foreign ministers of the six nations nominated three men to comprise that group: Franz Etzel, Adenauer's close friend and High Authority member; Armand; and Francesco Giordani, the head of the Italian Atomic Energy Commission. Monnet appointed Kohnstamm to be that group's secretary.[38]

The climate of peaceful coexistence between France and Germany facilitated the acceptance of Spaak's Intergovernmental Committee's report, named the Spaak Report, by the six nations at their Venice meeting on May 29, 1956. Five of the six strongly favored the common market but not Euratom. French opinion strongly supported Euratom but largely opposed the common market because of France's strong protectionist tradition. Since France would not proceed with the common market negotiations without Euratom, and Germany would not continue with negotiations on Euratom without the common market, Spaak proposed his committee continue to explore both ideas. Taking the report as a starting point, the six nations agreed to begin negotiating officially and charged his committee with drafting the appropriate treaties on both the Dutch proposal for a common market and Monnet's idea for a nuclear energy community.[39]

## Strong US Support for Euratom

Eisenhower and Dulles supported Monnet's effort to create a multinational program devoted to the peaceful uses of atomic energy because they attached great importance to European integration. As Eisenhower later wrote, "Euratom was one step. Then would come the effort toward economic union."[40] These leaders—along with Robert Bowie, then adviser to Dulles; Gerard Smith, the secretary of state's special assistant for atomic energy affairs; Robert Schaetzel, the Department of State official in charge of the peaceful uses of atomic energy; and John McCloy, then at Chase Manhattan Bank—shared Monnet's belief that institutions and programs that promoted economic cooperation among European nations were the most practical means of preventing future wars and promoting peace. As he had been in 1950, Bowie was especially helpful to Monnet. He told him what kind of collaboration was possible, how to gain support from the scientific community, and suggested ways to handle AEC Chairman Lewis Strauss, who strongly opposed Euratom.[41]

Not only did Euratom fit but it even furthered the foreign policy priorities of the Eisenhower administration. It built on the president's 1953 Atoms for Peace proposal, which offered other nations fissionable materials to be controlled by the International Atomic Energy Agency (IAEA) under UN auspices. The president understood that the Suez Crisis underscored Europe's need to develop atomic power rapidly as an alternative to Middle East oil and to the growing degree of Soviet influence in that area. Eisenhower also saw the plan as strengthening US-European ties, discouraging nuclear proliferation, and promoting the export of nuclear power reactors as a benefit to US firms. The president, moreover, sought a near-monopoly over the military atom. Resigned to the French nuclear weapons program, Eisenhower saw Euratom as imposing a nonproliferation policy on Germany while giving a "redeeming value" to what seemed an increasingly evil US engineering achievement. Schaetzel noted that this positive attitude toward Euratom established a kind of mystique built on "a belief in the magical powers of atomic energy, a real conviction that there were large benefits to be derived from atomic energy. Even the engineers and scientists believed that its cost would be so low that it would replace other means to generate electricity."[42]

Dulles at first remained cool to the idea of a European atomic pool. But both Eisenhower and Monnet eventually persuaded him that perhaps the practical hurdles he foresaw could be overcome. After meeting with Monnet several times in Paris at the end of 1955, the secretary of state became more committed to the idea and promised to do what he could to persuade the Germans and the British to support it. Dulles eventually gave Euratom priority even while supporting other forms of international atomic cooperation such as the IAEA; bilateral licensing agreements with European nations, especially with Germany; and the Organization for European Economic Cooperation. Dulles became convinced that only the community of six offered "promise of opening the way to a genuine United States of Europe." He had serious concerns about resurgent German nationalism, the weakness of France, and what he called its tendency to neutralism and defeatism. He well understood that Franco-German relations, while improving, needed constant encouragement. These problems, he came to believe, could be aided by a strong European atomic energy community, which would provide more immediate security and political significance than an economic community. On December 17, 1955,

Dulles even told Monnet that the United States would give Euratom fissionable material and technical information if it were supranational and would prevent the secret military use of nuclear fuel and its acquisition by France, Germany, or any other nation for manufacturing atomic weapons. In January 1956, Dulles stressed that the United States wanted to promote European unification to encourage "those forces now concerned with common development of atomic energy." He argued that if the atomic community succeeded, its members could proceed to other activities. "If they fail, the integration movement is apt to fall apart with little hope that it can be reconstituted, thus presenting a very bleak outlook for the future."[43]

Monnet traveled to Washington at Dulles's invitation in January 1957 to prepare for the visit of the three wise men and the eventual ratification of the Euratom Treaty. Monnet met several times with his close friend, who was recuperating from abdominal cancer surgery. He also spent hours with Strauss, who doubted Euratom could control the materials or safeguard classified information. Initially suspicious of Monnet, Strauss regarded French officials as serious security risks because of a pervasive belief in the US administration that the French bureaucracy was swarming with Communist spies. Most importantly, Strauss and his AEC colleagues did not want to give up direct US control of fissionable materials, which bilateral agreements sustained. AEC officials believed Euratom was a dangerous breach of the IAEA's universal inspection system, which would oversee the Atoms for Peace program. In addition, they believed it would generate activities outside the IAEA's supervision and destroy the inspection guidelines being constructed with the Russians in the United Nations.[44]

Dulles's strong support for Euratom muted but had not weakened Strauss's opposition to Euratom when Etzel, Armand, and Giordani arrived in Washington at the end of January 1957. In urging Strauss to be cooperative, Dulles wrote him that it was a "unique opportunity to assist the Europeans in carrying out a concerted effort to solve a major European economic problem in a framework which will promote political solidarity in Europe."[45] To facilitate the visit of the three wise men in January 1957, Monnet had sent letters to many of his American friends to ensure they understood the significance of this visit and asked them to treat Kohnstamm, his very close friend, as they treated him. Those who received these letters included André Mayer, a banker at Lazard Frères; McCloy; Donald Swatland of Cravath, Swain, and Moore; Gerard Smith; Bowie; and Dulles.[46]

On a trip to Washington in 1956, Monnet had befriended Schaetzel, believing he could be useful in securing US support for Euratom. This tall, intellectual diplomat and future ambassador to the European Communities was in charge of promoting the peaceful uses of atomic energy in the State Department. Soon they became close friends, dining together in each other's homes and sharing dreams of a unified Europe. In future years, whenever

Monnet returned to Washington, he would camp out in Schaetzel's office in the State Department, lean back in the chair, and put his feet on the desk while telephoning his many American friends. This Frenchman, Schaetzel confessed, was the most important influence in his life because he viewed him as a visionary who tirelessly strove for peace.[47]

Schaetzel escorted the three Europeans around the country on a schedule arranged by the AEC. Following meetings with industrialists, Eisenhower permitted them to meet with the heads of secret nuclear installations and laboratories at Shippingport, Pennsylvania, and Oak Ridge, Tennessee. After meeting with Dulles, the three met with Eisenhower on February 4, 1957. "The President told them," recorded Andrew Goodpaster, Eisenhower's closest adviser, "he thought Euratom was a great hope for the whole free world. He recalled that he has strongly supported a united Europe as a third great force in the world." Goodpaster noted the president "had urged Jean Monnet on, as he now urges this group on in the same direction." The president argued that "if they did not join together deterioration and ultimate disaster were inevitable. He had no hesitancy in declaring that the project would be to the benefit of the United States, of the Atlantic community, and of the world."[48] A few days later, Spaak brought a copy of the newly drafted Euratom Treaty to Washington to ensure it provided an adequate basis for future cooperation between the United States and ECSC nations. Dulles stated that the preliminary draft contained nothing "to preclude the subsequent negotiation of a fruitful cooperative arrangement between the United States and Euratom."[49]

## Completing the Treaties

Upon his return from Washington, Spaak held a series of meetings with foreign ministers of the six nations and experts in Paris in February 1957 to finalize the two treaties drafted by his committee. The Belgian had been an influential and effective chairman of the delegations in moving the discussions forward. Working closely with Uri, his principal assistant in designing the common market, Spaak made a great effort not to alarm the protectionists in France or the economic liberals in Germany. Adenauer and Mollet wielded the power in these difficult negotiations, and other government leaders generally went along with what they decided. As France was essentially protectionist, most of the French public opposed the removal of protections for agriculture, an essential sector of the common market. With the assistance of Foreign Minister Christian Pineau and Marjolin, his key adviser, Mollet developed a strategy to win as many concessions as possible for France from the other leaders while appeasing officials in Paris when they were denied.[50] As Marjolin recalled, he worked closely with Maurice Faure, the parliamentarian and Mollet's vice minister for Europe who led the French delegation. "For one year we worked on the drafting of what was to become the Treaty of Rome in a climate of trust and friendship," he wrote. "The essential difficulty that had to be overcome was the hostility of almost the whole of French public opinion to the removal, even gradual, of the protection which French industry enjoyed."[51] While many of the French demands were rejected or modified, the other five governments went a long way to accommodate Mollet, not only because they wished to ensure ratification, but most importantly because they knew there could be no workable common market without France. Since Franco-German reconciliation was the core of the European community, and that community was essential to German rehabilitation, both powers had to participate. They also realized that there was a better chance of obtaining a European treaty with the existing fragile French government than with a possible successor. Many in that government were motivated after Suez to conclude the treaties in order to lessen the humiliation suffered when the United States forced them to withdraw their troops from the Suez Canal Zone and to avoid a repetition of the EDC debacle.[52]

In the intergovernmental negotiations, the Germans never got too far out of line with the French. Adenauer followed this policy because he wished to maintain good relations with France and was willing to subordinate economic objectives to strategic considerations. Moreover, Adenauer enjoyed being on an equal footing with France. Most West German interests stood behind the chancellor in his European policy. He had won the support of the Social Democrats who believed as he did that the new community offered their nation and its booming economy a huge outlet for its industrial goods, in the same way it offered France some benefits for its agricultural sector.[53] Desmond Dinan contends that both France and Germany got what they wanted. The French government, namely the prime minister and foreign minister, favored both an agricultural and an industrial common market and used the promise of the former to get the latter. "Germany wanted an industrial common market above all but accepted an agricultural common market not only as a means of ensuring French participation but also for the sake of its own agricultural sector."[54]

The final treaties signed in Rome on March 25, 1957, creating the European Economic Community (EEC, now called the EC) and the European Atomic Energy Community (Euratom) reflect the vision of the six European leaders and Monnet of building through economic integration "an ever closer union among the peoples of Europe." While the leaders dealt with economic cooperation, the motives were overtly political. As Spaak pointed out in 1964, "Those who drew up the Rome Treaty . . . did not think of it as essentially economic; they thought of it as a stage on the way to political union."[55] After Messina, Hallstein wrote, "We are not integrating economies, we are integrating politics. We are not just sharing our furniture, we are jointly building a new and bigger house."[56] Marjolin, Pineau's special adviser throughout the negotiations, later wrote, "I do not believe it is an exaggeration to say that this date

*Franz Etzel (left) and Jean Monnet (right), mid-1950s.*

represents one of the great moments of Europe's history. Who would have thought during the thirties, and even during the ten years that followed the war, that European states which had been tearing one another apart for so many centuries and some of which, like France and Italy, still had very closed economies, would form a common market intended eventually to become an economic area that could be likened to one great domestic market?"[57]

The drafters modeled the institutions of the new EC on the ECSC and the Council of Europe. They established an institutional structure to do justice to both supranational and intergovernmental principles and incorporated both, even though the discredited term "supranationality" was not mentioned in the drafts or negotiations.[58] They modified and improved the ECSC models to make them more workable and acceptable to the leaders of the six. A nine-member Commission served as the supranational body, independent of national governments, to recommend policies, initiate and implement legislation, administer the treaty, and act as a brake on nationalism. The Council of Ministers, representing the national governments with one representative each, became the chief decisionmaking body, had the main burden of carrying out the Commission's policies through action and legislation, and acted as a check on the Commission. The Parliamentary Assembly of 142 representatives could censure the Commission by a two-thirds majority vote but was primarily an advisory body. The Court of Justice of seven judges, the interpreter of the treaties, handled all disputes arising from the three communities—the ECSC, EC, and Euratom—or between members, and had the final say on decisions regarding the treaties.

Both the French and German governments made great efforts to get these treaties ratified as quickly as possible. With memories of the EDC fiasco, Mollet placed the treaties before the National Assembly a week after they were signed. Monnet, who was not invited to Rome to join the signatories of the treaties, went instead to talk to the clerk of the National Assembly in Paris, Emile Blamont. This gentleman "operated the drawbridge to legislation" and had helped him earlier with the ratification of the ECSC Treaty. Blamont did so once again. The ratification procedures were streamlined so that when Mollet's government fell on May 21, 1957, the Foreign Affairs Committee's work on them was not interrupted during the interregnum and the Treaties of Rome were ratified by the Assembly the first week in July.[59] Monnet's Action Committee helped ensure their rapid ratification in all six nations by the end of 1957 as this vocal lobby used persuasive arguments with the legislators.

## Working to Achieve a "Financial Common Market"

In the summer of 1957, a request from French Finance Minister Félix Gaillard had stimulated Monnet to think also about a monetary union as a means to further European political integration. The French financial crisis brought on by the Algerian War, the long-standing balance-of-payments deficit, inflation, and a flight from the franc motivated the minister to seek Monnet's advice. Gaillard had worked in Paris in 1944–1945 as Monnet's *chef de cabinet* coordinating the distribution of US supplies. An admirer of this young *inspecteur des finances*, Monnet had written, "His intelligence and his exceptional ability to master difficult subjects enabled him to find brilliant and rapid short cuts" in the efforts to distribute badly needed supplies in France.[60]

Using his "brain trust" composed of Uri, Marjolin, Paul Delouvrier, and Marjolin's Belgian friend and Yale Professor of Finance Robert Triffin, Monnet developed a strategy in August 1957 to help solve some of France's financial problems. After discussions with Monnet in December, high-ranking Bank of France and Ministry of Finance officials concluded that immediate aid from international monetary institutions and the US government was required to enable their government to meet its obligations, help the economy recover, and prepare it for the implementation of the common market. As a result, Gaillard, who became prime minister in November 1957, sent Monnet to Washington in January 1958 as head of the French financial mission to seek a loan in order to gain time while some remedial measures could be enacted. Their second goal was to reschedule France's debts to the United States on the loans Monnet had obtained in 1945. The mission succeeded. The two governments concluded an agreement whereby the United States extended $274 million in financial aid to France, of which about two-thirds was new money. In addition, the US government postponed until 1981 the repayment of the 1958 and 1959 installments on the old loans.[61]

Adopting the ideas of Triffin and his brain trust, Monnet proposed to Gaillard in March 1958 that member states pursue a common financial policy to enable the free movement of capital among the EC countries. He argued that a European financial and money market with a European bank and reserve fund be established. His team had calculated that if member states pooled 20 percent of their gold reserves and foreign exchange, which would be freely convertible, they would be forced to coordinate their monetary and macroeconomic policies. Monnet hoped this would make it easier to achieve economic and political union. To Kohnstamm, he said, "Via money, Europe could become political in five years."[62] But as Gaillard's government fell in April, no such fund was established. Yet always optimistic, Monnet kept the idea of monetary union percolating through his Action Committee.[63]

Early in 1958, Monnet also pressured both Adenauer and Gaillard intensely about the need to choose Adenauer's colleague Hallstein as the first president of the EEC Commission. "We had not fought and won so great a battle in order to place the institutions in unreliable hands," he noted. "In appearance, those institutions were economic and technical, but their objectives were political."[64] The acceptance by the French government of Hallstein's appointment showed that Franco-German reconciliation had begun to affect some important decisions.[65]

Monnet's passionate and determined effort to launch a massive civil nuclear power program sponsored by the United States helped Europe stay on the road to unity. The Euratom Treaty, largely Monnet's creation, provided the necessary bridge from the ECSC to the new EEC. Urged on by the small group of determined French, European, and US Allies—Armand, Mollet, Spaak, Edgar Faure, Uri, Kohnstamm, Eisenhower, Dulles, Bowie, Schaetzel, and others—Monnet kept the concept alive with sheer political will in the face of determined opposition from Strauss and the AEC, the French nationalists and the CEA, and German nationalists. Some prominent French officials like Marjolin considered the common market the most important goal but Euratom of limited importance. Marjolin understood the political difficulties inherent in the conception and implementation of this atomic energy community and believed it would not likely be established. "The day when atomic energy would begin to be used on a significant scale was still far off," he wrote, ". . . and the problems of its civilian use were closely bound up with those of its military use, of which it was difficult even to speak."[66]

Nevertheless, Spaak and Monnet focused on Euratom because French opposition to a common market was strong when the negotiations began, and Euratom offered the French the time and a means for them to adapt to the common market idea. By promoting atomic energy cooperation through this civil nuclear power program, Euratom also provided a means to integrate Germany into Europe because it afforded the German Socialists the chance they needed to reverse their initial postwar stance of calling for German unification before and to some extent against Western European unity. As Duchêne argues, both the EC and Euratom treaties were essential as a package in the early negotiations because, if presented separately, each would have failed. Since the Germans were not especially interested in sectoral integration, they favored the EC Treaty, and since many French officials objected to the common market in 1955 and the first half of 1956, they supported Euratom. Tackling both schemes enabled Spaak, Beyen, and Bech to get the negotiations under way and allow them to continue. And Monnet's lobbying through his Action Committee helped ensure each treaty would be signed and ratified.[67]

Spaak and Monnet deserve much of the credit for devising a strategy to advance European integration after 1954 and successfully implementing it. Together these pioneering leaders capitalized on the anxiety resulting from the EDC debacle, generated new ideas, and kept the six foreign ministers meeting together and discussing plans for integration. Moreover, they wisely listened to Beyen, who stressed the need to integrate their entire economies. Together, these men spearheaded the advancement of the two schemes that became the Rome Treaties. Plotting and prodding, they kept the idea of European integration alive. When one idea did not please all the six, they used two.

Spaak ably led the diplomatic effort that culminated in the Rome Treaties and demonstrated enlightened leadership as head of the negotiations. Bech was also central to the bargaining process at Messina and Venice. But these men and the other representatives of the six nations could not have achieved success without Adenauer's consistent and continuous support, his farsighted diplomacy, and his strong domestic leadership. They also benefited from the improved atmosphere of peace and optimism generated by improvements in European economies in the 1950s, the US and British security commitments that reassured them they would not be abandoned, and improvements in Franco-German relations. As the ECSC had resolved some of the coal and steel conflicts that had embittered Franco-German relationships since the war and removed the main impediment to an economic partnership between the two nations,[68] French and German leaders were motivated to take additional steps. Prime Minister Faure's support and leadership with the Saar settlement in 1955 removed this issue from the policy debate. Moreover he wanted to make amends for some of the fiercely anti-German rhetoric that flowed in the national debates on German rearmament. With the WEU's solution to the question of defense, the French prime minister had recognized that his citizens, who were experiencing modernization and economic expansion in the mid-1950s, valued peace, compromise, and economic well-being more than problems with Germany and Europe.[69] International developments, argues Jeanne-Pierre Rioux, "strengthened French diplomacy's growing conviction that a new era in international relations had indeed dawned, one in which peaceful co-existence and co-operation were the most realistic policies for France."[70]

Once again, Monnet's US connections, especially Eisenhower and Dulles, provided his concept of an atomic energy community with the vital verbal support and diplomatic credibility it needed in spite of the political realities that made it unlikely to be established. Through many personal visits to Washington and by bombarding these two powerful leaders and his American friends with copies of his speeches and letters, Monnet lobbied incessantly for the efforts of the six nations to unify economically.[71] Eisenhower and Dulles furthered the integration process because they believed that the stronger and more unified Europe was, the greater share of the military and political burden it would bear in deterring Soviet advances in the Cold War. Eisenhower also understood that Western Europe had the human and economic resources to become a global power alongside the United States. These US leaders had also learned from the EDC debacle that integration initiatives had to come from the Europeans themselves, not from American pressure. But they also knew that US indifference or hostility to the integration process could possibly impede it.[72]

Even though Monnet was discredited and out of favor with much of the political elite in France after 1954 and other European leaders like Bech, he helped move European economic integration forward. While he did not participate in the negotiations, he contributed a new sectoral supranational institution that became one of the Treaties of Rome and created an international lobby for European integration. His method of employing intergovernmental committees to negotiate international agreements was incorporated at Messina and adopted by the Spaak Committee. And his strategy of fostering an institutional approach to solving international problems was embodied in the EEC Treaty. While he focused on Euratom and never thought a common market would succeed, he knew both treaties had to be presented together and ratified because the Rome Treaties were key steps on the road to political unity of Europe. And that unity, he believed, would be the ultimate guarantor of peace.

## Notes

1. Robert Marjolin, *Architect of European Unity, Memoirs 1911–1986* (London: Weidenfeld and Nicolson, 1989), p. 282.

2. François Duchêne, *Jean Monnet: The First Statesman of Interdependence* (New York: W. W. Norton, 1994), pp. 262–263.

3. Hans-Peter Schwarz, *Konrad Adenauer*, vol. 2 (Providence, RI: Berghahn Books, 1997), pp. 118–132; Desmond Dinan, *Europe Recast* (Boulder, CO: Lynne Rienner Publishers, 2004), p. 61; *FRUS*, 1952–1954, vol. 5, part 1, pp. 1295–1331.

4. Schwarz, *Adenauer*, vol. 2, pp. 118–132; *FRUS*, 1952–1954, vol. 5, part 1, pp. 1426–1456, 1464–1465.

5. Schwarz, *Adenauer,* vol. 2, p. 131.

6. Ernest R. May, "The American Commitment to Germany, 1949–1955," in *American Historians and the Atlantic Alliance,* ed. L. S. Kaplan (Kent, OH: Kent State University Press, 1991), pp. 52–80.

7. Andrew Moravcsik argues that the history of the European Community originated with the failure of the EDC. See his *The Choice for Europe: Social Purpose and State Power from Messina to Maastricht* (Ithaca, NY: Cornell University Press, 1998), p. 86; Dinan, *Europe Recast,* pp. 62–66.

8. Duchêne, *Jean Monnet,* pp. 265–269.

9. Ibid., pp. 267–270.

10. Ibid., pp. 273–274.

11. Jean-Pierre Rioux, *The Fourth Republic, 1944–1958* (Cambridge, UK: Cambridge University Press, 1987), p. 243; Schwarz, *Adenauer,* vol. 2, pp. 138–139.

12. Altiero Spinelli, *Diario europeo,* vol. 1: *1948–1968,* a cura di ed., Edmundo Paolini, trans. Piero Graglia (Bologna, Italy: Il Mulino, 1989), pp. 260–261.

13. Piero Graglia, interviews by the author, October 4, 2003, August 12, 2004, September 2, 2004, and February 8, 2005.

14. Dinan, *Europe Recast,* pp. 66–69; Duchêne, *Jean Monnet,* pp. 281–282.

15. Duchêne, *Jean Monnet,* p. 280.

16. Ibid., pp. 282–283.

17. Duchêne, *Jean Monnet,* p. 284.

18. Max Isenbergh, interview by Leonard Tennyson, April 20, 1981, Fondation Jean Monnet pour l'Europe Centre de recherches européennes, Lausanne, Switzerland.

19. Antonio Varsori, "Euratom, une organization qui échappe à Jean Monnet?" in *Jean Monnet, l'Europe et les chemins de la paix,* ed. Gérard Bossuat and Andreas Wilkens (Paris: Publications de la Sorbonne, 1999), p. 348.

20. Jean Monnet, *Memoirs* (New York: Doubleday, 1978), pp. 412, 419; Duchêne, *Jean Monnet,* pp. 264–269.

21. Duchêne, *Jean Monnet,* pp. 292–294.

22. Ibid., pp. 284–287.

23. Ibid., p. 288.

24. Monnet, *Memoirs,* p. 414.

25. Ibid., p. 417.

26. Ibid., p. 414.

27. Maria Melchionni, "Le Comité d'Action pour les Etats-Unis d'Europe: Un réseau au service de l'union européenne," in *Jean Monnet, l'Europe et les chemins de la paix,* pp. 221–251.

28. Ibid.; Duchêne, *Jean Monnet,* p. 288; see also Jean Monnet's "Informational Note: Why Create an Action Committee for the United States of Europe?" October 6, 1955, AMK 2/5/11, Fondation Jean Monnet; see also Eric Roussel, *Jean Monnet* (Paris: Librairie Artheme Fayard, 1996), pp. 693–696.

29. Pascaline Winand, "Eisenhower, Dulles, Monnet, and the Uniting of Europe," in *Monnet and the Americans,* ed. Clifford Hackett (Washington, DC: Jean Monnet Council, 1995), pp. 129–131.

30. Rioux, *Fourth Republic,* pp. 243–244.

31. Duchêne, *Jean Monnet,* pp. 293–294.

32. George-Henri Soutou, *The French Military Program for Nuclear Energy, 1945–1981* (College Park, MD: Center for International Security Studies at Maryland, Nuclear History Program, 1989), pp. 1–3.

33. Ibid., pp. 3–4.

34. Pascaline Winand, *Eisenhower, Kennedy, and the United States of Europe* (New York: St. Martin's Press, 1993), p. 87.

35. Duchêne, *Jean Monnet*, pp. 296–298.

36. Isenbergh, interview.

37. André Kaspi, interview by the author, September 24, 2008; Dirk Spierenburg and Raymond Poidevin, *The History of the High Authority of the European Coal and Steel Community* (London: Weidenfeld and Nicolson, 1994), pp. 55–57.

38. Duchêne, *Jean Monnet*, pp. 299–300.

39. Dinan, *Europe Recast,* pp. 69–70.

40. Dwight Eisenhower, *Waging the Peace, 1956–1961* (New York: Doubleday, 1965), p. 125.

41. Sherrill Brown Wells, "Monnet and 'The Insiders': Nathan, Tomlinson, Bowie, and Schaetzel," in *Monnet and the Americans,* ed. Clifford Hackett (Washington, DC: Jean Monnet Council, 1995), pp. 214–215.

42. Richard Hewlett and Jack Holl, *Atoms for Peace and War* (Berkeley: University of California Press, 1989), pp. 300–307; Robert Schaetzel, interview by the author, August 30, 1991.

43. Memorandum of Conversation among Dulles, Strauss, Bowie, Gerard Smith, Livingston Merchant, and others, January 25, 1956, *FRUS,* 1955–1957, vol. 4, pp. 390–399; Schaetzel, interview; Winand, *Eisenhower, Kennedy,* pp. 76–77.

44. Robert Bowie, interview by the author, August 15, 1990; Winand, *Eisenhower, Kennedy,* pp. 90–91; Duchêne, *Jean Monnet,* pp. 303–304.

45. John Foster Dulles to Lewis Strauss, letter, February 5, 1957, *FRUS,* 1955–1957, vol. 4, p. 510.

46. Winand, *Eisenhower, Kennedy,* pp. 95–96.

47. Schaetzel, interview; Wells, "Insiders," pp. 211–315.

48. Memorandum of Conversation of Dulles Meeting, February 4, 1957, and Memorandum of Conversation with the President, February 5, 1957, *FRUS,* 1955–1957, vol. 4, pp. 512–515, 516–518.

49. John Foster Dulles to Paul-Henri Spaak, letter, March 22, 1957, *FRUS,* 1955–1957, vol. 4, pp. 543–544.

50. Marjolin, *Architect of European Unity*, pp. 276–307; Dinan, *Europe Recast,* p. 73.

51. Marjolin, *Architect of European Unity*, pp. 283–284.

52. Dinan, *Europe Recast,* pp. 71–72.

53. Ibid., pp. 71–73.

54. Ibid., pp. 75–76.

55. Derek Urwin, *The Community of Europe* (London: Longman Group, 1991), p. 76.

56. Ibid.

57. Marjolin, *Architect of European Unity,* p. 306.

58. Hanns-Jurgen Kusters, "The Treaties of Rome, 1955–57," in *The Dynamics of European Union,* ed. Roy Pryce (London: Croom Helm, 1987), p. 94. While officially both are called the Treaties of Rome, in practice only the treaty establishing the EC, as the EEC came to be called, is known as the Treaty of Rome.

59. Duchêne, *Jean Monnet,* p. 306.

60. Monnet, *Memoirs,* p. 225.

61. Gérard Bossuat, "Jean Monnet et l'identité monétaire européenne," in *Jean Monnet, l'Europe et les chemins de la paix,* p. 370; *FRUS,* 1958–1960, vol. 7, part 2, pp. 1–2; Monnet, *Memoirs,* pp. 427–428; Duchêne, *Jean Monnet,* p. 312.

62. Duchêne, *Jean Monnet*, p. 312.

63. Bossuat, "Jean Monnet et l'identité monétaire européenne," pp. 370–376; Monnet, *Memoirs*, pp. 427–428.

64. Monnet, *Memoirs,* p. 426.

65. Dinan, *Europe Recast*, pp. 78–79.

66. Marjolin, *Architect of European Unity*, p. 284.

67. Duchêne, *Jean Monnet*, pp. 305–308.

68. John Gillingham, *Coal, Steel, and the Rebirth of Europe, 1945–1955* (Cambridge, UK: Cambridge University Press, 1991), pp. 297–298.

69. Rioux, *Fourth Republic*, pp. 240–243.

70. Ibid., p. 243.

71. With France's national interest always at the forefront of his mind, Monnet's letters to John Foster Dulles helped prevent the imposition of qualitative restrictions on the export of US steel scrap to the ECSC, which was needed to maintain steel production at a high level. See Winand, *Eisenhower, Kennedy*, pp. 65–68.

72. Jeffrey G. Giauque, *Grand Designs and Visions of Unity* (Chapel Hill: University of North Carolina Press, 2002), pp. 13–16.

# 8

# Promoting Closer Integration, 1958–1979

Since 1954, Monnet's influence and capacity to exert his will had diminished significantly in France and Europe. When Charles de Gaulle became president of France in June 1958, the seventy-year-old's stature declined still further. The newly elected leader was hostile to most of Monnet's initiatives and wanted relations with the United States on his own terms. He despised the concept of supranationality, had opposed Euratom since its inception, denied Euratom inspectors entry into French defense installations, and thwarted any transfer of essential power from the six member nations to the institutions of the European Community (EC). The president, supported by his colleagues at the French Atomic Energy Commission, did not tolerate restrictions on military weapons development because he was pursuing a nationalist nuclear policy. De Gaulle also viewed the development of the *force de frappe* (nuclear strike force) as a symbol of global power and an instrument of France's political independence.[1]

Monnet devoted his final decades to securing a lasting peace in Europe as though nothing in his status had changed. After the ratification of the Rome Treaties in 1957, this spry private citizen mobilized his Action Committee for the United States of Europe to combat the centrifugal forces of nationalism and to lobby leaders of the six Rome Treaty nations for full implementation of the common market. He never doubted that the political union of Europe, the ultimate guarantor of peace, could only be achieved through progress in economic integration. With his customary focus and intensity, he labored to galvanize opinion and stimulate action on both economic and political issues.

Monnet focused the Action Committee on strengthening ties among the political parties and trade unions of the six nations. While expanding this multinational network to include senior civil servants, ministers, and employers, he lobbied in several ways. He personally visited heads of state and their ministers to promote continued integration. In EC cities, he convened meetings to discuss position papers written by colleagues. Once a consensus was reached and resolutions were adopted by a vote of the Committee members present, he published them in the European press and mailed them to EC political leaders as well as to his American friends. When he asked members in 1958 whether the Action Committee should fold, he was heartened by the positive response. They overwhelmingly indicated that this multinational network's circulation of its papers and resolutions provided useful channels for confidential dialogue that didn't exist elsewhere. Invigorated by this news, he had the Committee tackle divisive political issues such as Euratom's future and the location of the EC's institutions. Monnet proposed that a "European District" be formed at a single site, resembling the federal district of Washington, D.C. But EC officials strongly opposed this idea, and a compromise resulted in Brussels as the location of the EC Commission and Strasbourg as the seat of the European Parliament; the Court of Justice and the European Coal and Steel Community (ECSC) remained in Luxembourg. In November 1959, the Action Committee called on the governments to speed up the implementation of the Rome Treaty. Monnet explained his reasoning:

> Since it was possible to go faster, it was necessary to do so—not merely to hasten the increase of trade among our six countries and improve their standard of living but also to arrive as soon as possible at a point when the Community would be ready to be enlarged and to share its prosperity with other countries in Europe and Africa. This would also bring closer the time when a political Europe could be built. These two objectives were now to become the chief concerns of the Action Committee and the main focus of my own work.[2]

Monnet emphasized to Max Kohnstamm how important he believed it was for Britain to join the Rome Treaty. He thought perhaps later the Scandinavians and maybe Poland could also join.[3]

## Support by the Ford Foundation

A Ford Foundation grant of $150,000 in 1958 for the Action Committee's Center of Documentation in Lausanne, Switzerland, to conduct research boosted the morale of Monnet and his able staff. Monnet received no salary for his work with the Committee, which was funded by its members, especially the German trade unions. But as he personally covered its deficits and championed the Committee's independence from governments, this was welcome news. The initiative for this grant had been taken by Shepard Stone, director of international affairs at the Ford Foundation since 1954. After working in the late 1940s as an editor of the Sunday *New York Times*, Stone had been re-cruited in 1949 by John McCloy, the high commissioner, to be the public affairs director of the United States High Commission for Germany. Since Stone had earned his doctorate at the University of Berlin, his mastery of the language and his German contacts made him useful to McCloy. After leaving Bonn in 1952 to become head of the Chase Bank in New York, McCloy served as a trustee of the Ford Foundation and supported Stone's appointment to that philanthropic organization. When McCloy became chairman of the board of the Ford Foundation in 1958, the two friends found themselves working closely together once more. In the 1950s and 1960s, their philanthropic orga-nization played a prominent role in the propaganda war against communism in Europe.

During those years, the foundation's staff was composed of international-ists who "understood the dependency of the United States on Europe as well as Europe's on the U.S.," recalled Stone. "It was obvious that the Ford Foun-dation should be interested in trying to help restore Europe. We saw that Euro-pean institutions needed help."[4] Stone's Eurocentric program worked to counter European hostility to American culture, evident in British and French journals, and anti-American attitudes among French intellectuals and journal-ists. It supported organizations that promoted cooperation among European governments, private organizations, and transatlantic institutions to foster ties with the United States. Stone also worked to fund a variety of initiatives to strengthen a new Atlanticism and publicize the virtues of the United States to Europeans through exchanges of leaders, intellectuals, and students.[5]

Stone traveled to Europe frequently in the 1950s and arranged to see Monnet, whom he had met through McCloy, every time he was in Paris. They had become good friends and shared behind-the-scenes information that was mutually beneficial. "He would always be interested in knowing what was happening in the United States," reported Stone. "That was his way of testing, of coming to some common conclusions of his own." While Monnet expressed some interest in Stone's visits to Eastern Europe, "he'd soon say, 'Let's get back to the main point,' which, of course, was Western Europe and the United States."[6] Since Stone, McCloy, and Monnet all worked tirelessly for Euro-pean-American cooperation, the Ford Foundation grant seemed a natural out-come of these friendships and part of the foundation's goals. Even though Monnet had hoped for a grant from this foundation, Stone said Monnet would never would have asked directly for it and explained:

> But if you told him this might be a possibility, he immediately showed inter-est. I would tell him to write something in the way of a request. Monnet thought even a paragraph or two was too long. Usually I dictated them for him. He wanted the Ford Foundation funds for his staff for the sake of inde-pendence. He didn't want to be beholden to the industrial side, to the politi-cal side, or to the labor unions.[7]

*Jean Monnet (left) and Max Kohnstamm in Luxembourg on the third anniversary of the Schuman Plan, May 9, 1953.*

Monnet had established the Center of Documentation in Lausanne to conduct research of immediate significance to the EC and provide detailed technical background and information about European integration problems for EC leaders and Action Committee members.[8] Grateful for the Ford Foundation's assistance, which came with no strings attached, Monnet had reassured Stone it would be used for the salaries of his research and administrative staff at the center. These funds enabled him to pay his talented, loyal colleagues like Kohnstamm, who gave up a promising diplomatic career to become the Committee's vice president. Jacques Van Helmont became its secretary general, and British journalists Richard Mayne and François Duchêne, who had previously worked with him, were hired to write most of the Action Committee's papers.[9] Monnet had made it clear to the Ford Foundation officials that, while the research center was financed by individual contributions like theirs, he accepted none from governments in order to maintain the center's independence and that the Committee itself was funded by its constituent political parties and labor unions.[10] University of Lausanne Professor Henri Rieben, an ardent federalist who had worked closely with Monnet in founding the Action Committee in 1955, became director of the center.[11]

Monnet exerted considerable influence over the Ford Foundation's European program in the mid-1950s and 1960s because of his close friendships with Stone and McCloy. Stone sought his advice concerning which institutions and universities in Europe to fund and which Europeans to invite to conferences or for speaking trips to the United States. The Ford Foundation renewed the original 1958 grant of $150,000 to the Lausanne center three times: in 1960, in 1963, and in 1965, for a total of $600,000. The foundation gave Monnet a further grant of $50,000 in 1968 for "the research and preparation of original materials on the European integration movement."[12] In 1957, as a result of Rieben's work with Monnet, it had earlier awarded the University of Lausanne $25,000 for research "relating to the practical problems of European integration." Stone found Monnet's colleague Kohnstamm a highly intelligent and important internationalist, corresponded often with him about their work with Monnet, and funded some of his trips to European capitals and the United States.[13]

Stone also expressed his gratitude for the introduction to Robert Marjolin's Belgian friend Robert Triffin, a professor of finance at Yale University. This academic impressed Stone with his enthusiasm for Monnet's idea of a European financial community. "He sees Monnet as the motor driving Europe forward and he believes we can make a large contribution in supporting this idea," wrote Stone. "Triffin made an excellent impression. His European-American background and his excellence in the field of economics can be of great use to us."[14] In a February 1959 letter to Monnet after a visit to Paris, Stone wrote, "The hours together with you are good for my sense of history, stimulating for my work, and above all, excellent for my soul."[15]

## Eisenhower's Unfailing Support for Euratom

Strong US support for Euratom facilitated Monnet's efforts to obtain an agreement with Washington essential for Euratom's viability. President Eisenhower had made Euratom a key element of his grand design for Europe and placed a high priority both on international cooperation on atomic energy and on European economic integration. However, Eisenhower did not seem to grasp that political forces in both the United States and Europe would make such international cooperation on atomic energy, as envisioned in Euratom, extremely difficult if not impossible to implement. In 1957 and early 1958, Monnet worked closely with his US friends to convince the Atomic Energy Commission (AEC) and Congress to conclude an agreement governing US-Euratom cooperation. Robert Schaetzel, the Department of State official in charge of the peaceful uses of atomic energy, and Kohnstamm, with Monnet's approval, decided the United States would take the initiative to get an agreement as rapidly as possible but make it appear to come from the Europeans.

Monnet left the negotiations to Kohnstamm, who prepared a draft agreement with Schaetzel. Euratom's designated president, Louis Armand, and the "Americanists" in the State Department, as Monnet's coterie of supporters were sometimes called, reviewed it. Once approved, Schaetzel wrote a memorandum to the president on January 28, 1958, recommending that a cooperative US-Euratom agreement be approved by him in principle. The memorandum outlined the proposed construction of several US-type reactors designed to produce one million kilowatts of energy for Euratom Treaty nations to be completed by 1962 or 1963. In addition, it specified that the Europeans would bear most of the cost with some US financing from loans, discussed how joint research could develop US-type reactors, and stated research results would be shared.[16] Both Kohnstamm and Schaetzel were cautiously optimistic that a program of cooperation between Euratom and the United States would be created and that a "new relationship" between the United States and Europe would materialize as a result. But they were painfully aware of the AEC's opposition to Euratom and that such a relationship might never materialize for many other reasons.[17]

After the president's approval, lengthy negotiations with Euratom representatives produced the June 17, 1958, Memorandum of Understanding, the basis for a US-Euratom agreement signed by the president and sent to Congress June 23. Because Eisenhower was adamant and believed so strongly in peaceful atomic diplomacy, he overrode the AEC's concerns about nuclear proliferation. And since he and John Foster Dulles had resigned themselves to French nuclear weapons production, he did not agree with the AEC's insistence on unilateral inspection rights to monitor and prevent Euratom from using US nuclear materials for military use. By the end of the summer, Congress had approved an international agreement with Euratom, pursuant to Section 124 of the Atomic Energy Act of 1954, which gave the United States the legal authority to enter into an agreement with a group of countries such as Euratom. Effective lobbying by Kohnstamm and Monnet's friends—Douglas Dillon, undersecretary of state for economic affairs, and George Ball—helped gain congressional approval in the fall of 1958. The Agreement of Cooperation between Euratom and the United States was finally signed in Brussels on November 8, 1958, in spite of the AEC's well-publicized opposition.[18] While the president and Dulles had committed the United States to sharing technology for peaceful purposes, neither seemed to acknowledge or be concerned about the possible consequences of the AEC's opposition, which they believed they could override.

## Euratom's Doom by French Government

While Eisenhower's support for Euratom never wavered, de Gaulle's hostility and his desire to pursue an independent nuclear weapons policy doomed it from the start. The French president probably did not kill Euratom outright because he feared such action would jeopardize his government's requests in the fall of 1958 and 1959 for information from the US government about the development of a French nuclear force and a nuclear-powered submarine.[19] Faced with Armand's illness the first year, Monnet persuaded de Gaulle during a November 11, 1958, conversation to appoint Etienne Hirsch as Armand's successor to head Euratom. Monnet's friend Guy Mollet, de Gaulle's minister for Europe, probably influenced this decision. The French president later firmly reminded Hirsch that "we are no longer in the era when Monsieur Monnet gave orders." And when, in early 1962, de Gaulle replaced Hirsch as Euratom's president with Pierre Chatenet, minister of the interior, he formally abandoned the US-Euratom program.[20]

Other factors contributed to Euratom's difficulties. Armand's illness, which meant little was accomplished its first year, was accompanied by a general weakening of support for a supranational element in the atomic energy field. Private industry, especially in Germany, vigorously opposed Euratom because it feared the consequences of a "supranational *dirigisme*" (state intervention). In addition, Euratom could not counter the growth of national nuclear programs in part because its members distrusted French motives. In 1955, the British had launched its nuclear power program, and, in 1959, West Germany and Italy began to build their own industries to prevent France's gaining too much dominance in that field. By the early 1960s, Euratom also suffered an increasing shortage of funding as the member states preferred to give priority to their own national programs.[21]

Antonio Varsori argues Euratom was doomed to fail because of flaws in Monnet's strategy. He states that Monnet never understood that Euratom was viewed by some in Europe as an instrument of European independence rather than a cooperative venture among Washington, Paris, and London. As a result, the US administration's strong public support of Euratom perhaps contributed to its failure. Because of Monnet's diminished influence, his opinion was not as highly regarded as when he was president of the High Authority. He also had less influence over the leaders of the six nations and the diverse opinions in the Action Committee, upon which he relied to promote Euratom. Varsori demonstrates that Monnet's insistence that Euratom's goals were purely pacific was another weakness in his strategy as was his demand that the assistance given the European nations would not be applied to military purposes. Moreover, he argues, Monnet's goal was too ambitious, and, as a result, he was unable to control the interaction of the many factors required for Euratom to become the community he envisioned.[22]

While some European Community member states remained suspicious of France's nuclear policy and worried about the environmental hazards and safety of atomic energy, the AEC and the US Department of State quietly limited some of the anticipated exchange of information despite the president's orders to the contrary. This hampered Euratom's effectiveness and contributed to its slow start. In addition, changing economic conditions in Western Europe and new oil discoveries in the Middle East, resulting in an abundance of cheap oil in the 1960s, diminished the need for nuclear power. A slowdown in Europe's economic expansion, combined with the increase in the consumption of oil as a substitute for coal, created an overproduction of coal in 1958 and a drop in its price. When new sources of natural gas were found in Europe, the demand for electricity leveled off. Moreover, when in 1967 the executives of the ECSC, the EC, and Euratom were merged by treaty and their executive bodies fused, Monnet saw Euratom along with the ECSC diminished in importance and marginalized.[23] Although saddened by this development but realistic about the fate of his two communities, Monnet advised Kohnstamm "not to cling to the forms of a discredited ECSC. If necessary, one might sacrifice this advanced patrol which has fulfilled the essence of a mission by acting as pathfinder [and] fall back on the strong points of the Common Market."[24] Once again, Monnet demonstrated he was pragmatic. He was able to move on and not let the marginalization of both the ECSC and Euratom prevent him from turning all his energies to the promotion of integration through the common market.

The US-Euratom agreement of 1958 nevertheless did enable Euratom to become an organization that promoted research on the peaceful uses of atomic energy. Although the Kennedy administration (1961–1963) had privately complained that this program drained US resources, the Johnson administration (1963–1969) continued to support Euratom. Additional agreements after 1958 expanded the supply of enriched uranium and plutonium for Euratom and provided for scientific research collaboration on breeder, or fast neutron, reactors. When the bilateral agreements between the United States and individual members of the six nations expired between 1965 and 1967, the United States merged them into one agreement with Euratom, which eliminated the necessity for bilateral safeguards and thereby demonstrated its support for integration. Pascaline Winand argues that the United States carefully protected its economic interests by "assuring that Western Europe remained dependent on the American supply of enriched uranium." Its policy had largely been successful, she argues, because by 1967, "the Europeans had not built any enrichment facilities for uranium, and the United States supplied about ninety-nine percent of the total amount of enriched uranium distributed among the Six for peaceful use."[25]

## The Inspirer and the General

The relationship between Monnet and de Gaulle remained complex throughout their lives. Both men were pragmatic, talented leaders who shared a deep love for their country and who harbored a somewhat distant but fluctuating respect for the other. While their relationship was usually contentious, manipulative, and competitive, they cooperated at times. Having worked together in London to persuade Churchill to agree to the unrealistic proposal for an Anglo-French union in 1940, each had aided the other at key junctures in their careers. In 1943, Monnet had been instrumental in helping de Gaulle emerge in Algiers as the leader of the French forces. As the new French president in 1945, de Gaulle had been seduced by and supported Monnet's ideas for the reconstruction and modernization of France.[26] Each of these pragmatic decisions had furthered not only their own personal goals but also France's national interest. But while they both worked to restore French influence in Europe after its humiliating defeat in World War II, Monnet and de Gaulle fundamentally disagreed on how to achieve that goal. De Gaulle wanted to restore his nation's prestige and independence through nationalist policies and increasingly resisted cooperation with the United States and some aspects of European integration. Monnet, on the other hand, believed France's interests were best served by European integration, reinforced by a close alliance with Washington, with France taking the leading role.

Monnet worked with and supported this strong-minded leader when be believed the general advanced France's national interest but attacked him when not. Monnet publicized in *Le Monde* his support for the September 8, 1958, referendum on de Gaulle's constitution because he shared the general's belief that the Fourth Republic needed a stronger government to preserve democracy and end the political instability. He also supported de Gaulle's referendum of January 1961 on Algeria because he understood the general was taking a pragmatic step to end the Algerian crisis in order to "safeguard our future" and "ensure government stability and authority."[27] He must have realized that only de Gaulle as a strong and respected general could give Algeria its independence and face the outraged French military. Because he also understood this bold leader's pragmatism often dictated his decisions, Monnet knew de Gaulle believed that a European organization that integrated Germany with Europe was indispensable for maintaining peace and that France had to progress economically to regain its status.[28] He applauded his president for fully implementing the provisions of the Rome Treaty early in 1958 by abolishing quotas and tariffs and creating the common market. When de Gaulle took steps to establish sound monetary and fiscal policies (including devaluing the franc by 20 percent in 1959), which were essential for the common market to function successfully, Monnet praised him and wrote, "The sensible and courageous monetary measures taken at the end of 1958 gave France back her self-confidence, and she took in her stride the first tariff cuts on the way to the full Common Market. The credit for this must go to General de Gaulle and Antoine Pinay . . . Minister of Finance, with Jacques Rueff as adviser."[29]

Monnet also understood that the fears aroused by the opening of the common market had been exaggerated. As economist Jean-Claude Casanova later noted, "It had became a necessity to be competitive abroad and not produce just for domestic consumption. Three or four years after France's entry, many Frenchmen were surprised not only that the economy had survived but that it was so strong."[30]

From 1959 to 1963, Monnet talked to the French president at the Elysée fairly frequently and to his advisers in order to keep channels of communication open.[31] He also maintained close touch with Couve de Murville, de Gaulle's foreign minister with whom he had worked in Algiers, and with Paul Delouvrier, whom the French president appointed as the delegate general in Algeria. Others like Prime Minister Michel Debré detested Monnet passionately, so the two avoided one another. But when Monnet found the president hostile to some aspects of European integration except on his own terms, the Cognac native spoke out and underscored their disagreements. In June 1959, he criticized de Gaulle's objective for atomic independence, charging he "was dealing cold-bloodedly with the United States on this issue." When de Gaulle in 1960 tried to reshape the EC through the Fouchet Plan, which called for coordinating forces and defense policies outside the Rome Treaties, Monnet shared with Paul-Henri Spaak his dismay at this ill-conceived maneuver. Since the leaders of the other five nations feared this initiative might weaken NATO as well as the EC and viewed it as another ploy by the imperious French president to seek domination of Europe, they killed it.[32]

Monnet's close relations with Americans had gained him power in Paris in the 1940s and early 1950s, but cost him respect and support among many of the French elites, especially after de Gaulle became president in 1958. Because this general widely propagated his own anti-Americanism, he accused Monnet of being an American agent, making secret deals, and being more loyal to the United States than to his own country. The general wanted a "European Europe" of sovereign states that cooperated with one another, not a "supranational Europe" or an "Atlantic Europe," which he accused Monnet of promoting.[33] De Gaulle denounced him for not giving him total support in 1940 in London, of wanting to give up some French sovereignty to Europe, and of "being jumpy like a goat" and "the man in the shadows." A few others accused Monnet of being more Anglo-Saxon than French, of favoring a united Europe over France, and of being an internationalist and not a French nationalist. Some even called him a traitor to his country because they claimed he placed European unity above France's national interests. Monnet's French colleagues who had worked with him in London, Algiers, and Paris, such as René Pleven and Mollet, knew these accusations were false. But this negative view of Monnet held by many of the elites prevailed even after his death in 1979.

## Loss of a Close American Friend

With a sad and heavy heart, Monnet flew to Washington at the end of May 1959. Dulles had died after a long battle with cancer, and Janet Dulles had asked him to be one of the honorary pallbearers, the only foreigner asked, at the funeral to be held at Arlington National Cemetery. It is a testament to Monnet's unusual personal skills that he developed friendships with so many different types of Americans among the powerful US East Coast elites. But his forty-one-year-old friendship with this stern Presbyterian was special for Monnet. It not only involved fairly regular contact through letters, telegrams, and frequent meetings in European capitals or the United States but also family gatherings, as their wives had become close friends. This tall, prominent international lawyer and statesman, whom others found insensitive, abrupt, and demanding and who was often criticized both at home and abroad, counted Monnet as one of his best friends. Monnet's admiration and feeling of warmth toward Dulles are revealed in his *Memoirs*:

> I appreciated his great ability . . . but above all, I admired his strength of character and the moral authority that he already commanded outside his professional sphere. . . . [He] was deeply religious and profoundly convinced that liberty is essential to civilization. I have always known him as decisive and inflexibly determined, just as history paints him and at the same time warm, fond of good living, and an affectionate friend. One day the world will come to see him, alongside Eisenhower, as a man of great stature, a symbol of willpower that aroused conflicting passions. But this was not Foster Dulles the man. The Dulles I knew and loved was like many other men, but greater and more upright than most.[34]

Monnet never forgot how Dulles had helped him survive financially during the 1930s by recommending him for consulting jobs and providing the financial backing for Monnet, Murnane, and Co. after the Frenchman returned from China. While they didn't always agree, they shared the fundamental belief that European integration was the best means of preserving postwar peace. And because of their close bond, Monnet usually found a way to win Dulles's support and successfully used him to help shape US policy toward Europe during the Eisenhower administration.

In a letter written to Dulles when he was hospitalized, Monnet paid a great tribute to his friend. Monnet reveals what he too hoped would be his legacy:

> It is very rare . . . that one can in life accomplish an effort that is conclusive. In fact, conclusion is static and contrary to life which is made of constant adjustments and changes. The real accomplishment is in the contribution that one can bring to the development of affairs of the world, and in the change in the psychology of men—and that you have done. You can look to your life and effort as having contributed to the development of the world at a vital moment of civilization when hesitancy might have fatally turned the course of events towards compromise first and then to the defeat of liberty as we know it. When our children will look back and consider the period we are going through, I believe they will consider the history of the last 10 years as

the "charnières" [hinges] in the course which the world will follow—and you as one of the main architects of it—and also the bravest.[35]

## Efforts to Create a New Atlantic Partnership

Monnet saw Europe "intimately linked" to the United States, asserts historian Gérard Bossuat, by common poltical values such as individual liberty.[36] The man from Cognac always believed the United States and Europe could be true partners in the Cold War era, and he worked diligently but unsuccessfully during the Eisenhower administration to achieve this goal. He discussed his partnership "theory" with his American friends as early as the mid-1950s.[37] Kohnstamm noted he personally shared Monnet's belief that "being a strong Atlanticist and a European were the same thing."[38] In his August 1959 letter to Eisenhower, Monnet stressed the need for a "partnership between the United States and a United Europe" in order to negotiate from a position of strength with the Soviet Union and to "build up a long term understanding between Russia and the West that might one day become an association." Monnet argued that the United States and Europe had to deal jointly with common problems.[39] He also hoped the EC could act as a unit and be the one voice for Europe, not as a collection of states, which would help it deal with Washington on equal terms.[40] Monnet also believed British membership in the EC would increase the chances of having a partnership of equals with the United States because, as he wrote to Konrad Adenauer four years later, they could settle together the problems of the common defense of the West.[41]

When John F. Kennedy became president in 1961, Monnet hoped to persuade the new US leader to establish a true Atlantic partnership with the EC. Monnet had reason to be optimistic that some concrete action would replace the platitudes of previous officials. His American network of friends and disciples permeated the new administration in key positions among both top-ranking and lower-level officials, especially in the State Department. George Ball, the top Europeanist in the new administration and the chief advocate of the Atlantic partnership concept, was given a surprisingly free hand in European affairs. As undersecretary of state for economic affairs in the State Department, Ball surrounded himself with a group of trusted officials who were longtime friends of Monnet and was affectionately called their "High Priest." Mockingly labeled by this new administration as the "Atlanticists," the " theologians," or "the Club," Monnet's friends under Kennedy included Averell Harriman, ambassador at large in 1961 who became undersecretary of state for political affairs in 1963; David Bruce, later appointed ambassador to Great Britain; Schaetzel, who became Ball's chief of staff; Henry Owen, State Department official given the responsibility to study the Atlantic partnership problem; Arthur Hartman, who became Schaetzel's deputy; John Tuthill, foreign service officer who became the liaison with European organizations; John Leddy of the Treasury Department; and Admiral John M. Lee of the Defense Department.[42] Tuthill later became US special representative to the EC. Dean Acheson was appointed by Kennedy to be his top foreign policy adviser on NATO as the chairman of the president's NATO Advisory Committee, and two Republican friends of Monnet were given key posts: McCloy became the president's principal disarmament adviser, and Dillon served as secretary of the treasury. Walt Rostow, a professor of economics, was appointed deputy special assistant to the president for national security affairs. He had met Monnet after the war in Washington through his brother, Eugene Rostow, an international lawyer and wartime Lend-Lease administration official who introduced them. Both Rostow brothers and Walt's wife, Elspeth, a professor of American studies and public policy, and Edna, Eugene's wife who was a psychiatrist, became very close family friends of the Monnets. Other relationships from the Truman era that Monnet resurrected to gain his objectives once Kennedy was elected included those with Paul Nitze, who had been director of policy planning at the State Department, and the Alsop brothers.

The Ball-Monnet connection proved important in August 1960 even before Kennedy's election. The presidential candidate asked Illinois Governor Adlai Stevenson to develop a plan of action for the first few months of his administration. To write the report, Stevenson commissioned Ball, who confidentially asked for Monnet's help in defining US policy toward Europe and outlining measures to strengthen US-European ties. With Schaetzel's help, Ball wrote a large part of this Foreign Policy Task Force report after also enlisting the advice of Kohnstamm and other European friends of Monnet. It included a plan to implement a "policy for Partnership between a United Europe and America within a strong Atlantic Community."[43]

Once Kennedy was elected, the Atlanticists in the State Department continued to work on a strategy for close relations with Europe while keeping in close touch with Monnet and his European colleagues, such as Walter Hallstein, Marjolin, and Hirsch. In the first three months of 1961, Ball and Tuthill, along with Robert Bowie, who was back at Harvard, traveled to Paris to see Monnet or visit him at his home in Houjarray. Ball also visited Kohnstamm and Duchêne at the Action Committee's Paris office. When Monnet came to Washington shortly after Kennedy's election, Ball hosted a dinner for him and included some of the top Kennedy advisers such as Rostow and McGeorge Bundy, national security adviser who served as While House intermediary to the Atlanticists in the State Department.

Ball soon discovered he was dealing with a president who was less interested in European unity than Eisenhower and Dulles. Although Kennedy knew little about European integration before he entered office, he was not particularly dedicated to that idea or convinced that it was inevitable or even desirable. Also, the concept of supranational institutions seemed strange and unfamiliar to him. Most importantly, he entered office particularly concerned about the US decline as the dominant economic power and the sharp drop in the US trade surplus since 1957. As a result, he feared the common market might have a negative effect on US trade and prestige.

In light of these concerns and skepticism, Ball worked hard to convince Secretary of State Dean Rusk and then the president of the need to rethink and develop a comprehensive economic policy in common with their Allies as the only hope for ensuring domestic prosperity and securing a free world.[44] He succeeded in part because Kennedy gave great weight to the State Department's views on Europe. Moreover, Kennedy admired the reputations, abilities, and intelligence of Ball and his colleagues and learned that Rusk acquiesced to Ball on most European, trade, and economic matters. Ball had totally embraced Monnet's central thesis that "European integration was an exorable process," writes David DiLeo. "He believed that the United States could prepare for it or be overrun by it."[45] Americans, he warned the president, "should act boldly and not sit back and be passive witnesses to the development of a closed, autarchic, incestuous 'continental' system." Ball had written Rusk that "unless we attempt some such *grand design* as I have outlined . . . we may be defeated . . . in conducting an effective foreign policy in the present age of change and uncertainty."[46] Ball had conceptualized the Atlantic partnership idea and defined it broadly to make it attractive to the president. He explained that it encompassed economic, political, and military cooperation, and was an essential complement to the progressive and more cohesive EC.[47]

Ball masterminded "the most constructive enterprise in pursuit of the Atlantic partnership," declares DiLeo, "the passage of the Trade Expansion Act of 1962 and the rethinking of American trade policy."[48] This piece of legislation called for a comprehensive reduction of tariffs, licenses, and restrictions as well as constructive political engagement with the nation's special interests. He thought the advance of European integration and the threat of higher duties were both a danger and an opportunity for the United States. Ball believed that this legislation would strengthen rather than weaken the common market and create the conditions in which the Europeans would bear more of the defense burden. But strong opponents to this trade initiative on both sides of the ocean added their voices to those opposed to European integration. "There were both Americans and Europeans whose reservations about a united Europe sprang from a conviction that an integrated Europe would inevitably become a third force," wrote Schaetzel. "The skeptics anticipated that instead of cooperating with the United States in a true Atlantic Partnership, a united Europe would become increasingly independent, with opposition to the United States deemed essential to a separate European entity."[49]

During the Eisenhower years, Monnet had ignored Acheson and concentrated on his friend Dulles. But Bruce had kept Acheson, his former colleague and friend, informed of Monnet's activities and the advances made in integration during the Eisenhower years. As Acheson believed that the Republican administration had not done enough to encourage European unity, he began to write articles and give speeches in the late 1950s on the need for a new European unity program. In hopes that a Democratic candidate would capture the White House in 1960, Acheson worked for the Democratic Party while advocating European unity and an Atlantic partnership.[50]

Monnet wrote Acheson immediately after Kennedy's election. He knew that Acheson and Ball were his two most valuable assets in Washington, and he leaned heavily on them to adopt his plan for an Atlantic partnership. Acheson jokingly remarked to journalist Joseph Alsop that he knew he was once more back in the influential White House circle because Monnet was using him again "to advance his united Europe cause." When he received a gift from the Frenchman, Acheson added, "Monnet was the only man he enjoyed being bribed by. . . . [H]e knew how to do it understated with flair."[51] In four meetings in Washington with Acheson in March of 1961, Monnet argued repeatedly that the West would be strengthened by uniting the United States and the "United Europe." As a result of the persuasive powers of Monnet and the lobbying of his Action Committee, Acheson became, along with Ball, a leading proponent of this new institutional initiative. These two men believed US leadership was essential to European integration. As a result, they both argued for greater US support of European political unification within a larger transatlantic framework that included Britain in the common market.

Acheson lobbied for the partnership both through his direct access to the president and through Ball. Kennedy responded positively to Acheson's suggestion, transmitted by Ball and supported by *Washington Post* publisher Philip Graham, and invited Monnet to the White House to promote the partnership idea. Acheson believed that such a visit would remind the president, who disliked de Gaulle, that the former French general did not represent the views of all Frenchmen. As a result, Monnet was invited in March 1961, not long after Kennedy's inauguration, to the first of three luncheons at the White House to discuss NATO, the common market, and the Algerian crisis.

Each of these men was impressed by the other. The president appeared interested in the Action Committee and Monnet's ideas on European unification.[52] Monnet found the president dynamic, intelligent, and thirsty for knowledge and conveyed his admiration to Adenauer. As always, he exaggerated the importance of the EC's role among the Western nations:

> Kennedy showed himself to be energetic and courageous. He saw Europe as his affair—his choice of advisers left no doubt of that. . . . The men around him have been well chosen . . . [and] they all have come to the same conclusion: that it is urgently necessary to organize the West—that is, the free world which essentially comprises continental Europe, Britain, the United States and Canada. But for all of them it is clear that the central core of this organization of the West is the European community, at the heart of which is unity between Germany and France.[53]

*President John F. Kennedy and Jean Monnet at the White House, March 26, 1962.*

## Monnet and the Kennedy Administration

Monnet returned to Washington at the end of March 1962 to sell his vision of the Atlantic partnership. He made appointments to see well-placed friends in the Kennedy circle, including Rusk, Dillon, Walt Rostow, Owen, Bundy, Schaetzel, Acheson, and Ball. Back in the US capital again in June, the Frenchman stressed that a united Europe would never be a rival of the United States but an equal partner united by a bond of common interest. That is why he urged the State Department to drop the term "Atlantic Community," a concept he believed implied one superpower with other small partners. At Acheson's home at the end of the month, Monnet revised a draft of a new Action Committee resolution on the Atlantic partnership, which was given to Ball, Rostow, Owen, and Schaetzel for review.[54]

Kennedy outlined his approach to European affairs, his "Grand Design" for the United States and Europe, in his "Declaration of Interdependence" speech in Philadelphia on July 4, 1962. This aspirational speech, a minimally revised version of Monnet's Action Committee resolution, clearly reflected the efforts of those who had worked on it a week earlier. The president boldly stated that, in foreign policy, he accorded top priority to Europe and strongly supported European unity because it was key to US success, security, and survival. He spoke about this Atlantic partnership between the United States and Europe as two pillars of democracy of equal weight, with leaders of equal voice. "We see in such a Europe a partner with whom we can deal on a basis of full equality in all the great and burdensome tasks of building and defending a community of free nations."[55]

Ball believed the speech had the potential for strengthening the partnership as well as meeting the fear held by some Americans of being cut out of Europe.[56] In retrospect, the speech was for Duchêne "the high-water mark of the ideology of integration."[57] Even though Acheson had been involved in writing both the Action Committee resolution and the speech, he intensely disliked the phrase "equal partnership" because his experience as a lawyer taught him that no partnership was ever equal. Monnet hastened to congratulate the president on his eloquent statement, which, he optimistically claimed, brought the hopes of many people in Europe into the realm of practical politics. In fact, it raised both expectations and apprehensions on both sides of the Atlantic.[58] In his July 11, 1962, letter, Monnet urged the president to deal with the issue of the monetary stability of the West. In his reply of July 17, 1962, to Monnet, Kennedy wrote, "I share your view that the problem of monetary stability is now of great importance, and our people here are moving forward with plans for improved joint action."[59]

The Kennedy administration made an effort to implement its twin policy goals of European unity and Atlantic partnership in the context of the British application to the EC. Economic factors, especially British declining export trade, the European Free Trade Association's lack of success in rivaling the European Community, and the fear of exclusion from the common market, motivated Prime Minister Harold Macmillan to apply for EC membership. Announced July 31, 1961, Britain's membership in the common market was "a farsighted effort to maintain British commercial prosperity," asserts political scientist Andrew Moravcsik.[60] Monnet believed it "laid the foundation for a potential restructuring of relations in the West" and would reinforce European unity and "increase the influence Europe could exert on the world's affairs."[61]

Monnet had labored hard to persuade British leaders to join the EC and met often with Edward Heath, who was appointed by Macmillan to lead the negotiations. Monnet believed Britain's membership was necessary to preserve the balance of power within the EC by providing a counterweight to Germany. Kennedy had followed Ball's advice and urged Macmillan, when he visited Kennedy in April 1961, to join the EC. When de Gaulle announced his veto of the British application on January 14, 1963, he shocked and infuriated London, Washington, and Monnet. American officials knew they too had been targeted because de Gaulle feared increased US influence in Europe through its British ally.[62] With his veto, argues historian Alfred Grosser, de Gaulle killed Kennedy's grand design.[63]

De Gaulle's veto influenced Kennedy's decision to consider seriously Bowie's 1960 proposal to create a multilateral missile force (MLF) under NATO. Written for the Foreign Policy Task Force, its purpose was multifold: to increase conventional forces within the alliance; reassure the Europeans that the US commitment to defend Europe remained firm; prevent the spread and maintenance of national nuclear forces in Europe, especially the emergence of a separate German nuclear force; and deflect the feeling of many in Germany that they were not participants in their own defense. To Ball and some in the State Department, the concept of a shared nuclear force was alluring on both political and security grounds.[64] Moreover, it offered Europeans a chance to help man the missile-bearing submarines and pay for nuclear forces that the United States would control. Monnet supported this proposal because it was designed to tie Western Europe more solidly to the United States in the nuclear field, satisfy German sensibilities, and undermine the French nuclear deterrent. After de Gaulle vetoed British common market entry, enabling the French to block a British contribution in the economic area, officials in Washington moved ahead on the nuclear front, exploring the MLF as a way of associating the British more closely with the continent. For Kennedy, MLF became a possible means of cementing Western unity ideologically and of maintaining US influence in Europe.[65]

While Kennedy's advisers on Europe continued to give conflicting advice, the president was never completely sold on the idea of MLF. Bundy forcefully argued it was both technically unfeasible and politically undesirable. The limited role allotted the Germans in MLF did not please those in Germany whom it was designed to satisfy as they believed their nation deserved a larger role in Western nuclear strategy. In addition, because of German opposition, a lack of interest in Congress, British reluctance to join, and Bundy's ability to persuade the president to abandon it, Kennedy did nothing about it.

The Kennedy White House remained nominally receptive to Monnet's advice on minor issues. After Monnet was awarded, with the president's blessing, the Freedom Award from Freedom House in New York on January 23, 1963, Kennedy wrote, "you come as the exemplar of disinterested service to Europe and to the Atlantic World."[66] In his address accepting the award, Monnet declared mankind must create new forms of relationships among countries to prevent war, which the common market had done. He claimed unity of the six nations had rapidly changed attitudes, and the process is "taking us faster and further than anyone would have dared to hope after the war."[67] When the administration in February 1963 conducted a review of US policy toward Europe, it planned a visit to Germany by Kennedy in an effort to revitalize the US-German connection. Monnet advised the president to accept the invitation from the new Socialist mayor of West Berlin, Willy Brandt, to visit that city. In addition, he recommended the president upstage de Gaulle by announcing his proposed June visit, which would occur before the general's. Monnet's advice, supported by McCloy and Bruce, was followed, and Kennedy arrived in Berlin ahead of de Gaulle. In Washington in early June 1963, Monnet helped the president develop some of the key themes for a major address on the United States and European integration given in Frankfurt on June 25, the day before Kennedy's Berlin Wall speech.[68]

Monnet was pleased that some of his suggestions appealed to the White House, but his hopes for more progress toward a concrete Atlantic partnership were dashed by an assassin's bullet that ended Kennedy's life that November. Upon hearing the news of his assassination, European leaders paid tribute to the young president. De Gaulle declared, "he was one of the very few leaders of whom it may be said that they are statesmen. He had courage and he loved his country."[69] Both Monnet and de Gaulle attended the president's funeral in Washington. The tall, statuesque general in military uniform and the short, dignified Atlanticist in his felt hat marched solemnly down Constitution Avenue to the Capitol behind the president's horse-drawn casket. Following the service, these two French leaders were seen engaged in an animated conversation at the State Department reception.[70]

Kennedy had come to admire Monnet and his resolve and even became a pragmatic but cautious supporter of European integration as a desirable objective for the unity of the West.[71] But the president remained "a bit skeptical of rigid supranational institutions in Europe," noted Arthur Schlesinger, his White House adviser. "Though he had the greatest affection and respect for Jean Monnet, he was not tied to Monnet's formulas—or those of anyone else."[72] Monnet was indeed disappointed that Kennedy's support of Atlantic unity remained idealistic rhetoric that was not converted into concrete action. As Ball himself later acknowledged, the grand design never became more than a figure of speech.[73] And neither Ball nor Monnet knew that Kennedy, in the months before his death, had expressed doubts about the major emphasis on Europe in his foreign policy and declared that the rest of the world was also important.[74]

Throughout the 1960s, Acheson and Monnet remained in touch. Forever optimistic, Monnet countered Acheson's complaints after the Cuban missile crisis about the West's weakness, de Gaulle's disturbing vetoes of British entry into the common market, and the slowness of the integration progress. In the latter part of the decade, Acheson grew disillusioned with both US and European leadership and found Monnet's optimism annoying. He doubted the common market would ever move forward politically or economically. Douglas Brinkley argues that both men "seemed to overestimate the possibilities of the Grand Design and Atlantic Partnership and deluded themselves about the realities of MLF . . . and underestimated their rival Charles de Gaulle." But even as Acheson's optimism dissipated, Monnet never lost hope or stopped advocating the advantages of a strong and united Atlantic community.[75]

## Challenges from the Gaullists

Under the Franco-German Friendship Treaty of January 22, 1963, signed by Adenauer and de Gaulle, both nations pledged to consult each other on foreign policy decisions, hold biannual summits, and develop an active youth exchange program. This agreement alarmed not only Monnet but many people in West Germany, including members of Adenauer's own Christian Democratic Union party, who disliked de Gaulle's anti-American and anti-EC policies and believed Adenauer was overly influenced by him.[76] Because this treaty stated that it superseded Germany's existing international agreements, which included NATO with its US security guarantee, Monnet was concerned. Along with officials in Washington, he feared being confronted by a closed French-German system that might conduct a policy independent of the alliance, such as courting the Russians or conspiring against NATO. That in turn could lead to the end of NATO and the disintegration of the common security it guaranteed. Monnet also worried that the general would "infect the Germans with the nationalism he personified" and "tempt them into playing off the West against the Russians." Above all, he believed de Gaulle's actions undermined his own efforts to ensure that Germany's bipartisan commitment to European unity continued.[77]

Just before Adenauer signed the treaty, Monnet had a long talk with him and Hallstein and insisted the chancellor do all he could to revive talks on British entry. But Adenauer ignored the advice. Monnet's fears about the agreement were confirmed by de Murville, who declared on February 23, 1963, that the six-member EU organization no longer existed because of the treaty: only the Franco-German relationship did. This angered Monnet.[78] Determined to counteract de Gaulle's action, he marched off to Bonn at the end of February to persuade individual Bundestag members to acknowledge the importance of the US security guarantee and remedy the negative effects of that treaty. Because the Bundestag politicians were under pressure from the United States to maintain the transatlantic security link and believed that their eighty-seven year-old chancellor had been seduced by de Gaulle,[79] they agreed in April to insert a preamble, which resembled a draft written by Monnet, in the Franco-German Treaty. The preamble asserted the supremacy of German-American security over other German international relationships and stated the treaty did not supersede Germany's existing international agreements.[80] The man from Cognac took pleasure in thwarting his own president on an issue he deemed of critical importance to France and Europe.

The relationship between the two exceptional French leaders who had the most influence on postwar France and the development of the European Community ended on a bitter note. De Gaulle's continued efforts to undermine the EC and NATO in the mid-1960s infuriated Monnet. As a result, he publicly announced he would vote against de Gaulle in the 1965 presidential elections, labored hard to persuade a candidate to run as president in the first election round, and supported Socialist François Mitterrand in the second. On December 2, three days before the first round, Monnet issued a communiqué to the press explaining his choice:

> Like many Frenchmen, I voted "yes" to the 1958 constitution, "yes" to the election of the President of the Republic by universal suffrage, and "yes" to the referenda on Algeria. On December 5, I shall not vote for General de Gaulle. His policy is leading us into the outdated path of nationalism and inevitably encouraging nationalism in other countries, in particular Germany. The future for Frenchmen is Europe. . . . I welcome the statements of François Mitterrand in favour of Europe and the support he brings.[81]

In the late 1950s and 1960s, Monnet's and de Gaulle's contrasting visions for postwar Europe stimulated debate in France and Europe. De Gaulle believed that the fundamental reality of international politics is the nation-state. His goal was to maintain a Europe of independent nation-states, which were highly nationalistic, free of supranationality and federalist pretensions, and independent of the United States. De Gaulle epitomized French nationalism and sought French leadership in Europe. As the general never trusted the United States to come to the aid of France if it were attacked with nuclear weapons, he argued that his country needed a nuclear deterrent in order to preserve its independence. In contrast, Monnet strove for a Europe that was basically antinationalist, united economically through concrete institutions based on the rule of law, and closely linked to the United States. Monnet believed France had a responsibility to lead Europe toward increased integration and unity where nuclear weapons were not needed. Moreover, Monnet had grave reservations about de Gaulle's nationalism and his despotic tendencies and believed nationalism had to be reined in to end wars in Europe.[82] As Stanley Hoffmann observed, "Today's European Community is an improbable—yet not ineffectual—blend of de Gaulle and Monnet."[83]

Throughout the 1960s, Monnet traveled often to Washington to see his many American friends and to ensure their continued support for European integration. He visited Shepard Stone, the Schaetzels, Bowies, Tuthills, Achesons, Balls, Eugene Rostows, Walt Rostows, McCloys, Bruces, Katharine Graham whose husband Phil died in 1963, and the Restons. Scotty, as James Reston was called, was a powerful voice at the *New York Times*, the nation's most prominent newspaper for much of the 1940s and 1950s, and was perhaps the most influential American journalist of his era. He and Monnet shared many qualities—drive, charm, judgment, and cunning—and both moved easily in the corridors of power. Reston admired his French friend's personal modesty, discipline, and relevance of thoughts to the problems of the twentieth century. Calling him a "doer" and "masterbuilder of the European Economic Community," Reston often wrote about Monnet's view of the EC—not as an end in itself but part of a process of change and only a stage on the way to a more organized world of the future. Jody Reston, Scotty's daughter-in-law, recalled an evening when Monnet joined the Reston family for dinner, which he did two or three times a year over many years. "Dressed in a casual way wearing a sport jacket and open-necked shirt, he was very humble and soft-spoken with no sign of ego," she said. "He spoke with passion, had great charisma, and was riveting. He seemed to adore Sally [Reston's wife] and was charmed by her. He paid attention to my husband, Dick, and me and the more he talked about his dreams for Europe's future, the more attractive he became."[84]

Katharine Graham wrote she enjoyed seeing Monnet during these years. "The thrill for me of being with him never disappeared as long as he lived," she recalled, as she found him "energetic and interesting, and I can testify to his virility. I especially loved the way he used the English language and his insightful comments on the American political scene." She added, "I recall his once telling me, after he had lunched with Bobby Kennedy, that he had been very impressed, saying 'The president had authority—Bobby has strength.'"[85]

Monnet's American friends also continued to visit him at Houjarray during the 1960s and 1970s. Robert Bowie remarked he enjoyed the dinners he and his family had with the Monnets, and he always found Silvia warm and welcoming. He recalled one occasion where his host embarrassed Silvia. Believing that Bowie's two young sons liked baked beans as much as he did, Monnet asked his wife in the middle of the meal to open a can of baked beans and heat them for the boys. Silvia protested, saying there was no need to feed these young men American food. But Jean was adamant and won the argument. The guests waited politely for the beans to be heated in the kitchen, and the young guests consumed them, without complaint, after they were served.

Bowie recounted with a smile that Monnet's love of America knew no bounds. He discovered that day that Monnet had boxes full of cans of Boston baked beans, specially ordered from the United States, stored in his cellar.[86]

## Keeping Alive the Idea of Monetary Union

Through the Action Committee and direct contact with the political leaders of the six nations in the 1960s and 1970s, Monnet tried to keep the idea of further integration through monetary union alive. In 1969, he lobbied both the new French President Georges Pompidou and German Chancellor Brandt about the need for a European reserve fund. Brandt, Monnet's political friend for a decade and member of the Action Committee, supported this idea because it demonstrated Germany's commitment to the EC while he pursued Ostpolitik, his policy of rapprochement toward the Soviet bloc. Brandt presented Monnet's proposals to the heads of government at the EC summit meeting in The Hague, December 1–2, 1969. Pompidou supported a monetary union because, as a former banker, businessman, and prime minister to de Gaulle, he understood that the events of 1968 that led to de Gaulle's not being reelected in 1969 had weakened the French economy. He also realized that its economic and monetary problems, which lowered France's international standing, made participation in the EC important. Moreover, Pompidou's devaluation of the franc and his recognition that the German currency and economy had become the main engine of growth in the EC meant he favored some coordination of the monetary policies of the six nations. The EC heads of government agreed at this summit on the principle of monetary union in the short term through cooperation in a European Reserve Fund, with full monetary union to be reached by 1980. They commissioned the premier of Luxembourg, Pierre Werner, to head the committee to plan the timetable. At the Action Committee's meeting in Bonn on December 15–16, 1969, Monnet not only congratulated the leaders on relaunching the EC after de Gaulle's departure but also encouraged them to bring about economic and monetary union.[87]

The adoption of Monnet's monetary union idea at the Hague summit was the result of Pompidou's pragmatic attitude toward Europe, Monnet's pressure on Brandt, and Brandt's desire to adopt the ideas of the Action Committee.[88] But tensions developed between Brandt and Monnet after the summit. German policymakers believed that a monetary union could only be set up after the economic policies of the member states had "converged." And because the French refused to abandon monetary sovereignty, Pompidou put the brake on a monetary union and decried Werner's 1970 report, which proposed a seven-stage plan to achieve economic and monetary union in ten years. As Jean-René Bernard, Pompidou's chief economic adviser, remarked, a European monetary zone had to be accompanied by a "dose of federalism," which did not appeal to the *dirigiste* French. As a result, Pompidou did nothing to implement the Werner report.[89]

Gérard Bossuat argues that both Triffin and Monnet shaped the foundation of European monetary union as it exists today, while Monnet's contribution to a monetary union occurred at the conceptual level between 1957 and 1974. In the early 1970s, Monnet pressed the heads of state incessantly through personal visits and his Action Committee, but his influence was proportional to the degree of confidence each leader had in him. While Brandt liked and admired Monnet, Pompidou did not. Bernard, whom Monnet met frequently, mocked his fanciful policies and joked, *"O pool charbon-acier, Benelux, Euratom! Nous peuplons le vacarme avec des mots fantômes."* (O coal and steel pool, Benelux, Euratom! We are filling the air with phantom words.)[90] Both Helmut Schmidt, the new German chancellor in 1974, and Valéry Giscard d'Estaing, who succeeded Pompidou that same year, credit Monnet as a source of Schmidt's 1978 proposal for the European Monetary System (EMS).[91]

The creation of the European Council by the heads of government stands as Monnet's final contribution to the European Community. He recognized the need to reform the EC's decisionmaking process, which had been hindered by economic crises in the early 1970s, and presented his plan, drafted by Van Helmont, to EC leaders in 1973. He recommended that the heads of government meet regularly to decide issues that were normally blocked at the Council of Ministers level, where each defended the position of his own government. The plan was not adopted until 1974 when Monnet's arguments convinced Giscard d'Estaing of the need to regularize summits or heads-of-government meetings. With the support of Schmidt, the EC leaders voted at the Paris Summit in December 1974 to create the European Council. This body, composed of the heads of government, was adopted in order to speed the decisionmaking process by having more frequent meetings at the highest level. Some consider it paradoxical that Monnet presented a plan in 1973 that highlighted the intergovernmental character of the Community system and maintained the influence of national governments over decisionmaking.[92] But always pragmatic, Monnet allowed his own thinking to evolve over the years when changing circumstances warranted it. As Eric Roussel has observed, "He was a federalist at the time of the High Authority but different when he suggested the creation of the European Council."[93] Monnet realized it was necessary to reinforce intergovernmentalism in the EC at that time because it seemed the only way to further integration, which had stalled in the 1970s.

## Dissolving the Action Committee

The Action Committee remained the "keeper of the European conscience," as Monnet viewed it, until the eighty-seven-year-old dissolved it in 1975.

*Jean Monnet at age eighty-four outside his home in Houjarray, Luxembourg, November 1972.*

Duchêne demonstrates that its influence as a political lobby, like Monnet's, went through several phases. After its creation in 1955 to 1958, Monnet and his Committee were viewed as a quasi-government and influenced issues such as Euratom and the proposal for a European district. During de Gaulle's presidency, Monnet's influence plummeted in Paris but his networks remained strong, and he continued to focus on keeping the idea of integration alive. In 1967, the Action Committee's proposal that a resolution in favor of British entry into the EC be placed before all parliaments passed unanimously. No group deserted the Committee, but new groups joined, such as the left-wing Italian Nenni Socialists in 1967 and the French Independent Republicans, non-Gaullist junior partners in de Gaulle's government led by Giscard d'Estaing in 1968. Through the Action Committee, Monnet helped keep the idea of integration alive in Germany after French President de Gaulle defeated British entry for the second time in 1967 and in succeeding years with diminishing success until 1975. The powerful German politician Herbert Wehner viewed the Committee as "a circle of friends . . . serving the same cause . . . and Jean Monnet's thinking and the work of the Action Committee were a treasure that could not be allowed simply to sink into oblivion."[94]

Monnet's concern for the welfare of his own nation as well as European unity never ceased. On January 8, 1975, he talked to Giscard d'Estaing about the need to keep Britain in the European Community in the face of efforts by the British Labour government of Harold Wilson to renegotiate the terms of British membership in the EC. Historian Klaus Schwabe argues Monnet believed that, as German reunification was likely a future possibility, he welcomed that event, provided it occurred within the framework of the EC. Schwabe asserts that Monnet viewed British membership as the way to guarantee the balance of power within an EC that included a united and stronger Germany and a weaker France.[95]

Monnet spent the last years of his life at his home in Houjarray. Lovingly cared for by Silvia, he welcomed friends, went for long walks, and enjoyed his grandchildren. But he nevertheless felt the isolation of retirement. Hesitant to write about his life when others had suggested it earlier, he was persuaded by one of his collaborators, François Fontaine, as well as other friends such as Bruce and Bowie in the 1970s, to complete his memoirs and thereby leave a written testament of his life and ideas. Monnet didn't like to write, so he eventually agreed to Fontaine's offer to write his memoirs for him because Monnet needed money. Monnet carefully reviewed and made changes to the text when necessary. Financial and political independence had been lifelong principles, so he had refused offers of paid directorships on boards. However, in 1960, he and his cousin had been forced to begin selling the family's controlling interest in J. G. Monnet and Co. And, as he had always lived beyond his means and had only a limited pension from his three years at the High Authority, his income was insufficient by the mid-1970s. So the fees and royalties of about $150,000 for his memoirs provided essential support from 1976 to 1978.

Monnet received several awards and honors from US organizations in the 1960s and 1970s but none from his own government before he died on March 16, 1979, at ninety years old. At Schmidt's initiative, the European Council had proclaimed him Honorary Citizen of Europe on April 2, 1976. His photo appeared on the March 26, 1979, cover of *Time* magazine and many articles were written about him in the US press declaring him the "Father of Europe." European leaders and dignitaries, including President Giscard d'Estaing, filled the small village church in Houjarray for his funeral along with some of his American friends, including Ball and McCloy. When the organist played "The Battle Hymn of the Republic," the popular American Civil War hymn, at the end of the service, these Americans looked at each other and smiled. It wasn't until November 9, 1988, when President Mitterrand ordered his ashes transferred to the Pantheon at a ceremony in Paris, that Jean Monnet was officially recognized by his government as a citizen who made an important contribution to his own country.

In the 1960s and 1970s, Monnet remained focused, determined, and persistent in pursuing his schemes to bring the EC countries closer together. From his seventies to eighties, except for the use of a cane and declining energy, he remained in relatively good health and a peripatetic, traveling regularly to the

EC capitals and Washington. Frailer in 1975 at eighty-seven years old, he could look back on the previous two decades with some satisfaction because he experienced successes along with the failures. He was most proud in his later years of his expansion of the Action Committee and its influential network. Its meetings and publications had strengthened ties among members and helped to provide a favorable political climate for the implementation of the common market clauses and general acceptance of new proposals in 1974, such as monetary union and direct elections. Monnet's constant prodding of the EC leadership resulted in a pledge to move toward monetary union and the creation of the European Council in 1974. While powerless in the face of de Gaulle's vetoes of British entry into the six nations, he and his Action Committee continued to lobby for British membership after Pompidou became president. In 1973, he happily celebrated British entry into the EC, one of his lifelong goals.

During his last years, Monnet acknowledged he had not accomplished all he had wished. Euratom failed to function as he had envisioned, although it remained a center for research. The idea of a strengthened Atlantic partnership as a pillar of the West in the Cold War era had remained only a verbal pledge on the part of Kennedy. Monnet had realized earlier than many the great need for a transatlantic relationship that went beyond trade and the security provided by NATO. And he remained convinced until his death that such a relationship was a strategically sound idea because it envisioned a powerful, democratic Western Europe together with the United States in opposition to the Soviet Union. He believed elites on both sides of the Atlantic had to maintain ties and nurture the shared Western values of democracy, human rights, and the rule of law. He told Tuthill shortly before he died that he hoped at least peace between France and Germany had been secured in Europe. Indeed it was. And he had played a critical role in that achievement.

In a lengthy interview several years before his own death, Max Kohnstamm reminisced about his many years of work with Monnet. For this Dutch diplomat, Monnet was a great humanist, philosopher, and man of action. He had been attracted to Monnet because the Frenchman understood the vicious cycle of wars that engulfed Europe and saw the need for change. "Working with Monnet you had the sense you were at the center of the world," said Kohnstamm. "Monnet always dealt with reality but provided hope through his focus on the future. He made you feel you could achieve something." Kohnstamm also admired his character. "He always had an open attitude, gave attention to process, possessed integrity, a sense of timing, and impressed others by a kind of solidity, but above all, by his magnetism and vision." Kohnstamm sensed his vision when he first met him—a vision not just of the European Coal and Steel Community but of the world. Monnet persuaded Hirsch, who had lost both his parents in Auschwitz, to work with him on building cooperation with Germany and breaking the cycle of violence. Monnet was also able to persuade the members of the German Socialist Democratic Party to back the ECSC because he showed a sympathetic understanding of their problems and their plight, Kohnstamm recalled. "We had an equal partnership for twenty-five years," concluded the Dutchman. "He told me once that he never would have succeeded in the negotiations with the Germans without me, as he would have been overwhelmed. But he never thanked me."[96]

## Notes

1. George-Henri Soutou, *The French Military Program for Nuclear Energy, 1945–1981* (College Park: Center for International Security Studies at Maryland, Nuclear History Program, 1989), pp. 6–8; Jean Lacouture, *De Gaulle: The Ruler 1945–1970* (New York: W. W. Norton, 1992), pp. 211–386; Stanley Hoffmann, review of Jean Lacouture, *De Gaulle: The Ruler 1945–1970*, in the *New York Times Book Review*, May 10, 1992, p. 3.

2. Jean Monnet, *Memoirs* (New York: Doubleday and Co., 1978), p. 430.

3. François Duchêne, *Jean Monnet: The First Statesman of Interdependence* (New York: W. W. Norton, 1994), p. 379.

4. Shepard Stone, interview by Leonard Tennyson, July 23, 1982, Lausanne, Switzerland, Fondation Jean Monnet pour l'Europe.

5. See Volker R. Berghahn, *America and the Intellectual Cold Wars in Europe: Shepard Stone Between Philanthropy, Academy, and Diplomacy* (Princeton, NJ: Princeton University Press, 2001), pp. 163–213.

6. Stone, interview.

7. Ibid.

8. Jean Monnet to Joseph McDaniel, Jr., letter, November 23, 1967, Ford Foundation Archives, New York, PA 58-0035, Reel R-0535.

9. Maria Grazia Melchionni, "Le Comité d'Action pour les Etats-Unis d'Europe: Un réseau au service de l'union européenne," in *Jean Monnet, l'Europe et les chemins de la paix,* ed. Gérard Bossuat and Andreas Wilkens (Paris: Publications de la Sorbonne, 1999), pp. 239–251.

10. Jean Monnet to the Board of Trustees of the Ford Foundation, letter, February 29, 1960, Ford Foundation Archives, New York, PA 58-0035, Reel R-0535.

11. Shepard Stone to Monnet, letters, January 16, 1958, December 27, 1962; and Stone Statement, August 17, 1962, Shepard Stone Papers, Dartmouth College Library; Duchêne, *Jean Monnet*, pp. 309–312, 339.

12. Willim Nims, Ford Foundation, to Jean Monnet, letter, January 26, 1972, Ford Foundation Archives, New York, PA 63-0434, Reel R-2348.

13. Stone interview; Berghahn, *America and the Intellectual Cold Wars*, pp. 197, 210–213, 336; Max Kohnstamm to Shepard Stone, letter, January 3, 1958, Ford Foundation Archives, New York, PA 58-0035, Reel R-0535.

14. Shepard Stone, memorandum, November 8, 1957, Ford Foundation Archives, New York, PA 57-0351, Reel R-0528.

15. Shepard Stone to Jean Monnet, letter, February 11, 1959, Shepard Stone Papers, Dartmouth College Library.

16. Pascaline Winand, *Eisenhower, Kennedy, and the United States of Europe* (New York: St. Martin's Press, 1993), pp. 104–105.

17. Max Kohnstamm to Jean Monnet, letters, February 10, 1975, and October 2, 1957; Robert Schaetzel to Kohnstamm, letters, November 26, 1957, and December 6, 1957, Papers of Max Kohnstamm, European University Institute Archives, Florence, Italy.

18. Richard Hewlett and Jack Holl, *Atoms for Peace and War* (Berkeley: University of California Press, 1989), pp. 410, 440–445; Winand, *Eisenhower, Kennedy*, pp. 100–108; Pierre Mélandri, *Les Etats-Unis et le "défi" européen* (Paris: Presses Universitaires de France, 1975), pp. 174–179; Duchêne, *Jean Monnet*, p. 303. See also article, "AEC Raises Objections to Accord with Euratom," *New York Times*, June 8, 1958.

19. *FRUS*, 1958–1960, vol. 7, pp. 2, 95, 122–126, 156–163, 189–216.

20. Duchêne, *Jean Monnet,* pp. 315, 333.

21. Duchêne, *Jean Monnet*, pp. 317, 333, 351; Robert Bowie, interview by the author, August 15, 1990; Hewlett and Holl, *Atoms,* p. 509; Winand, *Eisenhower, Kennedy*, pp. 124–125, 356–357.

22. Antonio Varsori, "Euratom, une organization qui échappe à Jean Monnet?" in *Jean Monnet, l'Europe et les chemins de la paix*, ed. Bossuat and Wilkens, pp. 350–356. See also Michel Dumoulin, Pierre Guillen, and Maurice Vaïsse, *L'Energie nucléaire en Europe: Des origins à Euratom* (Berne, Switzerland: Peter Lang, 1994), and Gérard Bossuat, *L'Europe des Francais 1943–1959: La IVe République aux sources de l'Europe communautaire* (Paris: Publications de la Sorbonne, 1996).

23. Hewlett and Holl, *Atoms,* p. 509; Winand, *Eisenhower, Kennedy*, pp. 124–125; Desmond Dinan, *Europe Recast* (Boulder, CO: Lynne Rienner Publishers, 2004), pp. 117–118.

24. Duchêne, *Jean Monnet,* p. 317.

25. Winand, *Eisenhower, Kennedy*, pp. 356–357.

26. J. B. Duroselle, "General de Gaulle's Europe and Jean Monnet's Europe," *The World Today* 22 (1966), p. 11.

27. Monnet, *Memoirs*, pp. 429–430.

28. Pierre Gerbet, "Jean Monnet–Charles de Gaulle: Deux conceptions de la construction européenne," in *Jean Monnet, l'Europe et les chemins de la paix*, ed. Gérard Bossuat and Andreas Wilkens (Paris: Publications de la Sorbonne, 1999), pp. 411–413.

29. Monnet, *Memoirs*, pp. 429–430.

30. Jean-Claude Casanova, interview by the author, June 28, 1984.

31. Melchionni, "Le Comité," p. 247.

32. Duchêne, *Jean Monnet*, pp. 318–320; see also Wilfred Loth, "Jean Monnet, Charles de Gaulle et le project d'union politique (1958–1963)," in *Jean Monnet, l'Europe et les chemins de la paix*, ed. Bossuat and Wilkens, pp. 357–367.

33. Gerbet, "Jean Monnet–Charles de Gaulle," pp. 411–412.

34. Monnet, *Memoirs*, p. 105.

35. Monnet to John Foster Dulles, letter, February 16, 1959, Dulles Papers, Box 141, Princeton University Library.

36. Gérard Bossuat, "Conclusion générale," in *Jean Monnet, l'Europe et les chemins de la paix*, ed. Bossuat and Wilkens, p. 499.

37. John W. Tuthill to Sherrill Wells, letter, June 24, 1992.

38. Max Kohnstamm, interview by the author, November 19, 2005.

39. Monnet to President Eisenhower, letter, August 14, 1959, Eisenhower Papers, Eisenhower Library.

40. Duchêne, *Jean Monnet*, pp. 322–323.

41. Monnet to Konrad Adenauer, letter, January 16, 1963, quoted in Richard Mayne, "Father of Europe: The Life and Times of Jean Monnet," unpublished manuscript, p. 496.

42. Winand, *Eisenhower and Kennedy*, p. 147; W. W. Rostow, "Kennedy's View of Monnet and Vice Versa," in *John F. Kennedy and Europe*, ed. Douglas Brinkley and Richard T. Griffiths (Baton Rouge: Louisana State University Press, 1999), pp. 281–287.

43. Winand, *Eisenhower and Kennedy*, pp. 140–160; Duchêne, *Jean Monnet*, p. 327; Robert Schaetzel, interview by the author, August 30, 1991.

44. David DiLeo, "George Ball and the Europeanists in the State Department, 1961–1963," in *John F. Kennedy and Europe*, ed. Brinkley and Griffiths, p. 263.

45. Ibid., p. 269.

46. Ibid., p. 263.

47. Ibid.

48. Ibid., p. 273.

49. J. Robert Schaetzel, *The Unhinged Alliance: America and the European Community* (New York: Harper and Row, 1975), p. 64.

50. Douglas Brinkley, "Dean Acheson and Jean Monnet: On the Path to Atlantic Partnership," in *Monnet and the Americans*, ed. Clifford Hackett (Washington, DC: Jean Monnet Council, 1995), pp. 88–89.

51. Ibid., p. 91.

52. Brinkley, "Dean Acheson and John Kennedy," in *John F. Kennedy and Europe*, ed. Brinkley and Griffiths, pp. 299–301; Brinkley, "Dean Acheson and Jean Monnet," pp. 92–93.

53. Monnet, *Memoirs*, p. 464.

54. Ibid.

55. John F. Kennedy, *Public Papers of the Presidents of the United States: John F. Kennedy, 1962* (Washington, DC: Government Printing Office, 1967), pp. 537–539.

56. Thomas Schwartz, *Lyndon Johnson and Europe* (Cambridge, MA: Harvard University Press, 2003), pp. 9–10; Department of State *Bulletin*, July 23, 1962, p. 132; Duchêne, *Jean Monnet,* pp. 327–329.

57. Duchêne, *Jean Monnet*, pp. 327–328.

58. DiLeo, "George Ball and the Europeanists," p. 264.

59. John F. Kennedy to Monnet, letter, July 17, 1962, Kennedy Papers, Kennedy Library.

60. Andrew Moravcsik, *The Choice for Europe: Social Purpose and State Power from Messina to Maastricht* (Ithaca, NY: Cornell University Press, 1998), pp. 164–165.

61. Monnet, *Memoirs*, p. 446.

62. Duchêne, *Jean Monnet,* pp. 323–329.

63. Alfred Grosser, *The Western Alliance: European-American Relations Since 1945* (New York: Continuum Press, 1980), p. 208.

64. DiLeo, "George Ball and the Europeanists," p. 277.

65. Winand, *Eisenhower, Kennedy*, pp. 218–226, 240–243; Charles Cogan, *Charles de Gaulle* (Boston: Bedford/St. Martin's, 1996), pp. 136–137; Duchêne, *Jean Monnet*, pp. 326–329; Robert Bowie, "Réflexions sur Jean Monnet," in *Témoignages à la mémoire de Jean Monnet* (Lausanne, Switzerland: Fondation Jean Monnet, 1989), pp. 81–88.

66. John F. Kennedy to Monnet, letter, January 22, 1963, AMK C 23/6/15 bis, Fondation Jean Monnet. This letter was probably drafted by George Ball.

67. Monnet, address, January 23, 1963, AML 192/54, Fondation Jean Monnet.

68. Winand, *Eisenhower, Kennedy*, pp. 335–340.

69. Lacouture, *De Gaulle: The Ruler*, p. 378.

70. Robert Schaetzel, interview by the author, August 15, 1990.

71. David DiLeo, "Catch the Night Train for Paris: George Ball and Jean Monnet," in *Monnet and the Americans,* ed. Clifford Hackett (Washington, DC: Jean Monnet Council, 1995), p. 158.

72. Arthur Schlesinger, Jr., *A Thousand Days* (New York: Fawcett Premier, 1965), pp. 781–782.

73. DiLeo, "George Ball and the Europeanists," p. 280.

74. Schwartz, *Lyndon Johnson,* p. 46.

75. Brinkley, "Dean Acheson and Jean Monnet," pp. 93–96.

76. Hans-Peter Schwarz, *Konrad Adenaue*r, vol. 2 (Providence, RI: Berghahn Books, 1997), pp. 596–687.

77. Duchêne, *Jean Monnet*, pp. 329–333. The agreement is also known as the Élysée Treaty.

78. Ibid., pp. 330–331.

79. Hans-Peter Schwarz, interview by the author, November 22, 2004.

80. Duchêne, *Jean Monnet*, pp. 329–333.

81. Mayne, "Father of Europe," p. 510.

82. Robert Marjolin, *Architect of European Unity: Memoirs, 1911–1986* (London: Weidenfeld and Nicolson, 1989), pp. 257–268; Gerbet, "Jean Monnet–Charles de Gaulle, pp. 411–433.

83. Stanley Hoffmann, "The Man Who Would Be France," *New Republic*, vol. 203, December 17, 1990, pp. 24, 29–35.

84. Jody Reston, interview by the author, April 22, 2007; articles by James Reston in the *New York Times,* November 8, 1978, March 18, 1979, and March 19, 1979.

85. Katharine Graham, *Personal History* (New York: Vintage Books, 1998), pp. 440–441.

86. Robert Bowie, interview by the author, September 19, 1990.

87. Desmond Dinan, *Ever Closer Union*, 2nd ed. (Boulder, CO: Lynne Rienner Publishers, 1999), pp. 59–64; Gérard Bossuat, "Jean Monnet et l'identité monétaire européenne," in *Jean Monnet, l'Europe et les chemins de la paix,* ed. Bossuat and Wilkens, pp. 379–385; Duchêne, *Jean Monnet,* pp. 334–335.

88. Eric Roussel, *Jean Monnet* (Paris: Fayard, 1996), pp. 868–869.

89. Bossuat, "Monnet et l'identité monétaire," pp. 385–387, 389–398; Duchêne, *Jean Monnet*, pp. 334–335; Jean-René Bernard, interview by the author, June 22, 1984.

90. Bossuat, "Monnet et l'identité monétaire," pp. 397–398.

91. Duchêne, *Jean Monnet,* p. 335; Giscard d'Estaing, in his speech at Georgetown University, May 17, 1997, stated that the idea of monetary union originated with Monnet.

92. Marie-Thérèse Bitsch, "Jean Monnet et la création du Conseil européen," in *Jean Monnet, l'Europe et les chemins de la paix,* ed. Bossuat and Wilkens, pp. 399–410; Duchêne, *Jean Monnet,* pp. 355–357; Monnet, *Memoirs*, pp. 502–513.

93. Eric Roussel, statement, "Table ronde," in *Jean Monnet, l'Europe et les chemins de la paix,* p. 490.

94. Duchêne, *Jean Monnet*, pp. 337–338.

95. Klaus Schwabe, "Monnet, la question allemande et l'ostpolitik," in *Une dynamique européenne: Le Comité d'Action pour les Etats-Unis d'Europe* (Lausanne, Switzerland: Fondation Jean Monnet, 2011).

96. Kohnstamm, interview.

# 9

# Jean Monnet:
# A Critical Assessment

Jean Monnet stands as one of the great leaders who shaped the twentieth century. By bringing rival nations together into an institutional framework for a joint economic endeavor, he helped break the cycle of hundreds of years of bloody conflicts and changed the course of European history. Motivated by his vision of a united Europe as the path to peace, he developed a grand strategy to achieve that goal. Because he believed in the transformative nature of economics, he argued that the best way to restructure politics and thereby achieve a lasting peace was through integrating economies. He thus became the single most important architect of European integration. This lengthy, incremental process culminated in the creation in 1957 of the European Economic Community (later the European Community, EC), now called the European Union.

The central element of Monnet's strategy was the establishment of effective international institutions. Since he identified nationalism as a central cause of European wars, he believed that peace in Western Europe could be achieved if this force could be channeled through institutions designed to create a new type of relationship among states. For Monnet, institutions were instruments of political and social change that could progressively alter thinking and reshape group psychology. He believed these organizations could break old patterns of thinking and behavior, transcend national divisions, and promote tolerance and understanding. But he knew such changes did not occur immediately. He wrote, "The unification of Europe, like all peaceful revolutions, takes time—time to persuade people, time to change men's minds, time to adjust to the need for major transformations."[1] He argued that such institutions were effective only if the nations involved created common goals and agreed to work for what he called the "general interest," or what was in their best collective interest. He argued that any decisionmaking body charged with

243

defining a general or common policy must be responsible to the group as a whole, not to a single member, and must accept responsibility for the effects of its collective decisions on each participating nation.

The European Coal and Steel Community (ECSC) remains Monnet's greatest achievement. This organization composed of six independent states demonstrated the effectiveness of international institutions with the power to make enforceable decisions in a clearly defined area. It was the pathfinder that led to a new order of Western European nations because it was a pragmatic way to link former enemies and involve them in a practical, limited economic endeavor of mutual interest. Because it was the first concrete step in Franco-German rapprochement, it revolutionized European international relations after World War II.

The design of this organization and its institutions grew out of Monnet's international experience. He learned during World War I that the Wheat Executive he devised produced what he called a creative force or new attitude—a spirit of cooperation—in the minds of the international civil servants who ran it. After the war, while working with the League of Nations, he experienced the weakness of this intergovernmental international organization where goodwill and good intentions were not enough: the League could not enforce policies in the face of a single national veto. To solve this problem, Monnet invented the first supranational organization, the ECSC.[2] What made it revolutionary was that its executive body, the High Authority, required consenting governments to share a part of their sovereign power for a common goal. Member states of the ECSC transferred to this common authority certain powers limited to the sectors of coal and steel, and the decisions taken by the majority of the nine High Authority members were imposed on all. Monnet also incorporated in this new community the principles of equality among states, the High Authority's independence from governments, and collaboration among the ECSC bodies rather than the subordination of one to the other. He devised a method, Stanley Hoffmann explains, that was "cautious and bold, pragmatic and ideological, and aimed at nations that had often been at war with one another" and were "proud of their past."[3]

The ECSC was truly a breakthrough in the process of European integration, because under Monnet's leadership, it became a functioning international organization even though it never achieved its original goal: to create a common market in coal and steel. By introducing the principle of supranationality into its institutional structure, he made the representatives of the six nations interact in a new framework. And by changing the context of their relationships, this community showed that habits of frequent consultation facilitated compromise. Moreover, it demonstrated that supranational cooperation in limited economic areas could serve as a brake on nationalism and that nations could survive and remain independent after sharing some national sovereignty. It also showed that some economic problems could be dealt with by this new approach. Monnet believed that peace did not depend solely on treaties and commitments, but rather on the creation of conditions that, although they may not change human nature, "are conducive to peaceful behavior towards others." By bringing nations together in institutions and by operating within a common set of rules and actions, he believed, a common spirit would evolve in that narrowly focused endeavor.

For Monnet, institutions were not static but dynamic, constantly evolving, and adjusting to changing situations. Monnet also thought they were "vital in cementing relations and creating democratic balances against abuse of power," notes François Duchêne. Monnet's dream was to make the international community a "civil society," or civil order of nations, governed by international institutions based on the rule of law.[4] He believed the new Europe, he wrote, could be built by the "same process as each of our national States—by establishing among nations a new relationship comparable to that which exists among the citizens of any democratic country: equality, organized by common institutions."[5] Hoffmann notes that the ECSC "aimed at transcending the nation-state" yet was "quite different from the classical federalism because it was functionally piecemeal and institutionally more technocratic than democratic."[6]

Social scientist Ernst B. Haas argues that Monnet set the paradigm for the study of European integration. In his 1958 book *Uniting of Europe: Political, Social, and Economic Forces, 1950–1957*, Haas analyzed the ECSC and used it to dissect the integration process. Haas, whom Hoffmann calls the first theorist of the Monnet method,[7] established the theory of neofunctionalism to explain how integration was taking place. Haas used concepts such as functionalism to describe forces that govern institutions at the supranational level and proclaimed these will "spill over" into the national level, generate counterpressures, and bind states more closely together.[8]

The term "functionalist" still persists as a description of the entrepreneur from Cognac. But those who knew him well, like Duchêne, understood how much he disliked academic theorizing, did not want to be tied to a formal definition that was the result of rationalization after the fact, and was not comfortable with, patient with, or respectful of the term "functionalism" as a description of his beliefs or an explanation of his actions.[9] Monnet was even leery of the term "federalist," most often used to label him, even though "federalism" describes what he hoped would eventually emerge from European integration. He also did not like the alternative term "supranational" or any term that might "prematurely tie him down." Because he never knew how he was going to solve a problem, Duchêne said, Monnet rejected categories that might interfere with "exploring the unknown as inventively as required."[10] But Monnet used both these terms freely in his writings and speeches. Etienne Hirsch noted that Monnet introduced the notion of federalism into the Schuman Plan even though he well knew that Europe was too diverse to federate like the United States. Duchêne asserted that the key for Monnet "was to keep the dynamic

going and for that, no means should be excluded." That meant not being wed-
ded to any term or method.[11] And Monnet's pragmatism ensured his thinking
evolved over his lifetime. After initially believing a common market could
never function, he strongly advocated its implementation after 1958 because it
showed surprising success. And his recommendation that the intergovernmental European Council be created in 1974 to further economic integration also
demonstrated this evolution.

Monnet's institutional approach to solving international problems was
incorporated at Messina and adopted by the Spaak Committee and signatory
nations of the Rome Treaties in 1957. The framers tried to balance national
sovereignty and supranational authority by incorporating both principles in the
institutional framework of the European Community. Its four institutions
were, with key modifications, modeled largely on those of the ECSC. The
Council of Ministers, the intergovernmental institution representing the individual nations, became the decisionmaking body. The Commission, composed
of international civil servants who executed and administered the Council's
decisions, was made the supranational institution. Monnet viewed the "constant dialogue" required between national governments and EC institutions as
the "keystone" of the system, inseparable from the decisionmaking process
and "the very essence of the Community's life." This is, he noted, "what
makes it unique among modern political systems."[12]

The Monnet Plan, as a strategy to restore France's influence through the
reconstruction and modernization of its economy, stands as another of his
important achievements. French historian Jean-Baptiste Duroselle asserts that
Monnet, although not an economist, was "a genius who was intuitive about the
economy."[13] Monnet used his business experience and knowledge about US
economic methods as well as US aid to successfully guide the French postwar
recovery. He had seen that, because of strategic miscalculations on the part of
French generals whose military training manuals had been studied by the Nazi
generals, his country was easily overrun by the Germans in 1940 and its economy ravaged by the war they executed.[14] While he detested the Nazis and
believed Germany's nationalism remained potentially dangerous, he did not
harbor negative feelings toward the German people and constantly stressed he
was uniting people, not states. He understood that for France to be respected
and restored to a position of influence and leadership in Europe, its democratic
tradition had to be preserved during the war and its economy modernized and
integrated with neighboring nations afterward. Monnet, like French Foreign
Minister Robert Schuman, viewed European economic integration as the
essential part of their national strategy to enhance France's interests by accel-
erating economic recovery and modernization, containing Germany and linking it to the West, and strengthening French influence within Europe and the
Atlantic alliance. By 1954, as French leaders had reconstructed their economy
through the Monnet Plan and had recast Franco-German relations through the

Schuman Plan and the ECSC, these achievements created goodwill and mutual interest between the two former enemies and enhanced French influence in the Western Alliance. Although not a member of the French government, Monnet played a key role in helping his nation's leaders shape French foreign policy in the postwar period.

Monnet never held a political office or joined a political party. His ability to change the course of events in twentieth-century Europe, however, remains a considerable achievement. It was Monnet's access to influence through connections to key French, European, and US leaders that gave him power. He gained the contacts and respect of many of his countrymen and foreign officials as a result of his international work on both continents, his contributions to his own government's policies and interests, and his unusual combination of talents. He was a man of integrity, intelligence, and great magnetism who dealt with reality but also provided hope for the future. He loved solving international problems. "He was a man of action with a particularly developed sense of the practical," Robert Marjolin wrote. "He was also . . . above all, a man of ideas. . . . It was this exceptional ability to conceive original ideas or ideas he was able to make appear original, combined with an extraordinary talent for putting them into practice, that largely explains the fascination Jean Monnet held for a great number of people from the most varied of backgrounds. He had a force of conviction I have never encountered in any other human being."[15]

Imaginative and persistent, Monnet had an uncanny ability to gain access to political leaders. Believing that men in power frequently lacked vision, he presented them with ideas that could be useful to them and often persuaded these men to adopt them as their own. His powers of persuasion were legendary. As Marjolin noted, "he knew how to combine, when necessary, the power of argument with a personal charm, graciousness and delicate tact that often disarmed those most predisposed to him."[16] Monnet was willing to take risks and did not fear failure because he believed it could be instructive and deserving of analysis. Never requiring recognition or acknowledgment or seeking political office, he did not pose a threat to leaders, treated most colleagues and politicians openly and honestly, and did not connive behind their backs. Because his mind was sharp and his personality charismatic, he attracted some of the ablest Frenchmen, Europeans, and Americans of his generation to work with him. Eric Roussel, Monnet's biographer who never knew his subject, stated he was fascinated to learn how much "of a grip Monnet had over people, even his enemies."[17]

Preeminent French intellectuals, economist Jean-Claude Casanova and Duroselle, have illuminated the qualities that made Monnet unique by comparing him with the other towering twentieth-century French leader, Charles de Gaulle. Duroselle asserts that both were men of power and of action but emphasized their power and influence derived from their different talents and sources.[18] He portrays de Gaulle as a brilliant military and political leader, as well as a philosopher, historian, talented orator, and writer with an extraordinary vocabulary and prose style. Elected to office, de Gaulle was a statesman with an intuitive sense of how to handle crises. By comparison, Monnet's power and influence, Duroselle contends, were derived not from the military or "the state," as with de Gaulle, but from his extraordinary "tapestry" of relationships with high officials, politicians, and journalists linked to men of power in Western states. He asserts that no one in the world has succeeded in becoming close to or gained the respect of so many heads of state and governments as Monnet, and that range of relationships was the basis for his achievements. Duroselle argues that Monnet's method of sharing, honing, and debating his ideas with close colleagues enhanced his creativity and flexibility and made many of his ideas attractive to men in power. Monnet attached more importance than de Gaulle to economic matters because he believed in the transformative nature of economics and advocated it as the best and most pragmatic way to transform politics.[19]

Casanova describes Monnet as a "pragmatic visionary" who was encompassed by his Americanophilism and more at ease with US democracy than British oligarchy. He argues that Monnet, unlike most French statesmen and diplomats, was indifferent to the cult of the state. His farsighted vision demonstrated his belief that uniting nations protected not only individual liberties and democracy by reducing the chance of war but ultimately Western civilization. Without him, Casanova states, Europe's history would have been more chaotic, and it might not have built the existing community institutional framework that is superior to the nations that comprise it. He asserts Monnet's greatness lay in "his lucidity, integrity, and his capacity to act, efficiently and rapidly, in a world that was more complex and more international than before." Casanova quotes French historian Alfred Sauvy's discussion of "great men" in French history to define Monnet. While Sauvy states that de Gaulle falls more in the tradition of Rousseau, in which one foresees nationalism, discord, and war, he asserts Monnet resembles Montesquieu, who stressed relationships, openness, communication, and exchange.[20]

The United States was a determining influence on Monnet's life, and his American friends helped him achieve his goals in Europe. Having become fascinated by the United States during his visits as a cognac salesman in the 1910s, he profited diplomatically and personally from the many connections with prominent Americans he developed during World War I and successive decades. In the World War II years and in the 1950s and 1960s, he had access to powerful Americans as he was very much a persona grata in the influential social, political, banking, journalistic, and legal circles in New York and Washington. On his regular visits, he always called on "well-informed friends," whom he described as "men who cannot afford to make mistakes. . . . I base my judgment on the wisdom of practical men."[21]

Since many prominent postwar US officials and other members of the mid-Atlantic elites clearly understood the importance of an integrated Europe as a bulwark against the Soviets, persuading US officials to support his ideas was often not difficult. They realized "their favorite Frenchman," in Robert Bowie's words, was an internationalist who shared their belief that the establishment of liberal international institutions after the war was the best way to achieve a lasting peace. Monnet's relaxed, intimate relations and close friendships with a wide range of US policymakers and establishment figures helped maintain cordial relations between the United States and Europe. It also allowed him to influence the formation of US foreign policy attitudes and hence shape US policy toward Europe. Just as he used his American friends to maintain US support for European integration, US officials in the Truman and Eisenhower administrations supported and used him to achieve their own diplomatic goals. To a great extent, they depended on him to sustain the progress toward European integration, which they believed essential to postwar peace and stability in Europe. In the eyes of many US officials, from the late 1940s and during the Cold War of the 1950s until de Gaulle came to power in 1958, it was indeed "Jean Monnet's Europe."[22]

Many American and European friends remained close to him until his death in 1979. While his circle of friends was vast, Monnet's relationships with key Americans were distinct from friendships with most other Europeans in their number, duration, and intensity. George Ball, John McCloy, and John Foster Dulles admired him professionally, especially for his ability to fuse pragmatism and idealism, which enabled him to develop a dynamic way to enact change. But they also remained close personal friends for many years. The Balls and McCloys looked after Silvia and the Monnet children at various times when Jean was away. And these families as well as those of Edna and Gene Rostow and Sally and James Reston remained close to Silvia and her children after Monnet's death. Edna Rostow had become a very close friend of Silvia's, and she continued to invite the Monnet children to visit them in Washington long after Silvia's death in 1982. Duchêne acknowledged that Monnet's relationships with his American friends were indeed special. Those Europeans who worked with Monnet, as he had done, knew they were part of his team and colleagues, but "none of us," he stated, were ever "friends of his like McCloy, Ball, and Dulles."[23]

Along with his successes, Monnet also suffered consequential defeats. His most important failures—the European Defense Community (EDC) and European Atomic Energy Community (Euratom)—had a significant impact on postwar French foreign policy. The EDC, known as the Pleven Plan, was created by Monnet to meet the demand of the Truman administration that Germany be rearmed and its troops placed under NATO in order to strengthen the European defense capability to counter a possible Soviet advance into Europe. As the French strongly opposed the re-creation of German army units, Monnet hastily created the Pleven Plan as an alternative to the US proposal. Even though it was not only conceptually flawed but militarily unsound and politically unworkable, Prime Minister René Pleven adopted it because it solved a diplomatic crisis. And as US officials forced West German Chancellor Konrad Adenauer to accept it, other ECSC nations reluctantly agreed to adopt it. But because the French could not tolerate German remilitarization under EDC terms, the French parliament refused to ratify the plan in 1954. Monnet acknowledged this failure. But as he explained in his memoirs, new opportunities sometimes "suddenly arise" and they can't be missed "simply because they were not expected so soon. . . . The question arose in 1950 when we were abruptly faced with the prospect of German rearmament. We seized the opportunity to try a new step forward on the basis of what otherwise might have been a setback for the process of integration that had barely begun. As has been seen, we failed."[24] This episode also demonstrated to Washington officials that even they, as representatives of the dominant Western power, the United States, did not always get their way.

President Eisenhower and Dulles, his secretary of state, were strong advocates of Euratom, which failed to become a viable international organization that fulfilled its original goal. By enthusiastically supporting Monnet's dream of a supranational community modeled on the ECSC to promote the peaceful uses of atomic energy, they were promoting their own policy goals of encouraging European integration and unity as a bulwark against the Soviets and keeping control of atomic sales to the continent. Eisenhower and Dulles encouraged Monnet and Belgian Foreign Minister Paul-Henri Spaak and other European leaders by promising concrete US support and the sharing of secret information. But they underestimated the strength of the opposition on the part of US Atomic Energy Commission Chairman Lewis Strauss and some bureaucrats in the State Department and ignored or didn't foresee the possibility that the president's orders might not be fully implemented or circumvented. Many other factors, including Monnet's own flawed strategy, caused its demise. Moreover, de Gaulle's opposition to Euratom, his policy of advocating nuclear energy for weapons development, and the desire of the other ECSC nations to build their own atomic energy facilities meant Euratom never became the supranational community envisioned by Monnet in which atomic energy was shared by European nations.

While the failures of these communities greatly disappointed their creator, each served a pragmatic purpose and ultimately allowed Monnet and other European leaders to achieve important steps in the process of economic integration. The EDC helped ensure the Schuman Plan negotiations were not derailed by postponing the discussion of contentious issues between France and Germany. And while the demise of the EDC dashed hopes on both sides of the Atlantic, its failure stimulated further integration efforts that led to the creation of the European Community. The Euratom idea also helped integration negotiations continue and advance between 1955 and 1957 and ensured that the EC Treaty, along with the Euratom Treaty, was signed in Rome. While Monnet's failures had an impact on French foreign policy, each contributed to his declining influence in French policy circles after 1954, a trend that he never reversed.

Another failed dream of Monnet's was the idea of the United States and the new EC being closely linked in a "partnership of equals." Monnet longed to give some permanency to the kind of close relationship he had with US government leaders in the Truman and Eisenhower administrations. For him, Atlantic partnership meant that the United States and Europe would share solid, supportive relations politically and economically as well as in the realm of defense. He knew realistically that they would never be equals in the economic sphere, nor could the Europeans alone defend themselves against Soviet encroachment. But his hope was that Europe would become strong enough politically and economically in order to avoid being dependent on the United States. For him, European integration was the path to greater strength and hence greater independence, at least in the economic sphere, and he worked tirelessly to construct a viable transatlantic community. He therefore saw no contradiction between being an Atlanticist—wanting Europe to be a vital partner of the United States and working with it to solve international problems— and an integrationist. While President Kennedy voiced the idea of the Atlantic partnership in his speeches, it was never more than a rhetorical objective. But Monnet's own close relationships with many prominent Americans helped dispel the negative view of the United States held by some European elites. While he never recaptured the effective and influential working transatlantic partnership he and McCloy created between 1949 and 1952, he contributed to the transatlantic community that came to life in the postwar period and demonstrated to both sides of the Atlantic the value of closer cooperation.

Monnet's usual method of working outside the political party system and behind the scenes with decisionmakers proved to be an asset in the 1940s and early 1950s but a liability later in his life. His established pattern of gathering a small group of carefully chosen colleagues together to develop, discuss, and hone ideas and then design a plan of action with them served him well. He had worked effectively as the leader of the small group, which served as his "brain trust," from 1945 until the first half of 1950 when the French political elites reached a consensus that economic reconstruction was necessary and that the growing crisis in 1949 in Franco-German relations had to be solved. Because he worked outside the French bureaucracies, bypassed parliament, distrusted politics, and reported directly to the government, his independence and his ability to act speedily to implement the decisions helped him gain influence with French leaders. Moreover, the unstable political system with the rapid turnover of French governments in the postwar period facilitated this access. But, in 1954, as a result of the EDC battles and other political factors, and as the French economy slowly recovered, the consensus that supported his leadership had diminished and some of his friends in leadership positions were no longer in office. In the mid-1950s and 1960s, Monnet found he had no political base and was victimized by his own earlier efforts to avoid party politics when he had to confront partisan battles, such as that over the terms of the Euratom Treaty. And when trying to implement Euratom in the late 1950s and 1960s, he found there were limits to his personal influence in the EC countries and to his ability to push the European idea with their elected leaders since no consensus existed beyond sharing atomic energy information. The inherent weaknesses in his policy of building Europe thus became evident. Moreover, as he worked outside party politics, there was no French political party or any political leaders to promote his legacy after his death.

As he grew older, he acknowledged some of his own failings. As president of the High Authority, Monnet had learned he could not successfully manage a large organization composed of individuals he did not choose. He admitted he was a bad manager. He also knew that to achieve results, he had had to persuade national leaders and the elites to adopt his ideas, and that, as a result, his behavior had been more didactic than democratic. Monnet also never believed it was his role to influence public opinion, even though he knew his ideas had to be honed and refined enough to be understood by the average Frenchman. He therefore targeted leaders and opinion makers with his Action Committee and left to its members the challenge of communicating to their publics. But he did understand the power of the press and cultivated prominent journalists and used them to publicize his ideas. In the late 1950s and 1960s, he used press communiqués and press conferences to publicize his plans, such as his announcement of his Action Committee in 1955 and his break with de Gaulle in 1965.

One personal failing he seemed never to have acknowledged was his occasionally harsh personal treatment of some of his younger colleagues and staff. None of his longtime colleagues, such as Duchêne, Max Kohnstamm, Richard Mayne, Hirsch, Pierre Uri, and Marjolin, have discussed this in their writings or personal interviews. But Dutch diplomat Dirk Spierenburg, historian André Kaspi who as a graduate student did research for Monnet's memoirs, Max Isenbergh, and Mayne's wife all have detailed occasions of this behavior. They reported that Monnet could be excessively demanding in terms of hours worked or calling colleagues away from an event such as a family picnic when he wanted their immediate presence at a hastily called meeting. They reported he could on occasion cruelly and insensitively berate a colleague or refuse to speak to or communicate over a period of time with an individual who disappointed or disagreed with him. Sometimes, if a person was no longer of any use to him, he would abruptly end that relationship without explanation. Mayne's wife said both her husband and Monnet's secretary suffered such inconsiderate treatment. She recalled Monnet had repeatedly demanded his pregnant secretary work late into the night for a period of time. Apparently this woman never complained to him because she was devoted to him. Shepard Stone recalled Monnet's "peculiarities with his staff." He noted his friend seemed "intimate yet cold-blooded. I used to say: 'Jean, it's marvelous working with you and having the feeling that one is a small footnote to history here. But let me tell you, I'd never in my life want to work *for* you. You're a slave driver and you don't recognize really how much people are doing.' He would reply, 'It isn't for me, it's for an idea.'" But even those who were temporarily ostracized or victimized by his temper or managerial style remained loyal to him, continued working with him, supported his goals, and eventually regained his friendship.[25]

However, the successes of Jean Monnet during his life as a businessman, financier, diplomat, and public servant dwarf his political failures and personal shortcomings. His achievements demonstrate how he translated ideas into actions of historical importance. As a result of his infinite patience for reconciliation, his optimistic and relentless pursuit of his goal to unite Europe, and his unusual ability to put his visionary goals and pragmatic principles into practice, this charismatic unconventional statesman was a man of action and influence. Most importantly, he helped to persuade European leaders to take the bold steps necessary to begin integrating their economies. As a result, he was instrumental in transforming the politics of twentieth-century Europe by bringing peace to its previously warring nations and establishing a community system that was superior to the nation-states it encompassed. His strong advocacy of democratic principles meant they were implanted in that international community. A pioneer for peace, Monnet demonstrated how one farsighted leader can truly make a difference and leave the world a better place.

## Notes

1. Jean Monnet, *Memoirs* (New York: Doubleday, 1978), p. 432.

2. Jean-Baptiste Duroselle, "Deux types de grands hommes: Le Général de Gaulle et Jean Monnet," *Collection "Conférences,"* no. 15 (Geneva, Switzerland: Institut Universitaire des Hautes Etudes Internationales, 1977), p. 11.

3. Stanley Hoffmann, "Review of *The Uniting of Europe: Political, Social, and Economic Forces, 1950–1957,* by Ernst Haas," *Foreign Affairs* 76, no. 5 (September–October 1977), pp. 226–227.

4. François Duchêne, interview by the author, September 20, 1994.

5. Jean Monnet, *Memoirs*, p. 383.

6. Hoffmann, "Review of *The Uniting of Europe*," p. 227.

7. Ibid., pp. 226–227.

8. Ernst B. Haas, *The Uniting of Europe: Political, Social, and Economic Forces, 1950–1957* (Stanford, CA: Stanford University Press, 1958).

9. Duchêne, interview.

10. Ibid.

11. Ibid.

12. Monnet, *Memoirs*, p. 432.

13. Duroselle, "Deux types de grands hommes," p. 21.

14. Ernest R. May, *Strange Victory: Hitler's Conquest of France* (New York: Hill and Wang, 2000).

15. Robert Marjolin, *Architect of European Unity: Memoirs 1911–1986* (London: Weidenfeld and Nicolson, 1989), p. 173.

16. Ibid.

17. Eric Roussel, "Table ronde," in *Jean Monnet, l'Europe et les chemins de la paix*, ed. Gérard Bossuat and Andreas Wilkens (Paris: Publications de la Sorbonne, 1999), p. 488.

18. Duroselle, "Deux types de grands hommes," p. 14.

19. Ibid., pp. 16–17.

20. Jean-Claude Casanova, "Jean Monnet, l'inspirateur," in *Overture, société, pouvoir, de l'Édit de Nantes à la chute du communisme,* ed. Emmanuel Le Roy Ladurie (Paris: Fayard, 2005), pp. 151–171.

21. Monnet, *Memoirs,* p. 271.

22. Alfred Grosser, *The Western Alliance: European-American Relations Since 1945* (New York: Continuum Publishing, 1980), pp. 97–128.

23. Duchêne, interview; Edna Rostow, interview by the author, January 29, 1994; W. W. Rostow, interview by the author, August 25, 1993.

24. Monnet, *Memoirs,* p. 432.

25. André Kaspi, interview by the author, September 24, 2008; Max Isenbergh, interview by Leonard Tennyson, April 20, 1981, Fondation Jean Monnet; Clifford Hackett, interview by the author, November 3, 2010 (Hackett knew and had talked to Richard Mayne's wife); Dirk Spierenburg and Raymond Poidevin, *The History of the High Authority of the European Coal and Steel Community* (London: Weidenfeld and Nicolson, 1994), pp. 55–56; Shepard Stone, interview by Leonard Tennyson, July 23, 1982, Fondation Jean Monnet.

# Bibliography

Acheson, Dean. Papers. Yale University Library.

Acheson, Dean. *Present at the Creation*. New York: W. W. Norton, 1969.

Adenauer, Konrad. *Memoirs, 1945–53*. London: Weidenfeld and Nicolson, 1965.

Alsop, Joseph. Papers. Library of Congress.

Ball, George. Papers. Princeton University Library.

Ball, George W. Interview by Leonard Tennyson, July 15, 1981. Lausanne, Switzerland: Fondation Jean Monnet pour l'Europe Centre de recherches européennes.

Ball, George W. *The Past Has Another Pattern: Memoirs*. New York: W. W. Norton, 1982.

Berghahn, Volker R. *America and the Intellectual Cold Wars in Europe: Shepard Stone: Between Philanthropy, Academy, and Diplomacy*. Princeton, NJ: Princeton University Press, 2001.

Bernard, Jean-René. Interview by the author, June 22, 1984.

Bidault, Georges. Papers. Archives nationales. Paris.

Bitsch, Marie-Thérèse. "Jean Monnet et la création du Conseil européen." In *Jean Monnet, l'Europe et les chemins de la paix*. Edited by Gérard Bossuat and Andreas Wilkens. Paris: Publications de la Sorbonne, 1999.

Bloch-Lainé, François, and Jean Bouvier. *La France restaurée, 1944–1954: Dialogue sur les choix d'une modernization*. Paris: Fayard, 1986.

Bossuat, Gérard. "Conclusion générale." In *Jean Monnet, l'Europe et les chemins de la paix*. Edited by Gérard Bossuat and Andreas Wilkens. Paris: Publications de la Sorbonne, 1999.

Bossuat, Gérard. *L'Europe des Francais, 1943–1959: La IVe République aux sources de l'Europe communautaire*. Paris: Publications de la Sorbonne, 1996.

Bossuat, Gérard. *L'Europe occidentale a l'heure américaine: Le Plan Marshall et l'unité européenne, 1945–1952*. Paris: Editions Complexe, 1992.

Bossuat, Gérard. *Faire l'Europe sans défaire la France*. Brussels: P.I.E.–Peter Lang, 2005.

Bossuat, Gérard. *La France, l'aide américaine and la construction européenne, 1944–1954*. 2 vols. Paris: Comité pour l'histoire économique et financière de la France, 1992.

Bossuat, Gérard. "Jean Monnet et l'identité monétaire européenne." In *Jean Monnet, l'Europe et les chemins de la paix*. Edited by Gérard Bossuat and Andreas Wilkens. Paris: Publications de la Sorbonne, 1999.

Bossuat, Gérard, and Andreas Wilkens, eds. *Jean Monnet, l'Europe et les chemins de la paix*. Paris: Publications de la Sorbonne, 1999.

Bowie, Robert R. Interview by François Duchêne, May 17, 1987. Lausanne, Switzerland: Fondation Jean Monnet.

Bowie, Robert R. Interview by Leonard Tennyson, June 16, 1981. Lausanne, Switzerland: Fondation Jean Monnet.

Bowie, Robert R. Interviews by the author, August 15, 1990, and September 19, 1990.

Bowie, Robert R. "Réflexions sur Jean Monnet." In *Témoignages à la mémoire de Jean Monnet*. Lausanne, Switzerland: Fondation Jean Monnet, 1989.

Brinkley, Douglas. *Dean Acheson: The Cold War Years, 1953–71*. New Haven, CT: Yale University Press, 1992.

Brinkley, Douglas. "Dean Acheson and Jean Monnet." In *Monnet and the Americans*. Edited by Clifford Hackett. Washington, DC: Jean Monnet Council, 1995.

Brinkley, Douglas. "Dean Acheson and John Kennedy: Combating Strains in the Atlantic Alliance, 1962–1963." In *John F. Kennedy and Europe*. Edited by Douglas Brinkley and Richard T. Griffiths. Baton Rouge: Louisiana State University Press, 1999.

Brinkley, Douglas, and Clifford Hackett, eds. *Jean Monnet: The Path to European Unity*. New York: St. Martin's Press, 1991.

Bruce, David. Diaries. Richmond, VA: Virginia Historical Society.

Burk, Kathleen. *Britain, America, and the Sinews of War, 1914–1918*. Boston: Allen and Unwin, 1985.

Bussière, Eric. "Jean Monnet et la stabilisation monétaire roumaine de 1929: Un 'outsider' entre l'Europe et l'Amerique." in *Jean Monnet, l'Europe et les chemins de la paix*. Edited by Gérard Bossuat and Andreas Wilkens. Paris: Publications de la Sorbonne, 1999.

Casanova, Jean-Claude. Interview by the author, June 28, 1984.

Casanova, Jean-Claude. "Jean Monnet, l'inspirateur." In *Ouverture, société, pouvoir, de l'Édit de Nantes à la chute du communisme*. Edited by Emmanuel Le Roy Ladurie. Paris: Fayard, 2005.

Catroux, Georges General. Papers. Paris. Archives nationales.

Churchill, Winston S. *Their Finest Hour*. Boston: Houghton Mifflin, 1949.

Clappier, Bernard. Interview by Robert Massip, November 11, 1980. Lausanne, Switzerland: Fondation Jean Monnet.

Clémentel, Etienne. *La France et la politique économique interalliée*. Paris: Presses Universitaires, 1931.

Cleveland, Stanley. Interview by Leonard Tennyson, June 12, 1981. Lausanne, Switzerland: Fondation Jean Monnet.

Cogan, Charles. *Charles de Gaulle: A Brief Biography with Documents*. Boston: Bedford Books of St. Martin's Press, 1996.

Cogan, Charles. *Oldest Allies, Guarded Friends: The United States and France Since 1940*. Westport, CT: Praeger, 1994.

Cohen, Stephen, S. Halimi, and John Zysman. "Institutions, Politics, and Industrial Policy in France." In *The Politics of Industrial Policy*. Edited by C. E. Barfield and W. W. Schambra. Washington, DC: American Enterprise Institute, 1986.

Cohrs, Patrick O. *The Unfinished Peace After World War I: America, Britain, and the Stabilisation of Europe, 1919–1932*. Cambridge, UK: Cambridge University Press, 2006.

Conant, Jennet. *The Irregulars: Roald Dahl and the British Spy Ring in Wartime Washington*. New York: Simon and Schuster, 2008.

Couve de Murville, Maurice. Interview by Antoine Marès, January 16, 1984. Lausanne, Switzerland: Fondation Jean Monnet.

Danchev, Alex. *Establishing the Anglo-American Alliance: The Second World War Diaries of Brigadier Vivian Dykes*. London: Brassey's Defense Publishers, 1999.

Danchev Alex. Interview with the author, July 1, 2009.

Danchev, Alex. *Very Special Relationship: Field-Marshal Sir John Dill and the Anglo-American Alliance, 1941–44*. London: Brassey's Defense Publishers, 1986.

Davenport, John. "M. Jean Monnet of Cognac." *Fortune* 2, no. 30 (1944), p. 125ff.

Dell, Edmund. *The Schuman Plan and the British Abdication of Leadership in Europe*. Oxford, UK: Oxford University Press, 1995.

Delouvrier, Paul. Interview by Antoine Marès, June 3, 1981. Lausanne, Switzerland: Fondation Jean Monnet.

Denton, Geoffrey, et al. *Economic Planning and Policies in Britain, France, and Germany*. New York: Praeger, 1968.

Diebold, William, Jr. *The Schuman Plan: A Study in Economic Cooperation, 1950–1959*. New York: Praeger, 1959.

DiLeo, David. "Catch the Night Plane for Paris: George Ball and Jean Monnet." In *Monnet and the Americans*. Edited by Clifford Hackett. Washington, DC: Jean Monnet Council, 1995.

Dinan, Desmond. *Europe Recast*. Boulder, CO: Lynne Rienner Publishers, 2004.

Dinan, Desmond. *Ever Closer Union*, 4th ed. Boulder, CO: Lynne Rienner Publishers, 2010.

Dinan, Desmond. *Origins and Evolution of the European Union*. Oxford, UK: Oxford University Press, 2006.

Dinan, Desmond, ed. *Encyclopedia of the European Union*. Boulder, CO: Lynne Rienner Publishers, 1998.

Duchêne, François. Interviews by the author, September 20, 1994, and September 13, 2002.

Duchêne, François. *Jean Monnet: The First Statesman of Interdependence*. New York: W. W. Norton, 1994.

Duchêne, François. "Jean Monnet's Methods." In *Jean Monnet: The Path to European Unity*. Edited by Douglas Brinkley and Clifford Hackett. New York: St. Martin's Press, 1991.

Dulles, John Foster. Papers. Princeton University Library.

Du Réau, Élisabeth. *Edouard Daladier*. Paris: Fayard, 1993.

Du Réau, Élisabeth. "Jean Monnet, le Comité de coordination franco-britannique et le projet d'Union franco-britannique: Les Moyens de vaincre le nazisme (septembre 1939–juin 1940)." In *Jean Monnet, l'Europe et les chemins de la paix*. Edited by Gérard Bossuat and Andreas Wilkens. Paris: Publications de la Sorbonne, 1999.

Duroselle, Jean-Baptiste. "Deux types de grands hommes: Le Général de Gaulle et Jean Monnet." *Collection "Conférences,"* no. 15. Geneva, Switzerland: Institut Universitaire des Hautes Etudes, Internationales, 1977.

Duroselle, Jean-Baptiste. "General de Gaulle's Europe and Jean Monnet's Europe." *The World Today* 22 (1966).

Eden, Anthony. *Full Circle: The Memoirs of the Rt. Hon. Sir Anthony Eden*. Vol. 1. London: Cassell, 1960.

Eden, Anthony. *Facing the Dictators: The Memoirs of the Rt. Hon. Sir Anthony Eden*. Vol. 2. London: Cassell, 1962.

Eisenhower, Dwight D. Papers. Eisenhower Library.

Eisenhower, Dwight. *Vital Speeches of the Day* 17, no. 20 (August 1, 1951).

Eisenhower, Dwight. *Waging the Peace, 1956–1961*. New York: Doubleday, 1965.

Ellwood, David W. *Rebuilding Europe: Western Europe, America, and Postwar Reconstruction*. London: Longman, 1992.

Fleury, Antoine. "Jean Monnet au Secrétariat de la Société des Nations." In *Jean Monnet, l'Europe et les chemins de la paix*. Edited by Gérard Bossuat and Andreas Wilkens. Paris: Publications de la Sorbonne, 1999.

Fondation Jean Monnet pour l'Europe. *Un changement d'espérance: La Déclaration du 9 mai 1950, Jean Monnet–Robert Schuman*. Lausanne, Switzerland, 2000.

Fondation Jean Monnet pour l'Europe. *Monnet, Jean–Robert Schuman, Correspondance, 1947–1953*. Lausanne, Switzerland, 1986.

Fondation Jean Monnet pour l'Europe. *Témoignages à la mémoire de Jean Monnet*. Lausanne, Switzerland, 1989.

Fontaine, Pascal. *Le Comité d'Action pour les Etats-Unis d'Europe de Jean Monnet*. Lausanne, Switzerland: Fondation Jean Monnet, 1974.

Ford Foundation Archives. New York City.

Frankfurter, Felix. Papers. Library of Congress.

Frankfurter, Felix. *Reminisces: Recorded in Talks with Dr. Harlan B. Phillips*. New York: Reynal, 1960.

Fransen, Frederic. *The Supranational Politics of Jean Monnet*. Westport, CT: Greenwood, 2001.

Gaddis, John Lewis. *Strategies of Containment: A Critical Appraisal of American National Security Policy During the Cold War*. Oxford, UK: Oxford University Press, 2005.

Gaddis, John Lewis. *We Now Know: Rethinking Cold War History*. Oxford, UK: Clarendon Press, 1997.

Gerbet, Pierre. *La Construction de l'Europe*, rev. ed. Paris: Imprimérie National, 1994.

Giauque, Jeffrey G. *Grand Designs and Visions of Unity*. Chapel Hill: University of North Carolina Press, 2002.

Gilbert, Mark. *Surpassing Realism: The Politics of European Integration Since 1945*. Lanham, MD: Rowman and Littlefield Publishers, 2003.

Gillingham, John. *Coal, Steel, and the Rebirth of Europe, 1945–1955*. Cambridge, UK: Cambridge University Press, 1991.

Gillingham, John. *European Integration, 1950–2003*. Cambridge, UK: Cambridge University Press, 2003.

Gillingham, John. "Jean Monnet and the European Coal and Steel Community: A Preliminary Appraisal." In *Jean Monnet: The Path to European Unity*. Edited by Douglas Brinkley and Clifford Hackett. New York: St. Martin's Press, 1991.

Gillingham, John. "Solving the Ruhr Problem: German Heavy Industry and the Schuman Plan." In *The Beginnings of the Schuman Plan 1950-5*. Edited by Klaus Schwabe. Baden-Baden, Germany: Nomos, 1988.

Graglia, Piero S. *Altiero Spinelli*. Bologna, Italy: Il Mulino, 2008.

Graglia, Piero S. Interviews by the author, October 4, 2003, August 12, 2004, September 2, 2004, February 8, 2005, and October 30, 2010.

Graham, Katharine. *Personal History*. New York: Vintage Books, 1998.

Grosser, Alfred. *The Western Alliance: European-American Relations Since 1945*. New York: Continuum Publishing, 1980.

Haas, Ernst. *The Uniting of Europe: Political, Social, and Economic Forces, 1950–1957*. Stanford, CA: Stanford University Press, 1958.

Hackett, Clifford. Interview with the author, November 3, 2010.

Hackett, Clifford. *A Jean Monnet Chronology*. Washington, DC: Jean Monnet Council, 2008.

Hackett, Clifford. "Jean Monnet and the Roosevelt Administration." In *Monnet and the Americans*. Edited by Clifford Hackett. Washington, DC: Jean Monnet Council, 1995.

Hackett, Clifford, ed. *Monnet and the Americans*. Washington, DC: Jean Monnet Council, 1995.

Hager, Barry M. *The Rule of Law: A Lexicon for Policy Makers*, 2nd ed. Washington, DC: The Mansfield Center for Pacific Affairs, 2000.

Haight, John M., Jr. *American Aid to France, 1938–1940*. New York: Atheneum, 1970.

Hancock, W. K., and M. M. Gowing. *The British War Economy: UK History of the Second World War*. London: H.M.S.O., 1975.

Harriman, Averell. Papers. Library of Congress.

Harryvan, Anjo G., and Jan van der Harst. *Max Kohnstamm: A European's Life and Work*. Baden-Baden, Germany: Nomos, 2011.

Hartman, Arthur. Interview by the author, October 15, 1990.

Hewlett, Richard, and Jack Holl. *Atoms for Peace and War*. Berkeley: University of California Press, 1989.

Hirsch, Etienne. *Ainsi va la vie*. Lausanne, Switzerland: Fondation Jean Monnet, 1988.

Hirsch, Etienne. Interview by the author, June 21, 1984.

Hirsch, Etienne. Interview by Theodore A. Wilson, June 30, 1970. Truman Library.

Hirsch, Etienne. "Témoignage de Etienne Hirsch." In *Témoignages à la mémoire de Jean Monnet*. Lausanne, Switzerland: Fondation Jean Monnet, 1989.

Hitchcock, William I. *France Restored, Cold War Diplomacy and the Quest for Leadership in Europe, 1944–1954*. Chapel Hill: University of North Carolina Press, 1998.

Hoffmann, Stanley. "The Effects of World War II on French Society and Politics." *French Historical Studies* 2 (Spring 1961).

Hoffmann, Stanley. "The Man Who Would Be France." *New Republic* 203, no. 24 (December 17, 1990).

Hoffmann, Stanley. "Obstinate or Obsolete?" *Daedalus* 95, no. 3 (1966), pp. 862–915.

Hoffmann, Stanley. "Review of *The Uniting of Europe: Political, Social, and Economic Forces, 1950–1957* by Ernst Haas." *Foreign Affairs* 76, no. 5 (September–October 1977), pp. 226–227.

Hogan, Michael. *The Marshall Plan: America, Britain, and the Reconstruction of Western Europe, 1947–1952*. Cambridge, UK: Cambridge University Press, 1987.

Hopkins, Harry. Papers. Roosevelt Library.

Ikenberry, G. John. *After Victory: Institutions, Strategic Restraint, and Rebuilding of Order After Wars*. Princeton, NJ: Princeton University Press, 2001.

Ikenberry, G. John. *Liberal Leviathan: The Origins, Crisis, and Transformation of the American World Order*. Princeton, NJ: Princeton University Press, 2011.

Iriye, Akira. *The Origins of the Second World War in Asia and the Pacific*. London: Longman, 1987.

Isenbergh, Max. Interview by Leonard Tennyson, April 20, 1981. Lausanne, Switzerland: Fondation Jean Monnet.

Janeway, Eliot. *The Struggle for Survival: A Chronicle of Economic Mobilization in World War II*. New Haven, CT: Yale University Press, 1951.

Jílek, Lubor. "Rôle de Jean Monnet dans les règlements d'Autriche et de Haute-Silésie." In *Jean Monnet, l'Europe et les chemins de la paix*. Edited by Gérard Bossuat and Andreas Wilkens. Paris: Publications de la Sorbonne, 1999.

Johnson, Lyndon B. Papers. Johnson Library.

Joxe, Louis. Interview by Roger Massip, May (n.d.) 1982. Lausanne, Switzerland: Fondation Jean Monnet.

Joxe, Louis. *Victoires sur la nuit: Mémoires 1940–1966.* Paris: Fayard, 1981.

Kaspi, André. Interview by the author, September 24, 2008.

Kaspi, André. *La Mission de Jean Monnet à Alger.* Paris: Publications de la Sorbonne, 1972.

Katz, Milton. Interview by Leonard Tennyson, January 28, 1988. Lausanne, Switzerland: Fondation Jean Monnet.

Kennedy, John F. Papers. Kennedy Library.

Kissinger, Henry. *Years of Renewal.* New York: Simon and Schuster, 1999.

Kohnstamm, Max. Interview by the author, November 19, 2005.

Kuisel, Richard F. *Capitalism and the State in Modern France.* Cambridge, UK: Cambridge University Press, 1981.

Kuisel, Richard F. Interview by the author, September 23, 2001.

Kuisel, Richard F. "The Marshall Plan in Action: Politics, Labor, Industry, and the Program of Technical Assistance in France." In *Le Plan Marshall et le relèvement économique de l'Europe.* Paris: Comité pour l'histoire économique et financière, Ministère des Finances, 1993.

Kusters, Hanns-Jurgen. "Jean Monnet and the European Union: Idea and Reality of the Integration Process." In *Jean Monnet et l'Europe d'aujourd'hui.* Edited by Giandomenico Majone, Emile Noel, and Peter Vand den Bossche. Baden-Baden, Germany: Nomos, 1989.

Kusters, Hanns-Jurgen. "The Treaties of Rome, 1955–57." In *The Dynamics of European Union.* Edited by Roy Pryce. London: Croom Helm, 1987.

Lacouture, Jean. *De Gaulle: The Rebel, 1890–1944.* Translated by Patrick O'Brien. New York: W. W. Norton, 1990.

Lacouture, Jean. *De Gaulle: The Ruler, 1945–1970.* Translated by Alan Sheridan. New York: W. W. Norton, 1992.

Lagrange, Maurice. Interview by Antoine Marès, September 28, 1980. Lausanne, Switzerland: Fondation Jean Monnet.

Lash, Joseph P. *From the Diaries of Felix Frankfurter.* New York: W. W. Norton, 1975.

Lefler, Melvin P. "1921–1932: Expansionist Impulses and Domestic Constraints." In *Economics and World Power: An Assessment of American Diplomacy Since 1789.* Edited by William H. Becker and Samuel F. Wells, Jr. New York: Columbia University Press, 1984.

Lefler, Melvin P. *The Elusive Quest: America's Pursuit of European Stability and French Security, 1919–1933.* Chapel Hill: University of North Carolina Press, 1979.

Leuchtenburg, William E. *The Perils of Prosperity, 1914–1932,* 2nd ed. Chicago: University of Chicago Press, 1993.

Lippmann, Walter. Papers. Yale University Library.

Lynch, Frances. *France and the International Economy from Vichy to the Treaty of Rome.* London: Routledge, 1997.

Lynch, Frances. "The Political and Economic Reconstruction of France, 1944–1947, in Its International Context." Ph.D. thesis, University of Manchester, 1981.

Macmillan, Harold. *The Blast of War, 1939–1945.* New York: Harper and Row, 1967.

Maier, Charles S. "The Politics of Productivity: Foundations of American International Economic Policy After World War II." In *The Cold War in Europe: End of a Divided Continent,* 3rd ed. Edited by Charles S. Maier. New York: Markus Wiener, 1996.

Maier, Charles S., and Gunter Bischof, eds. *The Marshall Plan and Germany*. New York: Berg, 1991.

Mandereau, Jean-Louis. "Témoignage de Jean-Louis Mandereau." In *Témoignages à la mémoire de Jean Monnet*. Lausanne, Switzerland: Fondation Jean Monnet, 1989.

Margairaz, Michel. "La mise en oeuvre du Plan Monnet (1947–1952)." In *Modernisation ou décadence*. Edited by Bernard Cazes and Philippe Mioche. Aix-en-Provence, France: Presses Universitaires de Provence, 1990.

Marjolin, Robert. *Architect of European Unity: Memoirs, 1911–1986*. London: Weidenfeld and Nicolson, 1989.

Marjolin, Robert. Interview by the author, June 13, 1984.

Massé, Pierre. Interview by the author, May 23, 1984.

May, Ernest. Letter to the author, December 19, 2003.

May, Ernest R. "The American Commitment to Germany, 1949–1955." In *American Historians and the Atlantic Alliance*. Edited by L. S. Kaplan. Kent, OH: Kent State University Press, 1991.

May, Ernest R. *Strange Victory*: *Hitler's Conquest of France*. New York: Hill and Wang, 2000.

Mayer, René. Papers. Paris. Archives nationales.

Mayne, Richard. "Father of Europe: The Life and Times of Jean Monnet." Unpublished manuscript.

Mayne, Richard. "Jean Monnet: A Biographical Essay." In *Monnet and the Americans*. Edited by Clifford Hackett. Washington, DC: Jean Monnet Council, 1995.

McCloy, John. Papers. Amherst College Library.

McGrew, Donald. Interview by the author, May 29, 1991.

Mélandri, Pierre. *Les Etats-Unis et le "défi" européen, 1955–1958*. Paris: Presses Universitaires de France, 1975.

Mélandri, Pierre. *Les Etats-Unis face à la unification européene, 1945–1954*. Paris: Pedone, 1980.

Melchionni, Maria Grazia. *Altiero Spinelli et Jean Monnet*. Lausanne, Switzerland: Fondation Jean Monnet, 1993.

Melchionni, Maria Grazia. "Le Comité d'Action pour les Etats-Unis d'Europe: Un réseau au service de l'union européenne." In *Jean Monnet, l'Europe et les chemins de la paix*. Edited by Gérard Bossuat and Andreas Wilkens. Paris: Publications de la Sorbonne, 1999.

Milward, Alan. *The European Rescue of the Nation State*, 2nd ed. London: Routledge, 2000.

Milward, Alan. *The Reconstruction of Western Europe, 1945–51*. Berkeley: University of California Press, 1984.

Mioche, Philippe. "Jean Monnet et les sidérurgistes Européens." In *Jean Monnet, l'Europe et les chemins de la paix*. Edited by Gérard Bossuat and Andreas Wilkens. Paris: Publications de la Sorbonne, 1999.

Mioche, Philippe. "L'Invention du Plan Monnet." In *Modernisation ou décadence*. Edited by Bernard Cazes and Philippe Mioche. Aix-en-Provence, France: Presses Universitaires de Provence, 1990.

Monnet, Jean. Interview by the BBC on *The Money Programme*, December 1971.

Monnet, Jean. *Memoirs*. New York: Doubleday, 1978.

Monnet, Jean. Papers. Lausanne, Switzerland: Fondation Jean Monnet pour l'Europe Centre de recherches européennes.

Moravcsik, Andrew. *The Choice for Europe: Social Purpose and State Power from Messina to Maastricht*. Ithaca, NY: Cornell University Press, 1998.

Moravcsik, Andrew, ed. *Europe Without Illusions.* Lanham, MD: University Press of America, 2005.

Morrow, Dwight. Papers. Amherst College Library.

Nathan, Robert. Interviews by the author, April 17, 1989, August 15, 1990, and September 15, 1990.

Nathan, Robert. Papers. Lausanne, Switzerland: Fondation Jean Monnet.

Nathan, Robert. "An Unsung Hero of World War II." In *Jean Monnet: The Path to European Unity.* Edited by Douglas Brinkley and Clifford Hackett. New York: St. Martin's Press, 1991.

National Archives. Washington, DC: US Department of State, Record Groups 59 and 286.

Nicolson, Harold. *Dwight Morrow.* New York: Harcourt, Brace, 1935.

Olson, Lynne. *Citizens of London: The Americans Who Stood with Britain in Its Darkest, Finest Hour.* New York: Random House, 2010.

Owen, Henry. Interview with Leonard Tennyson, June 30, 1981. Lausanne, Switzerland: Fondation Jean Monnet.

Perth, David Drummond, Lord. Papers. European University Institute. Florence, Italy.

Pflimlin, Pierre. "Jean Monnet que j'ai connu." In *Témoignages à la mémoire de Jean Monnet.* Lausanne, Switzerland: Fondation Jean Monnet, 1989.

Piétri, Nicole. "Jean Monnet et les organismes interalliés durant la Première Guerre mondiale." In *Jean Monnet, l'Europe et les chemins de la paix.* Edited by Gérard Bossuat and Andreas Wilkens. Paris: Publications de la Sorbonne, 1999.

Pleven, René. Interview by Roger Massip, May 28, 1980. Lausanne, Switzerland: Fondation Jean Monnet.

Pleven, René. "Témoignage de René Pleven." In *Témoignages à la mémoire de Jean Monnet.* Lausanne, Switzerland: Fondation Jean Monnet, 1989.

Plowden, Edwin, Lord. Interview by Richard Mayne, February 2, 1982. Lausanne, Switzerland: Fondation Jean Monnet.

Poidevin, Raymond. *Robert Schuman: Homme d'état. 1886–1963.* Paris: Imprimérie Nationale, 1986.

Pollard, Robert. *Economic Security and the Origins of the Cold War, 1945–1950.* New York: Columbia University Press, 1985.

*Public Papers of the Presidents of the United States: Dwight D. Eisenhower, 1953–1961.* Washington, DC: Government Printing Office, 1960–1961.

*Public Papers of the Presidents of the United States: John F. Kennedy, 1961–1963.* Washington, DC: Government Printing Office, 1962–1964.

Rioux, Jean-Pierre. *The Fourth Republic, 1944–1958.* Cambridge, UK: Cambridge University Press, 1987.

Roosevelt, Franklin D. Papers. Roosevelt Library.

Rostow, Edna. Interview by the author, January 29, 1994.

Rostow, W. W. Interview by the author, August 25, 1993.

Rostow, W. W. "Jean Monnet: The Innovator as Diplomat." In *The Diplomats, 1939–1979.* Edited by Gordon A. Craig and Francis Lowenheim. Princeton, NJ: Princeton University Press, 1994.

Rostow, W. W. "Kennedy's View of Monnet and Vice Versa." In *John F. Kennedy and Europe.* Edited by Douglas Brinkley and Richard T. Griffiths. Baton Rouge: Louisiana State University Press, 1999.

Roussel, Eric. *Jean Monnet.* Paris: Librairie Artheme Fayard, 1996.

Salter, James Arthur. *Allied Shipping Control: An Experiment in International Administration.* Oxford, UK: Clarendon Press, 1921.

Schaetzel, J. Robert. Interview by Leonard Tennyson, March 24, 1982. Lausanne, Switzerland: Fondation Jean Monnet.

Schaetzel, J. Robert. Interviews by the author, August 15 and September 12, 1990, and August 30, 1991.

Schaetzel, J. Robert. *The Unhinged Alliance: America and the European Community.* New York: Harper and Row, 1975.

Schlesinger, Arthur, Jr. *A Thousand Days.* New York: Fawcett Premier, 1965.

Schuman, Robert. *Apôtre de l'Europe (1953–1963).* Edited by Marie-Thérèse Bitsch. Peiterlen, Switzerland: Peter Lang SA, 2010.

Schwabe, Klaus. "L'Allemagne, Adenauer, et l'option de l'intégration a l'ouest." In *Le Plan Schuman dans l'histoire.* Edited by Andreas Wilkens. Brussels: Complexe, 2004.

Schwabe, Klaus. "Monnet, la question allemande et l'ostpolitik." In *Une dynamique européenne: Le Comité d'Action pour les Etats-Unis d'Europe.* Lausanne, Switzerland: Fondation Jean Monnet, 2011.

Schwabe, Klaus, ed. *The Beginnings of the Schuman Plan 1950–5.* Baden-Baden, Germany: Nomos Verlagsgesellschaft, 1988.

Schwartz, Thomas A. *America's Germany: John J. McCloy and the Federal Republic of Germany.* Cambridge, MA: Harvard University Press, 1991.

Schwartz, Thomas A. "Dual Containment: John J. McCloy, the American High Commission, and European Integration, 1949–1952." Unpublished paper.

Schwartz, Thomas A. *Lyndon Johnson and Europe.* Cambridge, MA: Harvard University Press, 2003.

Schwartz, Thomas A. "The Transnational Partnership: Jean Monnet and Jack McCloy." In *Monnet and the Americans,* ed. Clifford Hackett. Washington, DC: Jean Monnet Council, 1995.

Schwarz, Hans-Peter. Interviews by the author, November 22, 2004, and December 20, 2006.

Schwarz, Hans-Peter. *Konrad Adenauer: A German Politician and Statesman in a Period of War, Revolution, and Reconstruction.* 2 vols. Providence, RI: Berghahn Books, 1995, 1997.

Schwarz, Hans-Peter, ed. *Akten zur auswärtigen Politik der Bundesrepublik Deutschland.* Munich: R. Oldenbourg Verlag, 1997.

Sheahan, John. *Promotion and Control of Industry in Postwar France.* Cambridge, MA: Harvard University Press, 1963.

Sherwood, Robert. *Roosevelt and Hopkins.* New York: Harper and Brothers, 1948.

Shlaim, Avi. "Prelude to Downfall: The British Offer of Union to France, June 1940." *Journal of Contemporary History* 9 (1974): 44.

Smith, Don. C. *Jean Monnet: Father of Europe.* Documentary. Available at http://law.du.edu/index.php/jean-monnet-father-of-europe/documentary.

Soutou, Georges-Henri. *The French Military Program for Nuclear Energy, 1945–1981.* College Park: Center for International Security Studies at Maryland, Nuclear History Program, 1989.

Soutou, Georges-Henri. *L'Alliance incertaine: Les Rapports politico-stratégiques franco-allemands, 1954–1996.* Paris: Fayard, 1996.

Soutou, Georges-Henri. *L'Or et le sang: Les Buts de guerre économique de la Première Guerre mondiale.* Paris: Fayard, 1989.

Soutou, Georges-Henri. "La Sécurité de la France dans l'après-guerre." In *La France et l'OTAN, 1949–1996.* Edited by Maurice Vaïsse, Pierre Mélandri, and Frédéric Bozo. Brussels: Complexe, 1996.

Spierenburg, Dirk, and Raymond Poidevin. *The History of the High Authority of the European Coal and Steel Community*. London: Weidenfeld and Nicolson, 1994.
Spinelli, Altiero. *Diario europeo,* vol. I: *1948–1968*. Edited by Edmundo Paolini. Bologna, Italy: Il Mulino, 1989.
Stoffaës, Christian. *Politique industrielle*. Paris: Les Cours de Droit, 1984.
Stone, Shepard. Interview by Leonard Tennyson, July 23, 1982. Lausanne, Switzerland: Fondation Jean Monnet.
Stone, Shepard. Papers. Dartmouth College Library.
Su, Hungdah. "The Father of Europe in China: Jean Monnet and the Creation of the C.D.F.C. 1933–1936." *Journal of European Integration History* 13 (2007): 18.
Tennyson, Leonard. Interview by the author, June 30, 1981.
Truman, Harry S. Papers. Truman Library.
Tuthill, John. Interview by Leonard Tennyson, April 15, 1981. Lausanne, Switzerland: Fondation Jean Monnet.
Tuthill, John. Interviews by the author, June 13, 1991, and August 10, 1992.
Tuthill, John. Letter to the author, July 24, 1992.
*Une Europe inédite: Documents des Archives Jean Monnet réunis et introduits par Bernard Lefort*. Villeneuve d'Ascq, France: Presses Universitaires du Septentrion, 2001.
Uri, Pierre. Interview by Antoine Marès, October 13, 1981. Lausanne, Switzerland: Fondation Jean Monnet.
Uri, Pierre. Interview by the author, May 29, 1984.
Uri, Pierre. *Partnership for Progress: A Program for Transatlantic Action*. New York: Harper and Row, 1963.
Urwin, Derek. *The Community of Europe*. London: Longman Group, 1991.
US Department of State. *Foreign Relations of the United States (FRUS)*.
Vaïsse, Maurice. *L'Energie nucléaire en Europe des origins à Euratom: Actes des journées d'études de Louvain–la Neuve des 18 et 19 nov. 1991*. Berne, Switzerland: Peter Lang, 1994.
Vaïsse, Maurice. *La Grandeur: Politique étrangère du général de Gaulle, 1958–1969*. Paris: Fayard, 1998.
Vaïsse, Maurice, Michel Dumoulin, and Pierre Guillen. *L'Energie nucléaire en Europe: Des origins à Euratom*. Berne, Switzerland: Peter Lang, 1994.
Van Helmont, Jacques. Interview by Clifford Hackett, February 11, 1990. Lausanne, Switzerland: Fondation Jean Monnet.
Varsori, Antonio. "Euratom, une organization qui échappe à Jean Monnet?" In *Jean Monnet, l'Europe et les chemins de la paix*. Edited by Gérard Bossuat and Andreas Wilkens. Paris: Publications de la Sorbonne, 1999.
Wall, Irwin. "Jean Monnet, the United States and the French Economic Plan." In *Jean Monnet: The Path to European Unity*. Edited by Douglas Brinkley and Clifford Hackett. New York: St. Martin's Press, 1991.
Wall, Irwin M. *The United States and the Making of Postwar France, 1945–1954*. Cambridge, UK: Cambridge University Press, 1991.
Wells, Sherrill Brown. *French Industrial Policy: A History, 1945–1981*. Washington, DC: Department of State, 1991.
Wells, Sherrill Brown. "Monnet and 'The Insiders:' Nathan, Tomlinson, Bowie, and Schaetzel." In *Monnet and the Americans*. Edited by Clifford Hackett. Washington, DC: Jean Monnet Council, 1995.
Wells, Sherrill Brown. *Pioneers of European Integration and Peace, 1945–1963: A Brief History with Documents*. Boston: Bedford/St. Martin's, 2007.

Wells, Sherrill Brown, and Samuel F. Wells, Jr. "Shared Sovereignty in the European Union: Germany's Economic Governance." In *History and Neorealism*. Edited by Ernest R. May, Richard Rosecrance, and Zara Steiner. Cambridge, UK: Cambridge University Press, 2010.

Winand, Pascaline. "Eisenhower, Dulles, Monnet, and the Uniting of Europe." In *Monnet and the Americans*. Edited by Clifford Hackett. Washington, DC: Jean Monnet Council, 1995.

Winand, Pascaline. *Eisenhower, Kennedy, and the United States of Europe*. New York: St. Martin's Press, 1993.

# Index

Abadie, Jules, 81–82
Acheson, Dean: Atlantic partnership, 223–225, 227, 230; ECSC launch, 169; ECSC treaty ratification, 155; EDC failure, 177–178; Korean War and German rearmament, 140; Lend-Lease negotiations, 87; meeting Monnet, 56–57; Pleven Plan, 143; Schuman Plan, 127, 130, 132, 136
Action Committee for the United States of Europe, 194–196, 198, 204–205, 211–214, 225, 233–235, 252
Addis, Charles, 27
Adenauer, Konrad, 201, 205, 250; Atlantic partnership, 225; economic community cartels, 145; ECSC, 136–139, 146, 155, 157, 166(fig.); EDC Treaty, 176; Euratom support, 197; Franco-German Friendship Treaty, 230–231; German resistance to decartelization, 148–149; Monnet's retirement, 188; Paris Accords, 186; Pleven Plan, 142–143, 153–154; Schuman Plan, 127–128, 130, 133–135; the Korean War and German rearmament, 140
Administration of the ECSC High Authority, 165–167, 170–172
Agricultural common market, 202
Agriculture: Monnet Plan, 98–99, 102, 109

Airpower: Anglo-French cooperation, 50–52
Algeria, 69–81, 219
Allied High Commission, 129
Allied Maritime Transport Council (AMTC), 13
Allied Maritime Transport Executive, 13–14
Allied powers: Austrian reconstruction, 17–18; currency question with CFLN, 87–88; North Africa campaign, 69–75; postwar European policy, 84–86; resource allocation, 9–14; US wartime expansion of arms production, 61–66. See also World War II
Alphand, Hervé, 34, 73, 86–90, 139, 152; postwar European policy, 84
Alsop, Joseph, 225
Alsop brothers, 223
American Bosch Corporation, 37–38
Anglo-American Combined Statement, 62–63
Anglo-French Coordinating Committee (AFCOC), 50, 54–55
Anti-Communist activities, 104, 110
Apprenticeship, 7–8
Arbitration: Upper Silesia conflict, 17
Armand, Louis: Euratom proposal, 192–193; illness, 217; US support for Euratom, 200; Wise Men's group, 198

Arms race, 60, 128
Arsenal of democracy, 71
Assassination attempts on Monnet, concerns over, 80–81
Assassination, Kennedy's, 229
Atlantic Community, 227, 237
Atlanticists, 222–230
Atomic Energy Commission (AEC), 191, 196, 250
Atoms for Peace proposal, 199
Attolico, Bernardo, 13
Austria: reconstruction, 17–18
Awards and honors, Monnet's, 236
Axis powers, 70

Ball, George, 249; Atlantic partnership, 222–225, 227, 229–230; ECSC launch, 169; ECSC negotiations, 146; ECSC treaty ratification, 155; Euratom, 216; German rearmament, 140–141; Lend-Lease accords, 89; Monnet Plan, 116; Monnet's appeal for US loans, 174; Monnet's death, 236
Bancamerica-Blair Corp., 24–25
Bank of America, 24
Bank of China, 29
Bank of Shanghai and Hong Kong, 31
Baruch, Bernard, 15
Baudet, Philip, 30–31
Bech, Joseph, 190, 206
Belgium: ECSC launch, 164–165; ECSC negotiations, 136–137; ECSC voting rights, 150; Marshall Plan, 111
Benelux Memorandum, 189–191
Benelux states: Brussels Treaty, 186; ECSC treaty ratification, 155; EDC Treaty, 154; relaunching integration efforts, 190. *See also individual states*
Benon, Fernand, 10
Bernard, Jean-René, 233–234
Bernstein, Edward, 108
Berthelot, Philippe, 30
Bevin, Ernest, 111, 132
Beyen, Johan Willem, 188–190, 206
Bidault, Georges, 111, 120, 129–130, 176, 178
Billoux, François, 105
*Bismarck* (German battleship), 62
Blackwell, Basil, 18
Blair and Company, 21–25

Blamont, Emile, 204
Bloch-Lainé, François, 108, 114–116, 120–121
Blum, Léon, 103–104, 120
Blum-Byrnes Agreement (1946), 104
Bonnet, Georges, 18–19
Bonnet, Henri, 46, 81, 112
Bosch, Robert, 37–38
Bowie, Robert, 249; Atlantic partnership, 223, 228; ECSC launch, 169; ECSC treaty ratification, 155–156; Euratom support, 198–200; European integration, 232–233; Monnet's appeal for US loans, 174; Monnet's death, 236; Pleven Plan, 141–142, 151; Schuman Plan negotiations, 145–147
Brand, Robert, 25–27
Brandt, Willy, 229, 233
Brentano, Heinrich von, 196
Bridges, Edward, 50
Britain, 37; Anglo-French union proposal, 52–54; BPC supply coordination, 55; Chinese reconstruction plan, 30–32; decline of brandy trade, 20; EC entry, 235–236; EDC failure, 178; Euratom, 195–196; Franco-German air power gap, 45–46; industrial working groups, 98–99; nuclear power program, 217; Paris Accords, 185–187; Polish loans, 21–23; provisional French government, 80; Schuman Plan, 130–131, 135; support of Free French, 69–75; travel and business relations, 7–8; US aid during WWII, 64–66; US rearmament during WWII, 62–66; US-Atlantic partnership, 227–228; WWI resource allocation, 9–14; WWII Anglo-French cooperation, 49–52
British Purchasing Commission (BPC), 55, 60–61
British Security coordination (BSC), 64
Brooke, Allan, 76(fig.)
Bruce, David, 174(fig.); Atlantic partnership, 222, 224; ECSC ambassadorial appointment, 168–169; EDC Plan, 177; Marshall Plan funding, 113–115; Monnet Plan, 121; Monnet's appeal for US loans, 174;

Monnet's death, 236; Pleven Plan, 151
Brussels Treaty, 186
Bullitt, William, 32–34, 45, 47–48
Bundy, McGeorge, 223, 228
Byrnes, James, 104

Cadogan, Alexander, 31
Caffrey, Jefferson, 104
Caldor, Nicholas, 108
Camus, Albert, 77–78
Canada: BPC supply coordination, 55; early travels, 8–9; WWII arms production, 63
Cartels, 145–146, 148–149, 160(n58), 173, 179–180
Casablanca conference (1943), 70
Casanova, Jean-Claude, 247–248
Catroux, Georges, 75, 76(fig.), 77, 79, 83, 90
Cecil, Robert, 15
Central Powers, 9
CFLN. *See* French Committee for National Liberation
Chamberlain, Neville, 46, 50
Chaplin, W. H., and Co., 7–8
Chatenet, Pierre, 217
Chiang Kai-shek, 1, 26, 29, 31–32
China: development, 27, 36–37; reconstruction, 34; reconstruction assistance, 1; Sino-Japanese conflict, 29–30
China Consortium, 26
China Development Finance Corporation (CDFC), 31–33, 36, 38
China, Nationalist, 25–33; end of Monnet's involvement with, 38; National Economic Council, 26; secret negotiations with Britain, 36–37
Christian Democratic Union party (Germany), 230
Christie, Agatha, 52
Churchill, Winston, 2; Anglo-French union proposal, 52, 55; antipathy to de Gaulle, 80; CFLN creation, 84; North Africa situation, 70–71, 76(fig.); seeking US aid, 64–65
*Citizens of London* (Olson), 64
Civil society, international community as, 245

Clappier, Bernard, 129, 137
Clay, Lucius, 129
Clayton, William, 96, 103
Clemenceau, Georges, 14
Clémentel, Etienne, 12–15
Cleveland, Stanley, 113–115, 121
Coal market: Monnet Plan, 102–103, 119. *See also* European Coal and Steel Community (ECSC)
Cognac region, 5–7, 20–21
Cold War: threatening Franco-German balance of power, 128–130
Collective action, 8, 39; Austrian reconstruction, 18. *See also* Labor
Comert, Pierre, 46
Commission, EC. *See* European Commission
Common Assembly, 148, 150
Common Market, 3
Common market, coal and steel, 172–173
Communists (France), 96, 119–120, 194
Conant, James B., 197
Conflict: China, 36–38; Sino-Japanese, 29–30; Upper Silesia, 17. *See also* World War I; World War II
Constitutional referendum, 219
Consultative Committee of the ECSC, 167
Coppé, Albert, 164, 171
Corbin, Charles, 52
Council of Europe, 134, 203
Council of Ministers, 150, 166–167, 172, 246
Court of Justice, 148, 150–151, 167, 203–204, 212
Couve de Murville, Maurice, 74, 81–82, 84, 220, 230
Covington, Burling, and Rublee, 57
Coward, Noel, 64
Cromwell, William N., 36
Cuban missile crisis, 230
Cunningham, Andrew, 76(fig.)
Czechoslovakia: Austrian reconstruction, 17–18; Communist coup, 127

Dahl, Roald, 64
Daladier, Edouard, 2, 46–50
Darlan, Jean Louis, 70
Daum, Leon, 165
Dawes, Charles G., 21

de Bondini, Alexandre, 191
de Gasperi, Alcide, 166
de Gaulle, Charles, 2–3, 211; Anglo-
  French union proposal, 52–54; CFLN
  creation, 81–84; Euratom's demise,
  216–218; Franco-German Friendship
  Treaty, 230–231; Kennedy's German
  visit, 229; Monnet and Kennedy
  underestimating, 230; Monnet Plan,
  98–99, 120; Monnet's complex
  relationship with, 218–220; Monnet's
  declining influence, 235; North Africa
  situation, 74–76, 76(fig.), 77; postwar
  reconstruction, 86, 95–97; provisional
  French government, 79–81, 95–96,
  103; response to the Schuman Plan,
  135; Roosevelt's refusal to
  acknowledge CFLN, 87–88; source of
  power and influence, 248; US distrust
  of, 69–75; vetoing British EC
  application, 228
de La Grange, François-Amaury, 48
Debré, Michel, 220
Declaration of Interdependence
  (Kennedy speech), 227
Defense: NATO creation, 158(n7). *See
  also* Pleven Plan
Delcourt, Jean-Paul: Monnet Plan, 99,
  106(fig.)
Delouvrier, Paul, 100, 106(fig.), 204,
  220
Denis, Pierre, 17, 36
Diethelm, André, 81
Dill, John, 56
Dillon, Douglas, 178, 194–195, 216,
  223
*Dirigisme,* 144
Draper, William, 169
Drummond, David, 28, 31, 33, 36–37
Drummond, Eric, 15–16, 19
Duchêne, François, 214, 223, 227, 249
Dulles, Allen, 15
Dulles, Janet, 220–221
Dulles, John Foster, 14–15, 22, 36, 39,
  45, 174(fig.), 249; Anglo-French
  union proposal, 55; death of,
  220–221; ECSC launch, 168–169;
  EDC failure, 177–178; Euratom, 216,
  250; Monnet's failure to secure US
  loans, 175; supporting economic
  integration, 194; US response to the

Schuman Plan, 135–136; US support
  for Euratom, 199–201
Dumontier, Jacques: Monnet Plan, 99
Dykes, Vivian, 56

EC Treaty. *See* Rome Treaties
Economic community: Schuman Plan
  negotiations, 143–145
*Économie concertée,* 99
Economic Cooperation Act, 111
Economic Cooperation Administration
  (ECA), 112, 115
Economic crisis: France, 108, 204
Economic reconstruction, France. *See*
  Monnet Plan
Eden, Anthony, 76(fig.), 79–80, 185–186
Education: Monnet's, 6–7; Schuman's,
  132
Eisenhower, Dwight, 174(fig.), 250;
  building a new US-European
  partnership, 222–225; Euratom,
  198–201, 215–216; Monnet's appeal
  for loans, 173–175; North Africa
  situation, 69–75; Pleven Plan,
  151–153; Schuman Plan, 156
Erhard, Ludwig, 149
Ettori, Charles, 76
Etzel, Franz, 174(fig.), 203(fig.); ECSC
  High Authority, 164; Monnet's appeal
  for US loans, 174; US support for
  Euratom, 200; Wise Men's group, 198
Euratom (European Atomic Energy
  Community), 237, 249–250; Action
  Committee, 193–196; creation of,
  191–192; de Gaulle's opposition to,
  211, 216–218; financial common
  market, 205–206; France's nuclear
  policy threatening, 196–198; Rome
  Treaty, 202–204; Spaak proposal,
  188–189; US support for, 198–201,
  215–216
Euratom Treaty. *See* Rome Treaties
  (1957)
European Coal and Steel Community
  (ECSC), 2–3, 127–128, 165, 167,
  176–179, 212, 238; discrediting
  Monnet, 185; effectiveness of
  international institutions, 244–245;
  failures and successes of, 179–182;
  formulating the Schuman Plan,
  128–133; High Authority, 144; High

Authority's failure to secure US loans, 173–175; launching, 164–168; Law 27, 149; Monnet setting the tone for the High Authority, 170–172; Monnet's presidency, 163–164; negotiations, 139; policy failures, 172–173; political strengths of, 157; roots of, 129; scrap cartels, 173; Treaty of Paris, 150; Treaty ratification, 154–158; US support at the launching, 168–169; weighted voting, 150, 167

European Commission, 203–204, 212, 246

European Community (EC), 211–212; British membership, 227–228; creation of, 243; Parliamentary Assembly, 203–204; pursuing monetary union, 233–234; sovereignty and supranational authority, 246

European Council, 234; Honorary Citizen of Europe award, 236; Monnet's institutional approach to international problems, 246

European Court of Justice. *See* Court of Justice

European Defense Community (EDC): as blow to federalism, 190; as obstacle to French foreign policy, 176–177; crisis threatening Monnet's presidency, 176; failure to ratify, 177–179; Pleven Plan creation, 142; reasons for failure, 180–181; treaty negotiations, 155; US commitment to Germany and NATO, 187; weakening the European community, 185. *See also* Pleven Plan

European District, 212

European Economic Community: Rome Treaty, 202–204. *See also* European Community (EC)

European Federalist Movement, 168

European Free Trade Association (EFTA), 227–228

European Monetary System (EMS), 234

European Parliament, 212

Export-Import Bank, 32

Family, Monnet's, 5–7, 19–21. *See also entries beginning with* Monnet

Faure, Edgar, 189, 191

Faure, Maurice, 201

Federalism: EDC defeat as blow to, 190; Schuman Declaration, 245–246; through Euratom, 192–193

Financial crisis: France, 108, 204

Finet, Paul, 165

Fleming, Ian, 64

Fontaine, François, 25, 99, 167, 236

*Force de frappe* (nuclear strike force), 211

Ford Foundation, 212–215

Foreign Assistance Act (1948), 111

Foreign investment: China, 29–33, 37

Fosdick, Raymond, 16

Fouchet Plan (1960), 220

Fourastié, Jean: Monnet Plan, 99

Frachon, Benoit, 105

France, 201; Algiers negotiation over French unification, 75–81; Anglo-American war effort, 65–66; Anglo-French union proposal, 52–54; cartels, 160(n58); Chinese reconstruction plan, 30–31; de Gaulle and Monnet's differing goals for, 218–220; economic integration, 194; ECSC, 136–139, 144–145, 155, 165; EDC, 154, 176–179; Euratom, 192–193, 196–198, 216–218; financial crisis, 204–205; Franco-German air power gap, 45–48; growing distrust of Monnet, 156; inflation, 108–109, 119; Lend-Lease accords, 88–90; Marshall Plan, 111; Monnet's awards and honors, 236; Monnet's commitment to unity and French welfare, 235–236; North Africa campaign, 69–75; Paris Accords, 186–187; Pleven Plan, 151; Polish loans, 21–23; postwar aid, 86–91; postwar European policy, 84–86; postwar reconstruction, 95; response to the Schuman Plan, 135; Rome Treaty, 204; Roosevelt's refusal to acknowledge CFLN, 87–88; Schuman Plan, 130–131; the Korean War and German rearmament, 140–143; Vichy government, 53–54, 69–75, 81–82; WWI resource allocation, 9–14. *See also* de Gaulle, Charles; Monnet Plan

Franco-German air power gap, 45–46

Franco-German Friendship Treaty (1963), 230–231
Franco-German relations, 2, 15; Adenauer's response to the Schuman Plan, 133–135; air power gap, 45–48; Cold War tensions and the Schuman Plan, 128–133; ECSC, 127–128, 136–137, 157, 179–182, 244; Euratom, 199–200; monetary union, 206; Monnet's commitment to unification, 246–247; Monnet's dream of lasting peace, 237–238; Schuman Plan, 128–135, 250–251; US role in ECSC negotiations, 146; WWII North Africa campaign, 70
Frankfurter, Felix, 56–59, 71, 73, 174, 192
Free French, 69–76
Freedom Award (Monnet), 229
Freitag, Walter, 193
French Committee for National Liberation (CFLN), 75–76, 81–86, 91; Monnet's dismissal, 88; Roosevelt's refusal to acknowledge, 87–88
French Independent Republicans, 235
French Supply Council, 88–89, 117
Fulbright, J. William, 136, 175
Functionalism, 245
Funeral (Monnet), 236

Gaillard, Félix, 204–205; Monnet Plan, 97–98
Gaitskell, Hugh, 153
Gaullists, 194; growing distrust of Monnet, 156; legislative elections, 195; North Africa campaign, 70
Geneva Protocol, 18
Georges, Joseph, 76(fig.)
Germany, Nazi, 129; Franco-German air power gap, 45–48; overestimating airpower, 51–52; Upper Silesia conflict with Poland, 17; Vichy government's capitulation to, 53; WWI food shortages, 12–13
Germany, West: agricultural common market, 202; cartels, 160(n58); ECSC benefits, 179–182; ECSC creation and effectiveness, 127–128; ECSC High Authority, 144–145; ECSC launch, 165; ECSC negotiations, 136–139;

ECSC treaty ratification, 155; EDC failure, 178–179; establishment of, 129–130; Euratom, 193, 196–197, 217; Franco-German Friendship Treaty, 230–231; Kennedy's visit, 229; Marshall Plan, 111; monetary union, 206, 233–234; Monnet Plan, 102–103; multilateral missile force, 228; NATO membership, 158(n7), 189; Paris Accords, 185–187; Pleven Plan, 151, 153–154; rearmament, 140–143; Rome Treaty, 204; Schuman Plan, 133–135, 148–151; unification, 246–247, 251; US role in ECSC negotiations, 146–147. *See also* Franco-German relations
Giacchero, Enzo, 164–165
Giannini, Amadeo, 24
Giannini, Anna, 33–35, 37, 58–59, 97, 249
Giannini, Francesco, 24–25, 37
Giannini, Silvia de Bondini. *See* Monnet, Silvia
Giordani, Francesco: US support for Euratom, 200; Wise Men's group, 198
Giraud, Henri, 2; France's postwar reconstruction, 90; French Committee for National Liberation (CFLN), 81; North Africa situation, 70–76, 76(fig.), 77; provisional French government, 78–80
Giscard d'Estaing, Valéry, 234–236
Goering, Hermann, 47 Gouin, Félix, 103
Graham, Katharine, 57–58, 232
Graham, Philip, 57, 192, 225, 232
Grand Design, Kennedy's, 227, 229–230
Gruenther, Alfred, 169

Haas, Ernst B., 245
Hague summit, 233
Hallstein, Walter, 138–139, 205, 223, 230
Harriman, Averell, 65, 136, 222
Hartman, Arthur, 113–114, 121, 177, 222
Heath, Edward, 228
High Authority of the ECSC, 244, 252; creation of, 144; ECSC launch, 164–168; importance of, 157; Monnet setting the tone for, 170–172; Monnet's presidency, 163–164;

Monnet's retirement from, 188; treaty provisions, 150. *See also* European Coal and Steel Community
Hirsch, Etienne, 181(fig.), 245–246, 252; Atlantic partnership, 223; Euratom, 217; Euratom and ECSC extension, 188; Lend-Lease accords, 89; Monnet Plan, 97–99, 106(fig.), 107, 119; on Monnet, 237–238; postwar European policy, 84; Schuman Plan, 139; US role in ECSC negotiations, 146
Hitler, Adolf, 45–46
Hoover, Herbert, 14, 61
Hopkins, Henry, 59, 63–64, 71, 79
Hoppenot, Henri, 30
Hoppenot, Roger, 46
Hornbeck, Stanley, 34
Hudson Bay Company (HBC), 9, 11, 20–21
Hull, Cordell, 61, 71

Imig, Heinrich, 193
Institutions, international, 243–246; changing thinking and behavior, 180; ECSC negotiations, 137–138, 203; ECSC treaty provisions, 148
Integration, 190–198. *See also* Monnet Plan
International Atomic Energy Agency (IAEA), 199
International Ruhr Authority, 134
International Supply Commission (CIR), 11
Investment banking, 1, 21–25, 28–29
Isenbergh, Max, 191–192, 197–198, 252
Italy: Austrian reconstruction, 17–18; ECSC High Authority, 164–165; ECSC negotiations, 136–137; ECSC voting rights, 150; Nenni Socialists, 235; nuclear power program, 217

Jacob, Ian, 56
Japan: China's reconstruction, 27; conflict with Nationalist Chinese, 29–32
Javel, Fernand, 81
J. G. Monnet and Co., 19–21, 236
Johnson Act (1933), US, 48
Johnson administration: Euratom support, 219

Joxe, Louis, 18, 75–76, 78, 81–83

Kaplan, Léon, 89
Kaspi, André, 252
Katz, Milton, 58–59
Kennedy, John F., 226(fig.), 237, 251; assassination of, 229; Euratom support, 219; US-European partnership, 222–224, 226–230, 251
Kennedy, Robert, 232
Keynes, John Maynard, 15, 64
Kindersley, Robert, 9, 20, 25–27
Kohnstamm, Max, 214(fig.), 252; Atlantic partnership, 222–223; economic and political union, 188; economic integration, 194; ECSC staffing, 167; ECSC treaty negotiations, 148–149; Euratom, 216, 218; Ford Foundation funding, 214–215; Messina conference, 191; monetary union, 205; on Monnet, 237–238; Rome Treaty, 212; US support for Euratom, 200; Wise Men's group, 198
Korean War, 139–141
Kreuger, Ivar, 20, 23, 26, 36
Kung, H. H., 31–32, 37

La Chambre, Guy, 46–47
Labor, 193–195; Monnet Plan, 105, 119–120
Lacoste, Robert, 108
Lagrange, Maurice, 139, 147; ECSC draft treaty, 148
Laniel, Joseph, 178
Lazard Bank, 25–27, 33
League of Nations, 1, 15–19, 26, 30, 244; lack of authority, 16, 19
Lebrun, Pierre, 109
Leddy, John, 223
Lee, Higginson and Co., 35–36
Lee, John M., 223
Léger, Alexis, 69
Lend-Lease accords, 72, 86, 88–89, 91, 96–97, 99, 104
Lindbergh, Anne Morrow, 46–47
Lindbergh, Charles, 15, 46–47
Lippmann, Walter, 24, 56, 91(n2)
Loans: Austrian reconstruction, 17–18; Chinese reconstruction, 28–29; High

Authority's failure to secure US loans, 173–175; Monnet family's bankruptcy threat, 20; US investment banking, 21–24
*Loi Tréveneuc*, 79
Loucheur, Louis, 14
Luftwaffe, 51–52
Luxembourg, 212; ECSC launch, 165; ECSC negotiations, 136–137; ECSC voting rights, 150

MacArthur, Douglas II, 169
Macmillan, Harold, 72–74, 76(fig.), 228
Madariaga, Salvador de, 19
Marjolin, Robert, 201–202, 247, 252; Atlantic partnership, 223; Franco-German air power gap, 51; monetary union, 204; Monnet Plan, 97–98, 100–101, 106(fig.), 107, 119; postwar European policy, 84
Marriage, Monnet's, 34–35
Marshall Plan, 110–112, 120–121
Marshall, George, 57, 110–112
Massé, Pierre, 99
Massigli, Réné, 76(fig.), 80, 82
Mauclère, Eugène, 11
May, Ernest, 121
May, Stacy, 62–63
Mayer, André, 200; Monnet Plan, 120
Mayer, René, 49–51, 81, 130; High Authority presidency, 191; Monnet Plan, 108; postwar European policy, 84
Mayne, Richard, 214, 252
Mazot, Henri, 28, 36
McCloy, John, 23–24, 249, 251; assistant secretary of war appointment, 61; Atlantic partnership, 223; CFLN creation, 82; ECSC, 137, 155–156, 169; Euratom support, 199–200; Ford Foundation funding, 213, 215; French provisional government, 80–81; German acceptance of the Pleven Plan, 154; German resistance to decartelization, 149; increasing wartime arms production, 62; Monnet's death, 236; Monnet's return to France, 97; North Africa situation, 71, 73; Pleven Plan, 141–143, 151,

154; Schuman Plan, 129–130, 136, 145–146
McGrew, Donald, 121
Mendès-France, Pierre, 176–177, 185–186, 188
Merchant, Livingston, 169, 175
Messina conference, 190–191
Military action: European army, 140–143; Franco-German air power gap, 45–47; Korean War, 139–140; US support for the Pleven Plan, 151–153. *See also* European Defense Community (EDC); World War I; World War II
Millerand, Alexandre, 11
Mitterrand, François, 231, 236
Modernization, 96, 105. *See also* Monnet Plan
Mollet, Guy, 193–194, 196–197, 201, 217, 220
Monetary union proposals, 204–207, 233–234, 243
Monick, Emmanuel, 103
Monnet, Gaston (brother), 5, 20
Monnet, Georges (cousin), 20
Monnet, Henriette (sister), 5
Monnet, Jean-Gabriel (father), 5–6, 10, 20, 47
Monnet, J. G., and Co., 19–21, 236
Monnet, Maria Demelle (mother), 6, 19
Monnet, Marianne (daughter), 73, 78, 86–87, 97
Monnet, Marie-Louise (sister), 5, 34, 191
Monnet, Murnane, and Co., 36–38, 45, 221
Monnet, Robert (cousin), 20, 236
Monnet, Silvia (wife), 24–25, 27, 171(fig.), 249, 252; American ties, 232–233; Anna's American education, 58–59; custody battle, 37; de Gaulle and, 53; divorce and remarriage, 33–35; in Washington, 86–87; Monnet's death, 236; Monnet's dependence on, 78; Monnet's North Africa visit, 73; Monnet's return to France, 97, 191; Morrow on, 47
Monnet Plan, 2, 246–247; achievements and shortcomings of, 118–122; *économie concertée* approach, 98–99;

energy industry, 102–103, 108, 119;
finalization of, 105–107;
implementation, 107–108;
industrialization, 98–99, 102;
Marshall Plan aid for, 110–112;
modernization commissions, 98–99;
obstacles to execution of, 108–110;
origins of, 96–98; planning team,
99–101, 106(fig.); securing US loans,
103–105; setting goals, 101–103; US
input in implementing, 112–118
Moreau, Emile, 22
Morgan, J. P., 15
Morgenthau, Henry Jr., 48, 59, 64
Morrow, Anne, 15–16, 46–47
Morrow, Dwight, 15
Multilateral missile force (MLF), 228
Mumm champagne company, 20
Murnane, George, 35–38
Murphy, Robert, 70, 72, 74–76, 169
Murrow, Edward, 65

Nasser, Gamal Abdul, 196
Nathan, Robert, 61–64, 105–107;
Planning Committee of the War
Production Board, 63
NATO: creation of, 158(n7); EDC
failure, 178; Franco-German
Friendship Treaty, 230; German
membership, 189; German
rearmament, 140, 186; multilateral
missile force, 228; Pleven Plan,
152–153; Schuman Plan, 132–133
Nazi occupation, 38
Nelson, Donald, 63
Nenni Socialists (Italy), 194, 235
Neofunctionalism, 245
Netherlands: ECSC High Authority, 144;
ECSC launch, 165; ECSC
negotiations, 136–137; ECSC voting
rights, 150; Marshall Plan, 111
Neutrality Act of 1935 (US), 48, 50
New Deal, 139
*New York Times,* 232
Nicolson, Harold, 14
Nitze, Paul, 223
Norman, Montagu, 18, 22
North Africa, 54, 69–75, 86
North American Supply Committee
(NAS), 54

North Atlantic Treaty (1949), 129
Nuclear programs. *See* Euratom
Nuclear weapons: France, 196–198

Occupation Statute (Germany), 129, 149,
154, 186
Ogilvy, David, 64
Ollenhauer, Erich, 193, 195(fig.),
197
Olson, Lynne, 64
Organization for European Economic
Cooperation (OEEC), 111, 199
*Ostpolitik,* 233
Owen, Henry, 222, 227

Paris Accords (1954), 186
Paris Peace Conference, 14–15
Paris Summit (1974), 234
Pearl Harbor, 83
Pétain, Philippe, 53–54, 69–71
Petschek family, 37
Peyrouton, Marcel, 91(n2)
Pflimlin, Pierre, 109
Philip, André, 76(fig.), 80, 82
Pilotti, Massimo, 167
Pilsudski, Józef, 23
Pinay, Antoine, 130, 190, 219
Pineau, Christian, 201
Planning Commission for the Monnet
Plan, 171
Pleven Plan, 142, 182; German
acceptance, 153–154; US support,
151–153. *See also* European Defense
Community
Pleven, René, 23, 195(fig.), 249–250;
Anglo-French union proposal, 53;
CFLN creation, 83; Franco-German
air power gap, 45, 49; French
provisional government, 81; German
rearmament, 140–142; Monnet and de
Gaulle, 220; on Giraud, 74; Schuman
Plan, 130
Poincaré, Raymond, 22
Poland: loan program to, 21–23; Upper
Silesia conflict, 17
Pompidou, Georges, 233–234
Potthoff, Heinz, 165
Pricing policies, ECSC, 172
Protocol of abstention (League of
Nations), 18

Provisional government: France, 77–80, 84
Provisional Government of the French Republic (GPRF), 88–89, 95–96, 99, 103
*Psychology: Reflective Note* (Monnet), 85–86
Purvis, Arthur, 55, 60

Queuille, Henri, 108, 114

Rabier, Jacques, 100
Railroads: China, 32; Monnet Plan goals, 102
Rajchman, Ludwik, 22, 26, 30, 33–34
Ramadier, Paul, 108
Rand, William, 174(fig.)
Rearmament: German, 140–143, 151–152, 185–187; US, 61–66
Reconstruction: Austria, 17–18; China, 26–28; postwar France, 95. *See also* Monnet Plan
Reconstruction, Europe: Marshall Plan, 110–112
Resource allocation, 8, 55; Monnet Plan goals, 102; World War I, 9–14; WWII Anglo-French cooperation, 51. *See also* European Coal and Steel Community (ECSC); Monnet Plan
Reston, James "Scotty," 232, 249
Reston, Jody, 232
Reston, Richard, 232
Reston, Sally, 232, 249
Reuter, Paul, 139
Reynaud, Paul, 49, 52–53
Rieben, Henri, 214
Romania: loan program, 23
Rome Treaties (1957), 3, 206, 211–212, 246, 250–251
Roosevelt, Eleanor, 64
Roosevelt, Franklin, 2; CFLN creation, 82, 84; Franco-German air power gap, 47–49, 55–56, 60–61; GPRF recognition, 88–89; increasing wartime arms production, 62–66; North Africa situation, 69–75; refusal to acknowledge CFLN, 87–88
Rostow, Edna, 223, 249
Rostow, Elspeth, 223
Rostow, Eugene, 223, 249
Rostow, Walt, 222–223, 227

Rublee, George T., 13, 56
Rueff, Jacques, 219
Ruhr Valley, Germany, 102–103, 129–130, 134–135. *See also* European Coal and Steel Community
Runciman, Walter, 12
Rusk, Dean, 224

Saar policy, 18, 128, 195. *See also* European Coal and Steel Community
Salter, Arthur, 11–12, 16, 26, 28, 52, 54–55, 60
Sauvy, Albert: Monnet Plan, 99
Schaetzel, Robert, 181(fig.), 198–201, 215–216, 222, 227
Schlesinger, Arthur M., Jr., 229
Schmidt, Helmut, 234
Schuman, Robert, 246; commitment to democracy, 132; declining influence in France, 163; ECSC support, 157–158; Monnet's conceptualization of German revitalization, 129–133; Monnet's tribute to, 149; origins of the Schuman Plan, 127–128
Schuman Plan, 2, 127–128, 245–247; Adenauer's response, 133–135; economic community, 143–145; Korean War and German rearmament, 140; treaty negotiations, 136–139; treaty provisions, 148; US facilitating negotiations, 145–148; US response to, 135–136
Smith, Gerard, 198, 200
Smith, Walter Bedell, 169
Snyder, John, 113
Socialist Democratic Party (Germany), 238
Soong, T. A., 31
Soong, T. L., 31–32, 38
Soong, T. V., 26–28, 30–31, 33, 37–38
Sovereignty: France's postwar reconstruction, 89–90; High Authority, 144; limits of economic sovereignty, 14; Paris Accords, 186; supranational authority and, 131, 246; WWII French factions, 71–72
Soviet Union: ECSC creation and effectiveness, 127; EDC failure, 178; Korean War, 139–141; *Ostpolitik,* 233; Pleven Plan, 143; response to the Schuman Plan, 135; Silvia's divorce,

33–35; the Korean War and German rearmament, 140; Truman Doctrine, 110; US support for Euratom, 199

Spaak, Paul-Henri, 2–3, 189(fig.), 250; ECSC launch, 168; EDC failure, 185; Euratom and financial common market, 205–206; Monnet and de Gaulle, 220; Monnet's retirement, 188; relaunching integration efforts, 190–191; US support for Euratom, 201

Spaak Committee, 193, 197, 246

Spaak Report, 198

Spierenburg, Dirk, 174(fig.), 252; economic and political union, 188; ECSC High Authority, 144, 165; ECSC treaty negotiations, 147–148; Monnet's appeal for US loans, 174; Monnet's ECSC position, 171–172

Spinelli, Altiero, 165, 190

Stabilization program: France, 108–110

Steel market, 173; Monnet Plan goals, 102. *See also* European Coal and Steel Community (ECSC)

Stephenson, William, 64

Stevenson, Adlai, 223

Stimson, Henry, 61, 71

Stock market crash, 23, 25

Stone, Shepard, 212–213, 215, 252–253

Strater, Henrich, 193

Strauss, Franz-Joseph, 197

Strauss, Lewis, 199–200, 250

Strong, Benjamin, 22

Submarine warfare: World War I, 12–13

Suez crisis, 196, 198, 202

Suma, Yakichiro, 30–31

Supranational authority, 131; de Gaulle's opposition to, 211; economic community, 14; ECSC creation, 244; ECSC negotiations, 139; EDC rejection, 185; military community, 140–143; Monnet's objection to the term, 245; response to the Schuman Plan, 135; sovereignty and, 246. *See also* Euratom; European Coal and Steel Community

Supreme Allied Commander Europe (SACEUR), 140

Supreme Economic Council (WWI), 14–15

Swatland, Donald, 23, 200

Tariffs, 172

Taxation, 109

Temporary Council Committee of NATO (TCC), 153

*Time* magazine, 236

Tixier, Adrien, 81–82

Tomlinson, William "Tommy": ECSC launch, 169; ECSC treaty negotiations, 145–146; ECSC treaty ratification, 155; EDC plan, 176–177; Monnet Plan implementation team, 112–115, 121

Trade Expansion Act (1962), 224

Trade unions. *See* Labor

Transamerica Corp., 24–25, 36

Treaty of Paris (1951), 150

Treaty of Rome, 202–204

Triffin, Robert, 204–205, 215, 234

Truman Doctrine, 110

Truman, Harry: German rearmament, 139–141; Marshall Plan, 110–111; Monnet Plan, 96–97, 104; Schuman Plan, 156

Tuthill, John, 222–223, 237

United Kingdom. *See* Britain

United Nations Relief and Rehabilitation Agency (UNRRA), 87

United States: Algiers negotiation, 75–76; basis of Monnet's economic plan, 246; BPC supply coordination, 55–56; building a new US-European partnership, 222–225; CFLN, 82, 87–88; Chinese reconstruction plan, 30; de Gaulle's anti-Americanism, 220; de Gaulle's impression of, 96; decline of brandy trade, 20; Dulles's death, 220–222; economic mobilization, 106; ECSC, 137, 145–148, 155–156, 168–169; EDC treaty failure, 177–178; Euratom support, 191–192, 198–201, 215–216, 250; Euratom's demise in France, 217–218; Ford Foundation funding, 212–215; Franco-German air power gap, 47–49; Franco-German Friendship Treaty threatening united Europe, 232–233; French financial crisis, 204–205; French provisional government, 80; German acceptance of the Pleven Plan, 153–154; German

resistance to decartelization, 149; influence on Monnet, 248–249; investment banking, 21–24; Kennedy's commitment to a US-European partnership, 226–230; Korean War, 139–141; loans for the High Authority government, 173–175; Marshall Plan funding for France, 110–112; Monnet Plan, 96–97, 99, 101, 103–105, 108; Monnet's awards and honors, 236; Monnet's early travels, 8–9; Monnet's fascination with, 23–24; Monnet's financial consulting career, 35–39; North Africa situation, 69–75; Paris Accords, 185–187; partnership of equals, 251; Pleven Plan support, 151–153; post-WWII Franco-American relations, 2–3; postwar aid programs in France, 86; response to the Schuman Plan, 135–136; Romanian loan, 23; Roosevelt's recognition of the GPRF, 88–89; Roosevelt's refusal to acknowledge CFLN, 87–88; Schuman Plan, 130; Suez crisis, 196, 202; supranational military community, 140–143; wartime expansion of arms production, 61–66
United Vineyard Proprietors' Company, 5–6. *See also* J. G. Monnet and Co.
Upper Silesia, 17
Uri, Pierre, 201, 252; ECSC draft treaty, 148; Euratom and ECSC extension, 188; High Authority administration, 170–171; monetary union, 204; Monnet Plan, 99, 101, 107–109, 116; Schuman Plan, 139; US role in ECSC negotiations, 146
US response to the Schuman Plan, 136

Van Helmont, Jacques, 99, 113, 167, 214, 234
Vansittart, Robert, 52
Varsori, Antonio, 217
Vergeot, Jean: Monnet Plan, 99–100, 106(fig.)
Vichy government, 53–54, 69–75, 81–82, 91(n2)
Viviani, René, 10–11
Voléry, François: Monnet Plan, 106(fig.)
Voting rights, ECSC, 150, 167

W. H. Chaplin and Co., 7–8
Walker, Elisha, 24–25
Washington Conference System, 29–30
Wehrer, Albert, 165
Weiss, Louise, 19
Wellenstein, Edmond, 170
Werner, Pierre, 233–234
Western European Union (WEU), 186
Wheat Executive, 12–14, 244
Wilson, Harold, 236
Winant, John G., 56, 64–65
Wise Men's group, 198
World War I, 1–2, 9–14, 38–39; Monnet's American connections, 248–249; Schuman's service, 132; Wheat Executive, 12–14, 244
World War II: Algiers negotiations over French reunification, 75–81; Anglo-French cooperation, 49–52; Anglo-French union proposal, 52–54; BPC supply coordination, 55; Franco-German air power gap, 45–46; French provisional government, 75–83, 86–89; Monnet's American connections, 248–249; North Africa situation, 69–75; postwar European policy, 84–86; US wartime expansion of arms production, 61–66

# About the Book

How did Jean Monnet, an entrepreneurial internationalist who never held an elective office, never joined a political party, and never developed any significant popular following in his native France, become one of the most influential European statesmen of the twentieth century? How did he conceive of and become instrumental in achieving European integration? Addressing these questions, Sherrill Brown Wells's political biography also offers insights into the role of the fledgling community of European states in establishing peace in war-ravaged Europe in the aftermath of World War II.

**Sherrill Brown Wells** is professorial lecturer in history and international affairs at George Washington University. She is author of *Pioneers of European Integration and Peace, 1945–1963*.